NEW DIRECTIONS IN RHETORIC AND MATERIALITY
Barbara A. Biesecker, Wendy S. Hesford, and Christa Teston, Series Editors

Precarious Rhetorics

EDITED BY

Wendy S. Hesford

Adela C. Licona

Christa Teston

THE OHIO STATE UNIVERSITY PRESS | COLUMBUS

Copyright © 2018 by The Ohio State University.
All rights reserved.

Library of Congress Cataloging-in-Publication Control Number: 2018012919

Cover design by Angela Moody
Text design by Juliet Williams
Type set in Adobe Minion Pro

CONTENTS

ACKNOWLEDGMENTS

WE WANT TO thank all of the contributors to *Precarious Rhetorics* for their critical engagement and commitment to this volume. We would like to thank anonymous reviewers for their thoughtful readings of the manuscript in its early stages. Thanks also to Tara Cyphers for her editorial assistance and vision throughout the project. Wendy S. Hesford would like to thank the Yale University Gilder Lehrman Center for fellowship support during 2016–17. In addition, Hesford and Christa Teston thank Ohio State University for a research grant to offset the cost of production. Finally, we are so pleased that our volume serves as the introduction to the New Directions in Rhetoric and Materiality series.

Photographs by Tyler Jump/International Rescue Committee that appear in chapter 7 are reprinted with permission from the photographer. Cover photograph by Lukas M. Hueller is reprinted with permission from the photographer.

Rhetorical Recalibrations and Response-abilities

WENDY S. HESFORD, ADELA C. LICONA, and CHRISTA TESTON

OUR COLLECTION has come together in the midst of the rise of the global Right. It will likely be received and circulate in a global context wherein this ascendency has been consolidated through an entrenched hard-right populism, marked by xenophobia and racialized social orderings, and characterized by nativist, heteronormative, hypermasculine, and heteropatriarchal leadership styles and structures. Such structures are apparent in the authoritarian regimes of Tayyip Erdoğan in Turkey, Vladimir Putin in Russia, and most recently Donald Trump in the United States.[1] They are also present in the authoritarianism of British Prime Minister Theresa May, Abdel Fattal al-Sisi of Egypt, and Syria's Bashar al-Assad, as well as Prime Minister Rodrigo Duterte of the Philippines, President Nicolas Maduro of Venezuela, President Horacio Cartes of Paraguay, Prime Minister Narendra Modi of India, and China's Xi-Jinpin, all of whom are in one form or another engaged in increased militarization, new measures of securitization, and the simultaneous crackdown on oppositional voices and repression of dissent.

The hard-right populism this rise depends on is cultivated through the sowing of fear and suspicion and the production of devaluing discourses. In "The Dangerous Rise of Populism: Global Attacks on Human Rights Values," Kenneth Roth, director of Human Rights Watch (HRW), identifies Western populism and "unfettered majoritarianism, and the attacks on the checks and balances that constrain governmental power [as] perhaps the greatest danger today to the future of democracy in the West" (2). He writes, "Claiming to speak for 'the people,' [populists] treat rights as an impediment to their conception of majority will, a needless obstacle to defending the nation from perceived threats and evils" (1). Here Roth responds to fascist, (what some term "alt-right") and conservative arguments that assert that rights protect those who would do the nation harm: terrorist suspects, asylum seekers, migrants, and religious and ethnic minorities (Taylor 35–36). The Trump administration's airstrikes against Syrian airfields in the aftermath of Assad's chemical weapon attack on his own citizens reveal the tragic irony of Trump's Executive Order Protecting the Nation from Foreign Terrorist Entry into the United States, which bars the entrance of Syrian refugees fleeing Assad's and ISIS's violent attacks. The rise of the global Right is also the rise of economic nationalism, which depends upon extractions, evacuations, and erasures that can be traced to and through the legacies of settler state colonialism.[2] It is in this context that we bear witness to increasing and increasingly harsh restrictions on movement and mobility of entire populations and the politically induced causes and precarious conditions of displacement and dispossession.

As a counter to demagogues on the global Right, Roth argues, "responsibility lies with the public . . . to demand a politics based on truth and the values on which rights-respecting democracy has been built" (14). While we too are concerned about the "echo chambers of falsehoods" (14) and embrace public resistance to demagogues, we are also concerned that liberal internationalism, while aiming to counter human rights violations across the globe, has, in some instances, paved the way for the exceptionalisms upon which it depends. "The overarching and worst mistake liberal internationalists have made," as Samuel Moyn puts it, "is to believe that hegemonic ascendancy and military intervention by their own country could create a freer world. British liberals, especially in the age of William Gladstone, made that error in the nineteenth century, blithely assuming that the cause of humanity was served by the geopolitical advancement of a single nation (and empire)" (118). Moyn continues, "American liberals have repeated it in our time, never breaking with the exceptionalist outlook that cast the United States as uniquely virtuous" (118). Thus, we too are interested in critical engagement not only with the discourses and materiality of the global Right but also with the precarity of liberal internationalism in the late twentieth and early twenty-first century. We therefore turn to the concepts of precarity, precaritization, and precariousness to recalibrate liberal discourse and its foundational concepts.

Precarity has become a key concept in scholarly work devoted to the study of the affective, relational, and material conditions and structuring logics of inequality. Across disciplines, scholars employ theories of precarity to help explain the pervasiveness of problems related to labor, migration, biopolitics, securitization, global and settler-state governance, economies of war and violence, vulnerability, differentiated risk, poverty, debility, oppression, dispossession, and environmental degradation. Precarity helps us uncover and analyze "politically induced condition[s] in which certain populations suffer from failing social and economic networks of support and become differentially exposed to injury, violence, and death" (Butler, *Frames* 35). This collection mobilizes precarity as an analytic tactic for recalibrating how we understand, assume, and reconfigure divisions between liberal personhood/rights, inclusion/exclusion, victimization/agency, vulnerability/resistance, and human/nonhuman. A rhetorical approach to these divisions reconfigures them such that they can be understood as relational rather than as simply oppositional. Recalibrating for relationality, interconnection, interdependencies, and coalitional possibilities refuses social orderings and hierarchies that produce and secure systems of division that are bound by valuation and devaluation (Chávez; Licona; Licona and Chávez), and the "slow death" of particular peoples and populations (Berlant; Puar; Cacho).

Precarious Rhetorics features cross-disciplinary contributions that emphasize a materialist-rhetorical approach while also drawing on insights from scholars who work in feminist and transnational feminist studies, women of color feminisms, affect studies, critical disability studies, critical race studies, medical humanities, sexuality studies, queer migration studies, human rights and humanitarian studies, human and cultural geography, Native American and Indigenous studies, ethnic studies, and disability studies. Contributors draw from decolonial, cultural studies, and Indigenous scholars whose work is vital to understanding that researchers cannot isolate cultural practices—especially those threatened or made invisible through active erasures—from "other human economic, political, geographical, historical frameworks" that bear up and make such practices possible (Powell et al.).

When mobilized alongside theories of rhetoric and materiality, precarity draws attention to the material conditions from which liberal subjects emerge and to human and nonhuman inter- and intra-dependencies; it yields a generative model for the possibility of coexistence, an ethics based on an understanding of material and technological infrastructures and how they enable certain forms of being, becoming, and belonging. It also makes possible a politics of solidarity that is based on an understanding of shared precarity. And it recognizes ways in which vulnerability and precariousness may be mobilized as forms of resistance. Contributors' turn to precarity facilitates a renewed focus on materialism. Precarity as an analytic, we want to suggest, helps to bridge what are often viewed as distinct critical traditions, namely historical materialism and materialism of the body, and in so doing calls upon scholars in rhetoric and communication studies to reappraise concepts such as materiality, ontology, causality, political agency, embodiment, and power.[3]

Our collection is attentive to various power geometries, specifically how the rise of the global Right ushers in a reaffirmation of gendered and racialized politics and terror. Chapters call attention to the re/distribution of gendered and racialized vulnerabilities and their concomitant de/valuations that this rise has imposed especially with regard to violent displacements, dispossessions, and their various technologies. Chapters consider the rhetorical framings of refugees, asylum seekers, and im/migrants that can be criminalizing, pathologizing, or exceptionalizing and interrogate the consequences for how these populations are de- and revalued. Implicated in the production of dis/connectivities, im/mobilities, and vulnerabilities are various technologies, as they facilitate and enable economies of war, violence, and securitization.

Chapters herein consider not only im/mobilizations, but also the constellations of resistance that emerge in response to the rise of the global Right. Such constellations of resistance include "rhetorics of solidarity" and a rejection of the fiction of independence. Constellations of resistance recognize the conditions of and for interdependencies capable of responding to a hard-right populism that demarcates and "fixes" identities. We have selected contributions that draw on feminist materialisms, materialist economic frameworks, as well as those that engage critically with scholarship in new materialism. Rhetoricians attuned to materiality assume that all things—human, nonhuman, and extra-human—assemble (and, we argue, are assembled) to form the very conditions in and through which "human subjects are incorporated into systems of value" (Riedner and Mahoney 10). Rhetorical scholarship, therefore, takes seriously implications for how elements of a rhetorical situation bleed (Edbauer). Exploring and analyzing precarious rhetorics through the lens of materiality thereby necessitates critical attention to material ontologies (Barnett and Boyle), conditions, and vibrant matter (Bennett) that make possible human and nonhuman action and interaction (Rickert).

Our intervention in rhetorical studies' renewed interest in materiality is a deliberate attentiveness to unearthing the structures, and structuring forces, of inequity—inequities that both make possible and result from rhetorical situations' bloodshed. Furthermore, we hope that by resisting what some have critiqued as the fetishization of nonhuman objects, we've opened up space for joining extant conversations about the ethics of relationality. We recognize that while these conversations now enjoy a resurgence among rhetoric and communication scholars, they are not *new*. Conversations about materiality's suasiveness and concomitant ethics of relationality have taken place among Indigenous populations and people of color for centuries.[4]

Conversations about race, material rhetorics, and relationality have *had* to predate the so-called new material turn. After all, the United States was founded on racialized precarity. As we write this, plans to remove a statue of the Confederate general Robert E. Lee from the Emancipation Park (formerly Lee Park) in Charlottesville, Virginia, has sparked a weekend of violence on the University of Virginia's college campus. Hundreds of Nazis and white supremacists (under the guise of the "Unite the Right" movement) organized a rally that resulted in multiple bodily injuries and at least one homicide when they were confronted by counterprotestors.

But racialized precarity doesn't always march unabashedly around college campus rotundas, shouting "Blood and Soil" while armed with flaming torches. As several contributors demonstrate, racialized precarity is insidiously built into the United States' socioeconomic and educational infrastructures. Pérez, for example, examines the precarity of Black lives in structures of anti-Black racism. Coskan-Johnson interrogates how discourses of whiteness are mobilized in a way that stigmatizes non-white bodies as default perpetrators of violence against women. Greene and Swenson provide historical context for how economic insecurity became central to the United States' contemporary workforce. The contextualization of soft skills as individual job skills necessary for certain kinds of work generates a new precarity for those workers considered to lack those skills, and also slots those with the skills into a gendered and racial division of labor. Teston describes the ways racialized precarity embedded in genetics discourse affects biomedical treatment options, and by introducing the concept of wild refractions Licona offers the possibility of a critical intervention into the precarity that is produced by and produces a regime of distortion that otherwise functions to distort bodies of color, bodies of knowledge, and bodies of land.

Chapters in this collection share a common starting place by first recognizing the uneven distributions of power; they then, echoing Davis's notion of "response-ability" (200), respond to the fragility of human being—being that is perpetually entangled with and entrenched in infrastructural precarities. At the end of *Ambient Rhetoric,* a book frequently cited by rhetoricians with a renewed interest in materiality, Rickert confirms that, indeed, "nonhuman actants . . . have agency" (238). *Precarious Rhetorics* responds by asking: So, what now? What claims do Confederate statues, educational and economic infrastructures, and other nonhuman actants have on us? Answering Rickert's call to "attune . . . differently to world," chapters propose a series of rhetorical recalibrations—readjustments that force us not just to resee, but also to inhabit response-ability. In her contribution to this collection, Hirsu demonstrates not only how mobile technologies service the agendas of sovereign powers but also how they have contributed to the growth of networks of migrant activists, specifically how smartphones have enabled (or not) Syrian refugees to manage their precarious conditions. Attention to digital infrastructures in the pursuit of citizenship rights, protection, and movement enacts a materialism focused on accounts of human response-ability and its entanglement with "things," such as migrant vessels and mobile technologies.

As contributors engage a variety of subjects—structured and structuring inequalities, de/humanizing rhetorics of il/legality, resistance to social-symbolic injustices, settler-state governance, the displacement and disappearance of vulnerable human and nonhuman communities, statelessness, migrant crises, economic and institutional instability, digital interfaces, and the biomedical industrial complex—they animate anew classical and contemporary concepts in rhetorical theory, including ambience, kairos, akairos, the non-image, narrative, economic literacies, resignification, virality, ontologies, materiality, and co-construction. And they model a range of methodologies, including rhetorical, narrative, qualitative, and empirical analyses that elucidate the institutional and material-discursive machinations of precarity and activists' strategic, material-discursive mobilizations as forms of political resistance to precarious conditions.

VIOLENT RHETORICS: STATE TERROR AND POLITICAL RESISTANCE

Part I opens by drawing together the insights of critical theorists, philosophers, and rhetoricians who turn to concepts of precariousness, precarity, and precarization to understand state violence, terror, and political resistance. Contributors are particularly interested in how these concepts travel transnationally as instruments of domination to govern precarious "others" (migrants, refugees, detainees, and terrorist victims), preserve geopolitical borders, and legitimize the security logics and moral authority of modern nation-states. In *State of Insecurity: Government of the Precarious*, Lorey delineates three interrelated dimensions of the conceptual composition of the precarious, which help to frame the four chapters in part I. The first dimension of precariousness refers to the "socio-ontological dimension of lives and bodies" and social relationality, that is, the condition of "being with" other precarious lives (Nancy, qtd. in Lorey 12). The second dimension of precarity signifies the "distribution of precariousness in relations of inequity," and the third dimension, governmental precarization, points to modes of governing that destabilize individuals and communities, if not entire populations (12). Lorey's concept of "governmental precarization" is a particularly useful framework for understanding racialized state violence and gendered terror—themes at the heart of part I. Authors in part I contend that the study of governmental precarization not only demands a new ethics but also requires rhetorically informed methodologies.

In "Precaritization in the Security State: Ambient Akairos in Mohamedou Ould Slahi's *Guantánamo Diary*," Moore and Walzer focus on the geopolitical and rhetorical contingencies that shape Mohamedou Ould Slahi's *Guantánamo Diary* (2015)—the only account of post-9/11 Guantánamo written by a former detainee held captive for fourteen years. In this regard, Moore and Walzer embrace Lorey's notion of precarization as "living with . . . contingency" (1). Slahi's diary has been classified as protected information and was only released after nearly seven years of legal wrangling and with significant redactions. *Guantánamo Diary* began as notes for Slahi's attorneys, which he composed while in the third of his fourteen years of detention at Guantánamo Bay. Exposing false narratives used to sustain Guantánamo Bay as a prison camp, among them the "ticking bomb" scenario that has been called upon to rationalize torture, the diary, the authors argue, puts pressure on the genre of the first-person testimonial, where the privatization of justice often takes place. Moore and Walzer persuasively show how rhetoric materializes and manifests precarity through their analysis of the U.S. government's legal decisions that in effect justified the inhumane treatment of detainees. Methodologically, Moore and Walzer aptly extend Rickert's notion of ambient kairos in their characterization of akairos and the complex temporalities and materialities of precarity that the diary exposes, specifically how torture is legitimated outside the framework of exigency and exception, and how *Guantánamo Diary* operates within a framework of the inopportune. For example, *Guantánamo Diary* attests to the precarity of indefinite detention, and interrupts the progressive and triumphalist narratives of the state and "normative human rights" (22–23). Moore and Walzer's contribution therefore lies not only in their critical formulation of akairos as a concept and method to understand the instrumentality of state sanctioned violence; they also advance human rights scholarship in tracing the racialization of human rights institutionalization into securitization networks.

Likewise, in "Precarious Narratives: Media Accounts of Islamic State Sexual Violence," Hesford and Shuman turn our attention to the fusion of human rights and human security discourses. In their analysis of U.S. and U.K. media representations and UN reports on ISIS's enslavement of Yezidi women and girls, the authors identify how the descriptor "sex slavery" rhetorically reifies forms of American legal and moral exceptionalism and positions female Yezidi victims as precarious subjects. These precarious narratives, they argue, are themselves vulnerable to ideologies of rescue. The gendered ethno-religious vulnerability of Yezidi women and girls under radical Islamic theology, and the mobilization of the spectacle of sex slavery in both terrorist propaganda and human rights reporting, exemplify how the Yezidi crisis becomes intelligible within narrative representation, and specifically how narratives enable vulnerability to materialize in particular ways, in this case, by gendering terror and reproducing gendered precarity. Hesford and Shuman demonstrate how a framework of precarious rhetorics helps us to understand complex relationships between rescued and rescuer, the constitutive relationships among multiple narratives of victimhood, and the contradictory positions produced by narratives across geopolitical boundaries. In sum, these intersecting and often contradictory narratives in representations of ISIS's enslavement and rape of Yezidi women and girls prompt a return to a concept of ethical responsibility based on an understanding of the precarity of discourse.

In "Necropolitics as Foreign Affairs Rhetoric in Contemporary U.S.-Mexican Relations," McKinnon argues that transnational feminist rhetorical critics are uniquely situated to understand how precarious rhetorics activate neoliberal inter/national imaginaries and life and death logics that reinforce global political economic asymmetries and structures of power. McKinnon examines the ecology of foreign affairs making when the object of precarity and death is an entire nation-state. Through the analysis of entertainment and news media discourses as well as political discourse about U.S.-Mexico relations, McKinnon shows how necropolitics—a politic that focuses on decision making on "who may live and who must die" (Mbembe)—create material-discursive precarities. One of the ways that the U.S. government has managed risk around state sovereignty and borders, justified security-based initiatives, and propped up transnational capital's interests in the region has been through the construal of Mexico as a state rampant with narco-violence, brutal killings and mass graves, and citizens looking for safety elsewhere. McKinnon's focus on how precarious rhetorics function as part of a larger political economic ecology moves the study of foreign affairs rhetoric beyond the field's focus on a singular speech or political leader to consider how a range of political actors and diverse set of mediums and messaging strategies work in the macro-setting of global politics.

Part I concludes with Pérez's "Embodying 'I Can't Breathe': Tensions and Possibilities Between Appropriation and Coalition." Pérez, like McKinnon, draws readers' attention to the un/livability of particular and precarious bodies. She considers the suffocating powers of the state that render particular voices fatally inaudible. Focusing on the murder of Eric Garner, Pérez considers the organizing labor of his last words—"I can't breathe"—for multiple bodies and social movements across contexts. Pérez analyzes the circulation and appropriation of the #ICantBreathe hashtag that emerged after Garner's death. Specifically, Pérez offers an extended engagement with the rhetorics of coalition and coalitional gesture to consider the ways dominant and precarious bodies embody actions and produce alliances or appropriations and to what consequences. By unearthing the tensions between coalition and appropriation, and in moving readers through the messiness of coalitional performances and possibilities, Pérez makes both a theoretical and practical contribution to our volume that can inform movement accomplices and our gestures and practices of solidarity across social movements.

RESIGNIFICATIONS: MOVEMENT, MIGRATION, AND DISPLACEMENT

Chapters in Part II are critically aware of precarity as a theoretical construct that illuminates processes of differential valuations and devaluations as well as of redistributed vulnerabilities in an era of increasing transnational movements, migrations, dispossessions, and (forced) displacements. In different ways, each chapter interrogates myriad references Butler makes to precarious life and to "relations of proximity" in order to better understand the distortions that can structure such de/valuations and the related vulnerabilities they induce, especially through cohabitation. The four chapters in this section take up what Coskan-Johnson refers to as rapid resignifications and, relatedly, what Licona references as the seamless substitutions of one culprit for another in dominant social imaginaries. Such resignifications and facile replacements are manifestations of the precarious rhetorics that delimit how im/migrants, refugees, and asylum seekers can be seen and understood, even how they can move or not, particularly in an era of the rise of the global Right and its structuring il/logics.

Drawing from transnational feminist political, legal, and ethnic studies scholars and feminist philosophers and sociologists, contributors to part II highlight the rhetorically productive forces of post-9/11 contexts. Each contribution serves as a repudiation of circulating notions of the "exceptional" subject. Relatedly, chapters here also refuse oppressive rhetorics, including visual rhetorics, that circulate transnationally to produce fear and suspicion of those who have been forced to move and migrate through and into what

Butler references as the "radically uninhabitable" (*Precarious Life* xvii). Such refusals can be seen, for example, through distinct engagements with Cacho's considerations of the consequences of "repudiating criminality and recuperating social value" (13). Chapters in part II are analytically driven to work through the myriad ways social revaluations reproduce consequential delimitations and the conditions of possibility for resistances.

Coskan-Johnson begins "Reciprocal Flowers: Precarious Rhetorics of Solidarity on a New Year's Eve in Cologne" with reference to the gone-viral video that was created in response to reports of en masse sexual assaults on women reportedly by asylum seekers in Cologne, Germany, on New Year's Eve 2015. In the video, "How 100 Women Responded to the Attacks in Cologne with Love," German women exchange flowers with those assumed to be detained asylum seekers. The video's reproduction of simplistic understandings of the asylum seeker as either "good" or "bad" produces violent disavowals such that racially marginalized groups are forced to disavow refugees framed as "bad" in order for themselves to be viewed as potentially good, which leaves in place the divisions upon which such precarious valuations are predicated. In capturing what many see as an aspiring act of political resistance, Coskan-Johnson considers how the video functions as a disruption to "discourses of hate and division," as a "rhetoric of solidarity" it remains precarious (121). Drawing from Butler's notion of "unwilled adjacency" as the imposed intimacies and proximities of involuntary cohabitation, itself predicated on forced migrations, Coskan-Johnson considers how the precarious rhetorics of solidarity might and might not provide promising possibilities (Butler, "Precarious Life" 24).

Related to the contradictions that inhere in Coskan-Johnson's "rhetorics of solidarity," Lyon introduces the idea of co-opted vulnerability, which is at play in the rather anomalous and fraught public welcoming of refugees in Buffalo, New York. In "Reversals of Precarity: Rewriting Buffalo's Refugees as Neoliberal Subjects," Lyon notes, since 2003 the "more than 14,000 refugees [who] have resettled in the city of Buffalo," have come mostly from "Burma (Myanmar), Somalia, Bhutan, Iraq, and the Republic of the Congo" (128). She describes how many refugees embrace neoliberal values and highlights how the neoliberal imaginary at play in Buffalo functions as a technology of citizen creation, including how the notion of "we the people" is revealed as a consequential, and even distorting, rhetoric for both refugees and non-refugees. The reductive effects of such neoliberal discourses emphasize the economic value of refugees so that they are rhetorically framed as burgeoning entrepreneurs and, therefore, as exceptional citizen-subject saviors of a f(l)ailing economy. Lyon probes the many ways the economic needs and insecurities, traumas, and other vulnerabilities of many refugees go unrecognized. In refusing what she calls such neoliberal monologisms, Lyon introduces the paradox of possibility as a way of creating conditions for meaningful political engagements. Reminiscent of third-space, women-of-color feminisms, the in-between spaces theorized in both Lyon's and Coskan-Johnson's work is a generative space of possibility for engaging in democratic politics where meaningful deliberations of multiply-situated subjects might occur.

Hirsu's "'Where am I? Do you have WiFi?': Vital Technologies and Precarious Living in the Syrian Refugee Crisis" offers readers a nuanced understanding of the relationship between precarity, bodies, technologies, dis/connectivities, and im/mobilities within the Syrian refugee crisis. Working from an instrumentalist rhetorical frame and a new materialist perspective, she approaches smartphones as co-constitutive of human life and therefore as interactive techno-human assemblages that are embedded in the logics of capitalism and that make life matter. In considering the web of relations that exists in a technology-refugee assemblage and by resisting the reproduction of a techno-optimistic narrative, Hirsu creates a necessary conversation about precarity, asylum seekers, and digitality that asks readers to consider digital technologies as part of structural and structuring inequalities. She argues that in a "world of unsettling global movements and digital connectivity, precarity settles within techno-human assemblages that perpetuate sociopolitical inequalities and mask the entanglements of being in an unsafe world" (161). Hirsu is concerned with the obfuscating effects of visual representations of Syrian refugees with mobile technologies and calls for a more careful examination of techno-human assemblages in order to "make visible current conditions of precarity" (162). To create a more expansive human rights framework, and following Rickert, Hirsu articulates material conditions and vibrant matter to call for a repositioning of technologies as an interdependent part of the human ontology. This, she suggests, will allow for bodies structured in need to be seen not in opposition to technologies of connectivity but, rather, as fully implicated in them.

In "The Non/Image of the Regime of Distortion," Licona is also concerned with (manufactured) distortions of migrants, migration, borders, and borderlands spaces that permeate the U.S. social imaginary. Through images (what she terms "non-images") and fear-inflected discourses (treated here as monstrous rhetorics), U.S. publics are persuaded to believe—and to see—a story of movements and migrations composed of exclusively pathologized and increasingly only criminalized Others. The non-image, produced in what Licona theorizes as a "regime of distortion," relies on oppositional specular logics that are effectively and affectively mobilized and that have political and regulatory effects. Moreover, they constitute visual rhetorical arguments that function (1) to produce radical desires for new technologies and regulatory techniques of border securitization, and (2) secure conditions for the slow and social deaths of non-white bodies (see Puar). The regime of distortion, through which logics of seeing and believing function as systems of de/valuation, conditions the precariousness of the always-already and of the newly vulnerable. Licona suggests that practices of radical proximity and wild refractions might counteract the dispossessions that dominant imaginaries have continued to produce through the regime of distortion. This approach, Licona argues, can be understood as a kind of queer and affective visuality.

The four chapters that constitute part II call readers to be attentive to dominant discourses and technologies of fear, suspicion, and social division and their mediated distortions as precarious rhetorics that can function to effectively erase vulnerable people and places. They consider, too, various technologies of citizen making, of monster making, and of intra-activity, to carefully consider those populations that, as Butler and Cacho note, are differentially exposed to injury, violence, and slow and social death. In asking scholars what to make of such discursive contradictions and their material conditions/conditionings, these chapters begin to offer the possibilities for an expanded and expansive material-rhetorical framework for considering rights and justice. In part III, contributors focus on how precarity has become a means of "governing ourselves" (Butler, qtd. in Lorey vii)—particularly in everyday, institutional contexts and practices.

RHETORICAL NAVIGATIONS: INSTITUTIONAL AND INFRASTRUCTURAL INSTABILITIES

The contributors of the final four chapters in this collection leverage the explanatory power of precarity to uncover material-discursive phenomena that condition what is (or is not) accommodatable in educational spaces, what counts as "skill" in a postindustrial labor force, online abuse in digital environments, and how the biomedical backstage contributes to structuring inequalities and racialized medical practices. As Lorey argues, "Precarization means living with the unforeseeable, with contingency. . . . Neoliberal governing proceeds primarily through social insecurity, through regulating the minimum of assurance while simultaneously increasing instability" (2). Each chapter, therefore, highlights tactics and strategies for navigating instability— all of which are meant to reduce, or create the appearance of reducing, insecurities, but actually serve to reify if not mundanize infrastructural instabilities that are governed by neoliberal logics.

In response to the neoliberal university's attempts at ensuring equity through academic accommodations, Price's chapter, "The Precarity of Disability/Studies in Academe," troubles definitions of disability that rely on the appearance of a stable, disabled human body. Academic accommodations are made based on definitions of disability that rely on normative structures and fixed assumptions about how bodies, space, and time interact. Precarity helps Price to redefine disability in ways that recognize the unpredictable and often unequal ways that students and educators navigate the complexities of space, time, and what she calls "bodyminds." Price explores "unaccommodatable" disabilities—including, for example, severe depression, psychosis, and other unpredictable conditions ranging from multiple sclerosis to migraines. Such disabilities are, according to Price, quintessentially precarious. That such body-mind experiences resist formalized, stabilizing definitions of disability that are predicated on medicalized disease models—they are neither "physical" nor "mental"—makes them impossible to anticipate and accommodate. Understanding the precarity of unaccommodatable disabilities in institutions of higher education helps to challenge the heretofore inseparability of an accommodation model from goals for cure and profit, if not the full-on elimination of undesirable bodies. Price concludes by offering a theory of "crip spacetime," making room for an everyday ethic of care that recognizes independence (and concomitant definitions of accommodation in higher education) as a fiction.

In "'Are you Black, Though?': Black Autoethnography and Racing the Graduate Student/Instructor," Louis M. Maraj builds on the pivotal work of Black scholars in rhetoric, composition, and literacy studies in his methodological enactment of Black storytelling traditions. In his autoethnographic analysis of teaching composition at a historically white Midwestern university, Maraj highlights the institutional and embodied racial precarities that shape his relations with his students as a Black im/migrant able-bodied male graduate student instructor. Among the pedagogical insights that this chapter offers are critical reflections on students' identity negotiations, including expressions of stereotypical blackness and instances of cultural appropriation. Maraj discusses, for example, how he navigates the performance of difference in a context that entangles Black masculinity in a "self-defeating bind, all while working to subvert that paradox by embodying resistance" (215). Foregrounding Black feminist thinkers (Collins, Jordan, Lorde, Spillers), who prioritized a relational understanding of racial precarity long before scholarship's recent new materialist turn, Maraj aptly demonstrates the institutional mechanisms that regulate Black subjectivity. These include diversity initiatives that reify rather than contest systemic racism. As a form of resistant storytelling, "Are You Black, Though?," like Price's "The Precarity of Disability/Studies in Academe," importantly contributes to our understanding of academic precarities and difference within the neoliberal university.

Overlap between precarity, access, and ability are issues not just for the neoliberal university but also for the contemporary U.S. workplace. Motivated by economic insecurities that have emerged from what they see as the hollowing out of the U.S. middle class during the last forty years, Greene and Swenson, through a lens of precarity studies, explore which skills are deemed more or less valuable in the U.S. workforce. Their chapter, "Precarious Cooperation: Soft Skills and the Governing of Labor Power," frames so-called soft skills in terms of what they see as a shift in professional norms within post-Fordist policies of full employment. Unlike technical skills, soft skills reflect workers' flexibility and response-ability to contingencies of the contemporary workplace. Such skills are difficult to account for materially. In fact, at one time they may have been characterized as personality traits—for example, being adaptable, a skilled communicator, enthusiastic, a team player, or gifted in conflict resolution. Greene and Swenson argue that soft skills signify cooperation and accomplishment within larger organizational goals, which thereby serve to normalize capitalist modes of production. The championing of soft skills emboldens a new managerial class that is predicated on militaristic models of command, supervision, and leadership.

While Greene and Swenson are attuned to how soft skills, as modeled by the U.S. military, have become a precondition for employment in the U.S. workforce, in their chapter, "Complicit Interfaces," Tarsa and Brown zoom in on one soft skill in particular: digital communication in online spaces. Digital networks such as Facebook and Twitter harness the productive power of global capitalism in ways that, despite the promise of transcending barriers and ease of collaboration, are perilously precarious. Tarsa and Brown highlight how exploitations of race, class, and gender are built into the design of everyday digital interfaces. Tarsa and Brown productively pair scholarship in feminist media studies, critical race theory, and precarity studies in their call for "speculative redesign" of digital interfaces, which assumes that such interfaces do more than merely mediate online abuse (256). Digital interfaces are complicit in the very act of digital abuse.

Digital interfaces and other computational actors are central to human experience—especially in everyday health care practices. The computational medico-pharmaceutical industrial complex has ushered in the digitization of medical records, body data, and other key metrics for measuring health and wellness. Among such biomedical metrics are genetic evidences, which are increasingly used to manufacture arguments about how some bodies are more or less biologically vulnerable. In the final chapter, "Pathologizing Precarity,"

Teston interrogates geneticists' racialized computational methods to uncover how some bodies are rendered more or less pathologized or biologically "at risk." Teston describes that genetic evidences help to prop up arguments about Native American communities' increased risk for alcoholism and Black women's increased risk for deadly forms of breast cancer. Challenging their seeming objectivity, Teston first outlines how genetic tests are based on unwittingly racialized computational analyses of large data sets and then details how such analyses are supported in scientific laboratories through precarious rhetorics, including algorithms, big data, and computational-analytic procedures. Teston then pairs rhetorical theories that attend to materiality and computation (James J. Brown; Rickert) with precarity (Berlant; Butler, *Frames*; Lorey) to analyze how time and place "are both more dynamic and more integrated into our practices than we have recognized" (Rickert 43). Teston concludes that because human bodies are "porous and not discretely bounded" (Jayna Brown 326), care for human communities requires ongoing negotiations with constantly changing biologies, geographies, histories, environments, politics, and economies. Combined, these market, material, and computational actors help to structurally and scientifically recapitulate both the racialization of medical practice and the (de)valuation of non-white populations (cf. Holloway; Montoya; TallBear).

Each chapter in Part III contributes to rhetorical theory through rich illustrations of the ways material-discursive phenomena condition the very infrastructural insecurities that result in the slow death of certain populations. These chapters also model novel methods for uncovering and analyzing precarious rhetorics—interviewing tactics informed by a paradigm of accessible interdependent research (Price), autoethnography (Maraj), historiography (Greene and Swenson), speculative design (Tarsa and Brown), and rhetorical ontography (Teston). Each of the chapters in part III offers to readers a host of analytic constructs, claims, and methods for understanding how precarity operates in everyday, institutional spaces of human being.

Together the chapters in this collection compel us as rhetoric and communication scholars to recognize precarity and our inter-/intra-dependencies. Yet, as contributors also point out, such rhetorical recalibrations confer no guarantee. Recognition in and of itself is not "sufficient . . . to breach the ambiguities of ethics and violence" (Mills 153). But inhabiting a disposition toward responsiveness can hold the possibility of acting through an understanding of these long-standing if newly recognized inter-/intra-dependencies. Amid state-sponsored violence, terrorism, white nationalism, neoliberal political economies and subjectivities, technologies of citizenship, displacement, dispossession, and infrastructural instabilities, this collection demonstrates that when engaging critically with such material rhetorics—and when witnessed or otherwise experienced through the lens of precarity—new speculations emerge. Possibilities for becoming and belonging open up. Ultimately, recalibrating toward an ethic of responsibility and relationality disrupts precarious logics of independence that condition corporeal, physical, and affective abandonment.

NOTES

1. See Aciksoz and Korkman.
2. See Gómez-Barris.
3. See Coole and Frost for a discussion of how scholars are bridging critical traditions in turning to materialities "contingent modes of appearing" (27) and recognition of "materiality [as] relational, emergent" (29).
4. For more on radical, critical, and ethical relationality, see Simpson; Betasamosake Simpson; "Emergence" and TallBear's *Native American DNA*.

WORKS CITED

Aciksoz, Salih C., and Zeynep K. Korkman. "Grab 'Em by the Patriarchy." *Anthropology News* 58.3 (2017): 10–12.

Barnett, Scot, and Casey Boyle, eds. *Rhetoric, Through Everyday Things*. University of Alabama Press, 2016.

Bennett, Jane. *Vibrant Matter: A Political Ecology of Things*. Duke University Press, 2009.

Berlant, Lauren. "Slow Death (Sovereignty, Obesity, Lateral Agency)." *Critical Inquiry* 33.4 (2007): 754–80.

Brown, James J. "The Machine That Therefore I Am." *Philosophy and Rhetoric* 47.4 (2014): 494–514.

Brown, Jayna. "Being Cellular Race, the Inhuman, and the Plasticity of Life." *GLQ: A Journal of Lesbian and Gay Studies* 21.2–3 (2015): 321–41.

Butler, Judith. *Frames of War: When Is Life Grievable?* Verso, 2009.

——. *Precarious Life: The Powers of Mourning and Violence*. Verso, 2006.

——. "Precarious Life, Vulnerability, and the Ethics of Cohabitation." *The Journal of Speculative Philosophy* 26.2 (2012): 134–51.

Cacho, Lisa Marie. *Social Death: Racialized Rightlessness and the Criminalization of the Unprotected*. New York University Press, 2012.

Chávez, Karma R. *Queer Migration Politics: Activist Rhetoric and Coalitional Possibilities*. University of Illinois Press, 2013.

Coole, Diana, and Samantha Frost. *New Materialisms: Ontology, Agency, and Politics*. Duke University Press, 2010.

Davis, Diane. "Addressing Alterity: Rhetoric, Hermeneutics, and the Nonappropriative Relation." *Philosophy and Rhetoric* 38.3 (2005): 191–212.

Edbauer, Jenny. "Unframing Models of Public Distribution: From Rhetorical Situation to Rhetorical Ecologies." *Rhetoric Society Quarterly* 35.4 (2005): 5–24.

Gómez-Barris, Macarena. *The Extractive Zone: Social Ecologies and Decolonial Perspectives.* Duke University Press, 2017.

Holloway, Karla F. C. *Private Bodies, Public Texts: Race, Gender, and a Cultural Bioethics.* Duke University Press, 2011.

———. "Their Bodies, Our Conduct: How Society and Medicine Produce Persons Standing in Need of End-of-Life Care." *Journal of Palliative Medicine* 19.2 (2016): 127–28.

Licona, Adela C. *Zines in Third Space: Radical Cooperation and Borderlands Rhetorics.* SUNY Press, 2012.

Licona, Adela C., and Karma R. Chávez. "Relational Literacies and Their Coalitional Possibilities." *Peitho Journal* 18.1 (2015): 96–107.

Lorey, Isabell. *State of Insecurity: Government of the Precarious.* Verso, 2015.

Mbembe, Achille. "Necropolitics." *Public Culture* 15.1 (2003): 11–40.

Mills, Catherine. "Normative Violence, Vulnerability, and Responsibility." *Differences* 18.2 (2007): 133–56.

Montoya, Michael. *Making the Mexican Diabetic: Race, Science, and the Genetics of Inequality.* Berkeley: University of California Press, 2011.

Moyn, Samuel. "Beyond Liberal Internationalism." *Dissent* 64 (2017): 116–22.

Powell, Malea, Daisy Levy, Andrea Riley-Mukavetz, Marilee Brooks-Gillies, Maria Novotny, and Jennifer Fisch-Ferguson. "Our Story Begins Here: Constellating Cultural Rhetorics." *Enculturation: A Journal of Rhetoric, Writing, and Culture* 25 (2014): n. pag.

Puar, Jasbir K. *Terrorist Assemblages: Homonationalism in Queer Times.* Duke University Press, 2007.

Rickert, Thomas. *Ambient Rhetoric: The Attunements of Rhetorical Being.* University of Pittsburgh Press, 2013.

Riedner, Rachel, and Kevin Mahoney. *Democracies to Come: Rhetorical Action, Neoliberalism, and Communities of Resistance.* Lanham, MD: Lexington Books, 2008.

Roth, Kenneth. "The Dangerous Rise of Populism: Global Attacks on Human Rights Values." *Human Rights Watch World Report* (2017): 1–14.

Simpson, Audra. *Mohawk Interruptus: Political Life Across the Borders of Settler States.* Duke University Press, 2014.

Simpson, Leanne Betasamosake. "Land as Pedagogy: Nishnaabeg Intelligence and Rebellious Transformation." *Decolonization: Indigeneity, Education & Society* 3.3 (2014): 1–25.

Slahi, Mohamedou Ould. *Guantánamo Diary.* Ed. Larry Siems. Back Bay Books, 2015.

TallBear, Kim. "The Emergence, Politics and Marketplace of Native American DNA." *Routledge Handbook of Science, Technology, and Society.* Ed. D. L. Kleinman and K. Moore, 2014. 21–37.

———. *Native American DNA: Tribal Belonging and the False Promise of Genetic Science.* University of Minnesota Press, 2013.

Taylor, Letta. "Overreach: How New Global Counterterrorism Measures Jeopardize Rights." *Human Rights Watch World Report* (2017): 27–38.

PART I

VIOLENT RHETORICS

STATE TERROR AND POLITICAL RESISTANCE

CHAPTER 1

Precaritization in the Security State

Ambient Akairos in Mohamedou Ould Slahi's Guantánamo Diary

ALEXANDRA S. MOORE and BELINDA WALZER

IN HIS INTRODUCTION to Mohamedou Ould Slahi's *Guantánamo Diary*—the only account of secret rendition, torture, and indefinite detention written while its author was in captivity—the book's editor, Larry Siems, writes:

> Thirteen years ago, Mohamedou left his home in Nouakchott, Mauritania, and drove to the headquarters of his national police for questioning. He has not returned. For our collective sense of story and of justice, we must have a clearer understanding of why this has not happened yet, and what will happen next. (xlix)

In October 2017, Slahi was finally released from Guantánamo and transferred back to his family in Mauritania. However, his long overdue return does not diminish the significance of questions about "our collective sense of story and of justice" that the book raises. In this chapter, we read the narrative suspense generated by the book as contesting the rhetorical situation from which it emerges. That contestation has largely been framed by competing narratives of fear and vulnerability, each of which puts pressure on the concept of precarity as an index of endangerment.

On the one hand, Slahi's capture in November 2001 and the violence he suffered over fourteen years in the custody or at the behest of the U.S. government have taken place in a climate of exigency used to justify that treatment.

Slahi was once deemed one of the "worst of the worst," in the familiar words of Bush administration officials after the September 11, 2001, attacks—one whose disappearance, detention without charge, and abuse were deemed necessary to prosecute criminality and to secure the state against the purportedly existential threat of terrorism. This rationale, perhaps best encapsulated in the "ticking time bomb" scenario used to justify torture, is amplified by a rhetoric of fear in order to legitimate state violence that might otherwise be deplored. From this perspective, Slahi's book reads as a bid for leniency from a crafty and untrustworthy source or, given that Slahi was never charged with any crime and has now been released, as a tale of unfortunate "collateral" (Danner) in the "war on terror." Both interpretations maintain a climate of fear as the key index of rhetorical context, an index reflected in the naming of the war itself. As Marc Redfield has asked in his fine reading of *The Rhetoric of Terror*, "What might be made of the glide from 'terrorism' to 'terror'" (71) in the "war on terror"? If "terrorism" initially substituted a violent strategy for an identifiable enemy, the "glide" to "terror" further divorces the campaign from the political by targeting affect (Redfield 78). The "war on *terror*" reinforces what we frame here as the rhetorical ambience of fear and panic employed to fuel particular military and political actions.

On the other hand, and perhaps just as familiar as the rhetoric of fear underscoring the "war on terror," is the trope of the victim of human rights abuses who, gaining a public voice through the book's publication, seems poised to complete what Elora Halim Chowdhury refers to as the "'progress narrative,' the transformation of a victim to a survivor and then to an activist" (xvi). This resolution now appears imminent: over the summer of 2016, Slahi was granted a hearing by the administrative Periodic Review Board, which ruled unanimously that the "continued law of war detention of the detainee is no longer necessary to protect against a continuing significant threat to the security of the United States," thus making Slahi eligible for transfer "with appropriate security assurances" (Periodic Review Secretariat). Slahi's release makes good on that ruling. However, Slahi awaited transfer for eleven years from the same cell in which he wrote his manuscript in 2005 and six and half years after a federal district court judge granted his *habeas corpus* petition. Read as the penultimate chapter to a life of ostensible freedom (Slahi is still subject to unspecified security measures), *Guantánamo Diary* (in its original and now restored editions) presages the full agency of its author-subject.

Recognizing the significance of Slahi's release as well as the tremendous accomplishments of the manuscript in detailing his experiences and perceptions, we chart a different approach that does not rely on triumphalist, progressive temporalities of either state securitization or the agency of the liberal subject who has gained human rights through self-narration (e.g., Slaughter,

"Narration"). Wary of the state's ability to co-opt the language of precarity as well as of normative human rights discourse to assuage it, here we argue for a reading of *Guantánamo Diary*'s representation of precaritization as "an instrument of government" (Lorey 2).[1] Isabell Lorey defines precaritization as a form of neoliberal governmentality that operates primarily within national borders to manage populations by destabilizing select groups and privatizing risk. Precaritization requires what Lorey refers to as social hierarchization and segmentation to facilitate "political and legal regulations that are specifically supposed to protect against general, existential precariousness" (21–22). The "privilege[d]" protection of some is therefore predicated upon "a differential distribution of the precarity of all those who are perceived as other" (22). This designation clearly fits the Guantánamo captives as well as others targeted in the "war on terror" both in the United States and around the world. Mindful of Paul Amar's analysis of the role of intra- and transnational securitization networks in managing populations, we extend Lorey's argument to focus on the intersecting logics of precaritization and securitization, their transnational reach, and attempts to mask their normalizing effects. Precaritization and securitization, as tools of government that function intra- and transnationally to identify specific groups for endangerment ostensibly to protect the center, define the material and ambient contexts from which the book emerges and to which it speaks.

Whereas official U.S. rhetoric in the "war on terror" posited the attacks of September 11, 2001, as an extraordinary emergency that justified legal and political exception, we note that the language of emergency is crucial to normalizing the state's forcible precaritization of specific populations. Moreover, such targeting both activated an international network of black sites and torture surrogates *and* borrowed tactics already employed in the violent incarceration of racial minorities in the United States. At issue is not the severity and significance of the attacks of 9/11, but the government's decision to respond by exacerbating a climate of fear and then attributing it to a category of persons defined by identity rather than action. This twinned discourse of national precariousness and securitization directed specifically against Muslim men both in the United States and abroad has had two effects that bear on our argument: the precaritization of Muslim men (and boys) has led to some of the most egregious abuses in Guantánamo while simultaneously foreclosing analysis of the historical and geopolitical roots of the 9/11 attacks. Read in terms of debates over the future of the Guantánamo prison complex, this reading of precaritization suggests that Guantánamo does not so much guarantee either affective or material security for the United States and its citizens so much as it works to justify the ongoing mobilization of state violence by continually reproducing a "threat" to which that violence then responds. We take up rhetorical theories of kairos, akairos, and ambience to examine the tension between the language of emergency as a short-term and exceptional challenge to ever-increasing state power, on the one hand, and precaritization as the long-term normalization of state claims to *the right to harm* specific populations, on the other hand. These rhetorical analytics make visible the complex temporalities and materialities of precarity generated by the legal and procedural apparatuses that *Guantánamo Diary* exposes. We argue that an ambient akairotic approach, one focused on the ways in which *Guantánamo Diary* may be as read as inopportune speech in relation to its rhetorical context, contributes to a robust analysis of precaritization in an era of perpetual war.

Guantánamo Diary is the published form of a 122,000-word manuscript that Slahi handwrote in English, his fourth language, in 2005. It began as notes for his attorneys that he composed while in the third year of his detention at Guantánamo Bay. The writing itself emerges in complex ways out of the "Special Interrogation Plan" in 2003 and 2004 that then–secretary of defense Donald Rumsfeld approved for Slahi (Committee on Armed Services 135–41). Readers may surmise Slahi's egregious abuse provoked his desire to write as a form of witnessing, as when Giorgio Agamben states Primo Levi "becomes a writer so that he can bear witness" (16). However, we must also consider how Slahi's torture did not yield the "actionable intelligence" his interrogators sought but rather the apparent meltdown of the government's rationale for his treatment. In the manuscript, Slahi recounts when he broke under torture, telling his interrogators, "If you're ready to buy, I'm selling" (291), and produced over one thousand pages of forced confessions (283–84). Rather than provide the grounds for legal charges, Slahi's forced confessions resulted in the withdrawal of the lead prosecutor from his case and in the granting of privileges, including the writing materials necessary for the book and a small garden to tend in order to help Slahi recuperate from his yearlong torture and interrogation.

Deemed 'classified' and then 'protected' information, the manuscript was only released after six-plus years of legal wrangling and with significant redactions. Through a remarkably transparent process, Larry Siems edited the released text to its current 100,000 words, provided extensive footnotes for many of its 2,500 redactions, and made the original, handwritten redacted pages available on the book's website, www.guantanamodiary.com. Since his release, Slahi has "repaired" the original manuscript by reinserting the redacted text, and the Restored Edition, which makes both redactions and reinsertions visible was published in 2017. As such, *Guantánamo Diary* provides one man's testimony from dark chambers of kidnapping, torture, and indefinite detention without charge; however, that testimony is only made possible and legible by means of the privileges granted by his captors and the often contradictory editorial work of U.S. censors, Slahi, and Siems. Therefore, the book, as material object and narrative, documents a contested political and legal subjectivity in the making.

In what follows we focus on the original edition of the book first to consider how the rhetorical concepts of kairos, akairos, and ambience offer a framework through which to analyze that process of subjectivization in terms of the collaborative and contradictory text it yields, as opposed to a singular, agentic subject-as-voice. Second, we examine how the strategic precaritization of Slahi (and other detainees) takes place at the intersection of biopolitical and sovereign power. To do so, we show how temporal contradiction and the irruption of inopportune expression reveal the government's claim to the right to harm Slahi as one of Guantánamo's "population-subjects" (Lorey 24). Finally, we analyze moments of ambient akairos in *Guantánamo Diary* through its unusual dedication, its use of fable, and its redactions. Each in its own way functions as a form of precarious rhetoric that describes the material, psychological, and emotional endangerment of its subject. Even more important to our argument, however, are the ways in which these forms of precarious rhetoric, first, shift the context of the reader's encounter with the text, and second, disclose Slahi's precaritization as a rationale for state violence rather than as a means to a different end.

KAIROS AND THE POST-9/11 CONTEXT

Kairos, in its most straightforward definition, is the opportune moment traditionally juxtaposed to the chronological passing of time. It describes the fleeting present that denotes the specific moment to strike, here the "ticking time-bomb scenario," constructed in present tense, but recognizable only as it passes. It also describes the historical epoch, which for *Guantánamo Diary* might be the long history of the naval base as a gatekeeper of U.S. imperial interests since 1903 or, more briefly, the understanding of the September 11 attacks as a challenge to American exceptionalism that must be met with extraordinary measures. Kairos is therefore the recognition of how the surrounding conditions constrain or make possible an argument's legibility (Longaker and Walker 9). In other words, by grasping kairos, the rhetor can seize the moment and shift the frame to their own ends.

However, as Debra Hawhee notes, a more contemporary notion of kairos "enables a consideration of 'invention-in-the-middle,' a space-time which marks the emergence of a provisional 'subject,' one that works *on*—and is worked on *by*—the situation" (qtd. in Rickert 82). Thus, Hawhee "theorizes kairos less as a moment that we, as subjects, seize to our advantage than as an emerging situation that dissolves the a priori distinction between subject and object" (qtd. in Rickert 82). Kairos from this perspective can be understood less as a tool the rhetor can enact based on rhetorical acumen, and more as something that operates in what Thomas Rickert calls "ambient" terms.

According to Rickert, who traces the history of the term as it relates to materiality and spatiality, kairos has been materially emplaced and discussed in somatic terms since Homer's *Iliad*. He describes it in the form of an arrow finding its deadly mark (77–78), and in the form of "twelve axes set at precise intervals in a straight line" (Onians, qtd. in Rickert 78) through which Greek archers would conduct target practice, giving rise to the idiomatic use of "opening" or "nick" as a temporal moment (Rickert 78). This emphasis reminds us of the material, in this case corporeal, effects of state precaritization—the loss of freedom and physical abuse of those apprehended in the "war on terror"—as well as the need to extend that material emphasis to include the psychological and affective legacy inflicted upon targeted populations by power that acts "in the nick of time." Rickert emphasizes that the scholarly return to the concept of kairos in the latter half of the twentieth century has focused on the ability to manipulate kairos, to harness it as a rhetorical device (76), which ignores the important material and contextual—the ambient—situation that the rhetor may or may not be able to control. We turn to the concept of ambience as it relates to kairos here to understand the false temporal urgency upon which Slahi's torture was justified, as well as how the book emerges as much from its ambient context as from a single rhetor.

The tension inherent in an attempt to seize the moment for rhetorical invention (in this case to facilitate judicial and procedural intervention) in a context that cannot be fully controlled manifests in many of the Bush administration's responses to the 9/11 attacks. For example, read in terms of ambient kairos, President George W. Bush's February 7, 2002, memorandum in the Torture Memos skillfully addresses the pronounced climate of public fear and vulnerability in order to proclaim simultaneously both the importance of "our values as a nation" and the need to abrogate those values, namely U.S. commitments to international law: "this new paradigm—ushered in not by us, but by terrorists—requires new thinking in the law of war" (Bush). This rationale, which some continue to espouse, posits the attacks of 9/11 as an interruption of a normative history of legal warfare. Based upon the legal arguments of the U.S. Department of Justice (DOJ) in the Torture Memos, this "new thinking" also concludes that captives' treatment "should be consistent with the principles of Geneva" (Bush) although Bush, following the DOJ, has already determined that those principles do not legally apply. Whereas the DOJ reads international humanitarian law narrowly for limited meanings divorced from its larger impulse toward protection from harm, the president emphasizes the spirit of the law but not its instrumentation. Thus, the president ultimately reverses the logic presented by the DOJ in its memos, although they reach the same conclusion that the United States is not bound by Article III of Geneva in its treatment of detainees and the government may proceed with the assumption of their guilt. In the process, this logic achieves what Naomi Paik describes as "the savvy deployment of the law to produce new categories of subjects and flexible modes of governance" (156). In other words, the president's hollow rhetorical commitment to human rights masks the juridical production of inhumanity in the Torture Memos and subsequent legislation, not by dehumanizing Guantánamo detainees or casting them outside the law but in legalizing their abuse.

Coded in the language and logics of securitization and cultural difference, the categories of "unlawful" and "enemy" combatants and euphemisms such as "indefinite detention," "extraordinary rendition," and "enhanced interrogation" aimed to isolate already identified enemies—enemies whose identities were presumed to reflect their ideologies—and glean from them "actionable intelligence" to thwart future breaches of public safety. However, in so doing, these labels produce categories of persons who are not entitled to the protections of Geneva and instead are targets of precaritization (see, for instance, Luban 9–18) because the persons who will occupy those categories are always already "terrorists" before any investigation. It is, perhaps, because these categories are presented rhetorically and defended legally as self-evident, unassailable, and uninterrogatable through the syllogistic logic in which detainee equals enemy combatant equals terrorist that their population-subjects must be violently interrogated in order to justify their designations.

Because Slahi is already understood as a terrorist by his guards and interrogators, there is never an opportunity to convince otherwise. This paradox is described at the very beginning of the GTMO section of *Guantánamo Diary*, which details an exchange with a guard trying to justify Slahi's detention:

> "The rules have changed. What was no crime is now considered a crime." . . .
> "To me, you meet all the criteria of a top terrorist. When I check the terrorist check list, you pass with a very high score."
> I was so scared, but I always tried to suppress my fear. "And what is your ▉▉▉▉ check list?"

"You're Arab, you're young, you went to Jihad, you speak foreign languages, you've been in many countries, you're a graduate in a technical discipline."

"And what crime is that?" I said.

"Look at the hijackers: they were the same way." (192)

The logic of Slahi's detention is one based on proximity and guilt by association, but once he is inaugurated in the system, his "guilt" emerges from his detention alone. If the government thinks Slahi is a terrorist, then his ethos as a terrorist will always already undermine any logic advocating otherwise. Traceable onto a network of post-9/11 securitization alliances that include both domestic and international partners and black sites, Slahi's experiences include outsourced abuse through extraordinary rendition from Mauritania to Jordan and then to Afghanistan in 2001 and 2002; the legalization of torture as policy at Guantánamo; and the "successful" *habeas* petition in 2010—granted by Judge Robertson and then appealed by the Obama administration—that did not lead to his release. This range of legalized abuse works against the conception of a criminal tortured in response to the kairotic exigence that "justifies" any extralegal interruption, and paradoxically demonstrates instead the legality of his position. His detention in Guantánamo, authorized again and again by law and administrative procedure, determines his status as terrorist, and thus justifies his detention, simultaneously negating the possibility of staging an opportune claim otherwise.

AKAIROS AS AMBIENT INVENTION

According to Rickert, in ambient terms, "kairos is not simply the grasping of an opportunity that opens up for a rhetor; instead, the blurring of the interacting elements demonstrates a rhetor to be enmeshed with kairos and hence indistinguishable from it" (83). Similarly, as Walzer has previously demonstrated, kairos is also determined by propriety—the right place and time— such that even as it interrupts the status quo, it must still be recognized within the dominant framework of legibility. In this way, kairos offers exigence and an opportune interruption only when it is recognizable within a framework of legibility that is already determined and in turn helps to establish that legibility. Understanding *Guantánamo Diary* through ambience—as what Rickert might call a "vector of material-discursive force" (90)—enables us to see the ways in which the production of the book is materially enmeshed in the political circumstances out of which it emerges, and can expose the dominant narrative of national emergency that justifies both the naval bay's existence and Slahi's torture regiment. However, Rickert's notion of ambience and kairos as a reframing of the subject/object divide gets us only so far as an analytic to understand the intervention that *Guantánamo Diary* is making and the ways in which it emerges out of and discloses both Slahi's personal precarity and the state's work of precaritization. In other words, we are less interested in the implications of ambience as a metaphor that helps us understand the dissolving distinctions between subject and object. Instead, we take up Rickert's notion of ambience and extend it to the akairotic situation as a way to examine what happens when the ambient conditions that inaugurate the writing and the writer are materially, rhetorically, and structurally violent—that is, when the ambient rhetoric is as much harmful as it is productive of both subject and object.[2]

Building on Roland Boer's work, Walzer argues elsewhere that a more accurate opposition to kairos is not the chronological march of everyday time, but rather akairos, or the inopportune moment. If kairos is that which is "in the right and proper place and time," designating a sense of spatio-temporal propriety, then akairos is that which is "untimely and out-of-place" (Boer 117). This notion of akairos as untimely and inopportune understands akairos as still bound by the rhetorical logic of recognition, and yet simultaneously outside of it. Additionally, as Kelly Myers reminds us, akairos is not simply a failed timeliness, but is itself a rhetorical device (11). Moreover, as noted earlier, Rickert (and others, e.g., Catherine Eskin, 2002) argues that kairos can be understood as a concept always in flux, acting on the rhetor as much as the rhetor acts on it. In this way it becomes "embedded and embodied immersion rather than connection, dispersed and interactive flow, . . . conditions of possibility rather than static presence" (Rickert 91–92). Given Myers's and Rickert's readings of akairos and ambient kairos, respectively, we can understand akairos as also a mode of invention that is fully emplaced, embedded, and coproduced within material conditions, yet one that also potentially yields new contexts and meanings. Although one might understand akairotic rhetoric as simply subversive or resistant to the prevailing rhetorical situation and ethos, that view reinforces a notion of invention tied to the rhetor as an agentic subject. By focusing instead on *Guantánamo Diary* as a product of precaritization, we aim to put pressure on this reading of invention, to argue instead for a concept of invention as itself fundamentally ambient before it is agentic. We understand ambient akairos as the inopportune moment in material and rhetorical terms that stands to expose the very categories that determine legibility and thus the opportune. Ambient akairos, then, is that which reveals the ideological and procedural dictates of kairos, denaturalizing it and making it available for scrutiny. In doing so, akairotic invention can reorient the rhetorical situation, including the conditions of its own legibility. Such a reading emphasizes the material conditions of *Guantánamo Diary*'s founding and its complex process of authorship, including the ways in which Slahi emerges as a dynamic subject who is being formed by the experiences he recounts and who, until recently, has not been able to read or approve the book that bears his name.

Akairos, therefore, offers a way to understand the temporal and material circumstances that found *Guantánamo Diary*, to expose a regime that authorizes torture and abuse, and to account for ambient invention within a context that is actively working to condition and constrain the subject and his narration. We turn to three of the many textual strategies employed in the book—its dedication, use of fable, and redactions—to demonstrate not the power of the rhetor, although that is also impressive, so much as the process and effects of precaritization through which the text emerges.

TEXTUAL STRATEGIES OF AMBIENT AKAIROS

The original dedication in *Guantánamo Diary* reads as the following: "Mohamedou would like to dedicate his writing to the memory of his late mother, Maryem Mint El Wadia, and he would also like to express that if it weren't for Nancy Hollander and her colleagues Theresa Duncan and Linda Moreno, he couldn't be making that dedication." We begin our textual analysis with the book's dedication because of the way it signals the complex temporal, material, and political exigence and constraints under which *Guantánamo Diary* was produced. The dedication of the memoir is unusual because it is written not in first person, but in third person, which decenters the autobiographical "I" traditional to the genre of memoir or diary, while simultaneously expressing the urgency of that very subjectivity, even as it is mediated through the editor: "Mohamedou would like to dedicate" and "he would also like to express," as opposed to the more conventional "I dedicate" or the passive "This book is dedicated to." Additionally, the fact that Siems was prohibited from corresponding with Slahi in the preparation of the published book and that were it not for his lawyers, he "couldn't be making that dedication" to the memory of his late mother, who died during his captivity in Guantánamo, gestures in a few words to the layered temporalities, mediated agency, and simultaneous urgency operating in and through the text. "Couldn't be making"—the grammatical construct of continuous or progressive aspect formed by joining the present tense (to be) with the present participle (making)—denotes a dynamic action that is simultaneously present and future, while containing the sinister traces of the previous and continuing violence that prevents him from making the dedication in first person in the first place.

The book's dedication is one of several paratextual frames that also include images of the original handwritten pages (with redactions), a timeline, notes on the text, and the editor's introduction. The paratextual layers provide historical, legal, and linguistic context to the central narrative. Together they inform the reader that the book will not, in fact, provide direct access to its author-subject and his experience of torture and indefinite detention, nor will it offer a sense of closure provided in hindsight after the events are over. Rather, *Guantánamo Diary* offers a mediated and contested representation of the effects of precaritization of those deemed enemies of the state by someone who is currently experiencing that precaritization and who understands the ideologies that sustain it. While images of the original pages remind readers of the fraught materiality of the text (its status marked bizarrely as "~~UNCLASSIFIED~~" on the frontispiece), the timeline and introduction provide an immediate and larger framework, respectively, for the narrative that follows. This chronological and contextual material reestablishes an ambience of sociality or world-belonging that Slahi's treatment sought to deny, for example, when he was brought diapered, masked, goggled, earmuffed, gloved, and shackled to Guantánamo; in the attempts to erase his sense of time during his extensive interrogation sessions and terms in solitary confinement; and in the appeal by the Obama administration of Slahi's *habeas* petition that then stalled in the courts. Thus, the structure of the book represents the struggle between, on the one hand, the government's attempts to cast Slahi out of shared social, calendrical, and chronological time in order to justify a state of emergency as a kairotic temporal irruption, and, on the other hand, the narrative's efforts to demonstrate akairotically the ways in which these attempts, each of which gestures toward the indefinite length of his captivity, evinces the normalization rather than exceptionalism of his treatment.

If including Slahi's handwriting and life story is an attempt to render him more fully human and thus more worthy of the reader's consideration, then one might continue to the narrative itself to answer the question of who Slahi is. However, the book does not satisfy that inquiry readily as it details the process of subjectivization that emerges through the government's attempts to "break" him. As evidenced above in Slahi's discussion with the guard who has already predetermined that Slahi is a terrorist, before any investigation, the struggle throughout the book is over the government's attempt to justify precaritization as both a means and an end. Mark Danner memorably describes this solipsistic process as one featuring "zealous interrogators, untroubled by doubt, applying a relentless violence to conjure up a fantasy world born of the collective terrors of their own imaginations." In characterizing the paradox this creates for him as the target of violent precaritization—the necessary and impossible task of revealing the truth of a fantasy—Slahi turns to the literary device of the fable. It is an appropriate strategy, given that fables aim to convey moral truths through the fantastical devices of anthropomorphic animals.

At the beginning of chapter 2, the first chapter in the section titled "Before," which describes Slahi's time between January 21, 2000, and February 19, 2000, when, at the behest of the United States, he was detained for questioning in Senegal and Mauritania, Slahi tells a Mauritanian folktale about a "rooster-phobe" who is afraid because he thinks the rooster thinks he is corn. The story goes as follows:

> "Why are you so afraid of the rooster?" the psychiatrist asks him.
>
> "The rooster thinks I'm corn."
>
> "You're not corn. You are a very big man. Nobody can mistake you for a tiny ear of corn," the psychiatrist said.
>
> "I know that Doctor. But the rooster doesn't. Your job is to go convince him that I am not corn."
>
> The man was never healed, since talking to a rooster is impossible. End of story.
>
> For years I have been trying to convince the US government that I am not corn. (71)

This folktale serves as an all-too-real metaphor for the akairotic conditions under which Slahi narrates his story of extraordinary rendition and torture. It describes the difficult situation in which he has to argue the impossible despite a rhetorico-material framework that denies him the space from which to stage that claim. Herein lies the precarious material-discursive situation of the detainee who has committed no crime but whose very existence stimulates that sense of collective terror Danner describes. In this brief passage, Slahi likens himself to both the man and the doctor, unduly targeted as fodder in the "war on terror" and unable, like the doctor, to communicate with the rooster, despite knowing what the rooster thinks. The folktale describes the book and Slahi's challenge in his interrogation sessions of convincing the U.S. government of their misperception that he is a terrorist. The ambient akairotic framework exposes the precarity of his situation because it enables readers to see the paradoxical circumstance out of which he must stage his inopportune and seemingly impossible claim.

By describing this circumstance through the folktale, Slahi short-circuits the logic of his interrogators. In the context of Guantánamo, where guards and interrogators were working together to force Slahi to divulge a "truth" that will confirm the correctness of the actions being taken against him, the fable takes a different approach. It conveys a moral truth that is translatable to readers across the linguistic and national divides his interrogators find impassible; at the same time, it roots him in a Mauritanian oral tradition that he necessarily conveys in writing to reach a different audience. Moreover, Slahi's employment of fable to convey his circumstance functions akairotically to expose and undercut the search for personal truth through violent interrogation. Each time Slahi narrates his interrogations, the impossible rhetorical task of convincing the regime that he is "not corn" is reenacted, and the supposed telos of the sessions—to elicit information—is exposed as a flawed premise for justification. Instead, these textual moments demonstrate the authorization of inhumane treatment as policy.

As Hilary Neroni argues, "the believability of the effectiveness of torture . . . relies upon an extensive biopolitical ideological framework . . . largely structured around a particular conception of time"—what we could call kairotic exigence—that depends upon the chronology of the ticking clock: "the constructed urgency of the clock and its link to the ticking bomb provides the reason that a suspension of political rights is acceptable, a suspension that allows for the use of and even celebration of torture" (100). In attempts to "break" the subject, the clock serves as the catalyst and torture the means to get the body to reveal its inner truth. In other words, notwithstanding her critique of torture, Neroni's understanding of torture and biopower relies on the notion of ambient kairotic exigence that justifies this violence through temporal urgency and sees the material body as a hindrance to information gathering and, paradoxically, as a rhetorical source. However, when Slahi's experience of torture is placed in its larger context, when we see the coupling of torture and indefinite detention without charge, the stated justifications for his treatment are erased and the right to harm him as a member of a targeted population becomes an end in itself.

How, then, do we read Slahi's text as a combination of writing that is censored, edited, involuntary, and willed from conditions of extremity? As Chris Earle reminds us, scholarship on prison writing often reinforces a notion of subversion and recuperation by privileging narratives that tell the story of prisoners "reclaiming voice and subjectivity by enunciating opposition to the state and by critiquing the very terms by which they have been dispossessed" (50). These narratives provide a way to enact agency and rhetorical authority from the space of imprisonment, but this normative discourse of prison narratives assumes a conception of the liberal subject that does not adequately ask after its origins in rhetorical exchange and fails to account for writing that does not adhere to these conventions. The ability to seek address (and possibly *redress*), following Kelly Oliver and Diane Davis, is always already contingent on rhetorical reciprocation, "our very address-ability and response-ability" (Earle 52), rather than an implied sovereignty of the speaking subject. However, that reciprocity that precedes subjectivity and thus address-ability and response-ability is not evenly distributed, particularly in prison literature and even more narrowly in the context of Guantánamo, where Slahi's writings were automatically coded as classified and then protected (in the legal sense of restricted). As the extra-narrated dedication in *Guantánamo Diary* demonstrates, "the material and social world of the prison . . . threatens the address-response structure at the heart of subjectivity" (Earle 61). How, then, to stage a claim within an address-response structure that all but denies his speech and yet still draws attention to the ways in which his precaritization has become legalized status quo? We turn to the book's redactions for the way they manifest this process.

As we have argued thus far, *Guantánamo Diary*'s ambient invention is deeply conditioned by Slahi's material circumstances of indefinite detention, and perhaps nowhere is that context more legible than through the censoring black bars that regularly interrupt the narrative and can stretch for pages. The heavily footnoted redactions continue to remind readers, lest they forget, about the conditions of production and constrained invention the book underwent—from the original handwritten manuscript, to its redactions by the U.S. government, to its intercontextual editing by Siems. The redactions clearly demonstrate that *Guantánamo Diary* operates within the framework of the inopportune while simultaneously calling attention to the ambient conditions that deny Slahi a voice. More specifically, the redactions function as quintessential examples of precarious rhetoric in the text. They are precarious in their temporal disjunctions, logical inconsistencies, and ineffectualism, but even more importantly because they demonstrate (1) the state's efforts at securitization and precaritization to readers typically far removed from those processes, (2) Slahi's persistent vulnerability, and (3) the text's complex, akairotic ambient invention.

In terms of national security, the redactions are presumably employed to protect sources and methods of the U.S. military and intelligence agencies and their allies in the "war on terror" as well as the general reputation of U.S. forces. Although the process of the manuscript's redaction has not been revealed, we surmise that it included, first, intelligence screening by each of the agencies (who were often in conflict with one another) involved in what Siems describes as Slahi's "rendition, detention, and interrogation ordeal, which would be the FBI (or the Justice Department as FBI overseers), CIA, the

Department of Defense, and perhaps the State Department as well,"[3] and, possibly, review by the public affairs office of either each agency and/or the joint task force that operates the naval base (JTF-GTMO). Based on the official exemptions to U.S. Freedom of Information Act requests, sources and methods of redaction might also include disclosure of a confidential source, communication between agencies, and another person's privacy. Reading through this lens, one might presume the redactions are designed to protect information—about individuals, agencies, targets, and techniques—crucial to national security. From a rhetorical standpoint, then, the bars themselves function as kairotic interventions that underscore a threat against the United States that is at once nebulous (the censored text) and specific (Slahi himself).

However, the publication of the book is the result of a layered process of turning classified into unclassified speech, and, as Joseph Slaughter writes, "declassification is a process of revelation that entails concealment" ("Vanishing" 210). Although we agree that on one level the redactions indicate "political absence" (213), rather than read them solely as "untold stories" (218), as Slaughter does, we emphasize their rhetorical agency in narrative coproduction and as political presence. On a visual level, the redactions interrupt the narrative flow and transform the act of reading into one of deciphering. The work of deciphering focuses attention on the specter of a threat that further authorizes the redactions; however, deciphering, as opposed to more straightforward reading, requires a triangulating strategy of meaning-making that involves moving between the visible text, the redactions, and the extensive footnotes (and possibly additional research). In navigation, triangulation provides pinpoint targeting in relatively featureless terrain, an apt metaphor for how we can read the redactions as ideological and procedural markers of precaritization across the blanked-out spaces of Guantánamo. That the footnotes are culled from publicly available information undercuts the ostensibly protective authority of the censors, as much of what is barred has already been disclosed elsewhere. Moreover, both the redactions, as a result of the work of an untold number of anonymous censors, and the footnotes, inserted by Siems but culled from a multitude of attributed, often government sources, indicate the systemic (as opposed to purely individual) foundations of Slahi's story. Thus, the redactions perform the crucial work of demonstrating institutional violence and in disabusing readers of what Stephanie Athey has identified as the archetype of the torture narrative that involves solely the "dyad of torturer and tortured," thereby erasing the many functions of and participants in torture in its sociopolitical context (144).

The work of deciphering, of triangulation, provides a different context, both ambient and material, that transforms the redactions from protective, kairotic gestures to akairotic disclosures of precaritization. Slahi's harshest treatment took place over the year that began in late summer 2003, when military intelligence and the CIA took over his interrogation from the FBI. As is typical throughout the book, the abuse he suffered during this period remains legible: readers learn of his subjection to prolonged isolation, stress positions, sexual humiliation, beatings, a staged abduction, blaring music, and the use of temperature extremes, among other treatments. The few redactions of those techniques and their effects are largely ineffective as the larger context of the surrounding sentence generally makes them clear. Gender receives similarly odd treatment. For instance, the censors typically block feminine, but not masculine, nouns and pronouns. As a result, the redactions in these sections highlight rather than mask gender identity. Thus, when Slahi describes how "the two ████ took off their blouses, and started to talk all kinds of dirty stuff" (230), the redaction produces little ambiguity. In these instances, the redactions appear to be precarious in the sense of barely fulfilling any discernible function.

What the censors do protect more strenuously are the identities of participating guards and interrogators, raising the question of whether the black bars, like the masks many interrogators wear, are designed to guarantee privacy or impunity. Slahi understands that interrogators regularly employ aliases and disguise the government agency they represent, and indeed includes his own names for them, such as "the guy I call 'I-AM-THE-MAN'" (214). Here, footnotes often provide missing information. The most significant of these examples comes when Slahi meets the new chief of his "Special Projects Team": "He always tried to make me believe that his real name was ████, but what he didn't know was that I knew his name even before I met him: ████" (249). Footnotes, referencing the DOJ inspector general report, the Senate Armed Services Committee report, the army's Schmidt-Furlow report, and the investigative reporting by the *Wall Street Journal*'s Jess Bravin reveal that the new chief of Slahi's interrogation posed as "Captain Collins," but was the navy reservist Lt. Richard Zuley (fn 248–49). That the alias appears in three official reports but is redacted in *Guantánamo Diary* indicates a break between the book and its larger context and thus how the book works akairotically to unsettle that initial context and to make possible another. The redactions make visible a temporal disjunction—what is being denied has already been given—and although redacting "Captain Collins" is internally consistent, it is inconsistent and indeed illogical from the standpoint of national security.

Recent groundbreaking reporting by Spencer Ackerman in the *Guardian* (U.K.) demonstrates that the precariousness of the ineffectual redactions concerning Lt. Zuley signals a much more important task: that of understanding the network of forces that carry out precaritization to sustain the "securocratic state," in Allen Feldman's apt phrase (40). Ackerman describes how his investigation "unraveled from footnotes in Slahi's memoir and involve[ed] thousands of police and court documents plus interviews with two dozen veterans of both Guantánamo Bay and Chicago criminal justice" ("Guantánamo Torturer"). In a series of articles, Ackerman details Zuley's abuse of prison detainees from 1977 to 2007 (including 2003 and 2004, when he left Chicago to take over Slahi's case in Guantánamo) as a detective in the Chicago Police Department's Homan Square, "what lawyers say is the equivalent of a CIA black site" ("The Disappeared"). With reportedly "military-style vehicles, interrogation cells, and even a cage," Homan Square represents the "institutionalization" of "routinized" police abuse of predominantly poor people of color. Ackerman's reporting highlights the parallels between Zuley's mostly minority targets in Chicago and the "war on terror's" ghost detainees: "Unlike a precinct, no one taken to Homan Square is said to be booked. Witnesses, suspects, and other Chicagoans who end up inside do not appear to have a public, searchable record entered into a database indicating where they are" ("The Disappeared"). Zuley's use of techniques in Chicago such as shackling, threats to family members, and coercion, also familiar to Slahi's readers, resulted in involuntary confessions, wrongful convictions, mishandled evidence, and now—prompted by the exposé—new investigations into cases Zuley handled. Ackerman's most recent reporting concludes that over 7,000 people, of whom 82.2 percent were black and 11.8 percent Hispanic, were "disappeared" at the "off-the-books interrogation warehouse" ("Homan Square Revealed"). Thus, we can trace the concrete ways in which the black bars that sought to protect Zuley's alias and identity instead provoke, even necessitate, triangulated reading that exposes precaritization through military and police brutality and that links black sites within and across national borders.

Lorey analyzes the relationship between securitization and military-style precaritization in the neoliberal state to emphasize how ostensible protection can become a violent tool: the "state is not withdrawing from all formerly fundamental institutions of safeguarding," but limits those institutional investments to "police and military safeguarding, which in turn increasingly operate with disciplinary control and surveillance techniques" (64). According to Lorey, the result of this process is a fundamental shift of liberalism from "freedom and security" to "freedom and insecurity," such that "the state does not on principle limit freedom or combat insecurity, but both become the ideological precondition for governmental precarization" (64). This shift is evident in the involuntary confessions obtained through torture and abuse used to convict minorities in Chicago and in Zuley's treatment (again, authorized at the highest level of government) of Slahi. At their first meeting, Zuley presents Slahi with a forged letter that threatens his family if he does not cooperate: "You have two options: either being a defendant or a witness" (249). Slahi's unredacted "choice"—to which he responds, "I want neither" (249)—unwittingly reveals that the government does not know why it is holding him. This conclusion is supported by the book's documentation of the shifting allegations against him (he recruited 9/11 hijackers, participated in the Millennium Plot, etc.) and, most significantly, the pages-long redacted sections pertaining to his lie detector tests, which footnotes reveal are tests Slahi passes. Whereas the torture techniques are legible throughout the book, the redactions attempt to block notice of his lie detector tests and their results. Given that both context and footnotes offer evidence of these tests and the fact that Slahi was never charged with a crime, one may conclude that the treatments of both Slahi and his manuscript were not necessary to protect the nation, but just facets of a policy to harm one who has already been determined fit for precaritization.

To return to that "collective sense of story and of justice" (Slahi xlix) with which we began, we find that the text and its author-subject diverge in their conclusions. Whereas Slahi's release may signal a degree of justice, closure, and futurity for the individual, his personal (partial) freedom does not diminish the forces of precaritization that continue to operate in the name of security and through networks of legal, military, police, and administrative power. The ambient akairotic invention of *Guantánamo Diary* poses rather than answers the question of what a collective sense of story and justice might mean if many of its readers remain tethered to a "war on terror."

NOTES

1. Throughout this chapter, we use the more conventional English spelling of "precaritization" as opposed to Lorey's and her translator's "precarization."
2. Heather Hayes's work on "rhetoricoviolence" addresses this problem, but although we share her interest in rhetorical situations founded on violence, our focus here is on the climate of fear that serves as catalyst for the post-9/11 campaign of precaritization. Ambient kairos and akairos maintain the attention to the temporal dimensions of context and to the book as material rhetoric that emerges from that context and reorients it.
3. Personal email correspondence, "Re: mailing list," received by Alexandra S. Moore, 14 Oct. 2016.

WORKS CITED

Ackerman, Spencer. "Bad Lieutenant: American Police Brutality Exported from Chicago to Guantánamo." *The Guardian.* 18 Feb. 2015. <www.theguardian.com/us-news/2015/feb/18/american-police-brutality-chicago-guantanamo>. 19 March 2017.

———. "The Disappeared: Chicago Police Detain Americans at Abuse-Laden 'Black Site.'" *The Guardian*. 24 Feb. 2015. <www.theguardian.com/us-news/2015/feb/24/chicago-police-detain-americans-black-site>. 19 March 2017.

———. "Evidence from Chicago Detective's Cases Re-Examined for Multiple Exonerations." *The Guardian*. 19 Feb. 2015. <www.theguardian.com/us-news/2015/feb/19/evidence-chicago-detective-richard-zuley>. 19 March 2017.

———. "'Gestapo' Tactics at US Police 'Black Site' Rings Alarm from Chicago to Washington." *The Guardian*. 26 Feb. 2015. <www.theguardian.com/us-news/2015/feb/26/police-black-site-chicago-washington-politicians-human-rights>. 19 March 2017.

———. "Guantánamo Torturer Led Brutal Chicago Regime of Shackling and Confession." *The Guardian*. 18 Feb. 2015. <www.theguardian.com/us-news/2015/feb/18/guantanamo-torture-chicago-police-brutality>. 19 March 2017.

———. "Homan Square Revealed: How Chicago Police 'Disappeared' 7,000 People." *The Guardian*. 19 Oct. 2015. <www.theguardian.com/us-news/2015/oct/19/homan-square-chicago-police-disappeared-thousands>. 19 March 2017.

———. "How Chicago Police Condemned the Innocent: A Trail of Coerced Confessions." *The Guardian*. 19 Feb. 2015. <www.theguardian.com/us-news/2015/feb/19/chicago-police-richard-zuley-abuse-innocent-man>. 19 March 2017.

Agamben, Giorgio. *Remnants of Auschwitz: The Witness and the Archive*. Trans. Daniel Heller-Roazen. Zone Books, 2002.

Amar, Paul. *The Security Archipelago: Human-Security States, Sexuality Politics, and the End of Neoliberalism*. Duke University Press, 2013.

Athey, Stephanie. "The Torture Device: Debate and Archetype." *Torture: Power, Democracy, and the Human Body*. Ed. Shampa Biswas and Zahi Zalloua. University of Washington Press and Whitman College, 2011. 129–57.

Boer, Roland. "Revolution in the Event: The Problem of Kairós." *Theory, Culture, & Society* 30.2 (2013): 116–34. doi:10.1177/0263276412456565.

Bush, George W. "Memorandum: Humane Treatment of al Qaeda and Taliban Detainees." 7 Feb. 2002. <nsarchive.gwu.edu/NSAEBB/NSAEBB127/02.02.07.pdf>. 19 March 2017.

Chowdhury, Elora Halim. *Transnationalism Reversed: Women Organizing Against Gendered Violence in Bangladesh*. SUNY Press, 2011.

Committee on Armed Services, United States Senate. *Inquiry into the Treatment of Detainees in U. S. Custody*. 20 Nov. 2008. Washington, DC: U.S. Government Printing Office, 2009.

Danner, Mark. Rev. of *Guantánamo Diary*, by Mohamedou Ould Slahi. *The New York Times Sunday Book Review*. 20 Jan. 2015. <www.nytimes.com/2015/02/15/books/review/guantanamo-diary-by-mohamedou-ould-slahi.html>. 19 March 2017.

Davis, Diane. *Inessential Solidarity: Rhetoric and Foreigner Relations*. University of Pittsburgh Press, 2014.

Earle, Chris. "Dispossessed: Prisoner Reponse-Ability and Resistance at the Limits of Subjectivity." *Rhetoric Society Quarterly* 46.1 (2016): 47–65. doi:10.1080/02773945.2015.1104718.

Eskin, Catherine R. "Hippocrates, *Kairos*, and Writing in the Sciences." *Rhetoric and Kairos: Essays in History, Theory, and Praxis*. Ed. Phillip Sipiora and James S. Baumlin. SUNY Press, 2002. 97–113.

Feldman, Allen. *Archives of the Insensible: Of War, Photopolitics, and Dead Memory*. University of Chicago Press, 2015.

Hayes, Heather Ashley. *Violent Subjects and Rhetorical Cartography in the Age of the Terror Wars.* Palgrave Macmillan, 2016.

Longaker, Mark Garrett, and Jeffrey Walker. *Rhetorical Analysis: A Brief Guide for Writers.* Longman, 2011.

Lorey, Isabell. *State of Insecurity: Government of the Precarious.* Verso, 2015.

Luban, David. *Torture, Power, and Law.* Cambridge University Press, 2014.

Myers, Kelly. "*Metanoia* and the Transformation of Opportunity." *Rhetoric Society Quarterly* 41.1 (2011): 1–18. doi:10.1080/02773945.2010.533146.

Neroni, Hilary. *The Subject of Torture: Psychoanalysis and Biopolitics in Television and Film.* Columbia University Press, 2015.

Oliver, Kelly. *Witnessing: Beyond Recognition.* University of Minnesota Press, 2001.

Paik, A. Naomi. *Rightlessness: Testimony and Redress in U. S. Prison Camps Since World War II.* University of North Carolina Press, 2016.

Periodic Review Secretariat. Unclassified Summary of Final Determination. 14 July 2016. <www.prs.mil/Portals/60/Documents/ISN760/160714_U_ISN760_FINAL_DETERMINATION_PUBLIC.pdf>. 19 March 2017.

Redfield, Marc. *The Rhetoric of Terror.* Fordham University Press, 2009.

Rickert, Thomas. *Ambient Rhetoric: The Attunement of Rhetorical Being.* University of Pittsburgh Press, 2013.

Slahi, Mohamedou Ould. *Guantánamo Diary.* Ed. Larry Siems. Canongate Books, 2015.

———. *Guantánamo Diary Restored Edition.* Ed. Larry Siems. Back Bay Books, 2017.

Slaughter, Joseph R. "Narration in International Human Rights Law." *CLCWeb: Comparative Literature and Culture* 9.1 (March 2007). <docs.lib.purdue.edu/clcweb/vol9/iss1/19>.

———. "Vanishing Points: When Narrative Is Simply Not There." *Journal of Human Rights* 9.2 (2010): 207–23. doi:10.1080/14754831003761712.

Walzer, Belinda. "The Right Time for Rhetoric: Normativity, Kairos, and Human Rights." *The Routledge Companion to Literature and Human Rights.* Ed. Sophia A. McClennen and Alexandra Schultheis Moore. Routledge, 2015. 433–40.

CHAPTER 2

Precarious Narratives

Media Accounts of Islamic State Sexual Violence

WENDY S. HESFORD and AMY SHUMAN

ON AUGUST 14, 2015, the *New York Times* ran a front-page article, "Enslaving Young Girls," about the Islamic State's systematic rape of girls from the Yezidi community. The Yezidi, an ethno-religious minority of approximately 600,000, are the second largest non-Muslim community in Iraq. They are neither Muslim nor Christian. There is some dispute over their ethnic origin, and most scholars agree that they are a distinct ethnic and religious community (Phelps). "The Yezidi Human Rights Organization argues that Yezidi were 'forcefully misclassified as Arab' in ethnicity under the regime of Saddam Hussein and, more recently, under the control of the Kurdistan Regional Government they were 'wrongfully classified as Kurdish'" (Phelps 461). Many Yezidi live in the town of Sinjar that borders Iraq's Kurdish region, home to mostly Arabs and Kurds, who have jostled for control over the territory for centuries. The Yezidi have been targeted by Kurdish authorities in an effort to incorporate disputed territories in northern Iraq into the Kurdish region, and beginning in 2014 have been targeted by ISIS in its grab for territory after the fall of Mosul.

According to a 2016 UN Human Rights Council report, ISIS committed terrible atrocities against the Yezidi and other ethnic and religious communities, including Iraqi Christians, Shiite Muslims, and fellow Sunni Muslims. ISIS specifically targeted the Yezidi minority, whom they saw as infidels, as polytheists, with an oral tradition rather than written scripture. During its

August 2014 attack on Sinjar in northern Iraq, ISIS abducted hundreds of Yezidi women and girls and took many of them into Syria to be sold in markets as sex slaves. ISIS leadership emphasizes a narrow reading of the Quran and other religious rulings to justify the enslavement of Yezidi women and girls—a reading that Muslim scholars across the globe have condemned. ISIS has since developed an elaborate infrastructure for human trafficking and sexual slavery, which consists of a network of warehouses where victims are viewed and sold, transportation systems, how-to slavery manuals, and slave contracts notarized by the Islamic State–run Islamic courts (Callimachi A1). An estimated 360,000 Yezidi have been displaced; many are now in refugee camps, and approximately 3,500 women, girls, and some men remain in ISIS captivity.

Foreign correspondent Rukmini Callimachi opens the *New York Times* article with a graphic description of an Islamic fighter's rape of a twelve-year-old Yezidi girl, bound and gagged as the fighter "knelt beside the bed and prostrated himself in prayer before getting on top of her" (A1). The article concludes with the testimony of a thirty-four-year-old Yezidi woman who was repeatedly raped by a Saudi fighter in the Syrian city of Shadadi. The woman pleads with the Saudi fighter to stop raping another twelve-year-old girl, to which he responds, "She's not a little girl. She's a slave. . . . And having sex with her pleases God" (A13).

Callimachi reports that sex slavery is used as a "recruiting tool to lure men from deeply conservative Muslim societies, where casual sex is taboo and dating is forbidden" (A1). She writes, "In much the same way as specific Bible passages were used centuries later to support the slave trade in the US, the Islamic State cites specific verses or stories in the Quran or else in the Sunna, the traditions based on sayings and deeds of the Prophet Muhammad, to justify their human trafficking" (A13). Callimachi highlights the strategic use of religious doctrine to justify the enslavement of particular groups. Her analogy between ISIS's present invocation of Islamic doctrine and U.S. slave owners' invocations of Christian doctrine to justify slavery centuries earlier may serve to de-exoticize ISIS's religious rationale for the enslavement of the Yezidi and thus challenge the construal of the Muslim proclamation as exceptional. However, characterizations of ISIS's enslavement and rape of Yezidi women as symptomatic of repressed Muslim masculinities and framing acts of sexual violence as a epiphenomena of culture or psychology risk prioritizing sexual motives for terrorist acts over social-political causes and analyses (Puar and Rai 124). Such characterizations echo the liberal feminist lexicon of sexual slavery derived from early antiviolence platforms that universalized women's victimization and claimed that sexual violence against women arises from a "deep ideology of cultural sadism and female sexual domination" (Barry, qtd. in Suchland 30). Hence, in a close reading of the *New York Times* cover story "Enslaving Young Girls," we examine the precarious convergence of U.S. wars on terrorism and trafficking discourses (also see Madhavi).[1]

More broadly, we use the term "precarious rhetorics" to refer to the contradictory positions produced by narratives across geopolitical boundaries and to acknowledge the idea that these contradictions are not only not avoidable but also are supported by normative narratives that are susceptible to ongoing transformation. Specifically, in the context of tensions between Western, Yezidi, and ISIS conceptions of normative violence, the term precarious rhetorics is useful for describing the complex subjectivities of victim, perpetrator, and rescuer. In what follows, we examine these contradictions at multiple levels, both how they sustain discourses of precarity and violence and in terms of the precarity of the relationship among the interlocutors, for example, in characterizing victims as worthy of rescue.

Trafficking in human beings is a complex, global phenomenon, which scholars, journalists, activists, and government officials and politicians approach in a number of ways, including as an issue of migration or organized crime that affects state security, from a human rights perspective, as a form of modern-day slavery, and as a form of terrorism.[2] In contrast to the neo-abolitionist rhetoric that dominates the anti-trafficking campaigns of organizations such as Anti-Slavery International and Free the Slaves, recent coverage of the enslavement of Yezidi women and girls and the Chibok girls kidnapped by Boko Haram in Nigeria embed these discourses in national security and counterterrorist frameworks.

We characterize both the counterterrorist and neo-abolitionist discourses about modern-day slavery as precarious for several reasons. First, the analogy between human trafficking and slavery of the past takes on particular characteristics and political agendas in coverage of the U.S. "war on terror." The media emphasis on Islamic terrorism as a form of modern-day slavery, namely sex slavery, reinforces a sense of American moral exceptionalism. Similar to neo-abolitionist anti-trafficking campaign discourses, which easily slip into "teleological accounts of racial progress" (Hua 96), recent representations of ISIS's enslavement of Yezidi women and girls bolster a national U.S. mythology of progress, which ignores institutionalized sexism and racism in the United States and gendered and racialized state terror (101). Second, like Callimachi's link between the history of state violence (the Western institution of slavery) and present-day non-state violence (Islamic terrorism), representations of ISIS's enslavement of Yezidi women and girls pathologize sex slavery and sex trafficking, as Jennifer Suchland puts it in another context, as forms of "violence that circulate beyond the moral boundaries of the proper state" (6). Third, American exceptionalism—moral and political—supports the ontology of "sexual humanitarianism," a phrase coined by Nicola Mai, which we use here to describe the eroticization of violence and the gendering of terror and rescue in the U.S. international human rights imaginary. We employ the concept of trafficking sexual humanitarianism more specifically to point to the ways that sexualized vulnerability is mobilized—trafficked—as one dimension of a precarious rhetoric. In this precarious rhetoric, the human trafficking of female victims of Islamic terrorism, characterized as a form of modern-day sexual slavery, is invoked as a call for both military and humanitarian intervention. Sexual humanitarianism thrives on a lexicon of moral sentiments, graphically sexualized dichotomies between female victimization and male agency and between freedom and slavery, and heteronormative narratives of sexual danger and rescue (Vance 138).[3] Sexual humanitarianism operates within the violence against women abolitionist anti-trafficking framework, which calls for the protection of gendered vulnerability, and yet also "articulates with cultural scripts about female sexuality as . . . dangerous and inherently degrading" (Brysk 82). Sexual humanitarianism also operates within the occidentalist, counterterrorist discourses about U.S. strength and precarity.

In this chapter, we seek to elucidate the cultural and political work that representations of ISIS's enslavement and rape of Yezidi women and girls perform in the U.S. nationalist and international human rights imaginary. What ideologies and rhetorical contingencies make the Yezidi women's and girls' narratives legible to us, and how do we imagine them as legible within Yezidi culture? What facilitates and inhibits the circulation of these narratives? To what degree does the embedding of Yezidi women's and girls' rape narratives in U.S. news media reports about ISIS and the "war on terror" reproduce occidental ideologies?[4] Who is asked to protect these women? How do the narratives about the women's experiences frame them as victims, and how do the narratives position them with regard to Western feminist values in relation to Yezidi (patriarchal) and ISIS rationales for rape? How does their precarity become legible to us through what Catherine Mills describes (referring to Butler) as "normative regimes of social intelligibility" (150)? The multiple narratives about Yezidi women's experiences are not necessarily mutually intelligible across differences and to different audiences, and therefore their precarity may also be provisionally recognizable.

Specifically, we are interested in how the bodies of Yezidi women and girls in proximity to state and pseudo-state structures are differentially rendered vulnerable, and how these bodies become legally legible through their organization into narratives of sexual violence, anti-trafficking narratives chief among them. By combining narrative and rhetorical analysis, we aim to better understand how women and girls are positioned within terrorist and antiterrorist discourses as precarious. These precarious narratives are themselves vulnerable to gendered ideologies of rescue that position the West as a rescuer of Yezidi women victims (Agustín; Cojocaru; Bernstein; Shuman and Bohmer). The gendered ethno-religious vulnerability of Yezidi women and girls under radical Islamic theology, and the mobilization of the spectacle of sex slavery in both terrorist propaganda and human rights reporting, exemplify the trafficking of sexual humanitarianism and demonstrate the need for further study of the strategic mobilization and appropriation of gendered vulnerability and narratives of gendered terror.

CONSTITUTIVE RHETORIC: GENDERING TERROR AND VULNERABILITY

Constitutive rhetoric points to the capacity of language and symbols to create rhetorical community and to the process of calling into being a collective identity and sense of belonging (White). Constitutive rhetoric dates back to the Sophists; however, we locate our critical engagement to Maurice Charland's emphasis on how ideologies create political subjects through a "process of identification in rhetorical narratives that 'always already' presume the constitution of subjects." He continues, "To be constituted as a subject in narrative is to be constituted with a history, motives, and a *telos*" (140). As our work demonstrates, the limits of acknowledging a shared history and *telos* also compromises any possibility of constituting a subject that is mutually intelligible across differences. Building on Althusser's discussion, Charland observes that interpellation "occurs at the very moment one enters into a rhetorical situation, that is, as soon as an individual recognizes and acknowledges being addressed" (138). Constitutive rhetoric therefore points to how social subjects become intelligible within narrative representation and to the ideological effects of narrative and, more broadly, to narrative as rhetoric.

Narrative as constitutive rhetoric looks not only at how narrators position themselves and others in a particular account but also at how those positions re-instantiate or reconfigure dominant paradigms and ideological formations. Additionally, constitutive rhetoric focuses on how subjects affirm or contest their subject position(s) in any given text/context. For example, both U.S. mainstream news media coverage of ISIS's abduction, rape, and trafficking of Yezidi women and girls and ISIS terrorist propaganda converge in interpellating Yezidi as unified subjects—a configuration that fails to account for the greater complexity of their situations. Hence, we are also interested in who becomes a subject and under what conditions of intelligibility, producing what forms of precarity. We examine, therefore, how Yezidi women and girls are positioned as vulnerable on both Western cultural terms and how the Yezidi patriarchal culture of shame contributes to how the Yezidi women represent themselves and how they see their own precarity. Are these women regarded by Western journalists and human rights advocates as individuals who have been violated and who need to restore some sense of self and empowerment by speaking out (as they do in these *New York Times* articles)? Or are they vehicles for the West to further condemn difference, and to turn attention away from sexual violence and sex trafficking in the United States? A framework of precarious rhetorics helps us to understand complex relationships between rescued and rescuer and the constitutive relationships among multiple narratives of victimhood.

In highlighting the rhetorical constitution of Yezidi women's and girls' subjectivity in international and U.S. domestic news and terrorist propaganda, we demonstrate the rhetorical constitution of gendered precarity and the political and cultural agendas that these precarious rhetorics serve. The constitutive racist and ethnocentric rhetoric of ISIS unifies Yezidi as targets of extinction. Similarly, counterterrorist discourses, indebted as they are to the occidental rhetoric of savagery, exonerate the U.S. killing machine. This is not to deny the brutality of ISIS, but to draw attention to mutually constitutive rhetorics of terrorism and counterterrorism and to the precarity of the constitutive process itself.

We bring constitutive rhetoric into critical conversation with recent work in precarity studies to elucidate the engendering of terrorist and counterterrorist discourses and to explore the implicit and sometimes precarious discourses of human rights, national sovereignty, the protection of particular cultural groups, and the redemptive narratives produced by these discourses. We draw in particular from the work of critical theorists who focus on precarity as the basis for understanding human interdependencies, obligations, and ethical responsibilities (Berlant et al.), and who have turned toward concepts of precarity, precariousness, and precaritization as a way of accounting for contemporary forms of political violence and political subjectivity. Vulnerability and precarity studies includes work by feminist theorists, philosophers, and rhetoricians (see Gilson; Hesford and Lewis; MacKenzie; Murphy, *Violence*; Oliviero); queer theorists (Butler, "Perfomativity"); and critical legal theorists, who focus, in large part, on constructs of vulnerability (Fineman; Morawa; Turner). Precariousness, as employed by critical theorists, does not refer to an "existential sameness or equality" (Lorey, qtd. in Berlant et al. 172), but to social precariousness and relational difference. For example, in "On Being Beside Oneself," Butler highlights the "radically different ways in which human physical vulnerability is distributed across the globe" (57), and how "we are constituted politically in part by virtue of the social vulnerability of our bodies" (49). Deployments of discourses of vulnerability and precarity are mechanisms of state coercion and pseudo-state control as well as forms of resistance.

The *New York Times* cover story provides a critical occasion for us to examine the conditions for ascribing vulnerability and the question of how subjects benefit from or suffer the consequences of their attachment to the discourse of vulnerability and precarity and the politics of difference inherent to it.[5] The story highlights the rescue and redemption of the girls who have been "taken"—geographically removed from their homes, families, and region—by highly organized ISIS networks that involve the commodification and trading of women and girls. Yet the article also surrenders to the specter of culpable cultures to the degree that it focuses on Islamic cultural transgressiveness in locating "evil" in the people involved (ISIS), and thereby makes this a regionally/culturally specific "evil" rather than equating the "evil" with the geopolitical and sexual economies of terrorism and human trafficking. "Enslaving Young Girls" exemplifies the West's horror at the Islamic State's violation and commodification of Yezidi women and girls, even as the article simultaneously obscures some elements of Western culpability in demonizing Islam. Yezidi women and girls are depicted as fundamentally victims in the face of Islam; however, the coverage rarely attends to the fact that Yezidi culture is conservative and heteropatriarchal, which contributes to the revictimization of women and girls who are now culturally stigmatized by having been sexually violated. This is not to suggest that conservative Yezidi traditions are the cause of Yezidi women's and girls' vulnerability to Islamic terrorism, but to acknowledge how male spiritual leaders serve as cultural brokers in responding to their vulnerability.

Yezidi spiritual leader Baba Sheikh Khurto Hajji Ismail appealed on two occasions (September 6, 2014, and February 6, 2015) to Yezidi families to welcome women and girls who had been held as sex slaves back into the community. In what amounted to a doctrinal change in religious and cultural tradition, he said, "These survivors remain pure Yezidis and no one may injure their Yezidi faith because they were subjected to a matter outside their control. . . . We therefore call on everyone to cooperate with and support these victims so that they may again live their normal lives and integrate into society" (Human Rights Watch). As we discuss, at stake here is what counts as normal and who determines the boundaries and costs of the return to living "normal lives." The spiritual leader's appeal, which represents a break in traditional Yezidi marriage norms that forbid Yezidi women to marry or have sexual relations outside of their community or caste, importantly diminished the shaming of victims upon their return. Yet, in some instances, in an effort to sustain an "authentic" Yezidi identity, Yezidi religious leaders erase the trauma of sexual violence. Yezidi spiritual leader Baba Chawish explained: "Iraqi's Yazidis are already an extreme minority in the country. Losing thousands of Yazidi women and their children would be unsustainable. Now we've said that the door is open for everyone who has been raped they can still be purified and baptized . . . as if nothing happened to them" (George). While this "erasure" may aid the return of Yezidi women, it also risks the reinscription of a culturally gendered essentialism—the cultural arm of heteropatriarchal power.

Thus this "recovery" or "denial" narrative points to the threat of feminine sexuality itself, to purity and control of the female body, and to the survival of Yezidi traditional practices. The Yezidi patriarchs recognize sexual violence against Yezidi women and girls as a form of enemy contamination. In her scholarship on diversity in Iraqi Kurdistan, Sandra Phelps argues, "The body of Yezidi difference, threatened in so many accounts, secures its life within the body of the feminine subject" (470). This framework also grounds claims for understanding ISIS's dislocation of more than 150,000 Yezidi and kidnapping and killing of Yezidis as a crime against humanity—as genocide (Arraf 1). In other words, sexual violence and sex slavery are framed in both accounts in relation to the Yezidi struggle in Iraq for "maintenance of their identity as coherent, distinct, and unadulterated" (Phelps 470).

Although ISIS propaganda may solidify images of Islam as monstrous and barbaric, and thereby serve as a moral alibi for Western military-humanitarian interventions and occupations, its targeting of Yezidi women also fractures the monolithic schematic of the Muslim woman as the oft-repeated victimized identity category in Western discourse (Abu-Lughod; Moallem). These paradoxes compel us to move beyond the discourse of sexual humanitarianism and its emphasis on saving women or proclaiming women as no more than embodiments of regressive cultural traditions to think about the politics of representation as part of a series of state and pseudo-state practices that rework geopolitical boundaries and precarities (Fernandes 57). Narratives about the Yezidi women position them in several moral geographies (Modan; Hill)[6] of domestic and public spaces that not only do not align but that also are realigned. For example, as we will discuss, a woman rescued from ISIS slavery can remain a contaminated person. The gendered vulnerability of Yezidi women and girls and the mobilization of the spectacle of sexual violation in both terrorist propaganda and news reports demonstrate the need for further study of how vulnerability operates relationally and how norms and paradigmatic shifts in what counts as normal inhere in the discourse of sexual humanitarianism.

As a point of entry, we suggest that the framework of precarious rhetorics draws attention to the call and response of disproportionately vulnerable interlocutors in accounts of the Yezidi women. On the one hand, following Butler's call "to act from the place of vulnerability and the capacity to be undone by another" (*Giving* 136), the framework of precarious rhetorics examines how the Yezidi women are multiply positioned, as representatives of a global (Western-initiated) fight against slavery and trafficking and as locally caught in ISIS violence. On the other hand, as Ann Murphy argues, "recognition of vulnerability and relationality does not itself guarantee ethical responsibility" (*Violence* 153). In this discussion of media representations of the enslavement of Yezidi women, we show how vulnerabilities are reconstituted and realigned across geopolitical boundaries, and how those vulnerabilities invoke, sustain, and critique normative practice.

TRAFFICKING RAPE, RESCUE, AND RIGHTS NARRATIVES

U.S. and U.K. press coverage of ISIS's enslavement of Yezidi women and girls variously emphasizes sexual horror and slavery, and U.S. coverage additionally focuses on terrorist brutality. In their coverage, both U.K. and U.S. media sensationalize the rape of young girls. The transgressively young age of the girls also is repeatedly emphasized—a *Telegraph* headline proclaims: "Yazidi girls as young as eight raped as ISIL sex slaves" (Sherlock). An *AFP* report indicates that girls are sold for "a pack of cigarettes" or as little as ten dollars (Chulov); girls are given as "gifts" (Sherlock) or assigned negotiable "price tags" (Sherlock) for buyers, ranging from "a few tens of dollars for older women to $170 for children" (Spencer). Numerous articles describe girls stripped naked and evaluated as merchandise (Sherlock; Younis). A *Time* article reports that within the ISIS caliphate, not only is the systematic rape and sexual enslavement of non-Muslim women condoned, but survivors of ISIS abduction and rape have reported that "ISIS fighters believe that if a woman is raped by 10 Muslims, she will become converted" (Alter 1).

Although Yezidi girls' own testimonies are featured frequently in articles—often in order to lend shocking details to the accounts—a number of reports emphasize the girls' status as daughters or other female dependents, which likewise compounds the gendered humanitarian appeal. *The Daily Beast*, for example, described efforts by Yezidi families to negotiate for the release of their daughters through third-party brokers—notably, Canadian businessman Steve Maman, who has been described as the "Jewish Schindler." Maman's organization, Liberation of Christian and Yezidi Children of Iraq, has come under considerable criticism for its methods of "buying" Yezidi sex slaves into freedom (Wolf and Rubin).[7] The idea of "buying" girls for or into freedom is, of course, not new; indeed, many Western journalistic exposés focus on the white male undercover reporter as rescuer by virtue of the purchase of sex slaves (Kristof). Here the trafficking of sexual humanitarianism operates through monetary and human exchanges to reassert neocolonial heteropatriarchal authority in the presumed absence of local male protectors.

The relationship between outsiders offering rescue when insiders cannot protect themselves has further implications for the role of the outside reader. The point of the *New York Times* story, for example, is to inform outsiders, namely Westerners, about the horrific situations facing the Yezidi women. Outsiders understand the rape of these women within a larger narrative about institutionalized rape cultures—the rape of one group by another. The story's intelligibility depends on a concept of women's human rights—a concept that makes readers see a woman's experience as rape even if her perpetrator does not, and this includes rape as a form of warfare and mechanism of genocide.

The rapists categorize what they are doing as "drawing closer to God," rather than as rape, but both the rapists and the raped use the category of "slave." The stories told by both the journalists and the Yezidi women are part of a larger cultural narrative of sex slavery and terrorism, and part of the even larger narrative of sexual trafficking, extending to far-removed cultural and political contexts. The constitutive relationships among these multiple narratives intersecting, contradicting, and/or invoking other narratives destabilize monolithic narratives of victimhood that fail to account for the complexity of the rescuer/rescued relationship. Many of the journalistic accounts of the Yezidi women included embedded narratives told by the women themselves, and those sometimes include the voices of the perpetrators as well. These embedded narratives are multivoiced even when they attempt to create a unifying single-voiced, presumably factual, account. The *New York Times* article includes the third-person account of a rape and the girl's first-person account, including her reported dialogue with the rapist, who insists on the religious warrant for his actions. Their reported speech lends both veracity and power to the stories.

The precarious subject is often narrated by others, including by the perpetrators. From the framework of constitutive rhetorics, below we draw attention to the constitution of subjectivities and consider how the victims of rape position themselves, both in their described conversations with the rapists and in dialogue with the journalists, as well as how their victimhood is constituted and recontextualized by journalists and scholars. We are not challenging the accuracy of the journalists' and scholars' accounts; nor are we merely recommending that greater attention be paid to the Western perspective that frames the representations. We are arguing that these multiple stances and contradictory narrative positions are unavoidable and that we can gain understanding of the complexity of the production of the category of "victim" by attending to these multiple narrative positions.

The *New York Times* article begins with a narrative, told in the third person: "In the moments before he raped the 12-year-old girl, the Islamic State fighter took the time to explain that what he was about to do was not a sin." After explaining this, the story continues, "He bound her hands and gagged her. Then he knelt beside the bed and prostrated himself in prayer before getting on top of her. When it was over, he knelt to pray again, bookending the rape with acts of religious devotion." The account then turns to the girl's story. In her own words, "'I kept telling him it hurts—please stop,' said the girl, whose body is so small an adult could circle her waist with two hands. 'He told me that according to Islam he is allowed to rape an unbeliever. He said that by raping me, he is drawing closer to God.'"

Others featured in the story tell a similar story. For example, "'Every time that he came to rape me, he would pray,' said F, a 15-year-old girl. . . . 'He said that raping me is his prayer to God. I said to him, what you're doing to me is wrong, and it will not bring you closer to God, and he said, "No, it's allowed. It's halal,"'" said the teenager, who escaped with the help of smugglers after being enslaved for nearly nine months. The article reports, "F's account . . . is echoed by a dozen other female victims interviewed for this article." Both F and the twelve-year-old are quoted, and their first-person speech lends both veracity and power to the stories. Both of the girls also report what their rapists said. In F's account, she not only reports what he says, she quotes him saying, "No, it's allowed. It's halal." The girls' dialogues with their rapists included both requests to stop, because they were causing pain, and discussions of the religious teaching that, for the rapist, made the act acceptable. As listeners to these conversations, readers are positioned to reject the religious argument. Callimachi explained that Islamic scholars have repudiated the religious justification for enslaving and raping the women as well. She refers to a "lengthy how-to manual issued by the Islamic State Research and Fatwa Department" that describes the conditions that permit sex. Describing the manual, Callimachi notes, "Just about the only prohibition is having sex with a pregnant slave. . . . Beyond that, there appears to be no bounds to what is sexually permissible. Child rape is explicitly condoned." Citing a translation of the original manual article, they write, "It is permissible to have intercourse with the female slave who hasn't reached puberty, if she is fit for intercourse."

According to the journalists and the experts they cite, not only was sex with the girls sanctioned, it was the purpose of the conquest. "The offensive on the mountain was as much a sexual conquest as it was for territorial gain," said Matthew Barber, a University of Chicago expert on the Yezidi minority (qtd. in Callimachi). This documented cultural acceptance of the rapist's act—that is, that it isn't rape—would be rejected by most readers of the article. The Yezidi girls are positioned within what is proposed to be a universal framework that sees them as particular kinds of victims.

Our interest here is in how these contested categories position the victims of violence, and if deserving of rescue, from whom are they being rescued, for whom, and by whom? Further, and importantly, how do the victims categorize themselves, and how do they regard their survival and rescue? As Gayatri Spivak famously asked, are white people rescuing brown women from brown men? (297). Do these rescues exoticize and demonize the cultures the women come from? Or, in somewhat the same vein, do they fail to interrogate the cultural gendered institutions that regard women who have been raped as contaminated, and, for example, unmarriageable? Moreover, are these rescue narratives all-encompassing or are there narrative fissures that might serve as opportunities for resistance or cross-cultural affinities or solidarities? Discourses of sexual humanitarianism are always implicated in local cultural discourses as well as in global human rights and human security discourses, as we have shown, though in some cases, the dialogue between these discourses sustains contradictions, creating precarious rhetorics. In sum, we use the term "precarious rhetorics" to point to how contradictions between the precarious subject narrated by others, including perpetrators, and by the victims themselves are sustained by the collusion of legalistic (women's human rights), moralistic (humanitarian), and militaristic (human security) logics in representations of gendered vulnerability.

The journalistic accounts regard the ISIS rapists as living in a "totally fabricated universe" (Benhabib 175) in which rape is not rape, as is characteristic of totalitarian regimes, but the larger frame is the one in which people, in this case the Yezidi women, are regarded as not human subjects, as deprived of their humanity. In this frame, we need to also consider the conditions of the rescue. What subjectivity is restored? Are the Yezidi women rescued as raped women? Their subjectivity, before their capture and rape, along with that of their community, cannot be restored to its prior status. The only possible redemptive narrative is the larger narrative of liberation, a narrative of the West in which the Yezidi women are legible (rescuable) as outsiders. The narrative of rescue might be, for the rescuers, a redemptive narrative, but for those whose lives and communities have been shattered, often the only narrative is one of loss (Schiffrin 187).

As scholars and journalists reporting on trauma narratives have observed, for some victims, retelling the trauma narrative is a way of claiming ownership of their experiences, and for others, describing what they endured is retraumatizing. And for many it is both. Beyond the therapeutic purposes of talking about trauma narrative, the Yezidi girls tell their stories to reporters to inform Western readers of these atrocities and perhaps to inspire action. Callimachi describes her expectation that the girls would be reluctant to talk to her, and reports, "I interviewed this woman and I could tell there was something off, but she kept on saying, 'It's O. K., it's O. K., keep going.' But then about 20 minutes in, she basically admitted that the only reason she was talking was that a Yezidi elder had called her in and told her that the *New York Times* was very important and she really should talk" (qtd. in Allen). The Yezidi girls' stories seem to stand on their own as testimonies to atrocities, but, as we have shown, they are part of intersecting, sometimes contradictory narratives. The multiple speakers with their different agendas include (1) the conversation with the Yezidi elder who told the woman to tell the story—that conversation shaped the story, as did the interaction with the reporter (and, quite likely) her translator; (2) the reported conversation between the girls and their rapists; (3) the ISIS rules that permit intercourse with a slave; (4) the Islamic law that the ISIS rules purport to draw from the larger framework of sexual slavery, within the larger framework of sexual trafficking; (5) the reporter's accounts of her experiences; (6) the *New York Times* articles; (7) the concept of women's rights that makes us recognize the rape as a rape rather than as sanctioned intercourse with a slave; and (8) the competing narratives of the rescue of the Yezidi women and girls and the role of narrative in justifying genocide and in justifying interventions in genocide.[8]

These intersecting and often contradictory narratives in representations of ISIS's enslavement and rape of Yezidi women and girls help to elucidate a concept of ethical responsibility based on an understanding of the precarity of discourse. In *Precarious Life,* Butler claims that our primary vulnerability as human beings lies in the process of self-constitution, which for Butler is a process "given over to others" and to normative violence, that is, "the violent operation of normative regulation" (Mills 133, 135). The "violent operation of normative regulation" is discernable in both mass media representations of Yezidi women and girls as well as in ISIS's construal of Yezidi women and girls as "nonbelievers" because they do not practice Islam. Here we build on our earlier definition of the term "precarious rhetorics" to point to the rhetorical-material circumstances of mis/recognition and un/intelligibility, that is, how norms "govern intelligibility [and] allow for certain kinds of practices and action to become recognizable as such" (Butler, qtd. in Mills 138). If "recognition is mediated through the terms and names by which one is called into being as a subject," and if norms persist through "social rituals of bodily life," as Butler suggests, then resistance to normative regulation may involve the resignification or displacement of norms (Mills 137; Butler, qtd. in Mills 138). Further, displacement of norms is perhaps insufficient in the case of the Yezidi women's precarious subjectivity. Instead, we suggest that a constitutive rhetorics needs to consider the production of precarious subjectivities in situations of uncertainty, ambiguity, and contradictions that make any coherent subjectivity impossible.

CONCLUSION

As we grapple with both the violent force and precarity of normative narratives, we contemplate the extent to which we likewise can't escape the logic of the normative in our engagement with these representations. In highlighting narratives of innocence, terrorism, rape, victimization, rescue, and redemption that bolster sexual humanitarian appeals, we emphasize normative violence in accounts of subjection and subjectivation (Mills 143). But, as we also demonstrate, normative logics structure acts of resistance and yet are susceptible to transformation, especially when the norms themselves become sites of political agency. Precarious rhetorics reframe ethical responsibility as an ethical *response*. That response is already accompanied by the recognition of competing ethical concerns and critique based on skepticism of the possibility of universal human rights. In addition to the issues considered by Berlant and Butler, we want to observe the obligations interlocutors have to each other to better understand how their interdependencies are played out at every level from the engagement of the journalist with the victim to the discourses that they are invoking.

The humanitarian response is, first of all, a response, part of a precarious rhetoric that invokes demands, obligations, and misalliances among the interlocutors. The situated interlocutors of journalist and rescued victim, victim and her perpetrator, and survivor and her online audience (to list the most obvious examples) are not easily translated into more general relationships and positions between rescued and rescuer. In human rights discourse, the uneasy alliance between rescued and rescuer has fostered a conversation about idealism and skepticism as two alternative perspectives. When the idealism fails, in part because general pronouncements of human rights goals fail to materialize in actual situations, and in part as a challenge to the individual focus of human rights discourse, it has been replaced by discourses of skepticism, calling attention to some of the misalliances we discuss here. Of particular relevance here is the attention to individual victims and their stories as a vehicle for making the plight of Yezidi rape victims legible to Western audiences. We are not arguing that these stories are not accurate or not fully representative. Rather, we are suggesting that they can create a sense of legibility that masks more complex relationships, for example between rescuer and rescued. The challenge for scholars working at the intersection of transnational feminist, human rights, rhetoric, and narratives studies is not just one of "accurate representation" (Lyon 3) or inclusion, as Arabella Lyon notes in *Deliberative Acts*, "but about how differences (gender, race, ethnicity, religious affiliation, and so on) shape recognition, namely the movement of the conferring of subjectivity and humanity" (2).

In *Precarious Life*, Butler puts forth a notion of ethical responsibility grounded in "our mutual dependency" and "vulnerability established in that dependency" (145). Yet, for Butler, and we concur, "vulnerability itself can only appear within conditions of discursive regulation and recognition" (146). That is, vulnerability is only understandable, identifiable, "within the strictures of normative violence" (146). And, as we have shown, vulnerability is unevenly distributed. Hence the precarity of an ethics grounded in vulnerability, especially if vulnerability hinges on the idea of lack of choice or the incapacity to escape pain or injury. The quintessential figures of trafficked women, as Sally Engle Merry notes, are young women either lured and tricked or kidnapped and forced into sex work, both of which enable configurations of women as deserving the status of "victim." Framing sex slavery as a terrorist act echoes international recognition of rape as a crime of war (though the so-called caliphate of ISIS is not recognized as a sovereign nation engaged in conventional war), in which Yezidi are depicted as deserving victims in need of international rescue. The interviews and reports in mainstream media are part of this rescue; they reveal the particularities of Yezidi culture and help to mobilize support. At the same time, they can cast the Yezidi as a vulnerable mass who need Western reporters, advocates, and officials to protect and speak for them. Mitigating against this, the recent framing of sex slavery as a terrorist act also relies on the willingness of the victims to tell their stories; the Yezidi women and girls are historical and political actors with some control over the representation of their experiences. Despite Yezidi women's self-representations that highlight political agency and resistance, mainstream media frame both their stories and ethical responsibility in humanitarian terms and thereby partake in the broader (problematic) politics of empathy (LaCapra; Shuman).

We have considered the political work that gendered vulnerability serves. Images of vulnerable Yezidi women and children and stories of sex slavery have been normalized in discourses of terrorism. The reports we cited demonstrate a call for empathy with the women who have experienced this violence, a response notably absent for other refugee violence. Reports of violence are deployed across geographic and culturally perceived differences as a warrant for empathy toward some groups and fear of others, and the call for empathy toward others can become a warrant for fearing others; in other words, the various responses, whether empathy, fear, or retaliation, are linked and supported by constitutive rhetorics. The primacy of humanitarian logics—in the case of the sexual humanitarian response to the Yezidi women—partakes in the broader shift in international discourse from the normative legal regime of human rights to the normative moral regime of humanitarian appeals, although there is "considerable slippage of ideologies and practices between them" (Merry 198).

There are several slippages here, all significant for an ethical response to violence. In "Normative Violence," Mills asks: "What form might a nonnormative ethics take?" (148). She argues that "recognition of vulnerability and relationality does not itself guarantee ethical responsibility . . . [because] it is not sufficient in itself to breach the ambiguities of ethics and violence." (153). Ann Murphy identifies another slippage or ambiguity in this response. As she points out, vulnerability can "equally inspire abuse, intimidation, and violence. This ambiguity, which is a permanent, constitutive feature of corporeal vulnerability, prevents the appeal to embodied dispossession from yielding a normative ethics" ("Corporeal" 579). These ambiguities are a characteristic of precarious rhetorics. Our discussion of constitutive rhetorics demonstrates some of the slippage in making Yezidi rape victims legible to outsiders (Western feminists) as part of an already existing framework of rescued and rescuer. This framework always includes the implicit question of the extent to which the rescued are assumed to (or required to) subscribe to the ethics of the rescuer, and the kinds and degrees of victimhood that make one worthy of rescue. Ideally, we might understand our "constitutive obligations toward others" (Butler, "Frames of War" 14) as a two-way street, involving a dialogue and our mutual positioning of ourselves regarding each other, but in fact, conditions requiring rescue produce imbalances of the kind we are calling precarious rhetorics. In the precarious rhetorics about the Yezidi women, cultural shaming and other exclusions already accompany rape, which prevents the kind of constitutive subjectivities possibly offered by the rescuer. As Mills points out, the subject is "irremediably tied to others and to social norms in its very being" (134). In sum, although normative/non-normative binaries structure acts of power and resistance, we hold onto the promise of moving beyond normative/non-normative constructs and their legitimization of value. Precarious rhetorics acknowledge contradictions, imbalances, hesitations (Murphy, "Corporeal" 588), and impossibilities inherent in any account of violence and vulnerability, and in doing so, they destabilize both the engagement and the discourses they invoke.

NOTES

Wendy S. Hesford presented a version of this chapter at the 2015 "Representing Sexual Humanitarianism" workshop in Marseille, France. Hesford would like to thank the organizers of that event, Nicola Mai and Calo Giametti, for their generosity and critical engagement with an earlier version of sections of this chapter. Both Hesford and Shuman would like to thank OSU graduate student Kristin Ferebee for research assistance. Hesford would also like to thank the Yale University Gilder Lehrman Center for fellowship support in 2016–17, at which time she completed this essay.

1. Although Sunder does not address ISIS's enslavement and trafficking of Yezidi women and girls, the discursive fusion of the "wars" on terror and trafficking have resurfaced in particular ways in the political documentation of this crisis.
2. See Harrington's discussion of the problematic categories of trafficking in human rights discourse.
3. "Male and trans-sex workers are common and visible—but not in trafficking discourse." This absence is "arguably a product of trafficking discourse's beginnings in moral panics over the 'white slave trade' and has been reinforced by the radical feminist emphasis on gendered vulnerability" (Szörényi 22).
4. Claudia Brunner cites Fernando Coronil, who "conceives occidentialism as practices of representation that 'separate the world's components into bounded units; disaggregate their relational histories; turn difference into hierarchy; naturalize these representations, and thus intervene, however unwittingly, in the reproduction of asymmetrical power relations'" (958).
5. See Hesford and Lewis for an overview of distinctions between scholarship in feminist legal theory that focuses on vulnerability and scholarship by feminist philosophy and critical theorists who employ the terms "precarity," "precariousness," and "precarization."
6. Jane Hill (112) and Gabriella Modan (88–136) discuss how particular spaces in a narrative become associated with particular values, such as danger and safety or exploitation and other forms of exchange.
7. When asked whether the funds generated through his organization to rescue sex slaves may actually help perpetuate the problem, Maman claims: "ISIS is worth today—4 billion dollars. Do you think that my little meager two or 3,000 dollars per child is going to in any way or form help the power and might that ISIS may attain?" Maman claims that the rewards outweigh the inevitable risks.
8. See also Alter; Semple; Squires; Withnall; Wood.

WORKS CITED

Abu-Lughod, Lila. *Do Muslim Women Need Saving?* Harvard University Press, 2013.

Agustín, Laura. M. *Sex at the Margins: Migration, Labour Markets and the Rescue Industry.* Zed Books, 2007.

Allen, Erika. "Kidnapping and Sex Slavery: Covering ISIS' Religious Justification for Rape." *New York Times.* 14 Aug. 2015.

Alter, Charlotte. "A Yezidi Woman Who Escaped ISIS Slavery Tells Her Story." *Time Magazine.* 20 Dec. 2015. <http://time.com/4152127/isis-yezidi-woman-slavery-united-nations/>.

Althusser, Louis. "Ideology and Ideological State Apparatuses (Notes Towards an Investigation)." *The Anthropology of the State: A Reader* 9.1 (2006) [1970]: 86–98.

Arraf, Jane. "Islamic State Persecution of Yazidi Minority Amounts to Genocide, UN says." *Christian Science Monitor.* 7 Aug. 2014.

Benhabib, Seyla. "Hannah Arendt and the Redemptive Power of N." *Social Research* 57.1 (1990): 167–96.

Berlant, L., J. Butler, B. Cvejić, I. Lorey, J. Puar, and A. Vujanović. "Precarity Talk: A Virtual Roundtable." *TDR: The Drama Review* 56.4 (2012): 163–77.

Bernstein, Elizabeth. "The Sexual Politics of the 'New Abolitionism.'" *Differences* 18.5 (2007): 128–51.

Brown, Ryan. "Escaped ISIS Sex Slave Tells Congress of Horrors." *CNN Politics.* 21 June 2016. <http://www.cnn.com/2016/06/21/politics/escaped-yazidi-slave-isis-us-fight/>.

Brysk, Alison. "Rethinking Trafficking: Human Rights and Private Wrongs" *From Human Trafficking to Human Rights: Reframing Contemporary Slavery.* Ed. Alison Brysk and Austin Choi-Fitzpatrick. Philadelphia: University of Pennsylvania Press, 2012. 73–85.

Brunner, Claudia. "Occidentalism Meets the Female Suicide Bomber: A Critical Reflection on Recent Terrorism Debates: A Review Essay." *Signs* 32.4 (2007): 957–71.

Butler, Judith. "Bodily Vulnerability, Coalitions, and Street Politics." *Differences in Common: Gender, Vulnerability, and Community.* Ed. Joana Sabadell-Nieto and Marta Segarra. Rodophi Press, 2014.

———. *Frames of War.* Verso, 2009.

———. *Giving an Account of Oneself.* Fordham University Press, 2006.

———. "On Being Beside Oneself: On the Limits of Sexual Autonomy." *Sex Rights: The Oxford Amnesty Lectures 2002.* Eds. Nicholas Bamforth. Oxford University Press, 2005. 48–78.

———. "Performativity, Precarity, and Sexual Politics." *Revista de Antropología Ibero Americana* 4.3 (2009): i–xiii.

———. *Precarious Life: The Powers of Mourning and Violence.* Verso, 2006.

Butler, Judith, and Athena Athanasiou. *Dispossession: The Performative in the Political.* Polity, 2013.

Callimachi, Rukmini. "ISIS Enshrines a Theology of Rape." *New York Times.* 14 Aug. 2015. A1. <http://www.nytimes.com/2015/08/14/world/middleeast/isis-enshrines-a-theology-of-rape.html?_r=0>.

Charland, Maurice. "Constitutive Rhetoric: The Case of the *Peuple Quebecois.*" *Quarterly Journal of Speech* 73 (1987): 133–50.

Chulov, Martin. "Yazidis Tormented by Fears for Women and Girls Captured by Isis Jihadis." *The Guardian.* 11 August 2014.

Cojocaru, Claudia. "Sex Trafficking, Captivity, and Narrative: Constructing Victimhood with the Goal of Salvation." *Dialect Anthropol* 39 (2015): 183–94.

Davidson, Julia O'Connell. "Will the Real Sex Slave Please Stand Up?" *Feminist Review* (2006): 4–22.

Fernandes, Leela. *Transnational Feminism in the United States: Knowledge, Ethics, Powers*. New York University Press, 2013.

Fineman, Martha. "The Vulnerable Subject and the Responsive State." *Emory Law Journal* 60 (2010): 251–75.

George, Susannah. "Yazidi Society Changes to Try and Rescue a Generation of Traumatized Women." *PRI's The World*. 18 May 2015. <https://www.pri.org/stories/2015-05-18/yazidi-society-changes-try-and-rescue-generation-traumatized-women>.

Gilson, E. *The Ethics of Vulnerability: A Feminist Analysis of Social Life and Practice*. Routledge, 2014.

Harrington, Carol. "The Politics of Rescue: Peacekeeping and Anti-Trafficking Programmes in Bosnia-Herzegovina and Kosovo." *International Feminist Journal of Politics* 7.2 (2005): 175–206.

Hesford, Wendy S., and Rachel Lewis. "Mobilizing Vulnerability: New Directions in Transnational Feminist Studies and Human Rights." Spec. issue of *Feminist Formations* 28.1 (2016).

Hill, Jane. "The Voices of Don Gabriel: Responsibility and Self in a Modern Mexicano Narrative." *The Dialogic Emergence of Culture*. Ed. Dennis Tedlock and Bruce Mannheim. University of Illinois Press, 1995. 97–147.

Hua, Julietta. *Trafficking Women's Human Rights*. University of Minnesota Press, 2011.

Human Rights Council. "'They Came to Destroy': ISIS Crimes Against the Yazidis." 15 June 2016. <http://www.ohchr.org/Documents/HRBodies/HRCouncil/CoISyria/A_HRC_32_CRP.2_en.pdf>.

Human Rights Watch. "Iraq: ISIS Escapees Describe Systematic Rape: Yezidi Survivors in Need of Urgent Care." 14 April 2015. <https://www.hrw.org/news/2015/04/14/iraq-isis-escapees-describe-systematic-rape>.

Kristof, Nicholas. "Meet a 21st-Century Slave." *New York Times*. 25 Oct. 2015. Sunday Review: 9.

Labott, Elise, and Tal Kopan. "John Kerry: ISIS Responsible for Genocide." *CNN Politics*. 18 March 2016. <http://www.cnn.com/2016/03/17/politics/us-iraq-syria-genocide/>.

LaCapra, Dominick. "Trauma, Absence, Loss." *Critical Inquiry* 25.4 (1999): 696–727.

Lyon, Arabella. *Deliberative Acts: Democracy, Rhetoric, and Rights*. Penn State Press, 2013.

MacKenzie, C., ed. *Vulnerability: New Essays in Ethics and Feminist Philosophy*. Oxford University Press, 2013.

Madhavi, Pardis. *From Trafficking to Terror: Constructing a Global Social Problem*. Routledge, 2013.

Mai, Nicola. "Between Embodied Cosmopolitism and Sexual Humanitarianism: The Fractal Mobilities and Subjectivities of Migrants Working in the Sex Industry." *Borders, Mobilities and Migrations, Perspectives from the Mediterranean in the 21st Century*. Ed. V. Baby-Collins and L. Anteby. Peter Lang, 2014. 175–92.

Merry, Sally Engle. "Introduction: Conditions of Vulnerability." *The Practice of Human Rights: Tracking Law Between the Global and the Local*. Ed. Mark Goodale and Sally Engle Merry. Cambridge University Press, 2007. 195–203.

Mills, Catherine. "Normative Violence, Vulnerability, and Responsibility." *Differences* 18.2 (2007): 133–56.

Moallem, Minoo. "Muslim Women and the Politics of Representation." *Journal of Feminist Studies in Religion* 24.1 (2008): 106–10.

Modan, Gabriella Gahlia. "The Moral Geography of Mt. Pleasant." *Turf Wars: Discourse, Diversity, and the Politics of Place.* John Wiley & Sons, 2008. 88–136.

Morawa, A. "Vulnerability as a Concept of International Human Rights Law." *JIRD* 6.2 (2003): 139–55.

Murphy, Ann V. "Corporeal Vulnerability and the New Humanism." *Hypatia* 26.3 (2011): 575–90.

———. *Violence and the Philosophical Imaginary.* State University of New York Press, 2013.

Oliviero, Katie. E. "Thresholds of Vulnerability: Gesturing Beyond the Sensational." Paper presented at the Emory University School of Law, Vulnerability and Human Condition Initiative, 2011.

Phelps, Sandra Marie. "The Limits of Admittance and Diversity in Iraqi Kurdistan: Femininity and the Body of Du'a Khalil." *Totalitarian Movements and Political Religions* 11.3–4 (2010): 457–72.

Puar, Jasbir. *Terrorist Assemblages: Homonationalism in Queer Times.* Duke University Press, 2007.

Puar, Jasbir, and Amit Rai. "Monster, Terrorist, Fag: The War on Terrorism and the Production of Docile Patriots." *Social Text* 20.3 (2002): 117–48.

Schiffrin, Deborah. "Linguistics and History: Oral History as Discourse." *Georgetown University Roundtable on Languages and Linguistics.* Ed. Deborah Tannen and James E. Alatis. Georgetown University Press, 2003. 84–113.

Semple, Kirk. "Yazidi Girls Seized by ISIS Speak Out After Escape." *New York Times.* 14 Nov. 2014. <http://www.nytimes.com/2014/11/15/world/middleeast/yazidi-girls-seized-by-isis-speak-out-after-escape.html?_r=0>.

Sherlock, Ruth. "Yazidi Girls as Young as Eight Raped as Isil Sex Slaves, finds report." *The Telegraph.* 15 April 2015. <http://www.telegraph.co.uk/news/worldnews/islamic-state/11539492/Yazidi-girls-as-young-as-eight-raped-as-Isil-sex-slaves-finds-report.html>.

Shuman, Amy. *Other People's Stories: Entitlement and the Critique of Empathy.* University of Illinois Press, 2005.

Shuman, Amy, and Carol Bohmer. "The Uncomfortable Meeting Grounds of Different Vulnerabilities: Disability and the Political Asylum Process." *Feminist Formations* 23.1 (2016): 121–45.

Spencer, Richard. "Thousands of Yazidi Women Sold as Sex Slaves 'For Theological Reasons,' Says Isil." *The Daily Telegraph.* 13 Oct. 2014. <http://www.telegraph.co.uk/news/worldnews/islamic-state/11158797/Thousands-of-Yazidi-women-sold-as-sex-slaves-for-theological-reasons-says-Isil.html>.

Spivak, Gayatri. "Can the Subaltern Speak?" *Marxism and the Interpretation of Culture.* Ed. Cary Nelson and Lawrence Grossberg. University of Illinois Press, 1988. 271–311.

Squires, Nik. "Yazidi Girl Tells of Horrific Ordeal as ISIS Sex Slave." *The Telegraph.* 7 Sept. 2014. <http://www.telegraph.co.uk/news/worldnews/middleeast/iraq/11080165/Yazidi-girl-tells-of-horrific-ordeal-as-Isil-sex-slave.html>.

Szörényi, Anna. "Rethinking the Boundaries: Toward a Butlerian Ethics of Vulnerability in Sex Trafficking Debates." *Feminist Review* 107.1 (2014): 20–36.

Suchland, Jennifer. *Economies of Violence: Transnational Feminism, Postsocialism, and the Politics of Sex Trafficking.* Duke University Press, 2015.

Turner, Bryan. *Vulnerability and Human Rights.* Pennsylvania State University Press, 2006.

Vance, Carole S. "Thinking Trafficking, Thinking Sex." *GLQ* 17.1 (2010): 135–43.

Waters, Timothy William. "Yezidis vs. ISIS at the ICC: Why the Fight for Genocide Charges Is an Uphill Battle" *Foreign Affairs Magazine.* 29 March 2016. <https://www.foreignaffairs.com/articles/iraq/2016-03-29/yezidis-vs-isis-icc>.

White, James Boyd. *When Words Lose Their Meaning: Constitutions and Reconstitutions of Language, Character, and Community.* University of Chicago Press, 1984.

Withnall, Adam. "Former ISIS Sex Slaves Take Up Arms for Revenge, to Win Back Mosul and 'Bring Our Women Home.'" *The Independent* (UK). 10 Feb. 2016. <http://www.independent.co.uk/news/world/middle-east/isis-yazidi-sex-slaves-take-up-arms-for-mosul-fight-to-bring-our-women-home-a6865056.html>.

Wolf, Mat, and Shira Rubin. "How to Buy a Slave Girl From ISIS." *The Daily Beast.* 3 Sept. 2015. <http://www.thedailybeast.com/articles/2015/09/03/the-isis-slave-girl-buyback-schemes.html>.

Wood, Paul. "Islamic State: Yazidi Women Tell of Sex-Slavery Trauma." *BBC News Middle East.* 22 Dec. 2014. <http://www.bbc.com/news/world-middle-east-30573385>.

Younis, Nussaibah. "How Isis has Established a Bureaucracy of Rape." *The Guardian.* 15 Aug. 2015. <http://www.theguardian.com/commentisfree/2015/aug/16/isis-systematic-rape-sharia-justification-sex-slavery>.

CHAPTER 3

Necropolitics as Foreign Affairs Rhetoric in Contemporary U.S.-Mexico Relations

SARA L. McKINNON

THE YEAR 2005 was not a good year for U.S.-Mexico relations. Top national U.S. newspapers and media outlets began to home in on a unified narrative of Mexico as rife with drug-related violence and precariously on the precipice of collapse: "Border Police Chief Only Latest Casualty in Mexico Drug War; More Than 600 Killed This Year Despite Aggressive Crackdown" (Jordan and Sullivan); "Drug-Trade Violence Grips Acapulco" (Miller Llana); "Surge in Violence Shocks Even Weary Mexico; Drug Killings Nearly Doubled in Last Year" (Roig-Franzia); "With Beheadings and Attacks, Drug Gangs Terrorize Mexico" (McKinley). In response to both the violence and the rise in news reporting about violence, the U.S. Department of State implemented a travel alert to U.S. citizens, suspending unnecessary travel, especially in the northern Mexican states. Mexican officials were outraged by the implication of the alert, suggesting that it was a form of meddling in the business of the country. Once again, the United States was interfering with the sovereign right of its southern neighbor.

By March 2007, animosity seemed to have subsided and the neighbors were heralding their "cooperation" and "collaboration." Then-president George W. Bush met President Felipe Calderón in Mérida, Mexico, to begin talks for addressing security issues, violence, and drug trafficking. By October 22 of that same year, the presidents jointly introduced what they called the Mérida Initiative to the public. According to the joint statement, "Our shared goal is to maximize the effectiveness of our efforts to fight criminal organizations. . . . The Mérida Initiative represents a new and intensified level of bilateral cooperation" ("Joint Statement on the Merida Initiative"). In practice, the Mérida Initiative is an agreement between the United States, Mexico, and Central American countries to work together in curtailing and regulating drug trafficking through Mexico. Mexico is estimated to be the primary route for 95 percent of all cocaine reaching the United States. It is also reportedly a key producer or supplier for the growing U.S. heroine and methamphetamine markets. The collaboration between the countries focuses on what are described as the four pillars of collaboration: "1) disrupting the capacity of organized crime to operate, 2) institutionalizing the rule of law, 3) creating a 21st century border and 4) building strong and resilient communities" (Seelke and Finklea 7).

Contemporary history between the two countries demonstrates continuous contestation over the perimeters of sovereignty through insinuating necropolitical rhetorics of precarity and violence that often give way to gestures of collaboration and cooperation. While some moments of conflict cite real events, such as the escape of "El Chapo" Guzman from a maximum-security Mexican prison, others cite what Adela Licona in chapter 8 of this volume calls evidence emerging from a "regime of distortion." Whether actual, fake, or fictionalized in content, the repeated staging of Mexico as violently out of control and precariously close to collapse creates the friction; collaboration and cooperation are the life-giving resolves. I question in this chapter what is produced in the reverberations that these geopolitical oscillations create. What do precarious rhetorics do when produced at the level of geopolitics? And what do they mean for people's lives on the ground? I argue that the United States continuously uses necropolitical discourses of precarity and violence to warrant the need for involvement in its southern neighbor's activities. On the surface, collaboration and cooperation appear to neutralize sovereignty concerns and interstate asymmetries of power, yet they truly function to enable transnational capital's life.

Using an international political economy lens that examines the ecology of foreign affairs making, I question here what happens when the object of precarity and frailty is an entire country. To do this, I examine U.S. mediated and political discourse about Mexico since 2005, when the ramping up of messages about violence in Mexico began, questioning what is enabled when an entire state is figured as frail and precarious. The point of this analysis is not to consider the implication of the actual death of states, but rather what the rhetorical conjuring of frail and failing states provides as a necropolitical strategy to challenge sovereignty claims.

THE POLITICAL ECONOMY ECOLOGY OF FOREIGN AFFAIRS

More than thirty years ago, Deidre McCloskey called on rhetoric to examine with seriousness economics as a site of study. Contrary to popular belief and to what economists commonly believe, McCloskey argued that what economists do is fundamentally rhetorical. Deconstructing the rhetorical nature of the work of the economist, she offered two contributions to scholarly and commonsense knowledge of the politics of economics. First, economics is a symbol-based language, and as a language, it is addressing not matter of fact (as thinking about economics as a science might imply), but rather matter of human construction. The second contribution was to turn rhetoricians' attention to questions of the politics of economy. While it has been slow to emerge as primary field of interest, political economy has gained traction as an area of interest in studies of materialist rhetorics (Chaput; Cloud; Greene; May; McCann), transnational feminist rhetoric (Dingo; Dingo and Scott; Hesford), and American public address (Murphy; Rountree).

I want to suggest that rhetorical studies of foreign affairs rhetoric would do well to consider the political economy ecology in which global decision making and policy implementation happens. This involves examining the complex contestations, or frictions, that play out among a range of actors, and across a range of mediums, in order to assert global political-economic influence (Tsing). Rhetorical studies of foreign affairs has focused largely on the U.S. president as the most important actor in foreign policy making (Bostdorff and Goldzwig; Bryan; Chernus; Edwards; Edwards et al.; Hoover; Rottinghaus). Indeed, even when looking outside of the United States, foreign affairs rhetoric tends to focus on what presidents are saying and doing. Denise Bostdorff explains that this happens because "foreign locales are so distant and knowledge of them is far removed"; thus, "presidents must persuasively advance claims of crisis in order to prompt public support for their crisis policies" (1). I agree with Bostdorff and others that presidents matter greatly, and that they are significant actors in the political economy ecology of foreign affairs making. I also agree that a rhetorical analysis of foreign affairs should examine the way particular agendas are produced, promoted, or "brought to the attention" of publics (1). But in the contemporary global moment, there are numerous actors using a diverse set of mediums that convene to form the foreign affairs context. To analyze this context, we must attend to the ways the messages that presidents and other governmental actors make interact with those of nongovernmental actors, such as media makers and policy analysts. Furthermore, we must consider message mediums outside of the traditional bounds of foreign affairs making, such as the entertainment media landscape of movies and television, traditional news media, and social media. I suggest that we see this best by focusing in on various friction points, or crisis moments that arise in relations between states. This process is akin to Blake Scott's tracking of risk conflicts in the global pharmaceutical market. Drawing on Ulrich Beck, Scott explains that the global moment consists of "a world of conflicts around the distribution and management of risks" and global actors' "impulse to control" their personal risk (29). Conflict arises so commonly because global capitalism and industrial modernization led to intense integration, meaning that one actor's liberation from risk may be the burden of another. For Scott, the work of the rhetorician is to track the conflict, which means "capturing the movement and transformation of risks and their effects across a shifting web of local and global contexts and actors"; "such a tracking might also involve examining how the local-global publics who deploy and respond to risks shift and transform" (30). This is similar to Rebecca Dingo's call to look at the way discourses and arguments travel, network, and touch down, as well as Wendy Hesford's intercontextual method, which considers the way power dynamics in seemingly disconnected contexts form and articulate each other. I engage these methods to understand what animates conflict moments in the rhetoric of contemporary foreign relations between the United States and Mexico.

A constant and recurring trope in U.S. messages toward its southern neighbor is that of Mexico as unsafe and uncivilized. Historians of U.S.-Mexico relations Rachel St. John and Samuel Truett recount the wariness that U.S. citizens in border states felt during the times of Mexico's Revolutionary War (1910–1920) in regard to the potential for violent spillover. There were similar concerns of spillage with drugs during this period. Indeed, as St. John summarizes, the messages about Mexico as violent, rampant with drug smuggling, and as a primary source country for U.S. immigration problems are as historic as they are contemporary (202). I suggest that the consistent hailing of precarity towards Mexico, such as figuring the country as unsafe and faltering, has been a continuous way the United States has managed risk around concerns regarding state sovereignty and borders. It is a spatialized management strategy. This strategy uses precarious rhetoric to produce fear in audiences. This fear is then played on to justify the necessity for greater border enforcement, interstate surveillance, and security collaborations in order to contain the violence.

Sovereignty, typically conceived, refers to a state's internal control and external recognition as independent, with the shared understanding that states will stay out of other states' internal business. But clean lines conceived in theory often mean messy contours. In terms of sovereignty discourse, the messiness appears most obvious in talk about borders between one state and another, here and there. As Anne Demo writes, "Borders function as an index of sovereignty because their very presence (real or imagined) symbolizes claims of authority over a territorial entity. Contemporary border control imagery thus functions as a form of sovereignty discourse because it seeks to recast the transnational economic and social conditions of contemporary border life as an erosion of national autonomy" (295). Wendy Brown calls sovereignty something that has to be "theatrically and spectacularly performed" in order to appear godlike in its realness (29). As she explains in another passage, "There can be no 'sort of' sovereign, any more than there can be a 'sort of' God." (50). For political sovereignty to function, it has to be seen as existing a priori, as fact of being, not as a project of constant institution. States implement increasingly dangerous border policies, build walls, deploy drones, fill detention centers and prisons, and deport people, all in an effort to be seen as omniscient, and godlike in control (Allinson; Brown; Cacho; Wright). States and nations also circulate necropolitical messages in the struggle for sovereign control.

Necropower is waged when states and institutions create discursive and material precarity by deciding and implementing policy around "who may live and who must die" (Mbembe 11). Necropower works through actual political techniques and practices that make death, but it also functions as a particular discourse or a way of talking about and imagining people and places in "unreal" ways. Meditating on the difference between "real" lives and "unreal" lives, Judith Butler suggests that when "unreal" lives are touched with violence, the violence goes unmarked, and the fact that there was once a life also goes unmarked and unnoticed (35). As Butler explains, this unrealness is more than a "'discourse' of dehumanization that produces these effects, but rather . . . there is a limit to discourse that establishes the limits of human intelligibility. It is not just that a death is poorly marked, but that it is unmarkable. Such a death vanishes, not into explicit discourse, but in the ellipses by which public discourse proceeds" (35). Sometimes the vanishing is the result of details not covered. Rachel Riedner describes these subjects as the "ghosts" of neoliberalism, or the people whose lives are enmeshed in the intricacies of neoliberal global capitalism but who are completely absent representation as even present, or as person. Others vanish, as Licona in this volume shows, through the regimes of distortion that figure people and groups, either by direct association or tacit implication, in some monstrous way (i.e., terrorist, nacro-trafficker, criminal, prostitute). There may be a dead body, or a body part, but there is no subject. The death and the person "vanish" into the realm of the unreal.

For rhetorical scholars, analysis of the "unreal" means a shift to examine the ways lives and subjects are produced as "unreal," unvalued, and frail in order to prop up, or perform, that which is valued and ordered as "real," a priori, or godlike. As Lisa Marie Cacho's work on social death demonstrates, "value is made intelligible relationally"; "value *needs* negativity . . . [as] the 'object' of value needs an 'other'" (13). And try as we may to turn toward inclusionary politics to recover the unremarkable and unorderable, Cacho argues that *"there is no way out of this dilemma* because recuperating social value *requires* rejecting the other. Ascribing readily recognizable social value always requires the devaluation of an/other, and that other is almost always poor, racialized, criminalized, segregated, legally vulnerable, and unprotected" (17). Attentiveness to the discourse (and grammar) of necropower resonates deeply with the work of scholars examining processes of racialization through the ordering and valuing of human life in the global neoliberal order. In the West, communities of color are the primary targets of social death and vanishing practices, for "violence and whiteness constitute the intractable foundation of colonial sovereignty and its processes of subjection" (Thobani xv). Individuals and groups certainly die or are reduced to "flesh," but expungement also happens through the removal, or vanishing, of people from civic life (Cacho; Hartman; Spillers). I extend this work by showing the ways social valuing and vanishing practices extend to more than just particular groups and individuals. Neoliberalism doesn't just operate to order and value individuals. A primary global mechanism of neoliberalism is the ordering of states, political practices, and economies into the global social order. Precarity rhetorics are staged by nation-states toward other nation-states to suggest a sovereign as in need of intervention, assistance, and aid by external forces. This staging also performs a double move by making the rhetoric-producing state appear godlike in its sovereign ability to speak and do, and in those actions, to actualize what is "real" for the other state. I cue into this geopolitical social valuing and ordering to suggest that necropower, as a discursive strategy, plays out as sovereign states and their affiliates deploy precarity rhetorics toward other sovereigns.

FOREIGN POLICY FRICTIONS

The spectacularized narrative of violent and precarious Mexico reignited in 2005. By 2009, U.S. politicians and media were suggesting that Mexico, in total, might be at risk of death. "Drug violence has become so prevalent in Mexico," the *New York Times* reported, "that some experts warn that the country is on the verge of becoming a failed state" (Stolberg). A story that same year, also in the *New York Times,* suggested that Ciudad Juárez was particularly precarious: "'There's no square inch of the city that has been untouched by the violence,' said Lucinda Vargas, an economist who works by day to remake the city as executive director of Juárez Strategic Plan, but retreats to El Paso at night. 'There's a lot of evidence that Juárez, in a micro sense, is becoming a failed state. But I still think we haven't failed yet and that we could still rescue ourselves'" (Lacey, "With Force"). Other reports insinuated that Mexico was "'on the edge of an abyss' and 'could become a narco-state in the coming decade'" (Lacey, "Mexico"), and that the country was frighteningly similar to Columbia in the 1990s in losing control of rule of law to cartel leaders (*El Paso Times* Editorial Board).

News media telling these frail tales relied on two U.S. government reports that were published during the years of the Mérida Initiative formation. "In terms of worst-case scenarios for the Joint Force and indeed the world, two large and important states bear consideration for a rapid and sudden collapse: Pakistan and Mexico," the U.S. Joint Forces suggested in their 2008 document assessing the world's pending outlook and problems. The report began by describing the worries in Pakistan and then explained the Mexico context: "The Mexican possibility may seem less likely, but the government, its politicians, police, and judicial infrastructure are all under sustained assault and pressure by criminal gangs and drug cartels. How that internal conflict turns out over the next several years will have a major impact on the stability of the Mexican state. Any descent by the [*sic*] Mexico into chaos would demand an American response based on the serious implications for homeland security alone" (36). This forecasting was followed shortly by a 2009 document published by Strategic Studies Institute (SSI) of the U.S. Army War College entitled "Mexico's Narco-Insurgency and U.S. Counterdrug Policy." The paper begins by explaining, "Since 2006, Mexico has rapidly climbed the list of potential trouble spots for U.S. policymakers. Public security in that country has deteriorated dramatically of late. Drug-fueled violence has caused thousands of deaths, taken a severe psychological toll on the citizenry, and, in the estimation of some observers, brought Mexico to the edge of the failed-state precipice" (Brands iii).

In a post-9/11 context of terrorism and national security rhetoric, the commingling of Mexico and Pakistan is significant. The collision strengthens the imagination of Mexico as a warlike zone, unstable in its rule of law, and rife with rogue factions. The intimation is a challenge to the authority of Mexican sovereignty, a question mark concerning whether governmental officials are capable of handling their business. It simultaneously functions as a performance of U.S. sovereign power. The mere announcement of a message like this illustrates that the United States is godlike enough in its omniscient powers to know if another state may be frail and on the verge of death. These necropolitical messages of frailty assertively reinforce asymmetries of power between the countries. For U.S. audiences, the messages of unruly and unordered Mexico only prove the need for border enforcement and intervention so as to contain the disorder from violent spillage and contamination into the United States. The messages play off of anti-immigrant, border-enforcing messages that are prevalent in conversations about national U.S. immigration reform and national security (Cisneros; Dechaine; Hartelius), and they play off of the cinematic rhetoric of violence in news and entertainment media that positions the U.S. border space as vulnerable to violence and penetrable (Domínguez Ruvalcaba and Corona; Mercille). Once Mexico is conjured as failing in political discourse, especially alongside Hollywood-produced messages that reify this idea, then it is significantly easier to suggest that the country, in general, and the U.S.-Mexico border territory in particular, are in need of support, attention, and securitization.

Mexican officials were understandably upset by the insinuations of frailty and failure. "Absolutely not," President Calderón remarked. "Mexico is not a failed state" (Stolberg). The leader threw back with a jab of his own, reminding the United States that "New Orleans has a higher murder rate than his country as a whole" (Lacey and Thompson). Officials in the Obama administration quickly began work to smooth tensions. Secretary of State Hilary Clinton and President Obama both made trips to Mexico in 2009. For her part, Clinton assured the country by blaming the state death discourse on the Bush administration, explaining that "no official of the Obama administration had ever used the phrase 'failed state'" (Landler). The director of national intelligence reemphasized this message: "'Mexico is in no danger of becoming a failed state,'" he noted firmly. All U.S. officials affirmed their trust in President Calderón in "taking strong measures against the drug cartels" (Landler).

From this "failed state" rhetoric quickly reemerged the rhetoric that emphasized collaboration and cooperativeness between the countries in addressing security concerns, primarily through collaborative initiatives like the Mérida Initiative. In a joint press event between President Calderón and President Obama in 2009, both officials affirmed a commitment to working together. Obama called the trip "a new era of cooperation and partnership between our two nations, an era built on an even firmer foundation of mutual responsibility and mutual respect and mutual interest." Calderón emphasized, "As never before we have decided that the fight against multinational organized crime must be based on cooperation, shared responsibility, and in trust, a mutual trust. Both governments recognize that the Mérida Initiative is a very good starting point in order to strengthen cooperation in security. But we want to go beyond, we want to go further in order to liberate, to free our societies from the criminal activities that affect the lives of millions of people" (The White House). The public message warranting the Mérida Initiative collaboration between the countries was to "maximize the effectiveness of our efforts to fight criminal organizations—so as to disrupt drug-trafficking (including precursor chemicals); weapons trafficking, illicit financial activities and currency smuggling, and human trafficking" ("Joint Statement on the Merida Initiative"). The plan's primary method of implementing this anti-trafficking agenda was a ramping up of militarization and securitization throughout Mexico. In the early years, the plan paid for even more federal police and military on the streets. It also armed these officials with advanced technologies such as ion and gamma ray scanners, drug-sniffing dogs, surveillance technologies, Bell 412 helicopters, Blackhawk helicopters, and large transport aircrafts, to be used for securitization measures along the U.S.-Mexico border, in the interior states of the country, and along Mexico's southern border to limit immigration from Central America. Since 2008, the U.S. Congress has designated 2.5 billion dollars to the initiative, though the monies have come primarily through contracts to purchase U.S.-made technologies, weapons, personnel, and consultants in a double move that gives back to the U.S. military industry. While the 2.5-billion-dollar aid package seems significant, Mexico's economic contribution has surpassed that figure by billions each year. To give perspective, in the year after the initiative was implemented, Mexico spent over 12 billion U.S. dollars on crime and violence efforts. Currently, the figure is closer to 17 billion U.S. dollars a year (Institute for Economics and Peace 71).

Eight years into the Mérida partnership, and with both countries under new leadership, the foreign policy conflicts between the countries seem now almost routine and mundane. As has been made starkly clear, current U.S. president Donald Trump is a fan of using Mexico as a foil for most of the ills he perceives in the United States. He infamously stated on the campaign trail, "When Mexico sends its people, they're not sending their best. . . . They're sending people that have lots of problems, and they're bringing those problems with us. They're bringing drugs. They're bringing crime. They're rapists" (Schwartz), as well as a barrage of other messages framing the country as bad, violent, and ill-run. "In Mexico it is known as 'el efecto Trump,'" explained the *Guardian,* reporting on the impact that the shift in the executive office has had on the country (Carroll), which the head of the Bank of Mexico warned "could be a 'horror film' for the nation" (Lei).

Concern about *el efecto Trump* has also meant a rise in mediated discourse about the frailty of Mexico's economy. In the months surrounding the election and inauguration, U.S. media implied that Mexico might be "sliding," "sinking," and "taking a big hit under pressure from Donald Trump" (Kahn;

Showley). And as the *Economist* reported, "If Mr Trump declares economic war, things could get much worse. The economy could stumble into recession, just as Mexico is preparing for a presidential election in 2018" ("Donald Trump"). While these messages are not direct deployments of the frailty rhetoric, they do hold resonance. "Sinking" and "sliding" suggest that the sovereign is not able to keep control of what happens within its border territory. Try as it may, control slips out of grasp, sinks beyond reach. Help from something or someone with a firmer grasp or a deeper net may be necessary to again gain control. As with the hints of political collapse in 2009, the messages about Mexico's economic frailty position the United States as ripe for helping. Trump suggested as much in the early part of 2017 when he told Mexican president Enrique Peña Nieto that he would be willing to help the country with the "tough hombres" who were "totally out of control" (Miller et al.).

And yet, as with all necropower, there is always a life that exceeds the death frame and the wishes of the sovereign power enacting its will (Puar 35). Interactions around Trump's January 2017 executive orders to deport Mexican migrants and to make Mexico "pay for the border wall" set off a string of offensives that, in the coming years, may demonstrate the unwieldy way life appears when necropolitical messages are used to secure power against another sovereign in a globally integrated economy. On the same day that Trump released the executive order entitled "Border Security and Immigration Enforcement Improvements," President Peña Nieto gave a televised speech to the nation, entitled "Un mensaje para todos los mexicanos / A message for all Mexicans," where he speaks directly against the actions of the U.S. president:

> The 50 Mexican Consulates in the United States are now defenders of the rights of immigrants. Our communities are not alone. The Mexican government will provide them legal service and will guarantee the protection that they require. I call on legislators and civil society organizations to join efforts to support immigrants. Where there is a Mexican immigrant at risk who needs our help, there our country will be, just as we should. I am disheartened and deplore the decision of the United States to continue with the construction of a wall that has not brought us closer, but rather has divided us. Mexico does not believe in walls. And as I have said and will say once again: Mexico will not pay for a wall.[1] (Peña Nieto)

Throughout the speech, Peña Nieto uses *Mexicanos* to refer not just to those citizens living within the boundaries of the nation-state, but also to the global community of Mexicans, regardless of residency. Peña Nieto rebukes challenges to the state's sovereign power by inviting all Mexicans, regardless of residency, to be covered by the state's will and right to protect. In the face of extreme anti-Mexican and anti-immigrant rhetoric in the United States, the message positions the context as almost a state of emergency, offering protection and coverage to citizens and charging offices of the government to be "defenders of the rights of the immigrant." This part of the speech resembles those given by presidents or governors in the wake of natural disasters where emergency relief plans are put into play and government offices get to work facilitating aid distribution. Peña Nieto shifts the Office of the Consulate's role into an active stance, assisting country-persons, no matter where they live or their status.

The speech is also a sovereign rebuttal against the threat to "make Mexico pay" for a border wall. Peña Nieto states his answer plainly: "Mexico does not believe in walls," and "Mexico will not pay for a wall." The statement was what caught the most media attention, but it was what came directly after this portion of the speech that I believe speaks best to the risks of necropolitical discourse as a continuous foreign policy strategy in an integrated global economy.

> These executive orders also happen at a moment in time when our country is initiating conversations to negotiate new rules of cooperation, commerce, investment, security, and migration in the region of North America. This negotiation is very important for the strength, confidence and future of our economy and society. As the President of the Republic, I fully accept the responsibility to defend and take care of the interests of Mexico and Mexicans. It is my duty to be in charge of those problems and to confront these challenges.[2] (Peña Nieto)

Peña Nieto refers in an implicit way here to the renegotiation of the North American Free Trade Agreement (NAFTA), reminding the Mexican people, the United States, and the world that there are possibilities for economic partnerships, but that those partnerships must also "defend and take care of the interests of Mexico and Mexicans." This is not a gesture of assurance, but rather a subtle economic threat pitched at its trading partner to the north; while the valued resources of Mexico now primarily travel north to the United States, they might feasibly go elsewhere. One option in shifting current asymmetries of power between the countries is to reconsolidate global power around south-south relations. There are hints that conversations like these are already happening among Latin American countries. Mexico could also assert itself by stopping with the border enforcement strategies it currently operates along its southern border in order to prevent Central

Americans from migrating to the United States. It also includes diversifying the transnational political-economic partnerships that Mexico fosters. Mexico currently has over 1,000 free-trade partnerships with countries, but 80 percent of its exports move northward to the United States. This includes the country's agricultural products like avocado, limes, mango, and sugar, but also electronics like plasma televisions, Xbox gaming stations, and computers. In addition to continuing to state that Mexico "will not pay for a wall," the administration has begun exploring new possibilities for trade partnerships, for both its import and export industries. Mexico has begun talks with Brazil over defense contracts ("Trump Logra"), conversations with Japan about augmenting trade relations ("Videgaray Tiende La Mano"), and general talks with the United Kingdom for strengthening trade relations with the country (Hernández).

In the context of U.S.-Mexico relations, and decades of necropolitical messages about Mexico, we are perhaps on the cusp of shifts in political-economic relations between the countries. But, no matter if Mexico is in close alliance with the United States, China, or South American countries, it is clear that the hidden purpose of these foreign affairs conflicts is to maintain and manage the viability of transnational capital. Certainly, trade agreements, such as NAFTA, are ways that these countries maintain capital's viability. Security-based partnerships like the Mérida Initiative that both executive offices seem to agree are necessary serve as an additional way that transnational capital's sovereignty is secured. These partnerships, and the necropolitical messages that justify them, benefit transnational firms by providing firms with new ground to keep on extracting, completing what Immanuel Wallerstein called the endless cycle of accumulation.

In material terms, the rhetoric of violent Mexico, and the security-based initiatives that it justifies, enables what Dawn Paley calls "drug war capitalism." As she explains, the amplification of military and security around the country through these partnerships has coincided with the bulldozing of activism and investigative journalism in populist struggles around land and resources ownership. "The fact that there is a resource rush taking place in tandem with the militarization (and paramilitarization) linked to the drug war is an open secret," she writes, "one that provides a more adequate explanation of why governments (host and foreign) are promoting drug control strategies that do little to control drug trafficking or lessen consumption" (112). The Mérida Initiative, and the precarity rhetorics that justify it, serve transnational corporate and financial investors to secure their foothold and growth in the region. In particular, as Julian Mercille explains, the United States has used the Mérida Initiative to attempt to keep greater European and Chinese political and economic power at bay in the region (5). Mexican human rights advocate General

Francisco Gallardo agrees that "the context for Plan Mérida is this new world order where the US struggle for hegemony with China and the European Union" (Psmith). As these authors suggest, we must read state collaboration around security-based initiatives, such as Plan Mérida, as a part of the struggle over global power and the maintenance of the fiction of a sovereignty that's beyond question and reproach. Doing so helps to demonstrate the ways that the precarity rhetorics intermingle to prop up transnational capital's interests in particular countries and regions. As Paley explains, a similar process of readying a state was introduced decades earlier with another country known for its drug violence problem—Columbia. The rhetoric of the U.S.-derived Plan Colombia focused on curbing drug movement and violence in the country; the real effect was to grow U.S. foreign direct investment and political presence: "Foreign direct investment increased steadily following the launch of Plan Colombia. At the outset it was calculated at US$2.4 billion, and by 2011 it was more than US$13.4 billion, registering the fastest growth in Latin America; in 2012 it reached US$15.65 billion" (Paley 114–15).

While the early years of the Mérida Initiative emphasized securitization, increasingly the work of securing capital's life means shifting to what is called the second pillar of the initiative—"the institutionalization of rule of law" (Seelke and Finklea 7). As policy analysts for the initiative recently explained, "Whereas U.S. assistance initially focused on training and equipping Mexican security forces for counternarcotic purposes, it has shifted toward addressing the weak government institutions and societal problems that have allowed the drug trade to thrive in Mexico" (Seelke and Finklea 6). In practice, this has meant a complete overhaul of the federal and state judicial system, moving "from a closed-door process based on written arguments to a public trial system with oral arguments and the presumption of innocence until proven guilty" (Seelke and Finklea 13). The Mérida Initiative funded the U.S. Department of Justice's work with the Mexican Congress to revise its criminal procedure code, and Department of Justice training of prosecutors, investigators, and federal judges in the "accusatorial system." The Mérida Initiative has also funded reforms of law school curriculum and textbooks in the country.

Official record relies on the production of precarity to showcase the need for the reforms, suggesting that Mexico's legal system is an important piece in the disordered system and "hyper-violence engulfing certain Mexican states" (Committee on Foreign Relations 7). Yet there are geopolitical and economic motivations for the shift as well. As a report prepared by Secretary of State John Kerry for the Council on Foreign Relations explained, "The United States Government has been keenly interested in forging a cooperative law enforcement relationship with Mexican state-level and certain municipal-level authorities" (Committee on Foreign Relations 8). The "keen interest" I suggest is in exporting a U.S. "accusatorial" legal system that makes it significantly easier for lawyers trained and working in the United States, or for transnational corporations and legal firms, to navigate Mexico's legal terrain. As Deborah Weismann contends, "The practice of promoting rule of law programs in foreign countries has developed as a foreign policy subgenre" in the United States (Weissman 1472). While figured through seemingly "neutral" and "positive" rhetorics of need and cooperation, she writes that "rule of law programs implicate members of the legal academy and profession to cooperate with U.S. government agencies in an effort to make global judicial systems conform to the precepts of American legal values. That is, these programs propound the U.S. legal system as a model for the world, or at least that part of the world deemed to be of U.S. national interest" (1472). Precarity and security are the official record of why policies and partnerships like the Mérida Initiative are implemented with the hope that they will eventually facilitate the protection and security of life. As this analysis reveals, they are, indeed, securing something—capital's ability to survive and thrive.

CONCLUSION

Examinations of foreign affairs rhetoric often look at the influence of a singular speech or actor, yet I have shown in this chapter that in a globally integrated international political economy, we may need different tools of analysis to understand how rhetoric works in the macro-setting of global politics. I contend that by examining the political economy ecology of foreign affairs rhetoric within a particular context, through analysis of entertainment and news media discourses in tandem with political discourse, we gain a more complex understanding of what foreign affairs decision making and policy implementation looks like today. I have also demonstrated that by focusing on the conflict points between political actors within this broader political economy ecology, we gain insight into the geopolitical contexts where sovereignty is being managed and contested for accumulation of power and control. One particular way that states manage other states' sovereignty is through the deployment of necropolitical discourses in foreign affairs rhetoric. These messages might come through state actors, networked affiliates, or more diffuse means, such as circulation through the media or social imaginary. Whether deployed by the state actor directly or tacitly, necropolitical rhetorics of violence and frailty are used against entire countries to challenge the sovereignty of others and to perform the godlike omniscient power of the state doing the speaking and acting. In the context of U.S.-Mexico relations, necropolitical discourses justify the need for security-based collaborations in the region. But, when used as continuous strategies against other sovereigns, these messages can also have unintended effects. The sovereign being named as failing or sinking can forge life anew, building political-economic partnerships and coalitions with other states, or implementing policies that might impact greatly on the state waging the necropolitical strategies.

In the contemporary context of U.S.-Mexico relations, precarity rhetorics are deployed to suggest Mexico as unruly, unordered, and failing. Year after year, the friction of these rhetorics wears. The regular conflict causes strain to the relationship, and actors look elsewhere to forge new life. With U.S.-produced messages about Mexico as frail, sinking, and full of violent rapists, is it any wonder that governmental administrations might be seeking to forge political-economic relationships with other states? This is the process of making sovereignty in a densely integrated global economy. Sovereignty involves continuously performing as sovereign so as to make the sovereign appear godlike in its existence and facticity (Brown). Sovereignty is performed and conflicted over so that states can vicariously keep on living. A primary necessity for a sovereign's viability is the potentiality of transnational capital to keep on living.

Transnational capital's life must be constantly and continuously opened up, extracted, and renewed, and with that there are real effects. Necropolitical strategies may produce life for some, but the effect chain of a strategy bent on death and dying is quite obvious. Necropower is a strategy of brutal effects. With reports of over 80,000 murders in Mexico since the implementation of the Mérida Initiative in 2008 alone, it is no question that there are real effects. On the ground, Plan Mérida has scaled everyday militarism up to dramatic heights. People on their way to the market to pick up staples for dinner cross paths with pickup trucks, the beds packed with military or police officials, all sporting bulletproof vests and assault rifles. A Saturday outing at the ocean is speckled with securitized figures walking up and down the coast or kicking up sand as they zoom past on ATVs. And everyday commutes on the highway most certainly mean checkpoints where there will be more surveillance and weaponized security personnel. Daily life is increasingly, and spectacularly, militarized.

One of the things we know about militarization and securitization from feminist scholarship is the horrific effect it means for women, gays and lesbians, and transgender folk, as well as Indigenous and marginalized groups whose daily lives traverse these militarized spaces (Enloe, *Bananas, Maneuvers*). When daily life becomes securitized and militarized, those without power in a society bear the consequences through their bodies and lives.

Capital may keep living, and states may keep contesting to perform their sovereignty into existence, but to what and whose consequence? That is the question to which foreign affairs rhetoric must continuously attend.

NOTES

1. Author translated from "Los 50 Consulados de México en los Estados Unidos se convertirán en auténticas defensorías de los derechos de los migrantes. Nuestras comunidades no están solas. El Gobierno de México les brindará la asesoría legal, que les garantice la protección que requieran. Convoco a los legisladores y a organizaciones de la sociedad civil, a que sumemos esfuerzos para respaldarlas y apoyarlas. Donde haya un migrante mexicano en riesgo que requiera nuestro respaldo, ahí debemos estar ahí debe estar su país. Lamento y repruebo la decisión de Estados Unidos, de continuar la construcción de un muro que, desde hace años, lejos de unirnos, nos divide. México no cree en los muros. Lo he dicho una y otra vez: México no pagará ningún muro."

2. Author translated from "Estas órdenes ejecutivas también ocurren en un momento en que nuestro país está iniciando pláticas para negociar las nuevas reglas de cooperación, comercio, inversión, seguridad y migración en la región de Norteamérica. Esta negociación es muy importante para la fortaleza, certidumbre y futuro de nuestra economía y de nuestra sociedad. Como Presidente de la República, asumo plenamente la responsabilidad de defender y cuidar los intereses de México y los mexicanos. Es mi deber encarar los problemas y enfrentar los desafíos."

WORKS CITED

Allinson, Jamie. "The Necropolitics of Drones." *International Political Sociology* 9.2 (2015): 113–27.

Bostdorff, Denise M. *The Presidency and the Rhetoric of Foreign Crisis.* University of South Carolina Press, 1994.

Bostdorff, Denise M., and Steven R. Goldzwig. "Idealism and Pragmatism in American Foreign Policy Rhetoric: The Case of John F. Kennedy and Vietnam." *Presidential Studies Quarterly* 24.3 (1994): 515–30.

Brands, Hal. *Mexico's Narco-Insurgency and US Counterdrug Policy.* Strategic Studies Institute, 2009.

Brown, Wendy. *Walled States, Waning Sovereignty.* Zone Books, 2010.

Bryan, Ferald J. "Joseph McCarthy, Robert Kennedy, and the Greek Shipping Crisis: A Study of Foreign Policy Rhetoric." *Presidential Studies Quarterly* 24.1 (1994): 93–104.

Butler, Judith. *Precarious Life: The Powers of Mourning and Violence.* Verso Books, 2004.

Cacho, Lisa Marie. *Social Death: Racialized Rightlessness and the Criminalization of the Unprotected.* New York University Press, 2012.

Carroll, Rory. "Trump's Mexico Bashing May Backfire If Peso Plunge Forces Poor Migrants North." *The Guardian.* 21 Jan. 2017. <https://www.theguardian.com/us-news/2017/jan/21/donald-trump-mexico-us-immigration-border-wall>.

Chaput, Catherine. "Rhetorical Circulation in Late Capitalism: Neoliberalism and the Overdetermination of Affective Energy." *Philosophy & Rhetoric* 43.1 (2010): 1–25.

Chernus, Ira. "Franklin D. Roosevelt's Narrative of National Insecurity." *Journal of Multicultural Discourses* 11.2 (2016): 135–48.

Cisneros, J. David. *"The Border Crossed Us": Rhetorics of Borders, Citizenship, and Latin@ Identity.* University of Alabama Press, 2014.

Cloud, Dana L. "Fighting Words: Labor and the Limits of Communication at Staley, 1993 to 1996." *Management Communication Quarterly* 18.4 (2005): 509–42.

Committee on Foreign Relations of the United States Senate. "Judicial and Police Reforms in Mexico: Essential Building Blocks for a Lawful Society." 9 July 2012.

Dechaine, D. Robert. *Border Rhetorics: Citizenship and Identity on the U.S.-Mexico Frontier.* University of Alabama Press, 2012.

Demo, Anne. "Sovereignty Discourse and Contemporary Immigration Politics." *Quarterly Journal of Speech* 91.3 (2005): 291–311.

Dingo, Rebecca. *Networking Arguments: Rhetoric, Transnational Feminism, and Public Policy Writing.* University of Pittsburgh, 2012.

Dingo, Rebecca, and J. Blake Scott. *The Megarhetorics of Global Development.* University of Pittsburgh, 2012.

Domínguez Ruvalcaba, Héctor, and Ignacio Corona. *Gender Violence at the U.S.-Mexico Border: Media Representation and Public Response.* University of Arizona Press, 2010.

"Donald Trump's Presidency Is About to Hit Mexico." *The Economist.* 14 Jan. 2017. <http://www.economist.com/news/americas/21714397-protectionist-entering-white-house-mexico-ponders-its-options-donald-trumps>.

Edwards, Jason A. "Sanctioning Foreign Policy: The Rhetorical Use of President Harry Truman." *Presidential Studies Quarterly* 39.3 (2009): 454–72.

Edwards, Jason A., et al. "The Peacekeeping Mission: Bringing Stability to a Chaotic Scene." *Communication Quarterly* 59.3 (2011): 339–58.

El Paso Times Editorial Board. "Juárez Violence: Human Toll Defies Belief." *El Paso Times.* 23 Sept. 2010.

Enloe, Cynthia. *Bananas, Beaches, and Bases: Making Feminist Sense of International Politics.* University of California Press, 1990.

———. *Maneuvers: The International Politics of Militarizing Women's Lives.* University of California Press, 2000.

Greene, Ronald Walter. "Rhetoric and Capitalism: Rhetorical Agency as Communicative Labor." *Philosophy & Rhetoric* 37.3 (2004): 188–206.

Hartelius, Johanna E. "The Rhetorics of US Immigration: Identity, Community, Otherness." Penn State University Press, 2015.

Hartman, Saidiya V. *Scenes of Subjection: Terror, Slavery and Self-Making in Nineteenth-Century America.* Oxford University Press, 1997.

Hernández, Leticia. "Reino Unido Busca Con México Relación Profunda." *El Financiero.* 27 July 2017.

Hesford, Wendy. *Spectacular Rhetorics: Human Rights Visions, Recognitions, Feminisms.* Duke University Press, 2011.

Hoover, Judith D. "Ronald Reagan's Failure to Secure Contra-Aid: A Post-Vietnam Shift in Foreign Policy Rhetoric." *Presidential Studies Quarterly* 24.3 (1994): 531–41.

Institute for Economics and Peace. "Mexico Peace Index." 2016. <http://www.economicsandpeace.org>.

"Joint Statement on the Merida Initiative." U.S. Department of State Archives. 22 Oct. 2007. <https://2001-2009.state.gov/r/pa/prs/ps/2007/oct/93817.htm>.

Jordan, Mary, and Kevin Sullivan. "Border Police Chief Only Latest Casualty in Mexico Drug War; More Than 600 Killed This Year Despite Aggressive Crackdown." *The Washington Post.* 16 June 2005.

Kahn, Carrie. "Mexico Economy Sinks Under Pressure from Trump and Missteps by the Government." National Public Radio. 13 Jan. 2017. <http://www.npr.org/2017/01/13/509722798/mexico-economy-sinks-under-pressure-from-trump-and-missteps-by-the-government>.

Lacey, Marc. "Mexico: Foreign Minister Disputes 'Failing State' Label." *New York Times.* 16 Jan. 2009.

———. "With Force, Mexican Drug Cartels Get Their Way." *New York Times.* 1 March 2009.

Lacey, Marc S., and Ginger Thompson. "Between U.S. And Mexico, a Backyard Feud." *International Herald Tribune.* 25 March 2009.

Landler, Mark. "Clinton Reassures Mexico About Its Image." *New York Times.* 27 March 2009.

Lei, George. "Mexican Economy Facing Tough 2017 Even Without Trump's Wall." *Bloomberg.* 3 Jan. 2017. <https://www.bloomberg.com/news/articles/2017-01-03/mexican-economy-faces-tough-2017-with-or-without-trump-s-wall>.

May, Matthew S. "The Imaginative-Power of 'Another Materialist Rhetoric.'" *Communication & Critical/Cultural Studies* 12.4 (2015): 399–403.

Mbembe, Achille. "Necropolitics." *Public Culture* 15.1 (2003): 11–40.

McCann, Bryan J. "Therapeutic and Material <Victim> Hood: Ideology and the Struggle for Meaning in the Illinois Death Penalty Controversy." *Communication & Critical/Cultural Studies* 4.4 (2007): 382–401.

McCloskey, Deirdre N. *The Rhetoric of Economics.* 2nd ed. University of Wisconsin Press, 1998.

McKinley, James C. "With Beheadings and Attacks, Drug Gangs Terrorize Mexico." *New York Times.* 26 Oct. 2006.

Mercille, Julien. "The Media-Entertainment Industry and the 'War on Drugs' in Mexico." *Latin American Perspectives* 20.10 (2013): 1–20.

Miller, Greg, et al. "'This Deal Will Make Me Look Terrible': Full Transcripts of Trump's Calls with Mexico and Australia." *The Washington Post.* 3 Aug. 2017. <https://www.washingtonpost.com/graphics/2017/politics/australia-mexico-transcripts/?utm_term=.bad0e85bc341>.

Miller Llana, Sara. "Drug-Trade Violence Grips Acapulco." *Christian Science Monitor.* 14 Sept. 2006.

Murphy, John M. "Political Economy and Rhetorical Matter." *Rhetoric & Public Affairs* 12.2 (2009): 303–15.

Paley, Dawn. "Drug War as Neoliberal Trojan Horse." *Latin American Perspectives* 42.5 (2015): 109–32.

Peña Nieto, Enrique. "Un Mensaje Para Todos Los Mexicanos." 25 Jan. 2017. <https://www.gob.mx/presidencia/articulos/un-mensaje-para-todos-los-mexicanos?idiom=es>.

Psmith. "In Mexico, Opposition to Plan Merida Emerges." *StoptheDrugWar.org*. 2 May 2008. <http://stopthedrugwar.org/chronicle/2008/may/02/mexico_opposition_plan_merida_em>. 15 Aug. 2016.

Puar, Jasbir K. *Terrorist Assemblages: Homonationalism in Queer Times*. Duke University Press, 2007.

Riedner, Rachel C. *Writing Neoliberal Values: Rhetorical Connectivities and Globalized Capitalism*. Palgrave Macmillan UK, 2015.

Roig-Franzia, Manuel. "Surge in Violence Shocks Even Weary Mexico." *The Washington Post*. 29 Nov. 2006.

Rottinghaus, Brandon. "Presidential Leadership on Foreign Policy, Opinion Polling, and the Possible Limits of 'Crafted Talk.'" *Political Communication* 25.2 (2008): 138–57.

Rountree, J. Clarke. "The President as God, the Recession as Evil: Actus, Status, and the President's Rhetorical Bind." *Quarterly Journal of Speech* 81.3 (1995): 325–52.

Schwartz, Ian. "Trump: Mexico Not Sending Us Their Best; Criminals, Drug Dealers and Rapists Are Crossing Border." *RealClear Politics*. 16 June 2016.

Scott, J. Blake. "Track 'Transglobal' Risk in Pharmaceutical Development: Novaritis's Challenge of Indian Patent Law." *The Megarhetorics of Global Development*. Ed. Rebecca Dingo and J. Blake Scott. University of Pittsburgh, 2012. 29–53.

Seelke, Clare Ribando, and Kristin Finklea. "U.S.-Mexican Security Cooperation: The Mérida Initiative and Beyond." Congressional Research Service. 22 Feb. 2016. 1–31.

Showley, Roger. "Sinking Peso: Danger Sign to Economy?" *The San Diego Union-Tribune*. 20 Jan. 2017. <http://www.sandiegouniontribune.com/business/economy/sd-fi-econometer21jan-20170119-htmlstory.html>.

Spillers, Hortense J. "Mama's Baby, Papa's Maybe: An American Grammar Book." *Diacritics* (1987): 65–80.

St. John, Rachel. *Line in the Sand: A History of the Western U.S.-Mexico Border*. Princeton University Press, 2012.

Stolberg, Sheryl. "Obama Takes Aim at Finances of Three Mexican Drug Cartels." *New York Times*. 16 April 2009.

Thobani, Sunera. "Prologue." *Queer Necropolitics*. Ed. Jin Haritaworn et al. Routledge, 2014. xv–xviii.

Truett, Samuel. *Fugitive Landscapes: The Forgotten History of the U.S.-Mexico Borderlands*. Yale University Press, 2008.

"Trump Logra Que México Y Brasil Se Acerquen En Materia Militar." *El Financiero*. 8 Aug. 2017.

Tsing, Anna Lowenhaupt. *Friction: An Ethnography of Global Connection*. Princeton University Press, 2004.

United States Joint Forces Command. "The 2008 Joint Operation Environment: Challenges and Implications for the Future Joint Force." 25 Nov. 2008. 1–51. <https://us.jfcom.mil/sites/J5/j59/default.aspxhttps://us.jfcom.mil/sites/J5/j59/default.aspx>.

"Videgaray Tiende La Mano a Japón En Antesala De Tlcan 2.0." *El Financero*. 8 Aug. 2017.

Wallerstein, Immanuel Maurice. *World Systems Analysis: An Introduction*. Duke, 2002.

Weissman, Deborah M. "Remaking Mexico: Law Reform as Foreign Policy." *Cardozo Law Review* 35.4 (2014): 1471–1523.

The White House. "Joint Press Conference with President Barack Obama and President Felipe Calderon of Mexico." Office of the Press Secretary, 16 April 2009.

Wright, Melissa W. "Necropolitics, Narcopolitics, and Femicide: Gendered Violence on the Mexico-U.S. Border." *Signs* 36 (2011): 707–31.

CHAPTER 4

Embodying "I Can't Breathe"

Tensions and Possibilities Between Appropriation and Coalition

KIMBERLEE PÉREZ

I CAN'T BREATHE. The body calls out, from itself, about itself. *I Can't Breathe.* At the edge of a speech act, a performative doing (Austin). *I Can't Breathe.* Breath, required to speak. *I Can't Breathe.* A performative anticipation. *I Can't Breathe.* An announcement the body makes from itself, about itself, to another. *I Can't Breathe.* The announcement, a relation. *I Can't Breathe.* The relation, precarious. *I Can't Breathe.* Relations of precarity are dependent (Berlant 192). Racial precarity secures dependence through the maintenance of difference (Holland 3), misrecognition, invisibility, and hypervisibility (C. Smith 6), incarceration and terror (Cacho 121; Hartman 7). *I Can't Breathe.* A demand for recognition. *I Can't Breathe.* In precarity, recognition is incomplete, unwilling, perhaps impossible (Butler, *Precarious* 43–45; Butler, *Frames* 5–7). *I Can't Breathe.* A gesture of relation, otherwise, and elsewhere. In a moment. Of coalition.[1] A coalitional moment.

To resist, and to generate otherwise, and elsewhere, across lines of similarity and difference, is one potential of coalition. Coalition's potential materializes in what Karma R. Chávez theorizes as the coalitional moment, which "occurs when political issues coincide or merge in the public sphere in ways that create space to reenvision and potentially reconstruct rhetorical imaginaries" (8). This is to say that something, some things are apt to happen when political issues coincide or merge in the public sphere. A movement's taking up of the rhetoric of another is a political strategy, one of appropriation.

As with any strategy, the edges of appropriation can be mobilized in multiple directions, intersections, and relations. One edge of appropriation is in the service of coalition. As Chávez demonstrates, the DREAMers' deliberate appropriation of the LGBTQ rhetoric of the closet enabled visibility of the intersections of migration and sexuality, how the categories interanimate one another rather than parse them into separate categories (79–111). In this instance, appropriation produced a coalitional moment. Such openings depend on relational literacies, upon intentional modes of seeing and being, of mutual and cross-recognition beyond one's self and issues and across difference (Licona and Chávez). Relational literacies demonstrate the need for mutual understanding, the embodied knowledges and recognitions that rub against, that resist and remake, the conditions of precarity.

If one edge of appropriation is coalition, from "like me" to "with me," another edge is appropriation, which tips over to replacement, an eclipse of "like me" with "for me," "as me," "me." The potential at once pried open, now flattened; that which might have been reenvisioned and reconstructed is reabsorbed and recirculated in the service not of coalition but very often of power—of normativity, dominance, dependency, supremacy. Rather than subvert precarity, precarity is shored up. Recall the December 16, 2008, cover of the *Advocate* in the wake of the November elections that insisted "Gay is the New Black: The Last Great Civil Rights Struggle" (Gross). In this appropriation of black civil rights, gayness replaces, rather than intersects with, blackness. Replacement functions in the service of a separation that simultaneously refuses bodies that are both gay and black. Also foreclosed is the coalitional potential among and across differently racialized sexualities. Appropriation and coalition are not a binary, but a continuum of lines among political, relational, and embodied rhetorics and strategies. There is a tension between appropriation and coalition, one that must be closely tended, and traced through the ways that rhetorics are embodied, visibilized, and visualized. As Chávez further writes, "coalition is a liminal space, necessarily precarious, and located within the intermeshed interstices of people's lives and politics" (146). At and through the interstices of people's lives and politics lie the tensions and possibilities between appropriation and coalition. What I want to consider in this chapter are those tensions and possibilities as they are lived, as they are embodied, and as they are found in and through relations. I do so through three different iterations of representations and embodiments of "I Can't Breathe" in the wake of the murder of Eric Garner.

On July 17, 2014, Eric Garner was murdered at the hands of the New York City police. "I can't breathe," repeated eleven times, are understood to be among his final words. His final words, his insistence, his plea, from his body facedown on a public sidewalk in Tomkinsville, on Staten Island, New York, before he died in an ambulance and was pronounced dead at a hospital. After several police officers ignored Eric Garner's and others' insistent calls to action, making no physical intervention, offering no aid, waiting for an ambulance. After multiple police held Eric Garner down to handcuff him. After one officer put his hands around Eric Garner's neck in order to force his body to the street. After Eric Garner's insistence that "this ends today." After Eric Garner's precarity was always already doubled down at the intersection of race and economy.[2]

On December 3, 2014, the state announced a grand jury's failure to indict a police officer whose choke hold was in part responsible for Eric Garner's murder (Siff, Dienst, and Millman). The announcement was met with multiple demonstrations in New York City speaking back to anti-black racism and police brutality, and among the chants was "I Can't Breathe" (Goodman and Baker; Laughland et al.; Yee). Through their visual (posters/placards) and audible declarations, the demonstrations visibilize Eric Garner's body and voice and the conditions of his death, centering in public space the precarity of black bodies, and how precarity is materialized through police brutality. While Eric Garner's absent body no longer speaks as it no longer breathes, the collective agency of a public crowd relies on his absent body to mobilize resistance.

In the weeks following December 3, 2014, "I Can't Breathe" moved beyond the immediacy of the public demonstrations and was taken up by other, existing and intersecting movements. In what follows, I look at three specific sites where "I Can't Breathe" was, and continues to be, taken up through visual and embodied rhetoric. First, I look how two sites of labor take up "I Can't Breathe" and consider coalitional moments at the intersections of labor and race(ism). Next, I look to police and self-identified allies to show how Eric Garner's words are redirected to stabilize racial precarity, fixing blackness and black bodies as a threat to and forever outside, the nation. Finally, I turn to Pussy Riot's industrial ballad, "I Can't Breathe," to contemplate the possibilities of a transnational coalitional moment. My consideration and analysis of the appropriation of "I Can't Breathe" in these ways is in service of reflecting on how coalition is possible and practiced in resistance to anti-black racism. At the intersection of analysis and reflection is the necessary self-labor of coalition called for by queers, feminists, and people of color to account for our participation in, benefits and harms from, and bolstering of or resistance to structures of power. While I do not specifically locate my own body as a queer Chicana in relation to the sites below, it is through this embodiment that I approach them. It is to recognize that I (and you), as audience and consumer, as producer and recipient of anti-black and other racisms, am part of and implicated by the appropriation and coalitional potential of "I Can't Breathe." Through understanding myself, ourselves, and our relations, it is to argue we might further contemplate and participate in the relational and embodied potential of speech and the reconstruction of precarious relations otherwise and elsewhere.

COALITIONAL MOMENTS AT THE INTERSECTIONS OF LABOR AND RACE

Eric Garner embodied his precarity at the intersections of race and labor in the informal economy. At the intersections of race and labor in the formal economy, workers appropriate "I Can't Breathe" to mobilize coalitional moments. At one end of the wage spectrum, the fast-food worker movement, in their struggles for higher wages and unionization, incorporated "I Can't Breathe" into demonstrations and walkouts. At a much higher end, some professional athletes of the National Basketball Association (NBA) wore "I Can't Breathe" T-shirts during warm-ups to televised games. While the workers who make up these two sites of labor are vastly separated through discrepancies in their wages, income, and visibility/celebrity, the things that connect them make them worth discussing next to one another. Sports arenas and sporting events are worksites that bring the two in direct contact. Further, outside of the literal space they occupy, the cultural and popular imaginaries and commercialization of basketball often link sport celebrities with fast food. Finally, they share overlapping consuming and viewing that place the two sites of labor in relation to one another. The specific embodiments and rhetorical strategies of "I Can't Breathe" by fast-food workers and NBA players reveal similarities, differences, and the opportunities of and failures in coalitional moments.

Labor produces a relationship of exchange between employers and employees/workers. Because fast-food labor is low-waged work that fails to provide a living wage, one focus of the fast-food worker movement throughout 2014 was a demand for higher wages. During a December 4, 2014, demonstration and walkout, workers chanted, "I Can't Breathe" alongside other statements that called out the injustices of unfair wages. Shantel Walker, a fast-food worker, stated, "As fast food workers, we feel really upset about the [Eric Garner] decision," and said that "this is our way of showing the world how we feel at this time. We want to fight the powers that be so we can be" (Margolin). When fast-food workers demand higher wages in public, their audiences consist of fast-food employers, consumers, and other viewing publics.

In a coalitional moment, "I Can't Breathe" simultaneously expresses how wage injustices restrict the breath of fast-food workers and visibilizes the interconnection between wage injustice, racism, and police brutality. It opens possibilities for relations among workers, employers, and viewing and consuming publics to recognize those interconnections and to work across sites of difference to make change.

Fortifying the connection between labor, racism, and police brutality, days later, between December 7 and December 10, 2014, NBA players from the Chicago Bulls, Cleveland Cavaliers, Brooklyn Nets, Sacramento Kings, and LA Lakers entered pregame warm-ups wearing black T-shirts with white lettering reading "I Can't Breathe." In the NBA, players are contractually obligated to wear certain brands. Though not fined, those players wearing "I Can't Breathe" T-shirts did so in direct violation of their contracts (Holmes). While the NBA might have embraced the players' embodied performances as an opportunity to address the racism not only within the NBA but within the larger culture, its public responses refused the gesture. The NBA commissioner stated, "My preference would be for players to abide by our on-court attire rules" (Holmes). Rather than tending to the rhetorical gesture, stepping into the coalitional potential of the moment where labor is explicitly linked to rac(e)ism, the statement retreats into the employer/employee relationship through the rhetoric of rules, the contract that binds the two.

Skirting racism and the black players who perform at the intersections of race and labor, the commissioner reduces and relegates race to the personal. That he recognizes the players' rhetorical gesture about anti-black racism as important to them deepens the NBA's failure to see the employees as human beings whose race and labor render them precarious in an anti-black state. This is different than the players who themselves assert the personal. When Derrick Rose publicly attributed his actions to the personal, locating his motivation in his son's future (Harper), the difference is that Derrick Rose's son is black. And as a black child, he has the potential to become a black man living in an anti-black nation.

Professional, and other, athletes are political actors with complex ties to the nation and its publics. For black athletes, writes Nicole Fleetwood, "perhaps there is no other sector of culture and commerce where the legacies and practices of chattel slavery are more explicitly invoked in the contemporary era than the lucrative and highly elite world of professional sports" (81). Therefore, it is not surprising that both NBA management and players use the rhetoric of and appeals to the nation in framing acts of and responses to "I Can't Breathe." For example, the LA Lakers coach, Byron Scott, identified his team's actions as "freedom of choice and freedom of speech" but ultimately "their choice" (Holmes). Again, reducing the rhetorical gesture to the individual, this move draws on and maintains the intersections of the nation's neoliberalism and anti-black racism.

This stands in direct relation to appeals to the nation by players, such as LeBron James's call for the nation to address racism (Feeney). In contrast to Eric Garner, who can no longer breathe, NBA players like LeBron James are adept at using their breath in order to perform their labor while they are simultaneously black men whose breath is restricted in an anti-black state. LeBron James performs this irony through his position as what Nicole Fleetwood calls a "racial icon." Racial icons, Fleetwood explains, propel consuming publics to "want to *do* something" (4). Although Fleetwood is careful to caution against a unified "we," and notes that what "we" might feel compelled to do, feel, and see might be varied, what I read as LeBron James's coalitional gesture is an opportunity to "imagine and (temporarily) identify with blackness in ways that are not through minstrely, slumming, or parody" (20). This is to say that the NBA's consuming publics may, through LeBron James's status, be compelled to listen to and take up his gesture offered through his embodiment of "I Can't Breathe."

While without the iconic force of an NBA player, a similar move is present in the fast-food workers movement. Kendall Fells, organizing director of Fast Food Forward, a New York–based labor justice organization, insisted that the December 4, 2014, demonstration was "not just about fast food workers" but about linking the injustices of unfair labor practices and concerns of workers to the injustices of anti-black racism (Margolin). Appeals to and through the logic of nationalism remind us that while coalitional moments may hold the potential to subvert or resist normative or oppressive structures, they do so from within the confines of the nation (Chávez 150). Even those racialized subjects whose belonging is contingent often embody resistances that ultimately support existing structures, rather than creating new ones. The fragility of coalitional moments, then, is such that "coalitions or coalitional moments with only nationalist aspirations inevitably fail as they often reinscribe exclusionary norms with long-term impacts for people who should have supposedly benefited from the coalition" (Chávez 150). When workers, from NBA athletes to fast-food workers, call for social change, yet simultaneously do so through appeals to the nation, they necessarily participate in securing, rather than dismantling, the nation.

Perhaps one possibility of change from within the nation is through the kind of recognition that Fred Moten imagines through his reading of assassinated Black Panther Fred Hampton. Via Fred Hampton, Moten argues that coalition must include self-reflexivity and listening across difference. When fast-food workers and athletes rhetorically gesture toward the injustices of the nation from within the nation, there is the opportunity for viewing and consuming publics to recognize themselves as complicit with conditions and enactments of violence. For especially those viewing publics who might understand themselves as belonging to and participating in anti-racism and anti–white supremacy, it is important to maintain recognition that even as we critique the nation, we are never outside of it, and benefit from as much as we are harmed by it. Especially for white people, this would mean to locate resistance alongside privilege and alongside harm in the ways Mab Segrest theorizes and models. She argues that white supremacy does harm to white bodies and souls, that it cuts us off from feeling the kind of pain induced through inheriting and witnessing anti-black racism (157–75). Accounting for the harm of anti-black racism across race would be to pry open a coalitional moment, which might lead to other imaginaries, embodiments, and relations. It would be to turn not toward and through, but away from, false promises of the nation.

APPROPRIATING BREATH, SUFFOCATING STATES

The cumulative moments of police brutality and state-sanctioned murders of black people present an opportunity for the state to change itself, its practices, and its relations. However, to do so would be to radically reorganize relations between blackness and the state. If blackness exists in a precarious relation to the state, that relation is embodied through black people and the police. The precarity of this relation materializes police brutality. What alternate relations are possible when the police were founded to function as the state's "hunting institution," not subject to its jurisprudence (Chamayou 89–92)?

Whatever relations with the police that might have been altered and produced through "I Can't Breathe"—and indeed, the demands range from mandatory body cameras for police to implementing community policing strategies to abolition—here I want to focus on the ways it was taken up through the logic of precarity, which recognizes precarious bodies only as other, as threat (Butler, *Frames* 31). When recognized in a relation governed by threat, the potential for coalition is foreclosed; instead, the state understands *itself* as precarious, as vulnerable and under siege. Refusing the coalitional gesture, there is instead appropriation and redirection of "I Can't Breathe" from resistance to enforcement and performance of anti-blackness.

On December 4, 2014, the day after the non-indictment, and the day that began weeks-long demonstrations, the *New York Daily News* published a cartoon penned by Bill Bramhall (Bramhall; Mullin). The setting is a New York city sidewalk. Though there are no markers of where it is, the sidewalk figures as the one where Eric Garner lay before his death. Rather than the body of Eric Garner, it is the figure of Lady Justice lying on the ground, with the text bubble "I . . . Can't . . . Breathe . . ." She lies on her back, her blindfold intact, one arm stretched above her head, her scales of justice just out of reach. The other arm is splayed from her body, the sword of justice also next to her but out of her hands. What does it mean to depict Lady Justice out of breath, without the ability to breathe? What are the conditions of the restriction, and what does she anticipate will happen? To whom, and about what, is the gesture?

While the actual scene of Eric Garner's death included his body surrounded by at least six police officers and a number of other witnesses, in Bramhall's cartoon, Lady Justice is alone. Lady Justice embodies rugged individualism. Her responsibilities are singular, her own, rather than in relation. What the reader/consuming public witnesses here is the imminent death of justice. The visual communicates that Lady Justice cannot breathe, is suffering, is suffocating. If Lady Justice is suffering and suffocating, to what/whom does she appeal to make an intervention? What is the threat? One way to read such a depiction is as ironic, as somewhat of a wake-up call from Lady Justice to justice, reminding itself that it, and only it, has the ability to pick itself up and to make the change. However, if such a read is possible, it limits itself in a number of ways.

For one, the portrayal of justice as Lady Justice is to gender the state feminine. A feminized state is a state responsible for reproduction and rearing, while also in need of protection. A state in need of protection, a state that cannot breathe, is a state that is suffering/suffocating, a state under threat. While it may be victim to itself, and this would be a useful opening through which to enable a national conversation on its anti-black foundations, instead, the prone body of Lady Justice with the caption "I . . . Can't . . . Breathe" suggests she/the state is without agency or reparative measures to help itself and therefore seeking assistance beyond itself. Rather than taking off the blindfold and surveying the circumstances that she has created, she too is victimized, and the conditions of the legal system, its racist foundations, lie unexamined. The legal system, the state, may indeed be suffocating and in turn suffocating its constituents. This rhetorical frame relies on Eric Garner's dead body as a specter that circulates at the edge, and as a constant reminder of, death. It further raises the question of what happens to Eric Garner, to the black body. Even if there is a possibility within all this to open beyond the restraints of such a read, and there may just be, ultimately, Lady Justice in this depiction—the state—replaces the body of Eric Garner. The iconic image of a white woman takes the place of a black man. Rather than open coalition through appro-priation, through Eric Garner's erasure/replacement, coalition fails, relations foreclosed.

On December 10, 2014, another cartoon in service of the police and the state, redirecting and appropriating "I Can't Breathe," was posted by cartoon-ist A. F. Branco on the conservative platform website Legal Insurrection. The cartoon, "Every Breath Matters," also features a lone figure, this time a body buried at a gravesite. The grave marker is drawn as a police shield. The marker reads not the name of a police officer, but "POLICE," with the epigraph, "RIP, KILLED IN THE LINE OF DUTY" (Branco). Here *the* police are embodied, not *through* an individual, but *as* a collective individual, as slain individuals. Though dead, the collective speaks from beyond the grave in the text bal-loon that reads, "#WeCantBreathe." The shift from "I Can't Breathe" to "We Can't Breathe" might have opened beyond the individual in provocative ways; however, it uses the collectivity of the police as a unitary entity, bolstering the rugged individualism of the nation. This depiction underscores Chamayou's argument that the police are an extrajudicial site. Slain police are positioned not as a part of the nation but as working in service, read "in duty," to it. The duty positions itself against, rather than with and in relation to, black bodies.

Once again, the body of Eric Garner is replaced, this time with an entire force. For, while we might read a single grave marker as *a* slain officer, the implication is that *the police* can't breathe. If *the police* are unable to breathe, they are unable to perform their duty in service to anti-black racism. It relies on the logic of precarity to secure precarity, to position Eric Garner, and black bodies, and blackness, not as a victim of the police but as a threat to it, as the condition of its inability to breathe. It maintains black belonging as alter-ity (Holland 3), as enemies within. The slain police in this depiction figure as victims of blackness, in opposition to it. Ultimately, #WeCantBreathe is appropriated and recast in the service of a suffocating state under siege by blackness. Eric Garner's body is both erased and hypervisible, figuring other-wise, as responsible for both for the police death and, ultimately, his own, a now-extinguished threat.

If these cartoons' appropriation of Eric Garner's body and final words fig-ure the state and the police as victims to the state's own exertion of anti-black racism, then additional appropriations work from within that structure to simultaneously maintain the police as stable and secure protectors. On Friday, December 19, 2014, a rally of police supporters outside New York City's City Hall building were wearing black hoodies with "I Can Breathe" on the front and on the back, "Thanks to the NYPD" (Howell). These shirts resembled a shirt designed and produced earlier in the week by an Indiana police officer and designer, whose company produced and distributed ones with the slogan, "Breathe Easy, Don't Break the Law" (Ly).

Both slogans recognize and invert the call of "I Can't Breathe." If "I Can't Breathe" calls attention to the restriction of breath under conditions of anti-black racism and police brutality, to insist that "I *Can* Breathe" is twofold. On the one hand, the "I" called forth in "I Can't Breathe" is always a collective "I," even as it is the "I" of the body of Eric Garner. The collective "I" calls forth Eric Garner but does not replace him. Eric Garner exists alongside, with and through, the bodies of the living, through their embodied rhetorical gesture. Eric Garner is present. This is dissimilar to ways in which some people took up statements and images that circulated declaring "I am" or "We are" Trayvon Martin. While the Miami Heat and black congressmen wearing hoodies, heads bowed, used the now-iconic hoodies to summon Trayvon Martin, to declare "I am" or "We are" participates in a dangerous slippage between the living and dead. As Fleetwood insists, "Simply put, none of the hooded protestors is Trayvon Martin. *They are not the dead son of Sybrina Fulton and Tracy Martin. They are alive and their future outcomes are yet to be determined*" (22). Asserting "I Can Breathe," then, while wearing black hoodies, replaces the unbreathing bodies of Eric Garner and Trayvon Martin with bodies who can, and in fact do, breathe. Their breath takes away the possibilities of "I Can't Breathe," breathing new life into racial precarity.

Those bodies who can breathe are bodies who are not precarious. The "I" who can breathe, then, is also a speaking and intact subject. The "I" invokes the rugged individual who can breathe on his or her own and whose breath is enabled by the police, the police whose function is not to hunt that person, but to protect that person from threats, constructed and otherwise. For this "I," the breath is not restricted but is enabled, emboldened, and secure in relation to the state and to agents of the state, the police. To command an other to "breathe easy," to not break the law (yet another appropriated and redirected slogan), further secures the position of the law designed to protect that person. It refuses the reality of the informal economy, the only economy available to some people and the conditions under which someone like Eric Garner found himself working.

As I write about "I Can Breathe" and the "Breathe Easy" T-shirts (which remain available for purchase despite a recommendation by the local city council in December 2014 that the site cease sales), I cannot help but imagine and anticipate a response that reduces demonstrators, the designer/police officer, and consumers to a small population, as "not like me" or "not me." It is difficult not to anticipate questions of why I might not have included discussions of police officers, police departments, and even the federal Department of Justice and then-president Obama—of the people and sites who spoke and continue to speak in support of or in alliance with Black Lives Matter, through community policing, or in other ways against anti-black racism. Such discussions are important and perhaps even imperative. Such discussions may be coalitional moments in the making, in the doing. And yet, if such coalitional moments exist and are possible, they stand alongside embodiments and rhetorical gestures of appropriation and failed coalition, gestures that may be embodied by a few but that are permitted and consumed by many others, others whose silences and consumptions and those whose refusals to participate in dismantling anti-black racism, labor in the service of it, sanctioning and upholding it. And this, too, is imperative to recognize, to name, and to dismantle. Ultimately, appropriations of "I Can't Breathe" not only fail the coalitional gesture and the potential of the coalitional moment, they refuse it. Across and through these failures and refusals, racial precarity, and the anti-black nation, remains.

HOLDING TRANSNATIONAL BREATH

If and when the precarity of anti-black racism is secured at the national level, through agents and allies of the state, it is simultaneously witnessed and participated in beyond the nation. When the transnational meets the national at intersections of precarity, there is potential for a coalitional moment to take shape that resists oppression across, and makes connections among, national borders and boundaries. Regardless of the impetus or intention to forge coalition across transnational lines, to connect across lines of oppression and to make links that generate collective change or produce and demand alternatives, there is simultaneously risk. One risk of connection is conflation—flattening the particularity of any given situation in service of a universal statement or understanding of oppression. Yet another risk related to conflation is replacement, to appropriate the particularities in one situation and substitute another. Again, while appropriation may open coalition, it also holds the potential to conflate difference.

Transnational alliances among Russian and U.S. sites, such as through the cultural production of the band Pussy Riot's "I Can't Breathe" industrial ballad, are fraught and infused with histories between two nations that precede and continue to inform the current moment. Particularly around questions of civil rights and race, mutual accusations and demands between the United States and Russian governments have impeded and informed negotiations and relations between the two nations (Dudziak). This charged history infuses the present with narratives of one another, producing orientations through which citizens, and others related to the nation, are interpellated. Those orientations are deeply felt, even when they are challenged. In an interview, Pussy Riot members Nadya Tolokonnikova and Masha Alyokhina explain,

> For us it is important to have an independent opinion about what is happening in the United States not to sink into the phantoms of the Cold War, in which are still relations between Russia and the United States are build [sic]. The Russian propaganda machine has convinced us that the West and especially the US—is evil, is the enemy. To counter this irrational installation, we need to have an independent view of the situation in the US, because any one-sided position is ultimately losing. We have lots of things to notice in the media and politics of America, we would like to see in Russia, but this does not negate the fact that there are things that can and should be criticized. Things such as unjustified police violence. (Brown)

Pussy Riot's "independent opinion" and "independent view" of the United States, coupled with their presence in New York City in December 2014, led them to participate in some of the street demonstrations against police brutality, including the murder of Eric Garner. In New York to record an album at that time, their presence at demonstrations and in the surrounding politics was the catalyst for Pussy Riot to author the industrial ballad "I Can't Breathe." While "I Can't Breathe" does not identify Eric Garner by name, it references an unnamed "he" who in the first verse of the song is one who has "become his death / The spark of the riots / That's the way he's blessed / To stay alive / It never leads to an end / It's never getting quiet / If it's unfair, my friend / Make up your mind." In their lines "It never leads to an end / It's never getting quiet / It's unfair, my friend," one might read the traces of the long-standing rallying cry of Black Liberation, "No Justice, No Peace," which in and of itself is a potential moment, an opening for a transnational coalition. The ending of this verse transitions the opening referent from "he" to the listener, first calling the listener "friend" and thereby extending a relation beyond coalition to friendship, and also insisting that the listener "make up your mind."

What the listener must make up his or her mind about is ultimately, for Pussy Riot's "I Can't Breathe," the injustice of police brutality. Centering police brutality is a coalitional linchpin that connects Eric Garner to Pussy Riot, a transnational issue against which two nations and their oppressions might connect and unite. The call is to the listener to decide what to do about it. The context, through the lyrics, is New York City (the chorus repeats, "It's getting dark in New York City") and Eric Garner, whose last words as they were recorded on video close out the ballad. The final words of the ballad are not those of Pussy Riot and are not in their voices, but are those of Eric Garner, spoken by white American punk musician Richard Hell. Though the context of the lyrics specifically reference New York City and the United States, it is the videos for "I Can't Breathe," released coterminous with the ballad, that embody and enact its coalitional potential. This is to say that the ballad is not and does not provide a platform for Russian artists to speak on American issues. Indeed, it is the connections to be made among the U.S. and Russian context, of brutality and oppression that is the transnational link.

Two videos for "I Can't Breathe" were released in February 2015, each of which are worth considering on their own as well as alongside the other. One of the videos is a compilation of footage from anti-black racism and police brutality demonstrations. It includes tight close-ups of family members and friends of Eric Garner, looking directly into the camera. This video locates the disembodied lyrics of Pussy Riot singing/speaking/calling the events and the conditions in New York City. In some ways, it places the band in relation to realities of anti-black racism through their choice, and it is a choice they have and have made, to call attention to the issue. In an interview with *Billboard* magazine, they attribute their motivation to both their ongoing knowledge about police brutality in the United States as well as their presence in New York City in December 2014, and their participation in demonstrations throughout the month (Brown; see further interviews with and discussions of Pussy Riot and "I Can't Breathe," including Harding; Ohlheiser; Mullen). The band uses their position to speak about a nation in which they do not live, but through which (albeit contentious) connections between the two nations place them in relation to one another. Such a coalitional gesture in and of itself constitutes a transnational reach and site of awareness; they use their voice and stature as dissidents to call attention to issues of police brutality and the specificity of Eric Garner's (and others') murders. The potential to call awareness to not only police brutality but to anti-black racism, both in the United States and transnationally, is significant.

However significant that potential is and might be, through the site of their cultural production, ultimately, it is the other video of "I Can't Breathe" that both fails and limits that potential. In the other video, neither the body of Eric Garner nor the demonstrations, nor any black bodies, are featured. The only bodies present in this video are those of Nadya Tolokonnikova and Masha Alyokhina. From the opening, the camera pans across a Russian pack of cigarettes on top of a mass of dirt, a direct reference to the Russian Spring. As the camera continues to move backward, it rests on the open grave of the two women. They lie next to one another, each on their back, each dressed in the uniform of the Russian police. They do not look at one another, nor do they look in the camera. Their eyes are open. They are alive. They breathe. The tight frame of the camera depicts the claustrophobia of the grave in which they lie. Their bodies signify life and death, the in-between: their bodies are still yet highly stylized. Their hair coifed, makeup and lipstick on their preternaturally still faces, they are alive but about to be buried. As the lyrics unfold, the camera watches them from above as the dirt is tossed repeatedly and accumulates over their bodies. As the dirt shifts from a light dusting to burying them, their faces twitch, their chests heave. They do not resist. They do not rise up. As are the bodies of the oppressed, theirs are suspended between the conditions of life that restrict the breath, the slow death of suffocation imminent. Eventually, their bodies are completely covered with dirt. The camera pans to reveal a gravesite covered with the implements of their burial—shovels and such—but not the bodies who have done the labor of moving the dirt.

Even as the lyrics themselves call forth the body of Eric Garner and the conditions of anti-black racism and police brutality in the United States, black bodies exist solely as lyrical referents. The absence of blackness is striking and risks appropriating anti-black racism as a metaphor, or as a stand-in for the oppression and police brutality faced by Nadya Tolokonnikova and Masha Alyokhina. This is not to diminish their oppression, as certainly their bodies and labor are precarious in their lives and in relation to their country. However, it is to assign failure and appropriation to an otherwise possible coalitional moment that might have linked anti-blackness to police brutality.

The failure here is further evident through interviews with Pussy Riot. Across statements that I located on the topic, while Nadya Tolokonnikova and Masha Alyokhina consistently locate themselves as embodied presences during demonstrations, describing their awareness of and outrage against injustices and the murder of Eric Garner and others, they do so to emphasize connections between police brutality in the United States and across the globe. While cultural production of videos for "I Can't Breathe" stand on their own, extratextual statements made by Nadya Tolokonnikova and Masha Alyokhina in interviews and in a statement on the industrial ballad are instructive, and worth quoting at length here:

> Pussy Riot's first English song is dedicated to those who can no longer breathe. To Eric Garner and to all who suffer from state terror—killed, choked, perished because of war and police violence—to political prisoners and those on the streets fighting for change. We all have to protest for those who are silent, and we have to protest for each other, no matter the geography, no matter the borders.

"I can't breathe"—these are the last words of Eric Garner. Those words are his, but we hope they can also stand for us and for many around the world, for all who can't breathe because authorities act with impunity and feel invincible and above the law in using power to humiliate, intimidate, hurt, kill and oppress. We've known, on our own skin, what police brutality feels like and we can't be silent on this issue. (Brown)

From these statements, we see that what motivates Pussy Riot—a desire to "protest for those that are silent" and a refusal to "be silent on this issue" because they too have "known, on our own skin, what police brutality feels like"—materializes from a deeply embodied experience, and from that experience rises a need to connect with others who have experienced similarly. Such a move constitutes a coalitional gesture and through cultural production, a coalitional moment. The potential here is one that identifies and connects issues from the particular to their interdependence and in doing so effects consciousness and change.

However, in all the statements that I could locate from Pussy Riot on the issue, while police brutality features centrally, racism and anti-black racism do not. Coalition fails when police brutality in the United States and elsewhere are delinked. Refusal to speak about connections among and differences separating police brutality in the United States and elsewhere flattens and attempts to universalize police brutality. Such a move is both ahistorical and decontextual. It questions whether Pussy Riot are helping or "highjacking" resistances to anti-black racism and police brutality (Kornhaber).

Turning back to the video featuring the suffocating bodies of Nadya Tolokonnikova and Masha Alyokhin, the absence of blackness and black bodies relocates the body of Eric Garner with the bodies of two white women. Though their Russian bodies do not register in the same ways that U.S. American white bodies do, they cannot escape the signification and the displacement. While intersections of race, gender, and nation are ripe for coalitional moments, instead, the Russian context figures centrally. In the same interview, Pussy Riot identifies Russia as "burying itself alive in terms of the rest of the world. Committing suicide. Daily" (Brown). Breath, and the conditions that lead to its restriction, and murder, are redirected as metaphor and assigned back to a state that is, like the depictions of police in the above section, suffocating. Even as Pussy Riot speaks otherwise, elsewhere, such a move ultimately displaces bodies of those who suffer—actually and literally in the case of Eric Garner, and in precarity in the case of blackness and black bodies.

It is perhaps, then, to recuperate and contemplate the coalitional potential through the cultural production, necessary to maintain the two videos of

"I Can't Breathe" alongside one another. Alongside one another, the conditions of breath, of police brutality, of anti-black racism, and of precarity are copresent. The ways in which these conditions of oppression interanimate and maintain one another are visible, are consumable, and gesture toward one another, and toward the consumer of the production. Who consumes and audiences Pussy Riot may range from the transnational to the local, and across raced subjectivities.

Not only does the gesture reach across transnationally, it further reaches vertically and sideways, to the bodies of those who occupy, and act as, police. This is to recognize and to further contemplate ways in which Pussy Riot's members insist that "illegal violence in the name of the state kills not only its victims, but those who are chosen to carry out these actions" (Brown). Through this statement, Pussy Riot simultaneously recognizes the police as an extralegal and extrajudicial arm of the state as well as extends a welcome to those bodies that occupy the police. This is to refuse conflation of *the* police with *individual* police officers—to insist that individual police officers have an opportunity to resist structural constraints.

Ultimately, and however much it might be eclipsed through appropriation as erasure, it is the labor of anti–white supremacy and resistances to anti-black racism that make possible Pussy Riot's coalitional gesture in "I Can't Breathe." Appropriation, then, simultaneously has its limits as well as its possibilities. Coalitional gestures are neither pure nor complete on their own. They require ongoing labor across sites of difference as well as a turn within. Turning within enables the recognition "that this shit is killing you, too, however much more softly, you stupid motherfucker" (Stefano and Moten 140). Turning within allows not turning away from pain but into it in order to heal (Segrest 166–68). Turning within demands an understanding that within structures of anti-black racism, some of us can breathe and some of us cannot—and that we all, also, suffer. To recall and to suture these turns is to know, to feel, to embody, and to relate that oppressive structures are particular and widespread. And across their knowing, feeling, embodiment, and relating, they may meet but not eclipse the other. In this, across this, there is only, and always, *potential.*

NOTES

1. There is a long history of the study of coalition as method and practice, as an object of study in social movements and activism. While a review of that history is beyond the scope of this chapter, here I draw from people of color, queer, and feminist writings that detail,

theorize, analyze, embody, and enact coalition (see especially Bilge; Chávez; Hill Collins; Keating; Licona; Segrest).

2. Eric Garner was known to the police as someone who participated in the informal economy of selling loose cigarettes. The production and necessity of labor in the informal economy is part of the study of precarity. For a longer history of precarity and labor, see especially Angela McRobbie. One of the ways that police attempt to tamp down this and other aspects of the informal economy is through the logic of the broken windows approach to policing, which in part seeks not to address the structural issues that give way to informal economies, but rather to render the practices invisible, primarily through relocation outside the city's boundaries. See Jordan Camp and Christina Heatherton's edited collection *Policing the Planet* for further discussion of the history and impact of the broken windows theory and its relation to anti-black racism as well as the emergence of Black Lives Matter.

WORKS CITED

Adande, J. A. "Purpose of 'I Can't Breathe' T-shirts." *ESPN*. 10 Dec. 2014. <http://www.espn.com/nba/story/_/id/12010612/nba-stars-making-statement-wearing-breathe-shirts>. 1 June 2016.

Austin, J. L. *How to Do Things With Words*. Clarendon Press, 1962.

Berlant, Lauren. *Cruel Optimism*. Duke University Press, 2011.

Bilge, Sirma. "Theoretical Coalitions and Multi-Issue Activism: 'Our Struggles Will Be Intersectional or They Will Be Bullshit!'" *Decolonizing Sexualities: Transnational Perspectives Critical Interventions*. Ed. Sandeep Bakshi, Suhraiya Jivraj, and Silvia Posocco. Counterpress, 2016.

Booker, Brakkton. "Black Congressional Staffers Stage Walk Out Over Grand Jury Decisions." *NPR*. 11 Dec. 2014. <http://www.npr.org/2014/12/11/370156333/black-congressional-staffers-stage-walk-out-over-grand-jury-decisions>. 1 June 2016.

Bramhall, Bill. "Daily News Photos." *Daily News*. 1 June 2016. <http://www.nydailynews.com/opinion/bramhall-cartoons-december-2014-gallery-1.2028602?pmSlide=1.2032159>.

Branco, A. F. "Branco Cartoon—Every Breath Matters." *Legal Insurrection*. 10 Dec. 2014. <http://legalinsurrection.com/2014/12/branco-cartoon-every-breath-matters/>. 1 June 2016.

Butler, Judith. *Frames of War: When Is Life Grievable*. Verso, 2009.

———. *Precarious Life*. Verso, 2004.

Brown, Harley. "Pussy Riot Talk Eric Garner-Inspired 'I Can't Breathe,' and the Nascent 'Russian Spring.'" *Billboard*. 18 Feb. 2015. <http://www.billboard.com/articles/columns/pop-shop/6473148/pussy-riot-talk-eric-garner-inspired-i-cant-breathe-and-the>. 1 June 2016.

Cacho, Lisa Marie. *Social Death: Racialized Rightlessness and the Criminalization of the Unprotected*. New York University Press, 2012.

Camp, Jordan T., and Christina Heatherton. *Policing the Planet: Why the Policing Crisis Led to Black Lives Matter*. Verso, 2016.

Chamayou, Grégoire. *Manhunts: A Philosophical History*. Trans. Steven Rendall. Princeton University Press, 2012.

Chávez, Karma R. *Queer Migration Politics: Activist Rhetoric and Coalitional Possibilities*. University of Illinois Press, 2013.

Dockterman, Eliana. "See Congressional Staffers Stage a Powerful Walkout Over Grand Jury Decisions." *Time*. 11 Dec. 2014. <http://time.com/3630858/congressional-staffers-walkout-michael-brown-eric-garner/>. 1 June 2016.

Dudziak, Mary L. *Cold War Civil Rights: Race and the Image of American Democracy.* Princeton University Press, 2000.

Fast Food Forward Workers Committee. *Fast Food Forward.* 20 July 2017. <http://fastfoodforward.org/>.

Feeney, Nolan. "LeBron James Wears 'I Can't Breathe' Shirt During Warm-Ups." *Time.* 8 Dec. 2014. <http://time.com/3624684/lebron-james-i-cant-breathe-eric-garner/>. 1 June 2016.

Fleetwood, Nicole R. *On Racial Icons: Blackness and the Public Imagination.* Rutgers University Press, 2015.

Friedell, Nick. "Derrick Rose Wears Protest Shirt." *ESPN.* 7 Dec. 2014. <http://www.espn.com/chicago/nba/story/_/id/11990119/derrick-rose-chicago-bulls-wears-breathe-shirt-reference-eric-garner>. 1 June 2014.

Goodman, J. David, and Al Baker. "Wave of Protests After Grand Jury Doesn't Indict Officer in Eric Garner Chokehold Case." *New York Times.* 4 Dec. 2014. <http://www.nytimes.com/2014/12/04/nyregion/grand-jury-said-to-bring-no-charges-in-staten-island-chokehold-death-of-eric-garner.html?action=click&contentCollection=N. Y.%20%2F%20Region&module=RelatedCoverage&region=EndOfArticle&pgtype=article&_r=0 >. 1 June 2016.

Gross, Michael Joseph. "Gay Is the New Black: The Last Great Civil Rights Struggle." *The Advocate.* 16 Nov. 2008. <http://advocate.com/>. 20 Oct. 2017.

Harding, Luke. "Russian Punk Band Pussy Riot Release I Can't Breathe, Inspired by Eric Garner." *The Guardian.* 18 Feb. 2015. <https://www.theguardian.com/world/2015/feb/18/russian-punk-band-pussy-riot-i-cant-breathe-song-eric-garner>. 1 June 2016.

Harney, Stefano, and Fred Moten. *The Undercommons: Fugitive Planning & Black Study.* Minor Compositions, 2013.

Harper, Zach. "LeBron James, Kyrie Irving Wear 'I Can't Breathe' Shirts Pre-Game." *CBSsports.com.* 9 Dec. 2014. <https://www.cbssports.com/nba/news/photo-lebron-james-kyrie-irving-wear-i-cant-breathe-shirts-pre-game/>. 1 June 2016.

Hartman, Saidiya V. *Scenes of Subjection: Terror, Slavery, and Self-Making in Nineteenth-Century America.* Oxford University Press, 1997.

Hill Collins, Patricia. *Black Feminist Thought: Knowledge, Consciousness, and the Politics of Empowerment.* 2nd ed. Routledge, 2002.

Holland, Sharon Patricia. *The Erotic Life of Racism.* Duke University Press, 2012.

Holmes, Baxter. "Lakers Don 'I Can't Breathe' Shirts." *ESPN.* 10 Dec. 2014. <http://www.espn.com/los-angeles/nba/story/_/id/12007630/kobe-bryant-los-angeles-lakers-wear-breathe-shirts-warmup>. 1 June 2016.

Howell, Kellan. "'I Can Breathe—Thanks to the NYPD' Shirts Flood Pro-Police NYC Rally." *The Washington Times.* 20 Dec. 2014. <http://www.washingtontimes.com/news/2014/dec/20/i-can-breathe-thanks-to-the-nypd-shirts-flood-pro-/>. 1 June 2016.

"'I can't breathe': Eric Garner Put in Chokehold by NYPD Officer—Video." *The Guardian.* 4 Dec. 2014. <https://www.theguardian.com/us-news/video/2014/dec/04/i-cant-breathe-eric-garner-chokehold-death-video>. 1 June 2016.

"Indiana Cop Told to Stop Selling 'Breathe Easy' T-shirts." *NBC News.* 19 Dec. 2014. <http://www.nbcnews.com/news/us-news/indiana-cop-told-stop-selling-breathe-easy-t-shirts-n271581>. 1 June 2016.

Keating, Cricket. "Building Coalitional Consciousness." *NWSA Journal* 17.2 (2005): 86–103.

Kornhaber, Spencer. "Is Pussy Riot Helping the Eric Garner Cause or Highjacking It?" *The Atlantic.* 19 Feb. 2015. <https://www.theatlantic.com/entertainment/archive/2015/02/what-is-pussy-riot-doing-making-a-video-about-eric-garner/385643/>. 1 June 2016.

Laughland, Oliver, et al. "'We can't breathe': Eric Garner's Last Words Become Protestors' Rallying Cry." *The Guardian*. 4 Dec. 2014. <https://www.theguardian.com/us-news/2014/dec/04/we-cant-breathe-eric-garner-protesters-chant-last-words>. 1 June 2016.

Legal Insurrection. "About." 21 July 2017. <http://legalinsurrection.com/about/>.

Licona, Adela C. *Zines in Third Space: Radical Cooperation and Borderlands Rhetoric*. State University of New York Press, 2012.

Licona, Adela, and Karma R. Chávez. "Relational Literacies and their Coalitional Possibilities." *Peitho Journal* 18.1 (2015): 96–107.

Lugones, María. *Pilgrimages/Peregrinajes: Theorizing Coalition Against Multiple Oppressions*. Rowman & Littlefield, 2003.

Ly, Laura. "'Breathe Easy' T-shirts Stir Controversy." *CNN*. 19 Dec. 2014. <http://www.cnn.com/2014/12/17/us/breathe-tshirt-controversy/index.html>. 1 June 2016.

Mak, Tim. "Capitol Hill's Black Staffers Walk Out to Do 'Hands Up, Don't Shoot!'" *Daily Beast*. 11 Dec. 2014. <http://www.thedailybeast.com/capitol-hills-black-staffers-walk-out-to-do-hands-up-dont-shoot>. 1 June 2016.

Margolin, Emma. "Fast Food Workers' Strike Fueled by Other Low-Wage Employees, Eric Garner." *MSNBC*. 4 Dec. 2014. <http://www.msnbc.com/msnbc/fast-food-workers-strike-fueled-other-low-wage-employees-eric-garner>. 1 June 2016.

McRobbie, Angela. "Reflections on Feminism and Immaterial Labour." *New Formations* 70 (2010): 60–76.

Mullen, Jethro. "Pussy Riot Dedicates New Song 'I Can't Breathe' to Eric Garner." 19 Feb. 2015. *CNN*. <http://www.cnn.com/2015/02/19/us/pussy-riot-garner-video/index.html>. 1 June 2016.

Mullin, Benjamin. "4 Cartoonists on How Their Eric Garner Images Came Together." *Poynter*. 4 Dec. 2014. <https://www.poynter.org/2014/4-cartoonists-on-how-their-eric-garner-images-came-together/305659/>. 1 June 2016.

Ng, Alfred, and Thomas Tracy. "NYPD Supporters Wear 'I Can Breathe' Hoodies at City Hall, Sparking War with Demonstrators." *Daily News New York*. 19 Dec. 2014. <http://www.nydailynews.com/new-york/nyc-crime/suspect-arrested-assault-cops-brooklyn-bridge-article-1.2051361>. 1 June 2016.

O'Connor, Brendan. "'I Can Breathe": An Evening with the Men of #ThankYouNYPD." *Gawker*. 20 Dec. 2014. <http://gawker.com/i-can-breathe-an-evening-with-the-men-of-thankyo-uny-1673519049>. 1 June 2016.

Ohlheiser, Abby. "'I Can't Breathe': Pussy Riot's First Song in English Is About Eric Garner." *The Washington Post*. 18 Feb. 2015. <https://www.washingtonpost.com/news/arts-and-entertainment/wp/2015/02/18/i-cant-breathe-pussy-riots-first-song-in-english-is-about-eric-garner/?utm_term=.4a8dac51a3f9>. 1 June 2016.

Pincus, Eric. "Kobe Bryant: 'I can't breathe' Protest Not About Race but Justice." *LA Times*. 10 Dec. 2014. <http://www.latimes.com/sports/lakers/lakersnow/la-sp-ln-kobe-bryant-protest-not-race-but-justice-20141210-story.html>. 1 June 2016.

Segrest, Mab. *Born to Belonging: Writings on Spirit and Justice*. Rutgers University Press, 2002.

Sharpe, Christina. *In the Wake: On Blackness and Being*. Duke University Press, 2016.

———. *Monstrous Intimacies: Making Post-Slavery Subjects*. Duke University Press, 2010.

Siff, Andrew, Jonathan Dienst, and Jennifer Millman. "Grand Jury Declines to Indict NYPD Officer in Eric Garner Chokehold Death." *4 NBC New York*. 3 Dec. 2014. <http://www.nbcnewyork.com/news/local/Grand-Jury-Decision-Eric-Garner-Staten-Island-Chokehold-Death-NYPD-284595921.html>. 1 June 2016.

Smith, Aaron. "McDonald's Workers Rally in Times Square for $15 Minimum Wage." *CNN*. 14 April 2016. <http://money.cnn.com/2016/04/14/news/companies/mcdonalds-times-square-protest-15/index.html>. 1 June 2016.

Smith, Christina A. "Sorrow as Artifact: Radical Black Mothering in Times of Terror—A Prologue." *Transforming Anthropology Journal of the Association of Black Anthropologists* 24.1 (2016): 5–7.

Taylor, Keeanga-Yamahtta. *From #BlackLivesMatter to Black Liberation*. Haymarket Books, 2016.

Yee, Vivian. "'I Can't Breathe' Is Echoed in Voices of Fury and Despair." *New York Times*. 3 Dec. 2014. <https://www.nytimes.com/2014/12/04/nyregion/i-cant-breathe-is-re-echoed-in-voices-of-fury-and-despair.html>. 1 June 2016.

PART II

RESIGNIFICATIONS

MOVEMENT, MIGRATION, AND DISPLACEMENT

CHAPTER 5

Reciprocal Flowers

Precarious Rhetorics of Solidarity on New Year's Eve in Cologne

GALE P. COSKAN-JOHNSON

NEW YEAR'S EVE, 2015: international media outlets report that groups of men have attacked women at the central train station in Cologne, Germany. The reports are confusing. To be more precise, there is confusion about the category to which the men who perpetrated the attacks belong. For example, on January 6, 2016, the *CBC* reports, "Police . . . are investigating whether a string of sexual assaults and thefts during New Year's celebrations in Cologne is linked to a *known criminal network* in the nearby city of Dusseldorf" (emphasis mine). By January 8, 2016, a *New York Times* headline reads, "18 *Asylum Seekers* Are Tied to Attacks on Women in Germany" (emphasis mine). On the same day, *Reuters* offers the slightly amplified, "Nearly two dozen asylum seekers are among those suspected of involvement in mass assaults and muggings on New Year's Eve in Cologne" (Barkin and Carrel). Meanwhile, the *Telegraph* reports on a sense of public unease that outsiders might not be blamed for the attacks when they point out, "Police have been heavily criticized after apparent cover-up over [the] immigrant background of suspects involved in New Year's violence" (Huggler). It is important that the men who attacked women in Cologne on New Year's Eve in 2015 are constructed in media accounts as criminals, asylum seekers, or more generally, men of "immigrant background." It is important because statistical evidence suggests that in Germany, no particular race, ethnicity, or citizenship status characterizes male violence against women (European Union Agency for Fundamental Rights). Fatima El-

Tayeb reflects on this paradoxical quality in public discourse when she points out that the "continued inability or rather unwillingness to confront, let alone overcome, the glaring whiteness underlying Europe's self-image has rather drastic consequences for migrants and minority communities." What is clear is that mainstream reporting of the events in Cologne mobilized discourses of whiteness that framed violence against women as originating in non-white bodies in spite of an absence of substantial historical or contemporary evidence to support such a claim.

For example, eyewitness and victim accounts repeatedly describe the perpetrators of the attacks as "Arab-looking," "North African men," "migrants," and "foreign looking men," and one person explained that "they looked like 'refugees who'd just arrived in Germany'" (Brenner and Ohlendorf). Eventually, on January 11, 2016, the fact-checking site *Snopes.com* acknowledged the fraught nature of the public response with, "Did Refugees Ruin New Year's Eve? An outbreak of sexual violence across Germany during New Year's revelries is being popularly blamed on asylum seekers and migrants" (Binkowski). "Immigrant," "migrant," "asylum seeker," and "refugee" are terms that are precisely defined in official state and interstate discourses of transnational mobility. Each of these terms invokes peculiar and complex histories, geographies, and politics of mobility (UNESCO). Yet, in the brief description of media coverage here, these words appear to signify a kind of general, non-white foreignness, a "nonwhite presence" that in Europe always "seems to happen for the very first time" (El-Tayeb). Used interchangeably, they describe the men suspected of attacking women on New Year's Eve. What work does this dangerous migrant figure do in public discourse? Who benefits from its mobilization?

First, and perhaps obviously, these media reports reproduce a historically familiar figure, a dark and dangerous foreigner who deflects public attention from the violence of white, European men. However, it is also present in "progressive" voices like German feminist Alice Schwarzer, who insists that "immigrants already here" and "current refugees" require "enlightenment" (Schwarzer and Wizorek 3). Migration studies scholarship provides multiple examples of how full citizenship rights are limited or facilitated by a subject's location, real or imagined, in a racialized and unequal system of nation-states (Bosniak; Cisneros; Coskan-Johnson; Demo; Honig; Mountz; Nevins; Nyers; Sharma; Walia). This discursive process materializes when one of these terms is used to name a subject. Initial responses to the attacks in Cologne included multiple calls to "deport" the perpetrators. In fact, on July 7, 2016, Germany passed a "strict new rape bill" that included a provision to "more easily deport foreigners who are convicted of sexual assaults, a measure seen as a direct result of the Cologne attacks" (Payton). This law claims to protect women's bodies from male violence, but it does so by reifying the troubling perception that sexual assault on women in Germany is a problem primarily imported by men who are not "German," in spite of evidence to the contrary (European Union Agency for Fundamental Rights).

In this chapter, I examine another response to Cologne, represented by a video produced by the social justice organization Avaaz ("How 100 Women"). A progressive attempt to reclaim the "goodness" of the refugee, the video resists reactionary rhetoric in Germany and beyond. This video makes a gesture of solidarity in opposition to reactionary discourses, but I will argue that it also participates in a racialized terminological system of status (non)citizenship in which the "good refugee" deserves to be welcomed by an innocent and beneficent (Western) host. The core of this chapter is a critical rhetorical analysis of the Avaaz video as a precarious rhetoric of solidarity. With the video, an online activist community works to produce a narrative of street-based activism that will circulate online, influence conversations about "refugees," and reproduce a progressive online activist community that *cares* about refugees. My analysis suggests that this form of staged activism, framed to appeal to a general, politically progressive audience, makes use of commonsense tropes that enact rather than dismantle the figure of the dangerous foreign other. Ultimately, this chapter offers readers a critical rhetorical analysis of the Avaaz video as a precarious rhetoric of solidarity that brings feminist antiracist scholarship to bear on contemporary discussions of rhetorical theory.

In the section that follows, I unpack the phrase "precarious rhetorics of solidarity" that appears in my title and underpins my argument. I join a conversation taking place in rhetorical studies that views rhetoric as a force or energy that circulates, dissipates, and/or materializes effects (Chaput; Edbauer; Gries). I argue that this formation of rhetorical theory produces analytical tools critical to the examination of precarious rhetorics of solidarity. Finally, I turn to the video and examine it as a "viral video" embedded strangely in discourse. The video allows me to examine the discursive complexity of viral rhetorics and to explore the notion of precarious rhetorics of solidarity as a critical tool for resisting contemporary global rhetorics of exclusion.

A NOTE ON PRECARIOUS RHETORICS OF SOLIDARITY

After the Cologne attacks, people who looked like "asylum seekers" experienced an increase in precarity. In fact, by January 10, the *Telegraph* reported, "a group of immigrants and asylum seekers" had written an open letter to Angela Merkel stating, "We were appalled by what happened on NYE in Cologne and other towns nearby. We abhor the sexual assaults and petty thefts which took place and we denounce them" (English translation extracted from Rothwell). The same *Telegraph* article mentions that "a gang of men reportedly assaulted a group of Pakistani and Syrian asylum seekers" and claimed to be on a "'manhunt' for asylum seekers" (Rothwell). Lisa Cacho points out that "regardless of citizenship status, whether people of color deserve rights and resources is often questioned because those with social privilege often still interpret economic, social, political, and/or legal integration as a (conditional) 'gift'" (7). While only three out of fifty-eight suspects in Cologne turned out to be accurately described as "asylum seekers," the "open letter" and the retributive violence of the "manhunt" described in the *Telegraph* suggest that individuals who could be signified by the terms "immigrant" and "asylum seeker" perceived and experienced an increase in precarity as a consequence of the attacks on New Year's Eve.[1] It seems this discourse is haunted by the experience of Ida B. Wells, who, in Memphis, Tennessee, in 1892, responded to the brutal lynching of three black male friends, accused of raping white women, with, "Nobody in this section of the country believes the old thread-bare lie that Negro men rape white women" (Wells-Barnett 25). In the name of protecting (white) women from (black) male violence, the good citizens of Memphis threatened Wells's life and burned down her press. In the contemporary case, "gangs" of white men in Germany channel Wells's southern U.S. lynch mobs by instrumentalizing the female victims of the Cologne attacks to legitimate their own racist violence against people of color. These violent acts of (racial) solidarity are, at the very least, historically familiar, gendered performances of white racial domination that, in this instance, view "bodies assigned to Turkish and Arab 'origins' . . . as unassimilable in Germany" (Haritaworn).

Into this context, I introduce the phrase "precarious rhetorics of solidarity" to describe the fragility, the radical openness, and the self-reflexivity required by activism and scholarship that work collectively to critique discourses of exclusion and invent new ways of being social. The phrase mobilizes the notion of precarity, a concept that "situates inequality within broader historical shifts and social structures" (Paret and Gleeson 277), and it recognizes the charismatic richness of the term across scholarly disciplines. Paret and Gleeson point out that precarity has most commonly circulated in labor studies and is linked to "insecure work and insecure livelihoods" (278), but recently scholars have sought "a more expansive definition . . . synonymous with uncertainty and unpredictability" (280). For example, Bernhard et al. use the phrase "precarious migration status" to recognize that status citizenship remains qualified for particular kinds of subjects. The phrase collapses the citizen/noncitizen binary that fails to account for ways that contemporary Canadian immigration policy and procedures produce vulnerability (241). Finally, Judith Butler's *Precarious Life: The Powers of Mourning and Violence* marks a watershed moment for the term when she associates precarity with discourses that normalize "heightened surveillance of Arab peoples and anyone who looks vaguely Arab in the dominant racial imaginary" (39). As those who "look vaguely Arab" or who are linked to Islam come to embody the "terrorist," the precarity of their lives increases. Precarity, then, points to historically and socially produced vulnerabilities structured by racialized state discourses and fear of the Other. Precarious rhetorics are unpredictable because they are embedded in and potentially complicit with oppressive national imaginaries that exploit workers, noncitizens, and persons of color as tropes in the formation of dominant national imaginaries. "Solidarity," as a term of both interested and affective connection, retains radical potential when borrowed from the work of Chandra Mohanty, who calls for "political solidarity" as "a basis for cross-cultural comparison and analysis that is grounded in history and social location rather than in an ahistorical notion of culture or experience" (145). Mohanty's notion of solidarity urges subjects to reach across lines of difference to engage in radical acts of invention while remaining vigilant of the colonizing desire to rescue others, as if one were, oneself, free. To describe such practices as precarious rhetorics of solidarity is to recognize the moments in which they produce community and liberatory ways of being while remaining vigilant of the potential that they will also or instead reproduce the precarities that they seek to dismantle.

VIRAL SPEECH, SHARIA, AND A LEADING GERMAN FEMINIST

In what follows, I examine current formations of public rhetoric as viral economies while also considering Judith Butler's notion of "up-againstness." I suggest that the notions of viral speech and up-againstness, when associated with precarious rhetorics of solidarity, constitute useful methodological tools for analyzing rhetorics that circulate in contemporary public discourse, disrupt calls for solidarity, and work to divide friend from enemy along patriarchal, neocolonial lines. I ground this discussion by turning to a rhetorical analysis of the video "100 Women" as a text that exemplifies precarious rhetorics of solidarity when it strains earnestly toward the good while remaining complicit with gendered and racialized discourses of whiteness.

According to the *Oxford English Dictionary*, "virus" has its origins in classical Latin when it referred to "poisonous secretion, venom, virulent or malignant quality (of disposition or speech)." Viruses do damage. Viral speech is "malignant speech," it proliferates, it has violent tendencies. Sara Ahmed might call these words "willful" or "objects that do not allow subjects to carry out their will" (42). These willful words can put a stop to things. Viral speech mobilizes a hyperbolic sense of "presence," a term that Ralph Cintron places gently at a "scene of violence" (28), but I would suggest that the violence of viral speech is not "slight when compared to physical violence" (Cintron 28). Current usage employs the virus as an infection of the body or the computer, or as a technique of marketing. A virus interrupts the system it has entered because it replicates. The body's temperature rises, the computer becomes erratic, the product finds consumers who will find more consumers who will find more consumers. Poisonous speech, as virus, changes the nature of its host because it interrupts the business of living as usual. When a video goes viral, *Urban Dictionary* explains simply that it has gained "mass popularity through Internet Sharing, such as entertainment websites, e-mail messages or suggesting a friend watch it." A viral video is not figured as poison, but like Gorgias's ancient oratory or today's televised "infomercial," it captivates audiences in ways that are mysterious. To demystify such complex rhetorical processes requires critical methodologies that are equally willful, equally flexible, and fiercely historicizing.

To view rhetoric as a virus is to recognize the importance of spatiotemporal movement, complexity, and interconnection that has become current in contemporary formations of rhetorical theory (i.e., Royster's "critical imagination," Queen's "rhetorical fields," Wingard's "branded bodies," and Gries's attention to circulation and the "turn . . . toward futurity"). Edbauer makes use of the virus as an analogy to account for the ways that the rhetorical situation or "energy" of any public text relies on its interactions with other texts as a "mixture of processes and encounters" (13). Viral theories of rhetoric avoid treating discourses as discrete, isolated, or internally consistent. To understand how the New Year's Eve attacks in Cologne rippled through discourse and were mobilized by particular communities throughout the month of January 2016, one must identify tropes and trace their movement, circulation, and mutation through a wide variety of texts like one would trace microbes through a population in a viral outbreak. Rhetoric, in this sense, works through a "viral economy," and "the intensity, force, and circulatory range of a rhetoric are always expanding through the mutations and new exposures attached to that given rhetoric" (Edbauer 13). A viral notion of rhetoric recognizes that viruses are able to cross species boundaries to link a "baboon" to a "cat" because "rhetoric might manage to infect and connect various processes, events, and bodies" (Edbauer 14). The examination of viral rhetoric requires the identification of dissimilar yet linked texts, but it also notices missed encounters through which some texts appear to be inoculated against rhetorical exposure to other kinds of texts. In the case of Cologne, mainstream media foregrounded "shock" as the most reasonable response to the attacks by eliding extensive evidence that incidents of sexual assault at large public gatherings are not unusual in Germany (Moore).

In fact, among those who examine incidents of violence against women in Europe, the events in Cologne may be considerably less shocking, if no less horrifying. According to a European Union (EU) survey based on interviews with 42,000 women across the twenty-eight member states of the EU, "one in three women (33%) has experienced physical and/or sexual violence since the age of 15," (European Union Agency for Fundamental Rights 167), and in Germany, specifically, the percentage rises to the slightly above average 35 percent (28). What is more, the results of the survey "indicate relatively small differences between the respondents based on" a range of categories intended to identify immigrant background. The survey finds that

> women who are not citizens of their current country of residence have some-what higher rates of physical and/or sexual violence since the age of 15 by partners and non-partners, but there are no notable differences with regard to other forms of violence examined (stalking and sexual harassment since the age of 15; and physical, sexual or psychological violence before the age of 15). (European Union Agency for Fundamental Rights 188)

In other words, being an immigrant, asylum seeker, or refugee does not correlate with significantly higher rates of sexual violence. In fact, the study suggests that "immigrant" men who attack women in Germany have more in common with nonimmigrant men who attack women in Germany than they have with other "immigrants." EU survey "findings show that violence against women is an extensive but widely under-reported human rights abuse across the EU" (9), but public discourse resists the notion that men who are committed to patriarchal, sexual violence toward women belong together, regardless of their race, ethnicity, or geopolitical origins. Public discourse also evades other commonsense responses to the attacks that do not include "shock," such as "At Octoberfest, at Karnaval, we always have a lot of sexual crimes. . . . But society accepts that" (Moore). To sustain a sense of "shock" at the treatment of women on New Year's Eve in Cologne requires racialized public forgetting. El-Tayeb identifies this sort of "forgetting" as an "active process." Events are rendered "meaningless, without reference and thus without place in a collective memory," such that "every acknowledgement of a nonwhite presence always seems to happen for the very first time" (loc. 219). The "shock" of Cologne is sustained by the forgetting of both the sexual crimes rife at large public events like "Octoberfest" and a long history of mundane, everyday non-white presence in Europe.

Nonlinear, viral rhetoric articulates (always partially) the shifting environment in which a text circulates. Its complexity produces multiple points of entry for the work of critique, because "this circulating energy leaves discursive residues," and these residues "can be tracked in order to piece together the overdetermined relationships influencing the larger political economic moment" (Chaput 10). Viral rhetoric is less like an object to be described and "more like an unfolding event—a distributed, material process of becomings" (Gries). Yet, viral rhetoric often sustains hegemonic forms of remembering and forgetting. Its "rhetorical energy, inherited from past experiences, produces relations that are more often conservative than transformative" (Chaput 11). Viral rhetorics are precarious rhetorics because they embody an uncertainty and unpredictability that, yet, works to preserve existing power structures. Viral rhetorics interrupt the broad, recursive swath of a discursive formation when they make use of its material and energy. Viral speech works as an infinitely prolific enthymeme—it pulls from what is familiar and then molds the familiar into any number of novel assertions. Rhetoric as viral suggests that precarious rhetorics of solidarity that work to produce community across difference are precarious *because* they pull from "common" sense.

Chaput explains that "rhetorical energy acts conservatively because objects, like circulating energies, stay in motion until interrupted," and "the logic of emotional energy conserves and maintains power relations" (11). An examination of precarious rhetorics of solidarity seeks the energy of counter-rhetorics that interrupt the conservative energy of public speech. Tracing residues as a form of rhetorical analysis requires sifting the flow of public speech for interruptions, new trajectories, insurrectionary speech. Such critical practices would be attentive to course corrections, strange alliances, and moments that appear insurrectionary but may yet reinforce the conservative energy up against which they initially rose.

In "Precarious Life, Vulnerability, and the Ethics of Cohabitation," Judith Butler makes use of the term "up-againstness" to describe the "result of populations living in conditions of unwilled adjacency, the result of forced emigration or the redrawing of the boundaries of a nation-state" (134). Up-againstness involves strangers or groups of strangers becoming neighbors because circumstances, often traumatic or produced through violence, have dictated that they do so. Such groups experience "unwilled adjacency." Up-againstness describes the complexity of encounters between EU citizens and non-European asylum seekers who remain "new" and so constitutively different from the old (Western) European neighbors. This sense of up-againstness relies on the (mis)recognition of the familiar as the same and the ahistorical rewriting of the European past as ethnically pure and stable. This misrecognition comes into stark relief for "second and third generations" who "were born into their counties of residence" and whose "difference" is nevertheless "frequently framed as one of fundamental cultural opposition to everything Europe stands for" (Haritaworn). Sue Spearey points out that for Butler, "the dual sense of up againstness—as confrontation with ethical dilemma and as 'unwilled adjacency'—is bound up, in turn, with her related point about solicitations potentially being articulated in 'languages we may not understand or wish to understand'" (240). The question of whether or not a community responds ethically to bodies it never intended to press against is bound up in language, which is, in turn, embedded in questions of race, ethnicity, gender, and history.

For example, non-Arabic speakers in Europe, exposed to contemporary mainstream media, may have extensive but superficial experience with Arabic words like "Sharia" and "Allahu Akbar." Such words are often cited across mainstream media, social media, and popular culture; however, circulation leads to resignification. Resignification interrupts the ways these words have circulated in Arabic or Muslim contexts as ways of imagining and inhabiting a historical, ethical, and cosmological worldview rich with internal subtleties, variations, politics, and contradictions. In Western public speech, these words become transparent markers of terrorism, amorphous threat, and imminent violence. A memorial for the victims of a knife attack that took place in Munich on July 22, 2016, included the family and friends of at least three of the victims who were "of Turkish origin" ("Allahu Akbar"). *RT* reports, "The mood changes after cries of '*Allahu Akbar*' (literally, God is great) are heard at the gathering." The words "immediately cause a furor among a group of German males, who then respond by saying, "*Shut up with that 'Allahu Akbar' s**t, f**k you, mother f***er*" (italics in original). After some additional calls of *Allahu Akbar, RT* reports that the German men "question why the police are not intervening in the altercation." I am interested, specifically, in how this phrase is taken up by the "German males" as words that require police intervention. I make no claims about the intentions of the friends of the victim, and I recognize that the movement of this phrase from Arabic to Turkish would require its own complex analysis of rhetorics, geographies, histories, and politics. Nevertheless, here we find that resignification produces meanings that move virally through German language discourse, working to invite uptake that legitimates the violent response of white patriarchal culture to the "original" speakers.

Perhaps more troubling, Alice Schwarzer, "the grande dame of German Feminism" (Schwarzer and Wizorek), gave an interview to *Spiegel Online* after the Cologne attacks. She uttered the following words:

> We need to finally be proactive in enlightening people from Islamic cultural groups. And this applies to immigrants already here as well as to current refugees. The German constitution stands above the Sharia. Schools need to offer classes on gender equality. (3)

To follow the logic that leads Schwarzer to the apparent non sequitur, "the German constitution stands above the Sharia," it is necessary, first, to establish that she is not working from a definition of the word "Sharia" based in Islamic law, tradition, or current scholarship.[2] Rather, she pulls from a public discourse that is shaped by "the supposed contemporary Judeo-Christian affinity and alliance against the lethal threat of radical Islam . . . naturalized and implied to be traditionally present, despite all historical evidence to the contrary" (Haritaworn). Schwarzer uses the figure of the dangerous Muslim foreigner to legitimate her refusal to engage with communities of color, and in the process, she makes common cause with white supremacy. In the passage, Schwarzer's assertion is preceded by a statement that sets up a binary between a "we" and "people from Islamic cultural groups." The "we" that Schwarzer invokes does not include Muslims, whom she positions as requiring "enlightenment" that the "we" can provide. "We" Christians need to enlighten those Muslims. The second sentence of the passage racializes the binary when it includes "immigrants already here." It is not clear what "already here" means—the phrase feels slippery in Schwarzer's speech. Can "immigrants" be born in Germany? Schwarzer asserts the need for "gender equality" classes in schools and "an alternative to young men with a penchant for violence." In other words, when compared to "us," Muslims are sexist and violent. If Schwarzer's use of the word "Sharia" takes up a viral residue, there must be traces of that use elsewhere. Interestingly, in response to attacks in Brussels in March 2016, then-U.S. presidential candidate Donald Trump responded, "They want Sharia law. They don't want laws that we have. They want Sharia law" (Weissmann). Trump's "we" and "they" appear to adhere to a compatible categorical system as that employed by Schwarzer. Trump subsequently and infamously called for a "total and complete shutdown of Muslims entering the United States." The fact that Trump, despite being subsequently elected president of the United States of America, is widely known as a misogynist and a racist, while Schwarzer is "Germany's leading feminist" (Schwarzer and Wizorek), illustrates the stickiness of viral rhetoric and its ability to link Trump's "baboon" to Schwarzer's "cat." We might note that, from the perspective of a native Arabic speaker, the circulation of complex terms like "Allahu Akbar" and "Sharia" seems to have infected them with a virus, an extreme catachresis that not only transforms and simplifies meaning, but in turn, weaponizes them for use against individuals who show visible signs of being linked to their previous iterations.

RESPONDING TO 100 WOMEN RESPONDING

As of June 22, 2016, "How 100 Women Responded to the Attacks in Cologne with Love," a video posted five months earlier by the social justice organization Avaaz, had been viewed 1,966,527 times, had received 15,173 "likes," and had been shared 41,795 times. The Facebook post was followed by 1,700 comments. The video's quantitative data provides an opaque glimpse into the quality of its reception, but clearly the video has entered public discourse—it drew viewers, and a significant percentage of them made a record of their response by leaving a comment. The video went "viral." I first encountered this video on my own Facebook timeline on January 28, 2016. I "liked" it, and I "shared" it. Five of my "friends" liked it too. All of us came up against this video from within the odd private/public virtual space of social media, where we find the qualities that characterize public rhetoric, namely, "an open network" that involves "a mixture of processes and encounters" (Edbauer 13).

When I viewed "How 100 Women Responded to the Attacks in Cologne with Love," in which "women" and "refugees" exchange flowers, it brought tears to my eyes. Though the video does not depict suffering directly, it impinged upon me as an "ethical solicitation" (J. Butler, "Precarious Life" 135). My eight-year-old felt its pathos—she said, "Giving flowers is nice and it feels nice when someone gives you a flower." The video works to assert a rhetoric of solidarity; in the aftermath of the events at Cologne, it depicts the mutual rejection of violence, retributive or otherwise. It interrupts ideologies that intersect with Samuel Huntington's infamous and ubiquitous contribution to the Western imaginary, "Clash of Civilizations," that imagines and positions a chasm of difference between an ahistorical and internally homogenous Christian West and Muslim East. The "common sense" of a racialized public discourse reproduces that chasm in the named groups of the video, "refugees" and "women." In the video, it seems, the individuals named "refugee" seek asylum in Germany from Syria or Iraq or Afghanistan, and the "women" are German, though neither group exhibits overt markers of nationality, and the first group also includes women. A nagging discomfort followed my tears, and it moved me to critically examine my tender feelings and my participation in the circulation of the video. Just what sort of response does the video solicit, and what viral residues does it contain? As a text embedded in a system of other texts, a complex rhetorical network of visual, textual, embodied, and entangled causes and effects, to what extent does this video reproduce precarity with its rhetorics of solidarity? Does this scene in which putatively Christian German women and not-German, Muslim refugees exchange flowers against the backdrop of sexual assault in Cologne interrupt oppressive rhetorics of transnational migration that figure contemporary (male) refugees as always potential terrorists and/or sexual predators? What kinds of rhetorical work does this video, as a particular kind of virus, do to disrupt, interrupt, or conserve current (precarious) rhetorics of transnational migration?

First, "How 100 Women Responded" is the product of an online social justice organization called Avaaz. *The Economist* describes Avaaz as "an online campaigning organization that's halfway between an NGO and a megaphone" (R. Butler). Its website can be viewed in seventeen languages (Avaaz—The World in Action). Avaaz claims 20 million members, of which I am evidently one, "as all [membership] requires is that you 'take an action once'" (R. Butler). Avaaz describes itself as "a global web movement to bring people-powered politics to decision-making everywhere." The organization's stated purpose is to pursue issues of social justice by mobilizing online tools and social media through traditional forms of social activism. Consequently, Avaaz has accrued significant material and financial resources through online donations, as they "receive no money from governments or corporations" (Avaaz). Their website's "About Us" page explains that "campaign ideas are polled and tested weekly to 10,000-member random samples—and only initiatives that find a strong response are taken to scale." In effect, Avaaz pursues activist projects that have been tested by focus groups, like commercial products bound for market. Before producing the video "How 100 Women Responded," the group would have consulted online members through polls or some other online voting system to be certain that the project had significant support in the "Avaaz community." Evidently, the video arrived on the Avaaz Facebook page with some prior assurance that it would be received positively.

The video was posted on the Avaaz Facebook page on January 23, 2016. The attacks took place in the context of a "refugee crisis" in Europe that had followed the civil war in Syria (see "Syria"). As visual rhetoric, the post entered a rich and dynamic network of circulating images of war, of people fleeing war, of people packed into boats, of lines of people crossing Europe, and of Germans welcoming asylum seekers with a "spirit of generosity and compassion" (Bell). That the reported attacks took place in Germany is important, because Germany has accepted the highest number of asylum seekers fleeing wars in North Africa and the Middle East, and Chancellor Angela Merkel paid a political price for that decision (Feldenkirchen and Pfister). Gathering together three events, the video builds them into a narrative: (1) the NYE attacks in Cologne, (2) a scene in which "refugees" hand out flowers to "women," and (3) an event organized by Avaaz in which "women" hand out flowers to "refugees." The narrative works to produce a particular way of understanding the three events by weaving them into a story of reciprocal gift giving that responds to violence with "love." In doing so, it interrupts the gendered and racialized "hate" that has characterized much of the wider public response to Cologne. By staging a performance in which Europeans and (Arab) refugees turn to each other and embrace, the video interrupts xenophobic narratives that place blame on the non-European foreigner for social and economic problems in Europe. Yet, as Honig reminds us, "interruption is an odd sort of doing, not always a sort of doing, in fact" (3). Interruptions can be intentional, involuntary, unconscious, "but sometimes interruptions just happen as a side effect or by-product of other doing" (Honig 3). The video performs a rhetoric of solidarity between the two groups, interrupting Huntington's clash, but at the same time, it is a *precarious* act of solidarity, because its controlling binary is linked, residually, to Butler's precarious subject who "looks vaguely Arab" (*Precarious Life* 39), like the "refugees" in the video. The narrative fails to undo neocolonial discourses that essentialize "the East," because it fixes its subjects in a binary in opposition to "Germans," leaving intact an ahistorical version of Europe that, via Stuart Hall ("Europe's Other Self"), El-Tayeb describes as appearing "as a largely homogeneous entity, entirely self-sufficient, its development uninfluenced by outside forces or contact with other parts of the world."

The video is framed by the following blurb:

> The Cologne attacks on NYE shocked Germany. But now hundreds of women are responding with an unprecedented act of love. Like and share if you think this message is what our world needs right now.

The first sentence makes an assumption about the online media literacy of the viewer—by referring to "the" Cologne attacks, the text invites a viewer who has already encountered them.[3] The video invites the social media–savvy viewer to commiserate in a shared sense of "shock" about the extreme nature of the New Year's Eve incident. The notion of shock imagines a community that shares surprise and disbelief in response to the events in Cologne on New Year's Eve 2015. The video anticipates that the viewer is aware that the perpetrators were identified as asylum seekers and refugees. This act of identification relies on a wider frame of "public outrage" about the events in Cologne, and it recognizes that the outrage has been directed, specifically, to the always racialized "refugees" and "asylum seekers" rather than more generally to men who commit violence against women.

The first five-second cut of the video depicts a stark scene in black and white of the globally reported incident in which gangs of male asylum seekers or refugees were accused of sexually harassing and assaulting German women on New Year's Eve. In that footage, a chaotic scene is accompanied by street sounds, the whine of fireworks, and overlaid on the screen appear the words, "The Cologne attacks on women shocked Germany." Uneven camera movement suggests the immediacy of footage taken by a cell phone. The scene is brief and lacks overt evidence of violence—it could be stock footage of any nighttime street party. The frame relies on an audience for whom the audio-visual reference of disorderly crowds, the piercing whine of fireworks, and a police car positioned in the foreground will be obvious and automatic, because it links visually to the "viral" event in Cologne. The scene invokes a "we" that agrees about the "shocking" nature of the attacks.

At the five-second mark, the video cuts to black. The street sounds recede and are replaced by the upbeat chords of an acoustic guitar. The mood in the video changes instantly, perhaps because, as John Oliver has pointed out, "jangly guitars simply make anything more plausible" ("Chickens"). The following words appear on screen: "Refugees responded in a beautiful way / they handed out flowers to women / to express their respect and gratitude." The video cuts back to the street, but now there is color and it is daytime. The viewer sees a close-up shot of a man giving a flower to a woman as they embrace and laugh. The pathos of the scene requires an audience that will perceive the man as a refugee (vaguely Arab), and the women as white and ethnically German. In this way, the scene builds a sense of warmth and human connection across perceived difference. In effect, the "bad refugee" visually referenced in the first five seconds of the video is rehabilitated and replaced by the "good refugee." The interactions are close, intimate, and infused with a kind of joyfulness. A piano joins the jangly guitar as the video cuts to scenes of evidently German women giving flowers to, again, men whom the viewer is meant to perceive as refugees—though it is difficult to point out exactly what, visually, marks them so. There is a close-up focus on faces; many women are resolute, some are young and some are older, some smile, others laugh. One blond-haired woman speaks to the camera in German, and her words are translated onscreen: "We are an open country and you're still welcome here."

The "still" in this sentence is chilling. It appears to refer the viewer back to the first five-second clip, it acknowledges the "bad refugee" that the clip constructs, and it forgives the "good refugee" for the existence of the bad. Because Germany is "open," the people will forgive the presence of the bad refugees in order to welcome the good ones. An older woman, marked as not-German by her hijab, covers her face and begins to cry. Another woman in hijab receives a flower through the bars of an enclosure, smells it, and sighs with evident pleasure. These two women are both marked as non-German by the resignified hijab—it is worth noting that the hijab is really the only way this narrative can visually communicate the (religious) difference of the women. Within the frame of the video, their headscarves work to mark them as part of the refugee community rather than part of the community of "German women."

What does this exchange of flowers mean? The text of the video gives a simple, if not simplistic answer: "Their acts carry a simple message for all of us / sometimes all we have to do is reach out to each other / for love to triumph over fear." A woman with her back to the viewer hands a flower to a smiling boy. The camera follows the boy and it fixes on a man standing between two women posing for a photo. There are more close-up scenes of children, old people, and young people, and everyone is smiling or looking resolute. The video ends with the close-up of a boy in a hoodie smiling and giving the camera a thumbs up. To what extent does this video risk producing the refugee as El-Tayeb's "excitedly cuddled object" that "is nevertheless regularly mishandled"? Given the speed and efficiency of the Avaaz activism machine, may this object "well be discarded depending on its imminent uses"? (El-Tayeb). The juxtaposition of allegedly refugee women, men, children, and old people and German women is important here to the message of the video—it allows the video to interrupt "rumors and misinformation" that "have been an integral part of anti-refugee campaigns across the world" (Binkowski). Such rumors have contributed to widespread fears, seemingly materialized amidst the shock on New Year's Eve in Cologne, that refugee men are too numerous and dangerous to allow into the European home. The specter of the dangerous brown male body persists even in the face of concrete knowledge, such as that produced by the EU survey. If it is true that "one in three women (33%) has experienced physical and/or sexual violence since the age of 15; one in five women (18%) has experienced stalking; every second woman (55%) has been confronted with one or more forms of sexual harassment," and if "given this, violence against women cannot be seen as a marginal issue that touches only on some women's lives" in Germany (European Union Agency for Fundamental Rights 167), then why do refugees need to hand out flowers to apologize for those among them who share patriarchal views of women's bodies with their German, male counterparts? Why isn't the "shock" directed toward the wider category of *men who commit violence against women*?

CONCLUDING THOUGHTS, OR THE SHOCKING PROCESSES OF FORGETFULNESS

One interesting insight that emerged in the aftermath of the attacks on Cologne is that "most of what happened that night in Cologne [was] not actually a crime" (Moore). Chantal Louis, editor of *Emma*, a feminist magazine in Germany, explained to *BuzzFeed*, "The German Law accepts that a man generally has the right to touch a woman, to have sexual intercourse with a woman. It's his right, unless the woman shows her resistance very, very, strongly" (Moore). Presumably, the sexually empowered "man" of German law was imagined as white, given that it took attacks attributed to non-white foreigners in Cologne to inspire the passing of tighter rape laws. German law now "classifies groping as a sex crime and makes it easier to prosecute assaults committed by large groups" ("Germany Rape Law"). It is encouraging that Germany is examining ways that its laws do or do not protect women from male violence. However, it is troubling that the laws protecting women from assault in a country in which "only one in 10 rapes is reported" ("Germany Rape Law") did not warrant change until the perpetrators were figured as overwhelmingly and hypervisibly non-white and non-German.

In another section of her *Spiegel* interview, Alice Schwarzer makes a claim about the importance of naming. She explains,

> The threat of being accused of racism gave birth to false tolerance. Once, about 20 years ago, a police officer in Cologne told me, 'Ms. Schwarzer, 70 to 80 percent of the rapists in Cologne are Turkish.' I was very upset and said: 'Then good God, why don't you bring the issue up?' Because only after you call a problem by its name can you change it. And then he said, no way, not politically opportune. So you see, the police have long been extremely frustrated by these hush-ups. I think that's changing now, and that's a good thing. (Schwarzer and Wizorek 3)

In this passage, we gain some insight into the problem of figuration into which the Avaaz video intervenes. Schwarzer works from within rhetorics of the everyday and commonsense. One might call her to task for her lazy form of citation, the reference to an unclear and somewhat distant past ("20 years ago"), a vague sense of authority (a "police officer in Cologne"), and a hyperbolic if not absurd use of unsupportable statistics ("70 to 80 percent"); however, it is troubling that she replicates a similar claim from one who ought not be easily linked to a "leading German feminist." Then–president elect Donald Trump said, "When Mexico sends its people, they're not sending their best

... they're bringing drugs, they're bringing crime. They're rapists. And some, I assume, are good people" ("Full Text"). If Schwarzer's Turks are rapists as Trump's Mexicans are rapists, could Schwarzer and Trump be imagining the same community and producing the same "we," in spite of their differences? Is theirs, too, a precarious rhetoric of solidarity? It seems to be a kind of solidarity at work when a "we" asserts the need, the right, and the ability to teach other "cultural groups" to be more civilized, or more *like* "us" or, conversely, to build a wall to keep "*them*" out. I have worked here to make sense of the ways that the Avaaz video disrupts public discourses of hate and division by producing a love story between refugees and German women; however, as a rhetoric of solidarity, it is precarious, because its "refugee" remains a gendered, apolitical, and eternally grateful figure, haunted by his "bad" brothers.

NOTES

1. Five months after New Year's Eve 2015, Yermi Brenner and Katrin Ohlendorf, after a comprehensive investigative process, concluded the following:

   A more accurate description of what happened last New Year's Eve might be: several dozen young men, many of North African origin, are suspected of sexually assaulting and robbing hundreds of women in the crowd. The crimes were made possible by the crowded New Year's Eve conditions in and around Cologne's main train station. They appear to have been further facilitated by poor coordination among the different police forces responsible for responding to the situation.

2. I lack the knowledge, experience, and space to explain a "true" meaning of Sharia; however, a good start for those interested might be Asifa Quraishi-Landes's "Five Myths About Sharia" from the *Washington Post,* June 24, 2016.

3. See "Germany Shocked."

WORKS CITED

Ahmed, Sara. *Willful Subjects.* Duke University Press, 2014.

"'Allahu Akbar' Calls at Munich Memorial Trigger Angry Reaction." *RT International: Question More.* 27 July 2016. <www.rt.com/news/353566-munich-attack-video-allah/>. 25 Aug. 2016.

Avaaz. "Avaaz—The World in Action." 2014. <secure.avaaz.org/en/>. 25 Aug. 2016.

Barkin, Noah, and Paul Carrel. "Asylum Seekers Among Suspects in Cologne's New Year Violence." *Yahoo! News.* 8 Jan. 2016. <www.reuters.com/article/us-germany-assaults-idUSK-BN0UM0U420160108>. 6 Jan. 2017.

Bell, Matthew. "What's Behind Germany's Welcome Spirit for Refugees? And How Long Will It Last?" *PRI's The World.* 16 Dec. 2015. <www.pri.org/stories/2015-12-16/whats-behind-germanys-welcome-spirit-refugees-and-how-long-will-it-last>. 6 Jan. 2016.

Bernhard, Judith, Carolina Berinstein, and Luin Goldring. "Institutionalizing Precarious Immigration Status in Canada." *Citizenship Studies* 13.3 (2009): 239–65.

Binkowski, Brooke. "Are Refugees Overwhelmingly Young and Male?" *Snopes.com*. 29 Mar. 2016. <www.snopes.com/refugee-invaders-meme>. 25 Aug. 2016.

Bosniak, Linda S. "Human Rights, State Sovereignty and the Protection of Undocumented Migrants Under the International Migrant Workers Convention." *International Migration Review* 15.4 (1991): 737–70.

Brenner, Yermi, and Katrin Ohlendorf. "Time for the Facts: What Do We Know About Cologne Four Months Later?" *The Correspondent*. 2 May 2016. <thecorrespondent.com/4401/time-for-the-facts-what-do-we-know-about-cologne-four-months-later/740617958817-a498b7c3>. 6 Jan. 2017.

Butler, Judith. *Precarious Life: The Powers of Mourning and Violence*. Verso, New Left Books, 2004.

———. "Precarious Life, Vulnerability, and the Ethics of Cohabitation." *The Journal of Speculative Philosophy* 26.2 (2012): 134–51.

Butler, Robert. "The Man Behind Avaaz." *The Economist 1843*. May/June 2013. <www.1843magazine.com/content/features/robert-butler/man-behind-avaaz>. 25 Aug. 2016.

Cacho, Lisa Marie. *Social Death: Radicalized Rightlessness and the Criminalization of the Unprotected*. New York University Press, 2012.

Chaput, Catharine. "Fear, Affective Energy, and the Political Economy of Global Capitalism." *Entertaining Fear: Rhetoric and the Political Economy of Social Control*. Ed. Catherine Chaput, M. J. Braun, and Danika M. Brown. Peter Lang, 2010. 1–22.

"Chickens." *Last Week Tonight with John Oliver*. HBO: New York. 17 May 2015. <www.youtube.com/watch?v=X9wHzt6gBgI>. 25 Aug. 2016.

Cintron, Ralph. "'Gates Locked' and the Violence of Fixation." *Towards a Rhetoric of Everyday Life: New Directions in Research on Writing, Text, and Discourse*. Ed. Martin Nystrand and John Duffy. University of Wisconsin Press, 2003. 5–37.

Cisneros, Josue David. "Contaminated Communities: The Metaphor of 'Immigrant as Pollutant' in Media Representations of Immigration." *Rhetoric and Public Affairs* 11.4 (2008): 569–601.

Coskan-Johnson, Gale. "Troubling Citizenship: Arizona Senate Bill 1070 and the Rhetorics of Immigration Law." *Present Tense: A Journal of Rhetoric in Society* 2.1 (2011). <www.presenttensejournal.org/wp-content/uploads/2012/03/Coskan-Johnson.pdf>. 2 April 2017.

Demo, Anne. "Sovereignty Discourse and Contemporary Immigration Politics." *Quarterly Journal of Speech* 91.3 (August 2005): 291–311.

Edbauer, Jenny. "Unframing Models of Public Distribution: From Rhetorical Situation to Rhetorical Ecologies." *Rhetoric Society Quarterly* 35.4 (2005): 5–24.

El-Tayeb, Fatima. *European Others: Queering Ethnicity in Postnational Europe*. Kindle ed. University of Minnesota Press, 2011.

European Union Agency for Fundamental Rights. *Violence Against Women: An EU-wide Survey, Main Results*. Publications Office of the European Union, 2014. <fra.europa.eu/sites/default/files/fra-2014-vaw-survey-main-results-apr14_en.pdf>. 6 Jan. 2017.

Feldenkirchen, Markus, and Rene Pfister. "The Isolated Chancellor: What Is Driving Angela Merkel? *Spiegel International*. 25 Jan. 2016. <www.spiegel.de/international/germany/why-has-angela-merkel-staked-her-legacy-on-the-refugees-a-1073705.html>. 25 Aug. 2016.

"Full Text: Donald Trump Announces a Presidential Bid." *Washington Post*. 16 June 2015, <www.washingtonpost.com/news/post-politics/wp/2015/06/16/full-text-donald-trump-announces-a-presidential-bid/?utm_term=.32e5b9902cd2>. 6 Jan. 2017.

"Germany Rape Law: 'No Means No' Law Passed." *BBC News.* 7 July 2015. <www.bbc.com/news/world-europe-36726095>. 25 Aug. 2016.

"Germany Shocked by Cologne New Year Gang Assaults on Women." *BBC News.* 5 Jan. 2016. <www.bbc.com/news/world-europe-35231046>. 25 Aug. 2016.

Gries, Laurie E. *Still Life with Rhetoric: A New Materialist Approach for Visual Rhetorics.* eBook. Utah State Press, 2015.

Hall, Stuart. "Europe's Other Self." *Marxism Today* 35.8 (1991): 18–19.

Hall, Stuart. "The West and the Rest: Discourse and Power." *The Indigenous Experience: Global Perspectives.* Eds. Roger Maaka and Chris Andersen. Canadian Scholar's Press, 2006, 165–73.

Haritaworn, Jinthana. *Queer Lovers and Hateful Others: Regenerating Violent Times and Places.* Kindle ed. Pluto Press, 2015.

Honig, Bonnie. *Antigone, Interrupted.* Cambridge University Press, 2013.

"How 100 Women Responded to the Attacks in Cologne with Love." *You Tube.* 23 Jan. 2016. <www.youtube.com/watch?v=S07PIs5dyNo>. 1 Feb. 2016.

Huggler, Justin. "Cologne Sex Attacks: City's Police Chief Removed from Post over Violence." *The Telegraph.* 8 Jan. 2016. <www.telegraph.co.uk/news/worldnews/europe/germany/12088994/Cologne-sex-attacks-Two-immigrant-suspects-arrested-carrying-note-in-German-and-Arabic-saying-I-want-to-have-sex-with-you.html>. 6 Jan. 2017.

Huntington, Samuel P. "The Clash of Civilizations?" *Culture and Politics.* Palgrave Macmillan, 2000. 99–118.

Mohanty, Chandra Talpade. "Women Workers and the Politics of Solidarity." *Feminism without Borders: Decolonizing Theory, Practicing Solidarity.* Duke University Press, 2000. 139–68.

Moore, Jina. "Why the New Year's Attacks on Women in Germany Weren't Even a Crime." *BuzzFeed News.* 26 March 2016. <www.buzzfeed.com/jinamoore/cologne-attacks-on-women?utm_term=.ec78b7vYMV#.hmAblMK9NR>. 6 Jan. 2017.

Mortimer, Caroline. "Cologne: Three out of 58 Men Arrested over Mass Sex Attack on New Year's Eve Were Refugees from Syria or Iraq." *The Independent—Europe.* 15 Feb. 2016. <www.independent.co.uk/news/world/europe/cologne-only-three-out-of-58-men-arrested-in-connection-with-mass-sex-attack-on-new-years-eve-are-a6874201.html>. 25 Aug. 2016.

Mountz, Alison. *Seeking Asylum: Human Smuggling and Bureaucracy at the Border.* University of Minnesota Press, 2010.

Nevins, Joseph. *Operation Gatekeeper and Beyond: The War on "Illegals" and the Remaking of the U.S.-Mexico Boundary.* Routledge, 2010.

Nyers, Peter. "Abject Cosmopolitanism: The Politics of Protection in the Anti-Deportation Movement." *The Deportation Regime: Sovereignty, Space, and the Freedom of Movement.* Ed. Nicholas Genova and Nathalie Peutz. Duke University Press, 2010. 413–31.

Paret, Marcel, and Shannon Gleeson. "Precarity and Agency Through a Migration Lens." *Citizenship Studies* 20.3–4 (2016): 277–94.

Payton, Matt. "Germany Passes Strict 'No Means No' Rape Law in Response to Cologne Attacks." *Independent.* 7 July 2016. <www.independent.co.uk/news/world/europe/rape-law-germany-reichstag-mps-vote-strict-no-means-no-rape-law-cologne-attacks-a7125101.html>. 6 Jan. 2016.

Rothwell, James. "Cologne Sex Attacks: Mob Attacks Group of Migrants in 'Manhunt' for Suspects." *The Telegraph.* 11 Jan. 2016. <http://www.telegraph.co.uk/news/worldnews/europe/germany/12092354/Cologne-sex-attacks-New-Years-Eve-cases-rise-to-more-than-500.html>. 15 Feb. 2018.

Said, Edward W. *Orientalism.* Vintage, 1979.

Schwarzer, Alice, and Anne Wizorek. "A Feminist View of Cologne: 'The Current Outrage Is Very Hypocritical.'" Interview by Christine Hoffmann and Rene Pfister. *Spiegel Online: International.* 21 Jan. 2016. <www.spiegel.de/international/germany/german-feminists-debate-cologne-attacks-a-1072806.html>. 25 Aug. 2016.

Sharma, Nandita. *Home Economics: Nationalism and the Making of "Migrant Workers" in Canada.* University of Toronto Press, 2006.

Spearey, Susan. "Fostering Receptivity: Cultural Translation, Ethical Solicitation, and the Navigation of Distance in J. T. Rogers' *The Overwhelming.*" *Safundi* 17.2 (2016): 231–48.

"Syria: The Story of the Conflict." *BBC News.* 11 Mar. 2016. <www.bbc.com/news/world-middle-east-26116868>. 25 Aug. 2016.

Trump, Donald J. "Donald J. Trump Statement on Preventing Muslim Immigration." 7 Dec. 2015. <www.donaldjtrump.com/press-releases/donald-j.-trump-statement-on-preventing-muslim-immigration>. 25 Aug. 2016.

United Nations Educational, Scientific and Cultural Organization (UNESCO). "Learning to Live Together: A Glossary of Migration Related Terms." <www.unesco.org/new/en/social-and-human-sciences/themes/international-migration/glossary/>. 6 Jan. 2017.

"Viral Video." *Urban Dictionary.* 29 Aug. 2006. <www.urbandictionary.com/define.php?term=viral%2Bvideo>. 25 Aug. 2016.

"Virus." *OED Online.* Oxford University Press, June 2016. <en.oxforddictionaries.com/definition/virus>. 25 Aug. 2016.

Walia, Harsha. *Undoing Border Imperialism.* Anarchy Press, 2013.

Weissmann, Jordan. "Donald Trump Calls Brussels a 'Horrible City' After It's Attacked by Terrorists." *Slate Magazine.* 22 Mar. 2016. <www.slate.com/blogs/the_slatest/2016/03/22/donald_trump_calls_brussels_a_horrible_city_after_it_s_attacked_by_terrorists.html>. 25 Aug. 2016.

Wells-Barnett, Ida B. "Southern Horrors." *African American Classics in Criminology and Criminal Justice* (2002): 25.

CHAPTER 6

Reversals of Precarity

Rewriting Buffalo's Refugees as Neoliberal Subjects

ARABELLA LYON

> "Our country has a lot to learn from this 'City of Good Neighbors.'"
> —Samantha Power, U.S. ambassador to the UN (qtd. in Zremski, "UN Ambassador")

SINCE 1951, first in the UN Convention and then in the U.S. Immigration and Nationality Act 208(a), a refugee is defined by persecution, well-founded fears, and an unwillingness or inability to return home. By legal and state-sanctioned definition, refugees' lives move from the human condition of precariousness to precarity, a move that Judith Butler characterizes as a shift from a primary human vulnerability to the political and hence contingent state of precarity. As she observes, "precarity designates the politically induced condition in which certain populations suffer from failing social and economic networks of support and become differentially exposed to injury, violence, and death" (*Frames* 25, *Notes* 33). By international precedent, precarity marks a refugee's position in failed networks and the resulting exposure to violence. Butler also recognizes the violence inherent in *designating* another's precarity, as it offers a fantasy of mastery as it denies the vulnerability of all bodily life. Against the dangers inherent in precarity, she considers the potential of precarity as a concept that "cuts across identity categories . . . thus forming the basis for an alliance focused on opposition to state violence" (*Frames* 32). Since it focuses on "differential subject formation" and "differential distributions," she argues that precarity has the potential to create a different type of political coalition, one that would *not* require "agreement on all questions of desire or belief or self-identification" (32). Rather radical alliances might be founded on difference and evade the maps of identity politics and multiculturalism. In Butler's reckoning, precarity has the potential to violate and to liberate.

In my investigation of refugee rhetoric in Buffalo, New York, I employ Butler's robust, decade-long analyses of precariousness or vulnerability, precarity, and political agency. Her foundation offers a lens for examining why the U.S. ambassador to the UN, Samantha Power, among others, would praise one city, Buffalo, as offering a model program for refugees (see epigraph). Still, in following Butler, I worry that she is not consistent in her distinctions, sometimes conflating vulnerability with precariousness (Mills 45, 48–49). Butler herself writes that "precariousness and precarity are intersecting concepts" (*Frames* 25). Not to deny the generative aspects of Butler's blurred vocabulary, but to be more precise, I engage Erinn Gilson's concept of epistemic vulnerability, a form of precariousness essential to identity formation. Building from Butler, Gilson draws out three definitions of vulnerability. The common understanding of vulnerability, for instance in normative rights projects, minimizes the qualities of vulnerability as it emphasizes harm and injury (309–10). Vulnerability indicating hurt and grievance can be considered a negative, a political or socioeconomic *lack* that characterizes oppressed and marginalized people. In response, Gilson extensively reviews the literature that supports a second sense of vulnerability as a common condition and an ambivalent—not negative—term, a definition similar to Butler's. Gilson characterizes ambivalent vulnerability as "a more general term encompassing conceptions of passivity, affectivity, openness to change, dispossession, and exposure" (310). Moving beyond ambivalent vulnerability, Gilson then posits a positive, epistemic vulnerability. Epistemic vulnerability is constitutive, attending to "the way in which we become who we are through our openness to others" (319). This third vulnerability asks that an individual be open to not knowing, being wrong, and yet venturing; attends to affective and embodied knowing; and most significantly, engages a willingness to alter "not just one's ideas and beliefs, but one's self and sense of one's self" (325–26). Epistemic vulnerability demands an attitude of full engagement and willingness to change.

In this inquiry, I use Butler's definition of precarity as a political condition resulting from failed social and economic networks, creating differential exposure to injury, violence, and death. "Precarious" is used as a synonym with an ambivalent vulnerability, acknowledging the universal state of potential violation and liberation. In analyzing Buffalo's engagement with its refugee population, I also employ both negative vulnerability and epistemic vulnerability to understand the constraints and possibilities on representing and so engaging the Other. Through this vocabulary, I critique the media's rhetorical framework for charactering refugees in Buffalo, a model city for resettlement.

National and local media regularly represent Buffalo's refugees as entrepreneurial saviors of the decaying city. The refugee, no longer vulnerable, repairs the Rust Belt city. Such representations deny precarity and reveal the rhetorical technologies of citizen-making. Paradoxically, as the self-sufficiency of refugees is imagined, if not demanded, the precarity of Buffalo's long-term residents is exposed. Thus, the drive to portray self-sufficient refugees reveals the underlying failure of neoliberalism. The dynamics and implications of the rhetorical reversal of precarity are significant for understanding the success of Buffalo's resettlement programs.

By what rhetorical strategy does the media construct precarious refugees as neoliberal subject-citizens who can revitalize a city? What are the benefits and costs of constructing refugees as economic saviors? Ultimately I argue that although humanitarian frameworks often frame refugees through negative vulnerability and precarity for one set of political purposes, successful resettlement of refugees may depend on minimizing, if not denying, these characteristics. Furthermore, the paradox inherent in reversing precarity potentially provides Buffalo's inhabitants with shared geographies as it promotes epistemic vulnerability and the possibility of critique. In the end, "precarity" is a term particularly useful in rhetorical and political strategy, readily manipulated to reverse and redefine privilege.

BUFFALO AND THE REFUGEE CRISIS

Understanding rhetorical responses to the refugee crisis is particularly urgent. The UN High Commission for Refugees (UNHCR) reports, in 2015, a record 65.3 million refugees; over 50 percent are children. The rate of people fleeing war and persecution rose from six per minute in 2005 to twenty-four per minute in 2015; about 34,000 people are displaced every day. In one day alone, June 23, 2016, 4,500 migrants were rescued from dozens of small boats in the Mediterranean Sea.[1] In this context, I examine the rhetorical strategies supporting what has been called a model program for resettling refugees. News outlets from NPR to Yahoo to the *Middle East Eye* join Ambassador Power in praising the city of Buffalo and Erie County's resettlement of refugees.[2] Buffalo's commitment to welcoming refugees is significant; one might study the city's recently formed Office of New Americans, its first chief of diversity, the Buffalo Police Language Access Program, the commitment to providing refugee children with 25 percent of the spots in the summer youth camp, the city's *New American Study: A Strategic Action Plan to Advance Immigrant and Refugee Integration and Success,* or the White House report, *Bright Spots in Welcoming and Integration: A Report by White House Task Force on New Americans,* which recognized Buffalo as a Bright Spot, a preferred community for refugees.

Since 2003, significantly more than 14,000 refugees have resettled in the city of Buffalo, a city of just over 250,000 (Miller). Buffalo has been accepting over 1,300 refugees per year, but many who were initially settled elsewhere later moved to create critical cultural mass. The largest portions come from Burma (Myanmar), Somalia, Bhutan, Iraq, and the Republic of the Congo; three hundred invited Syrian refugees will add to the diversity.[3] A decade ago, Buffalo media occasionally worried about the precarity of refugees and their economic cost to the precarious county. Now, however, it reports that refugees have stabilized the city's shrinking population; revitalized the city's West Side, where 90 percent initially settle; and provided an international economic network.[4] For example, in a 2016 *Buffalo News* editorial, Michael Weiner, the president of the United Way of Buffalo and Erie County, observed that Buffalo has gained from refugee entrepreneurship, cultural exchange, global connection, addition to the tax base, reversing population decline, and replenishing the nineteen- to forty-four-year-old demographic. Tracking recent immigration and change on Buffalo's West Side, sociologists Robert M. Adelman, Watoii Rabii, and Aysegul Balta Ozgen also observe that community organizations and local media both emphasize trends in housing and economic development, entrepreneurialism, and multiculturalism.

In my analysis, I focus primarily on the *Buffalo News,* daily circulation 139,000, studying more than thirty-five articles published from October 2009 to January 2017. During that period, the *Buffalo News* increased its coverage of resettlement and changed its reporting pattern from one of public education and economic worry to celebrations of refugee entrepreneurship, culture, and cuisine. The *Buffalo News* offers a synecdoche of the local media. Certainly it is not the only outlet emphasizing the economic value of refugees. For instance, the January 2016 *Buffalo Spree,* a glossy magazine usually promoting elegant housing and fine dining, invites readers to "Meet Buffalo's Newest Residents and Find Out How They Are Enriching Our Community." Tellingly, it emphasizes refugee contributions to employment, education, and urban revitalization over trauma and vulnerability, as the use of "enriching" suggests.

BUFFALO'S GEOGRAPHY AS RHETORICAL SPACE

Although representations of refugees may help to structure their acceptance, large parts of Buffalo's success with resettlement stem from material conditions, such as inexpensive housing stock, a good public transportation system, and an established infrastructure of social services that settle and assist refugees. Four different resettlement agencies—Catholic Charities, International Institute, Jewish Family Services, and Journey's End—offer support for the first three to six months, but then a myriad other community services, from the area's seven colleges and universities to multiple health care centers, provide ongoing support for English language skills, job placement, housing, medical care, and so on. For example, three linked programs— Hope Refugee Services, HomeFront, and M&T Bank Corp—have designed a program to support refugee home buyers in saving, understanding the U.S. financial system, and obtaining credit (Epstein). As well, a supportive city and county government facilitates resettlement. In 2015, Mayor Byron W. Brown created an Office of New Americans, and County Executive Mark Poloncarz created a New Americans Advisory Committee.[5] Poloncarz also supports the hiring of county workers fluent in immigrant languages, as refugees represent sixty languages, and he has personally welcomed refugees on many occasions.

Another consideration: Buffalo is a border town, easily characterized by its borders, both internal and international. With an increased fear of terrorism and increasing numbers of economic migrants and refugees, national concern for secure borders has grown, resulting in exclusionary asylum processes. Certainly borders are dividing lines, created and maintained by the nation-state, but the nature of division is not singular. For example, although Gloria Anzaldúa articulates the transformative power of borders, acknowledging their liminality and human resistance to either/or epistemologies, she primarily sees the U.S.-Mexican border as a painful, open wound, writing, "the U. S.-Mexican border *es una herida abierta* where the Third World grates against the first and bleeds" (25). Carol Bohmer and Amy Shuman emphasize that the character of borders, boundaries, and crossings varies. Even as it has been affected by post-9/11 regulation, the U.S.-Canadian border is a permeable border. Buffalo is a small city, just over 250,000 residents, on the edge of Canada's population center, 12.2 million residents of prosperous southern Ontario. Metropolitan Buffalo has three bridges with Canada, bridges inadequate to the flow of traffic. The two nation's flags often fly together, the two anthems are played at sports events, and the local news announces exchange rates, crossing times, and Canadian holidays as it reports temperatures in Fahrenheit and centigrade. International economic and cultural exchanges occur every day and have for centuries, the flow of traffic following the currency rates.

Contrasting Buffalo's permeable international borders, as a nineteenth-century city, Buffalo has historically defined neighborhoods or borders within, and its internal (socioeconomic and cultural) borders may be more multi-faceted in that their interpenetrations create and hail differences. Neighborhoods become a means of containment, identity formation, and relationship building, and thus the assemblage of refugees in the West Side facilitates their cultural preservations through community organizations, shops, newspapers, and places of worship even as it limits their contact with the more established populations. That 90 percent of refugees live in the West Side may help local acceptance in that refugees' negative vulnerability and precarity remain invisible throughout much of the city, conveniently hidden on the West Side.[6] The cultural, racial, and socioeconomic differences among Buffalo's neighborhoods interact complexly. More than simple geographic boundaries, borders qualify divisions and control migrations as they shape and regulate political, cultural, economic, and social relationships. If the acceptance of Canadian shoppers and business partnerships signifies a fully sanctioned relationship, I demonstrate that sanction also extends to the West Side's refugees through a transformative paradox based in reversing precarity.

Following Sandro Mezzadra and Brett Neilson, I consider borders to provide an epistemic viewpoint that gives critical residents on both sides the possibility of seeing "how relations of domination, dispossession, and exploitation are being redefined" and understanding "the struggles that take shape around these changing relationships" (18). Fostering epistemic vulnerability, borders invite or demand a willingness to alter one's beliefs, and as sites of struggle, borders can produce redefinition and changed relations. Knowledge of other ways of being is exchanged at borders, and hence, borders potentially offer opportunities to reinvent global politics. The struggles and stresses of the borders may accentuate all three aspects of vulnerability and precarious relationships, but they may also produce an "in-between," Hannah Arendt's term for the positional space that "relates and separates men at the same time" (52). The in-between delineates the scene of recognition, where people are positioned—related and separated—by a common lifeworld of objects, symbols, events, and actions. The shared space in-between begins relationships through the acknowledged presence of a shared world. Before recognition, "without an explicit demand or precluding of full recognition" (53), the in-between offers the potential to find shared acts and words, not the demand for them.[7] As I discuss in *Deliberative Acts,* through being seen and heard from different positions, interlocutors may come to better decisions, but there is no demand for deliberation in the space of in-between. Hence, Buffalo's openness to resettlement and familiarity with borders facilitates both the creation of in-betweens and the *possibility* of shared acts and words, the possibility of epistemic vulnerability.

PRECARITY REWRITTEN AS ECONOMIC POTENTIAL

U.S. citizens are often celebrated as self-reliant, entrepreneurial, and civically engaged; alternatively, refugees are often characterized as precarious (Cacho; Mezzadra and Neilson; Ong; Powell). In reversing these commonplaces and denying the precarious lives of refugees, paradoxically the Buffalo media carves refugees a more secure place in the city by including them in an imagined community and representing them as enriching the wider region. Perversely, in reifying refugees' embrace of neoliberal values, the media acknowledges Buffalo's economic difficulties and the failure of neoliberalism in the Rust Belt. That is, the media, as part of the technology of citizen formation, frames the grounds of recognition in terms of the dominant political rhetoric. If international and urban borders contribute to the construction of an in-between, the press frames the potential acts in terms of the existing discourses and concerns.

Significant, early coverage of refugees occurred in the business section of *Buffalo News*, more geared toward educating readers about resettlement than to including refugees in the neoliberal polity. In October 2007, two linked essays presented refugees as negatively vulnerable; still, the titles reveal a concern with the transition from precarity to potential, from past to future: "Refugees from the World's Most Troubled Nations Find New Homes in Buffalo," and "Fleeing Wars and Persecution, Refugees Pursue Their Dreams Here." The differences between the two essays and how they imagine refugees might be seen through the verbs in the titles. Ordinary language philosopher Gilbert Ryle analyzes the difference between terminus verbs and process verbs. Terminus verbs, like "find," designate an endpoint of action; the refugees have ended their troubles in finding a home. Process verbs, like "seek" and "pursue," describe ongoing action and open possibility; the second essay's title reveals a commitment to ongoing action by the refugees in that they will continue to pursue dreams until they are reality. This difference is evident in the body of the articles, too.

In the first essay, "Find New Homes," journalist Jay Rey provides an educational overview of the history and resettlement of refugees. He discusses challenges in the schools, laments the difficult job market, and analyzes strained social services, observing that the federal government only covers initial costs. His analysis is in the present tense, giving a subtle sense that identity is fixed.

For example, the last few lines introduce a woman from Burundi and her surprise that her neighbors are "mostly white people," an ending that clearly emphasizes difference and confirms her precarity in the lack of home and community. The second essay, "Pursue Their Dreams," balances community education with refugee dreams and obstacles. Journalist Jay Tokasz discusses western New York's tradition of German, Irish, Italian, and Polish immigration. In doing so, he gestures to the cultural heritage of his readership and its knowledge of difficult migrations. Emphasizing transitions, he intertwines the voices of two African refugees (Somalia and Sudan) with that of a Somali immigrant who has graduated from the University at Buffalo as a way of predicting their productive futures. Although he notes that some local residents are concerned "about immigrants not fitting in and being a drain on city and county resources," the essay discusses the interviewees' jobs and ambitions; tellingly, it quotes Mohamed A. Mohamed, a University at Buffalo graduate: "If you bring those people, they become taxpayers." Here the move from refugee to taxpayer-citizen is a given end.

These early articles recognize loss and negative vulnerability, but one can see two trends emerging. First, the second essay marks the rapid conflation of refugee and negative vulnerability to immigrant and employment. In leaving behind issues of trauma and persecution, the press emphasizes becoming an employed, taxpaying American, an identity given as a basic, healing good. Second, the economic value of refugees to the city displaces their economic need and precarity. The economic value emerges as a potential counterweight to the cost of their negative vulnerability. Media themes of neoliberalism develop as Buffalo grows as a resettlement city and the abilities of refugees become more visible. Concerns about costs to the city and worry about early trauma all but disappear. Only one exception can be found; a 2015 article addresses cost concerns in response to the cutting of services. Mark Sommer's first sentence emphasizes the negative vulnerability of the refugees: "Dr. Myron and Joyce Glick nearly two decades ago opened a health clinic on Buffalo's West Side to help refugees fleeing war-torn countries and poverty-stricken conditions." Note the sentence includes both local history and commitment as it emphasizes the trauma and material need of refugees. The theme of trauma does not disappear as the article proceeds to discuss the services of the Jericho Road Community Health Center, its small price tag, and possible political reasons for its funding cuts. Still the concern with precarity is couched in terms of economic expediency. County Executive Poloncarz is quoted as arguing not only for humanitarian concerns but for economic pragmatics: "These organizations help people become self-sufficient. . . . If we can spend a tiny amount of money like this we can save millions in the long run on public assistance costs."

Aside from the 2015 report on funding cuts, the *Buffalo News* has increasingly focused on the economic development of individual refugees and cultural tourism. This trend emphasizes what the refugees give the city, creating a citywide awareness of an in-between, a relationship where the city is the shared world. Significantly, in ignoring negative vulnerabilities and emphasizing the common lifeworld of the in-between, the paper gestures toward an epistemic vulnerability where there is an economic and culture openness to others, though not fully an attitude of engagement and desire to change oneself, but an openness to a changed city and citizenship. In this vein, even international news becomes tied to Buffalo's economy and citizenship, the world imagined through the shared space of the city, as in a report on local response to Burma's move to democracy (Zremski, "Former"). Through interviews with eighteen former political prisoners celebrating at a local Buddhist monastery, Zremski demonstrates the shared value of democracy. Despite the obvious political and international frame and the potential for representing negative vulnerability, the economic significance of refugees remains; the article notes that 8,000 Burmese refugees have "helped to revive swaths of the West Side and Black Rock/Riverside." Although acknowledging Burma's ethnic wars, which caused 140,000 Burmese to become refugees, the article connects that negative vulnerability to the revitalization of Buffalo, moving quickly from the refugees' precarity to their contributions to the city.

Although the contribution of cultural tourism is sometimes the focus—for example, "West Side Mural Honors Buffalo's Burmese Community" (Dabkowski)—the mutual economic benefits of home ownership (Epstein) and entrepreneurship are more common topics. Invariably, coverage of the West Side Bazaar combines both economic and cultural messages, and thus it has become a mechanism for presuming joyful resettlement, one in which refugees leave behind the political complexity of precarity and the trauma of negative vulnerability to become neoliberal citizens, contributing to the U.S. economy and global trade. Perhaps for this very reason, since the West Side Bazaar opened in 2011 (http://www.westsidebazaar.com/), it has received attention from local newspapers, magazines, television, and radio, and from national outlets such as *USA Today*, NPR, and *Yahoo News*. Housed in an old grocery, the collection of micro-loan start-ups—stalls, tabletops, and a food court—is sometimes imagined as the center of revitalized Buffalo, a cultural contact zone, and the entrepreneurial spirit of refugees and immigrants.[8] Initially a grant-driven project of Westminster Economic Development Initiative, the bazaar identifies both cultural and economic missions for itself.[9] Its website describes it as "a local, regional, and national attraction" and "an International Market and food destination." More tellingly, it self-describes as "a small business incubator where new business owners could find a safe, nurturing, and inexpensive environment to develop their business with guidance in the ways of running an enterprise successfully." Initially it housed six new business owners from Rwanda, South Sudan, Peru, Indonesia, and the United States; in five years, it has grown to sixteen businesses. It has hosted fifty businesses in a city of 10,000 refugees, suggesting that its fame exceeds its impact. Although I would not diminish the accomplishments of the West Side Bazaar—it has launched successful shops and restaurants—the attention to the small incubator is symptomatic of the fantastic transformation of the refugee into a neoliberal subject, capable of receiving a micro-grant and establishing a competitive business.

Although this transformation can happen, for thousands of refugees the economic, psychological, and social changes are more fraught. The narratives produced by the media are selected carefully and are simple, focusing on the individual entrepreneurial refugee as an ideal. For example, Zelalem Gemmeda first appeared in the *Buffalo News* in February 2015, when she won the Entrepreneur of the Year Award from Rich Products, a local company, the award consisting of a certificate and $500 (Sapong, "Ethiopian"). Among her recognized accomplishments is advocating for the seven day a week opening of West Side Bazaar. Nine months later, an extended interview emphasizes the fulfillment of her American dreams (Radlich). As her children receive scholarships leading to college, Gemmeda continues working in the food court of the West Side Bazaar, preparing food with Ethiopian spices sent by her sister. This representation of an entrepreneurial refugee frames her identity between an international transfer of spices and her son's graduation from Colgate University, offering her as evidence of opportunity in Buffalo, successful globalization, and the easy integration of refugees into the U.S. economy.

DISCARDING PRECARITY?

As long-term residents eat and shop at the West Side Bazaar, how do they imagine the shopkeepers? Do they accept the media's neoliberal representations or wonder why this particular in-between is more referenced than, say, the schools? Why do members of the dominant culture seek this particular space? Is the consumption a synecdoche for the global capitalism and an easy way to deny its failure in Buffalo and the economic vulnerability of citizens, both resettled and native-born? In her desire to understand precarious lives, Butler would have us "interrogate the emergence and vanishing of the human at the limits of what we can know, what we can hear, what we can see, what we can sense" (*Precarious* 151). Unlike more intimate places such as mosques and temples, the West Side Bazaar has come to represent a public sphere constituted in what can be comfortably known, shown, and said by long-term residents. For many, it is the limit of initial engagement, the limit of who can be recognized. At this moment, in Buffalo, the neoliberal values espoused by the media seemingly deny the politics of precarity as they facilitate one kind of interaction in between new and established residents. The consequences of this recognition are not benign, as they demand a normalization of consumer capitalism and a denial of trauma, identity, and economic insecurity. That is, when the refugees are repurposed as arriving to save the great U.S. city, their negative vulnerability is unrecognized, as is their agency in self-naming. What might be epistemic vulnerability *seemingly* is rescripted as openness to commercial success.

In what follows, however, I assume that commercial spaces, due to their transactional nature, predominately function as in-betweens, but they also do the significant work of eroding borders between locals and refugees and between nationalities among refugees. That is, commercial spaces—real and imagined—can create an in-between, a shared world of things, both material and cognitive. In *Deliberative Acts,* I appropriate Hannah Arendt's concept of the in-between as the scene of recognition and potentially deliberative and transformative space (54–59, 92–97). The in-between both relates and separates people in the present tense; it is less a social meeting, a table between us, than a temporal tension between the past and future. Being seen and heard by others potentially shifts participants and pushes them to new positions, or at least, toward acknowledging their own position. As I wrote, "the deliberative present creates a temporal gap and spatial positioned potential where the citizen agent is vulnerable to her own acts as well as the acts of other interlocutors in-between" (55). In the in-between, people position themselves in ways that might lead to epistemic vulnerability, to not knowing and being wrong and yet venturing. The West Side Bazaar, as a jumble of cultures, sometimes can be viewed as exotic, but it also positions visitors in ways that can challenge beliefs about the nature of Buffalo, refugees, and local economics. Epistemic vulnerability creates possibility. That is, even at the limits of what we humans can know, hear, see, and sense, there is a potential shifting of understanding in our positions.

The dynamic potential of the in-between, particularly at the borders, relates to Butler's more pessimistic observation that "not only is there always the possibility that a vulnerability will not be recognized and that it will be constituted as the 'unrecognizable,' but when a vulnerability is recognized, that recognition has the power to change the meaning and structure of vulnerability itself" (*Precarious* 43). That is, vulnerability—given its three semantic fields—is not stable, especially as dispersed across relationships. At first glance, within the technology of the West Side Bazaar, both vulnerability and precarity's political potential are transformed to opportunities for service and economic development, both for a city and for an individual refugee. The meaning and structure of a refugee's negative vulnerability is shifted to entrepreneurial strength. One might hope the West Side Bazaar might provoke ambiguous or epistemic vulnerability—perhaps its practices do—but its primary representation is as a site of consumer capitalism. Obviously a rhetoric that diminishes precarity and promotes neoliberal values can be easily criticized as co-optive or exploitative. In denying precarity, history, and all other ways of being human, neoliberal discourses achieve a self-sustaining momentum and monological power, hiding deeper paradoxes, a theme to which I will return. Currently being successfully resettled refugees denies the trauma, the history, and the birth culture as it subsumes them under the dominant discourse, privileging their economic self over any broader intersection of being and any community of origin. In denying who refugees were and are, the rhetoric of neoliberalism creates new (false) identities in the service of dominant values and communities, values and communities distant, even alien, from the lives of refugees, and yet it is hard to critique the pure effectiveness of Buffalo's successful model of resettlement. Something works here.

Ignoring the struggles of refugees is disturbing, but their inclusion in the wider Buffalo community is a significant accomplishment. I maintain inclusion is a necessary accomplishment for successful resettlement whether achieved through glorifying the high school soccer successes of Somalian refugees in Lewiston, Maine, or shopping the bakeries of Little Bosnia in St. Louis, Missouri.[10] Not all cities have succeeded in welcoming and including refugees, and if a neoliberal rhetoric of inclusion limits the terms of recognition, it also offers a collective identity, one that lays a groundwork for "inter-ests," not selfish interests, but Arendt's term for granting what relates and binds us to others (182). The neoliberal articulation of resettlement pragmatically succeeds in that refugees are placed in relationship to a people and a community, and while other positives of such rhetorical strategy may be harder to grant, I want to understand the positive possibilities of this strategy, through considering the constitutive power of "we the people," a power that necessarily excludes some, but in the Buffalo case, includes refugees, makes them visible, and recognizes them. Furthermore, in making them economic saviors of the city, the discourse reconstitutes the identity of the precarious refugee, inverting the inherent hierarchy of negative vulnerability and reimagining refugees as migrants central to the city's health. As Butler observes, "the discursive move to establish 'the people' in one way or another is a bid to have a certain border recognized, whether we understand that as a border of a nation or as the frontier of that class of people to be considered 'recognizable' as a people" (*Notes* 5). Concerned with how "the people" become performative and politically self-determining, Butler understands "we the people" as linguistic autogenesis, beginning a process of identifying "needs, demands and desires" (169). Hence, when the media revise refugee identity, they recognize them within the borders of city and citizen. The process of political formation begins.

Chantal Mouffe's work on agonistic democracy, democratic citizenship, and political community is explicit on the discursive nature of shared community. Both of us discern dangers in the prevalence of neoliberal ideology and its ubiquity; still, she tellingly observes, "neo-liberal dogmas about the unviolable [*sic*] rights of property, the all-encompassing virtues of the market and the dangers of interfering with its logics constitute nowadays the 'common sense' in liberal-democratic societies" (6). The ubiquity of market logic makes it all but impossible to elude; hence, its strategy must be confronted and addressed. In the face of such pervasive "common sense" and its self-sustaining momentum, what is achieved in rewriting refugees as neoliberal subjects? Could they be recognized without that common sense? By including refugees in mainstream values, Buffalo's media—wittingly or unwittingly—includes them in the community, or at least the social collective, and authorizes their participation in city institutions. In opposition to valorizing all differences, a move that would evade politics, Mouffe would have us acknowledge that collective identities are part of the agonism of politics. I tentatively offer that, despite its inequity, at this moment in U.S. politics, scripting the collective identity of neoliberal subjects may be necessary to including refugees and creating an identity where they have the potential of politics. There are two interlocking concepts here: (1) relations of power and (2) the imperative of at least some shared political and ideological space.

First, as well recognized, power is not external to identity or relationships, but rather constitutes identities and relationships. In the media's construction of a relationship between established citizenry and newly arrived refugees, the relationship itself becomes a means of interaction. It is a relationship sanctified by capital, the state, and media representations, but contaminated with hegemony and misrecognition. The relationship is flawed in that the recognition is distorted through a required American dream, entrepreneurship, and a falsely inverted hierarchy where refugees save America. Even so, the relationship should not be discarded abruptly because it serves to authorize the foundational moves toward a shared politics. As Mouffe writes, "politics aims at the creation of unity in the context of conflict and diversity: it is concerned with the creation of an 'us' by the determination of a 'them'" (101). Hear echoes of Butler's "we the people." The Buffalo media does not designate a "them," but one might assume that the inherent "them" are neither Buffalo long-term residents nor recent arrivals committed to a more economically stable city. In accepting the creation of an "us," a power-based relationship, Mouffe dismisses a model of endless antagonism and diversity as diminishing the possibility of politics. Instead, she understands struggle within democratic politics through a shift from seeing opponents as enemies and rather conceiving them as adversaries with whom one shares common ground on the democratic principles of equality and liberty. Of course, equality and liberty are liberal values, not neoliberal values. At this moment, however, neoliberalism is such a dominant regime that it may be the Other's first step toward finding inclusion and adversaries rather than antagonism, enemies, or pity. Through the false imaginary of neoliberalism, rather than dwelling in negative or ambiguous vulnerability, refugees are imagined as open to the city's established values, imagined as embracing a constitutive, epistemic vulnerability that creates possibilities, such as new identities, for refugees themselves. In turn, by being open to the knowledge of refugees, long-term residents also are positioned in a space of epistemic vulnerability and potential identity change. The relations of power change.

Second, the imperative of at least some shared political and ideological space is an important, but fraught political concept.[11] As both a refusal of the drive to consensus and a modulation of antagonism, pluralism with agonism may be safer and more productive for precarious populations than direct identification with cultural rupture, language loss, and (post)colonial dependency. Yes, the cost of reframing identity from precarity to entrepreneurship denies refugee trauma and posits too facile a cultural engagement and identity change, one in service to an unexamined status quo. Still, Butler observes, precarity has the potential to create a different type of political coalition, one that would *not* require "agreement on all questions of desire or belief or self-identification" (*Frames* 32). Balancing the potential of a rich agonistic pluralism with the dangers of exclusion is a troubled undertaking. In the face of the refugee crisis, the discourse of neoliberalism—in its ubiquity—provides a rhetorical tool for creating inter-ests. When people in Buffalo announce that their city is a model for refugee resettlement, they acknowledge both inclusion and pluralism, neither a simple accomplishment.

PARADOXES ABOUND

Disregarding refugee precarity and cultural difference paradoxically creates an in-between where refugees become an acknowledged part of the city. In pragmatically accepting the construction of economic and political engagement, however, one should be hypervigilant about how "the imaginary is guided and channeled within the communication machine" (Hardt and Negri 33). The rhetoric of capitalism extends into the life itself and serves to blind us to possible resistance. Seemingly the imaginary of this self-sustaining communication machine, a monologic power, hides the failures of its logic. For example, one might consider how Buffalo's citizens accept a substantive equality with refugees—one founded in shared inter-ests—without attending to other significant problems of equality and economics. Neoliberalism might be imagined as a form of life that founds a particular political community, but its strident, rhetorical presence cannot completely bury its structural failure. In focusing on entrepreneurial successes, the media ignores facts, such as Buffalo's poverty rate. Buffalo is the third poorest city in the United States, just behind Rust Belt sisters Detroit and Cleveland: 41 percent of blacks and 45 percent of Asians and Hispanics live in poverty (Rey, "More Than"). Further, 82 percent of its students are labeled "economically disadvantaged," and close to 54 percent of its children live in poverty.[12] In focusing on the successes of a few refugees, the dominant discourse fails to name the precarity of all of Buffalo's poor, both native-born and refugee, but that poverty does not evaporate.

A further failure of logic: perhaps the media seeks to create relationships between equals, but in fact, the refugee is imagined as more powerful and more able to navigate the failed Rust Belt economy than the long-term residents. In simply resettling vacant parts of Buffalo, replacing the missing youth demographic, and developing small shops, the refugees replace populations who fled for better economic environments. In doing so, they are constructed as saviors of a city and creators of a new economy. This narrative of fluid migration ignores both earlier histories and the forces that control lives, pushing people across borders. When jobs were lost in the collapse of manufacturing, the demographics and economy of Buffalo changed, and poverty grew, revealing the failure of unregulated capitalism. Refugees are sent to Buffalo because of its inexpensive housing and need for population, but they must create their own jobs because of its high unemployment rates and poorly paying jobs.

Implicit in the representation of refugees is the claim that the Buffalo economy needs to be saved, and saved by geopolitical actions outside its bor-

ders. In characterizing war and forced migration as a source of U.S. development, even as it creates community, the media implicitly omits the failures of
neoliberalism and U.S. policies as it rearticulates failures as opportunities, just
not opportunities for long-term residents. The momentum and monological
power of neoliberal rhetorics hides deeper paradoxes as to the honest possibilities of individual entrepreneurship. If long-term residents cannot revitalize
Buffalo, by what logic can vulnerable refugees be expected to do so? Rather
than see the paradox as a problem to be resolved, I would join others, such
as Mouffe and Bonnie Honig, in suggesting that paradoxes are productive
in disrupting monologs and monologics, revealing cultural conflicts, creating
deliberative or political moments, and calling forth citizen response.[13] Paradoxes can disrupt single answers and push interlocutors to define inter-ests
and commit to struggles over meaning. The rhetorical strategy of transforming precarity and vulnerability to equality, even salvation, offers a lens into
the technology of citizen creation and neoliberal monologism, but more significantly its paradox reveals the fissure in the monolog and so might stop
its totalizing momentum.[14] The paradoxical construction of refugees saving
precarious U.S. cities, once revealed and analyzed, disrupts the stability of
neoliberal valuations and opens new possibilities for critical responses.

RESPONDING TO NEOLIBERAL MONOLOGUES

As Brett Neilson and Ned Rossiter argue, the experience of precarity creates the conditions from which "differential capacities and regimes of value
emerge" (64). Similarly, Gilson writes, "vulner*ability* is not just a condition
that limits us but one that can *enable* us" (310). Vulnerability can be "a condition of potential" (311). Just as paradoxes are productive, so too can be precarity. Of further interest, across different experiences of precarity, in the current
global economy, precarity is becoming a norm and not an exception (Neilson
and Rossiter 68). Both the new and long-term residents of Buffalo struggle.
As the denial of precarity can mark a productive social leveling and allow
for a social collective, its denial can obliterate the enabling potential of precarity to change values. Currently the precarity and precariousness of both
populations is framed in such a way that neither can escape the demands of
self-sufficiency. Even so, the articulation of the paradox of refugee vulnerability and self-sufficiency allows for critique. That critique potentially redefines
the terms of welcoming resettlement. If it is not possible to escape the neoliberal frame and the legal requirement of refugee economic self-sufficiency,
the critique can nudge the in-between and the nature of inter-ests toward
engagements that foster epistemic vulnerability and offer potential for politi-

cal change. Shared space (in-between) and inter-est initially represented in the neoliberal subject extends to both refugees and Buffalo's long-term residents the right to appear and be recognized. It offers a potential position for critique, a moment revealed by paradox.

Lisa Duggan calls for a critical response to neoliberalism, one dependent on integrating cultural and identity issues with the political economy; she hopes for a new social movement leading to a new global politics. As she rightly claims, the discourse of neoliberalism permeates cultural and identity politics: "Neoliberalism was constructed in and through cultural and identity politics and cannot be undone by a movement without constituencies and analyses that respond directly to that fact. Nor will it be possible to build a new social movement . . . as long as cultural and identity issues are separated, analytically and organizationally, from the political economy in which they are embedded" (3). At the end of *Empire*, Michael Hardt and Antonio Negri make a similar call, although they are more optimistic in their demand for action, "absolute democracy in action." They too defer defining future political events, proposing that "the multitude through its practical experimentation will offer models and determine when and how the possible becomes real" (410, 411).

I have heard their calls, but I do not have a model, a new social movement. Whose imaginary will become the future remains unclear. I simply analyze local cultural and identity issues and offer a few glocal observations. First, if refugees become "we the people" through neoliberal imaginings, the productivity and efficiency of that rhetorical strategy are worthy of attention, but glib inclusion—even if it facilitates politics—is not in the service of a new politics. It diverts attention from failed economic histories and the struggles of precarity. Second, refugees, who are defined by precarity, may not be the ideal agents for building the social movement or providing the analyses that link cultural and identity issues with the political economy. Their inclusion in the city and the country is fragile and new, most Buffalo refugees arriving in the last five years. The demands of vulnerability, in all three manifestations, may require their attention. The analyses and critiques—as well as the political response to neoliberal failures—are more likely to arise from their children, activists, the media, academics, and other long-term residents. Third, as offered here, acknowledgment of mutual vulnerability—both of refugees and the long-term residents—achieves an acknowledgment of a shared form of life as well as the acknowledgment of the mutual cost of global capital. In apprehending and acknowledging common, if not universal, human vulnerability to failed economies and states, Buffalo is potentially positioned to create a community better able to address political, economic, and social violence. The interdependency of neighbors across borders may create a social collective capable of shared agency and political effect. As Butler observed, "From where might a principle emerge by which we vow to protect others from the kind of violence we have suffered, if not from an apprehension of a common human vulnerability?" (*Precarious* 30).

NOTES

1. http://www.bbc.com/news/world-europe-36611059
2. In addition to local voices celebrating Buffalo's success, national news acknowledges Buffalo's reception of refugees. See Joel Rose's piece on NPR's *Morning Edition,* Katie Couric's *Yahoo News* video, Laura Kirkpatrick in *PassBlue,* a CUNY Graduate Center publication that covers the UN, and James Reinl in *Middle East Eye* on Buffalo's welcoming of Muslims.
3. See "Editorial: Erie County Merits Praise for Offer to Resettle Suffering Syrians."
4. As early as 2003, in an effort to revitalize the West Side, the city developed a project with pushcart venders, reportedly Latino immigrants. See Biddlecom.
5. See Miller.
6. Conscious of the damaging effects of borders, Buffalo's International Institute plays with the idea of borders in the title of its annual food-center fundraiser. "Buffalo without Borders" suggests that the problem of borders and the difficulty of their irradictation is worth a night of consideration.
7. "Nepantla," sometimes translated as "in-between," is a Nehuatl term arising in colonization. As used by Anzaldúa, its connotations include distress, dislocation, and oppression. With different cultural origins and connotations, it highlights Arendt's ambivalent sense of a shared space that both relates and separates.
8. See Couric; Rose; Preval.
9. In 2007, WEDI was begun by members of the Westminster Presbyterian Church. In 2009, concerned West Side agencies, business owners, and residents met and planned to encourage business on the West Side, becoming the West Side Stake Holders. The two joined with the mission of nurturing micro-businesses (Sapong, "Helping"). WEDI now has eleven full-time employees, a zero percent default rate on micro-loans, and a high success rate on grants (interview May 2016).
10. See Bass; Rivero.
11. See Miranda Joseph's *Against the Romance of Community* and Michaele L. Ferguson's *Sharing Democracy* for overviews of community, commonality, and their alternatives. Ferguson outlines the difficulties with a democratic requirement of commonality as opposed to loose concepts, such as collective enactments. My *Deliberative Acts* similarly critiques consensus and argues for a performative model of deliberation.
12. http://data.nysed.gov/enrollment.php?year=2013&instid=800000052968; http://www.dailypublic.com/articles/01202015/staggering-poverty-facing-buffalo-students
13. I discuss the productivity of the political paradox in *Deliberative Acts* (152–68, 175–77).
14. Like Rousseau's paradox of origins (democracy needs good men to make good laws, but needs good laws to make good men), one can see the paradox of the neoliberal citizen (one needs entrepreneurs to make good economies, but one needs good economies to make entrepreneurs).

WORKS CITED

Adelman, Robert M., Watoii Rabii, and Aysegul Balta Ozgen. "Immigrants and Neighborhood Change on Buffalo's West Side." Immigration and Refugee Research Institute Conference. University at Buffalo, SUNY, Buffalo, New York. 16 May 2016.

Anzaldúa, Gloria. *Borderlands/La Frontera: The New Mestiza.* 3rd ed. Aunt Lute, 2007.

Arendt, Hannah. *The Human Condition*. University of Chicago Press, 1958.

Bass, Amy. "How Soccer Made Refugees American." *CNN*. 19 Nov. 2015. <http://www.cnn.com/2015/11/19/opinions/bass-immigrants-soccer-maine/>. 21 March 2017.

Biddlecom, Brendan. "An Old Approach to Building a New City: Buffalo's New World Market Aims to Improve Life on the West Side . . . One Street at a Time." *Artvoice* 2.14 (April 2003): 8–10.

Bohmer, Carol, and Amy Shuman. *Rejecting Refugees: Political Asylum in the 21st Century*. Routledge, 2008.

Butler, Judith. *Frames of War: When Is Life Grievable?* Verso, 2009.

———. *Notes Towards a Performative Theory of Assembly*. Havard University Press, 2015.

———. *Precarious Life: The Powers of Mourning and Violence*. Verso, 2004.

Cacho, Lisa Marie. *Social Death: Racialized Rightlessness and the Criminalization of the Unprotected*. New York University Press, 2012.

City of Buffalo. *New American Study: A Strategic Action Plan to Advance Immigrant and Refugee Integration and Success*. February 2016. <https://www.ci.buffalo.ny.us/files/1_2_1/Mayor/NewAmericansStudy.pdf>.

Couric, Katie. "Buffalo's Big Back." *Yahoo News*. 15 Jan. 2016. <https://www.yahoo.com/katiecouric/buffalos-big-comeback-201146847.html>. 17 March 2017.

Dabkowski, Colin. "West Side Mural Honors Buffalo's Burmese Community." *Buffalo News*. 6 Aug. 2015. <http://buffalonews.com/2015/08/06/west-side-mural-honors-buffalos-burmese-community/>. 17 March 2017.

Duggan, Lisa. *The Twilight of Equality? Neoliberalism, Cultural Politics, and the Attack on Democracy*. Beacon, 2003.

"Editorial: Erie County Merits Praise for Offer to Resettle Suffering Syrian Refugees." *Buffalo News*. 12 Sept. 2015. <http://buffalonews.com/2015/09/12/erie-county-merits-praise-for-offer-to-resettle-suffering-syrian-refugees/>. 17 March 2017.

Epstein, Jonathan D. "Saving for a New Home Away from Home." *Buffalo News*. 19 April 2009. <https://www.highbeam.com/doc/1P2-21700967.html>. 17 March 2017.

Ferguson, Michaele L. *Sharing Democracy*. Oxford University Press, 2012.

Gilson, Erinn. "Vulnerability, Ignorance, and Oppression." *Hypatia* 26.2 (2011): 308–32.

Hardt, Michael, and Antonio Negri. *Empire*. Harvard University Press, 2000.

Honig, Bonnie. *Emergency Politics: Paradox, Law, Democracy*. Princeton University Press, 2009.

Joseph, Miranda. *Against the Romance of Community*. University of Minnesota Press, 2002.

Kirkpatrick, Laura E. "In New York State, a City Willing to Settle Refugees the Right Way." *Passblue*. 20 Oct. 2015. <http://www.passblue.com/2015/10/20/in-upstate-new-york-a-city-willing-to-settle-refugees-the-right-way/>. 17 March 2017.

Lyon, Arabella. *Deliberative Acts: Democracy, Rhetoric, and Rights*. Penn State University Press, 2013.

Mezzadra, Sandro, and Brett Neilson. *Border as Method, or, the Multiplication of Labor*. Duke University Press, 2013.

Miller, Melinda. "Refugees and Locals Try to Bridge Language Barrier to Make Buffalo More Welcoming." *Buffalo News*. 7 May 2015. <http://buffalonews.com/2015/05/06/refugees-and-locals-try-to-bridge-language-barrier-to-make-buffalo-more-welcoming/>. 17 March 2017.

Mills, Catherine. "Undoing Ethics: Butler on Precarity, Opacity and Responsibility." *Butler and Ethics*. Ed. Moya Lloyd. Edinburgh University Press, 2015. 41–64.

Mouffe, Chantal. *The Democratic Paradox*. Verso, 2000.

Neilson, Brett, and Ned Rossiter. "Precarity as a Political Concept, or, Fordism as Exception." *Theory, Culture, & Society* 25.7–8 (2008): 51–72.

Ong, Aihwa. *Buddha in Hiding: Refugees, Citizenship, and the New America*. University of California Press, 2003.

Powell, Katrina M. *Identity and Power in Narratives of Displacement*. Routledge, 2015.

Preval, Jeff. "Unique Places: West Side Bazaar." *The Tennessean*. 3 Jan. 2016. <http://www.tennessean.com/story/life/2016/01/03/unique-place-westside-buffalo/78237654/>. 25 March 2017.

Radlich, Jane Kwiatkowski. "People Talk: Woman's American Dream Lands Her at West Side Bazaar." *Buffalo News*. 15 Nov. 2015. <https://buffalonews.com/2015/11/14/people-talk-womans-american-dream-lands-her-at-west-side-bazaar/>. 17 March 2017.

Reinl, James. "Muslim Refugees in Buffalo Defy Stereotypes." *Middle Eastern Eye*. 1 Feb. 2016. <http://www.middleeasteye.net/news/muslim-refugees-buffalo-defy-expectations-1322216507>. 17 March 2017.

Rey, Jay. "In the Arms of Buffalo: Refugees from the World's Most Troubled Nations Find New Homes in Buffalo." *Buffalo News*. 21 Oct. 2007. <http://buffalonews.com/2015/10/21/in_the_arms_of_buffalo_refugees_from_the_worlds_most_troubled_nations_find_new_homes_in_buffalo>. 17 March 2017.

———. "More Than Half of Buffalo Children Live in Poverty, New Census Figures Show." *Buffalo News*. 1 Oct. 2016. <http://buffalonews.com/2016/10/01/half-buffalo-children-live-poverty-new-census-figures-show/>. 17 March 2017.

Rivero, David. "This City Let in Tens of Thousands of Mostly Muslims Refugees. Here's What Happened." *Fusion*. 25 Nov. 2015. <http://fusion.net/story/238682/the-miracle-of-little-bosnia/>. 21 March 2017.

Rose, Joel. "Resettled Refugees Help To 'Bring Buffalo Back.'" NPR *Morning Edition*. 2 Dec. 2015. <http://www.npr.org/2015/12/02/458007064/resettled-refugees-help-to-bring-buffalo-back>. 17 March 2017.

Ryle, Gilbert. *Dilemmas*. Cambridge University Press, 1954.

Sapong, Emma. "Ethiopian Refugee Wins Entrepreneur of the Year Prize." *Buffalo News*. 2 Feb. 2015. <http://buffalonews.com/2015/02/02/ethiopian-refugee-wins-entrepreneur-of-year-prize/>. 17 March 2017.

———. "Helping Grow New West Side Businesses." *Buffalo News*. 17 Aug. 2014. <http://buffalonews.com/2014/08/17/helping-grow-new-west-side-businesses/>. 17 March 2017.

Sommer, Mark. "County Slashes Aid to Organizations that Serve Buffalo's Refugee Population." *Buffalo News*. 3 Dec. 2015. <http://buffalonews.com/2015/12/02county_slashes_aid_to_organizations_that_serve_buffalos_refugee_population/best/>. 17 March 2017.

Tokasz, Jay. "Fleeing Wars and Persecution, Refugees Pursue Their Dreams Here." *Buffalo News*. 22 Oct. 2007. <http://buffalonews.com/fleeing_wars_and_to_organizations_that_serve_buffalos_refugee_population/best/>. 17 March 2017.

United Nations High Commission for Refugees. "Global Trends." 2015. <https://s3.amazonaws.com/unhcrsharedmedia/2016/2016–06–20-global-trends/2016-06-14-Global-Trends-2015.pdf>.

Weiner, Michael. "Buffalo's Support of Immigrant Benefits Everyone." *Buffalo News*. 23 Jan. 2016. <http://buffalonews.com/2016/01/23/another-voice-buffalos-support-of-immigrants-benefits-everyone>. 17 March 2017.

White House Task Force on New Americans. *Bright Spots in Welcoming and Integration: A Report by White House Task Force on New Americans.* 2016. <https://obamawhitehouse.archives.gov/sites/default/files/docs/bright_spots_report_63016.pdf>.

Zremski, Jerry. "Former Political Prisoners Cheer Burma's Move to Democracy." *Buffalo News.* 15 Nov. 2015. <http://buffalonews.com/2015/11/15/former-political-prisoners-cheer-burmas-move-to-democracy/>. 17 March 2017.

———. "UN Ambassador Says Buffalo's Refugees Offer Lessons to Nation." *Buffalo News.* 22 Nov. 2016. <http://buffalonews.com/2016/11/22/un-ambassador-says-buffalos-refugees-offer-lessons-nation/>. 17 March 2017.

CHAPTER 7

"Where am I? Do you have WiFi?"

Vital Technologies and Precarious Living in the Syrian Refugee Crisis

LAVINIA HIRSU

"WHERE CAN I buy food and water?" "How do I register?" "Do you have WiFi?" (International Rescue Committee, "What Refugees Ask"). According to the International Rescue Committee (IRC), these are the first questions Syrian refugees[1] ask upon arrival on the shores of Greece. Having survived dangerous journeys, they try to make sense of their new lives by reconnecting to the world. Smartphones,[2] in particular, are among the first objects that refugees use to find a secure path and contact their families. These are vital objects in a struggle for life and social place, any place that would allow them to affirm their humanity and to live "a life worth living" (Butler, *Frames* 53).

Articles in major Western newspapers, messages on social media, and viral photographs have all confirmed the vital role of mobile phones in Syrian refugees' lives. Countless reports have presented the journeys of migrant boats that made it safely to the shore because they were guided by GPS technologies and other signaling apps installed on migrants' phones. Such stories demonstrate the importance of smartphones in the Syrian refugee crisis; yet the vitality of these objects hasn't been remarked without contestation: If migrants can afford to buy expensive phones, why should we think that they are dispossessed? Why should we try to deploy supplementary resources to meet their basic needs of food, shelter, and security? How can we imagine the precarious living conditions of Syrian people when the things they carry prove the contrary? In this chapter, I argue that the public debate around the role of smartphones has adopted *a rhetoric of material assets* that views smartphones as vital tools with contested sociopolitical capital. Within this framework, smartphones are sometimes presented as valuable assets that point to the refugees' abilities to manage their precarious conditions. However, such framing not only simplifies complex accounts of human struggle but also obscures the fragile circumstances in which refugees make their journeys, their rights and critical needs, and the very precarious nature of their lives.

By focusing on phones as vital tools, public representations of refugees in the media and on social networks tend to obscure deeper ontological relations between people, objects, networks, and (infra)structures. A rhetoric of material assets hides and misrepresents the refugees' struggles by directing public attention toward a limited set of relations between humans and objects. Beyond the photographs of stranded boats, there are deeper connections that need to be made visible so the reader/viewer can begin to understand the precarious conditions refugees are forced to face. For this reason, I turn to new materialism and use Jane Bennett's notion of "vitality" and Karen Barad's concept of "intra-action" to analyze the debate on smartphones in the Syrian refugee crisis. In order to understand how vital mobile phones are for the migrants, I propose that we situate these objects within fragile and always changing assemblages of human bodies, technologies (digital and non-digital), structures of support (be they social, infrastructural, or political), and other entangled objects that make human life *matter*.[3] Against an instrumentalist rhetoric, I argue that smartphones, just like boats, tents, food, and clothes, do not merely *support* those who own them; they are entangled in discursive and material relations that make the fabric of life. A new materialist view of human-object relations allows us to gain a more profound understanding of the nature of precarious living and consider ethical guidelines toward human life and its constitutive technologies.

The analysis becomes even more relevant if we situate it in the historical context of the emergence of cell phones. An instrumentalist rhetoric toward these material objects is deeply embedded in the logics of capitalism. The mobile phone was initially perceived as a symbol of class, stability, and prestige, "an elitist device mainly used by middle and upper class males" (Lacohée, Wakeford, and Pearson 205). With a continuous history of development in the United Kingdom, the United States, and the Nordic countries (Denmark, Norway, and Sweden) (see Agar's *Constant Touch*), the mobile phone has gradually become a common Western material object that transitioned from being an exclusive artifact to "an artefact of mass consumption" (Lacohée, Wakeford, and Pearson 208). Co-opted into what Mirowski calls "everyday neoliberalism," the cell phone is nowadays an essential material possession associated with notions of (global) mobility, customization, and self-management. Smartphones, in particular, feed into notions of individualism and neoliberal self-determination with their "ability to be reconfigured and repurposed by individual users through their choices of downloadable apps and content" (Watkins, Hjorth, and Hoskinen 666). However, these attributes are neither homogenous nor evenly available to all. Smartphones in the hands of Syrian migrants carry differential material and ideological weight, indexing different understandings of mobility and individuality that challenge the logics of the "Western" consumer culture and demonstrate competing assumptions about ties between material culture and humans on the move.

SMARTPHONES: TOOLS FOR MEASURING PRECARIOUS LIVING

> Some lives are grievable, and others are not; the differential allocation of grievability . . . operates to produce and maintain certain exclusionary conceptions of who is normatively human. (Butler, *Precarious* xiv–xv)

In the context of an unprecedented influx of migrants at the gates of Europe in 2015, public outlets such as social media and major Western news channels published a series of articles and photographs that showed refugees talking on smartphones. These accounts were meant to open a public debate around their vital needs and to question the legitimacy of their urgent claims for protection based on their ownership of smartphones. The wide range of news articles and online public responses that followed embraced a rhetoric of material assets whereby smartphones were presented as contested mediating tools that refugees used purposefully to manage their precarious conditions.

The analysis of 342 English-language news media entries reported on the vital nature of smartphones (see the report by Gillespie et al.). Many migrants who attempt to cross the European borders use GPS, Google maps, Facebook, WhatsApp, and Viber to navigate through the waters (Graham). The phone becomes "a lifeline, offering access to information and services put in place to help them, as well as keeping in touch with loved ones left behind" (Marr). Once on the shore, migrants use their phones to find crucial information about the registration process, affordable accommodation, medical help, humanitarian aid (Abrougui, Othman, and York), and local language and currency exchange rates (Graham). With the help of these tools, migrants can access websites such as Google's Crisis Info Hub app and Refugeeinfo.eu that centralize information on how to transit different European countries. *Arriv-*

ing in Berlin—A Map Made by Refugees, for instance, is a collective online map, developed by Hamidullah Ehrari, Mohammad Yari, Farhad Ramazanali, and Alhadi Aldebs, which aims to give migrants reliable information on how to explore the resources available to them.

The phones enable refugees to continue their journey safely from one location to another based on shared experience communicated through social media (Von Habekuß and Schmitt). Through WhatsApp messaging, for instance, refugees can receive antifraud messages (Favell) and identify reliable smugglers who would not just take their money and leave them at the mercy of the waves. Life-and-death information is sent via wireless networks (Williams). Some of the migrants can communicate back with their relatives to notify them about their location and living conditions (Wall, Campbell, and Janbek 12), while others use websites such as Trace the Face, set up by the International Committee of the Red Cross (ICRC), to reconnect with their friends or relatives who have gone missing during displacement.

With so many uses, smartphones are indeed "the refugee's most valuable tool" (Von Habekuß and Schmitt). However, if smartphones represent objects that facilitate access to other material resources and services, their owners are implicitly portrayed as agents in control of their conditions. Central to the migrants' experience, smartphones appear to function as material instruments that "enable [refugees] to mitigate or resolve uncertainties of everyday working life in relation with others" (Harney 541), vital linking points between the refugees and a wealth of structures of support. This view positions migrants as managers of their own conditions, and the relations to the smartphones reflect the assumption that refugees can carve their own paths. The vitality of smartphones depends on a human-centric framework that turns phones into objects that people use in order to achieve their goals. In other words, the rhetoric of material assets is about humans doing things with objects.

At its most basic level, this proposition implicitly opposes the notion of precarity that presupposes humans' *inability* to act on things, or their lack of access to various resources. However, the refugees represented as owners of smartphones seem to contradict this definition of precarity. Messages on social media and other public outlets emphasized the refugees' abilities to self-manage, and their claims for humanitarian aid were questioned. A Twitter post, for instance, that was quickly circulated on major news platforms, reported: "Photographers dramatizing #Europe's SUDDEN #migrant influx. Most well dressed, smoking, #smartphones, don't look like #refugees to me. @CNN" (Williams). An article in the *Daily Dot* explains the logic behind this message: "Critics suggest that those who are fleeing mass casualties, political oppression, and extreme destitution shouldn't be carrying around these devices—because it signals that they really don't need help after all. The idea is that what they're facing couldn't be *that* bad if they still have their cell phones" (Williams). In other words, the possession of phones seemed to collide with what it means to be a refugee and the "claims of urgency" made by those caught in the migrant crisis (cf. Azoulay). The use of smartphones invalidated their owners' stories about the precarious circumstances in their home countries. To put it simply, having smartphones meant having the material resources that could potentially ensure more secure lives than the ones described by the refugees themselves.

The rhetoric of material assets establishes clear relationships that divide and differentiate. As one article put it, "It's because the refugees many of us have conjured in our imaginations are starving and wearing tattered clothes, relics of a cultural past that helps separate them from us" (Williams). A common view defines the refugee status as one built on relations of lack and dispossession. According to Williams, the common definition of a refugee implies a relationship of distance (both temporal and spatial) from the viewers or readers. The refugees' imagined spaces serve as a counterpoint based on which us-other divides can be perpetuated and justified. Smartphones, as objects that define contemporary conditions of connectivity, establish different relationships: they are at the core of infrastructural support, they index modern living, and they are believed to have the power to overcome distance. Connecting devices do not establish the same relationships with the human body that ragged clothes would. Nobody would question the presence of tents, blankets, or worn-out strollers in the migrants' journeys because these objects are part of the conventional narrative of precarious living in different unknown spaces. These objects can also be part of the story of human movement under conditions of unstable resources (material, financial, emotional, etc.). Therefore, for many readers on social media who took a critical stance vis-à-vis technology use, "refugees with cell phones" read as a cacophonous phrase. The copresence of smartphones and migrants indicated a contradictory relationship between bodies caught in structures of need and objects that build connectivity and bring other things within reach.

To debunk the argument that smartphones indicate privilege via material possessions, a variety of newspaper articles tried to reestablish the vital nature of these devices. Public commentaries tried to demonstrate that smartphones actually save lives, put them back on a provisory course, and cannot be viewed as tools of power. According to James O'Malley, "You don't need to be a white westerner to own a relatively cheap piece of technology." To those who believe that smartphones are objects that only rich people have, O'Malley offers a cost evaluation to demonstrate that there is nothing special about having such a device: "It's also possible to pick up the second generation iPhone—the iPhone 3G—for around £25, and despite being a few years old is still perfectly serviceable. There are more mobile phones than people in the world so chances are that anyone who can afford a phone (like millions of Syrians) already own one." The public's questioning of smartphones, Audra Williams notes, points to an even deeper public concern: "They [cell phones] symbolize normalcy for many Westerners, and we unconsciously let ourselves believe that these mass-produced possessions are part of what isolates us from the tragedy we see happening to others—always others—on the news." Embedded in the process of Othering, smartphones represent symbolic tools used to differentiate between "us" and "them," between those who have such tools and those who should not own them. Holding these divides betrays a politics of differential allocation of moral value onto objects that are meant to establish social hierarchies (see Butler, *Frames* 32)—a point that I will return to in the following sections.

Although divided on whether smartphones are tools of human agency, self-management, or social power, the rhetoric of material assets adopted in social and news media outlets seemed to reduce the migrants' profound vulnerabilities and struggles. Photographs taken at different points of arrival focused viewers' attention on smartphones alone, excluding from the debate more important questions about the nature of refugees' unstable conditions and uncertain future. Tiffany Dykstra notices a similar process behind the competing discourses of the refugees' experiences. Although public outlets tend to present different views on refugees' critical needs, they all seem to end up "recreating conditions of bare life[4] and precarity through discourses of disposability" (Dykstra 31). Instead of promoting rich public debates on how to engage with migrants' calls for humanitarian support, public mainstream discourses aggravate the precarity of their lives. From the lens of an instrumentalist rhetoric, refugees are those who need to be kept alive because they do not have the means to do so. Any material objects that prove the contrary (in this case, the smartphone) extract refugees from their precarious conditions and position them in self-managerial roles.

Dykstra argues that such representations dangerously disconnect the public from "the material and historical systems of power that are responsible for the [refugees'] condition" (46). Once the migrant experience becomes reductively a problem of having or not having a smartphone, more complex conditions of precarity are obscured and refugees' desperate calls are no longer heard. Dykstra finds this disconnect highly problematic because "even with sufficient calories to sustain their bodies, refugees continue to suffer within and outside of the camps" (Dykstra 32). Precarity cannot be simply measured by the number of refugees who are sheltered and fed, nor by the number of

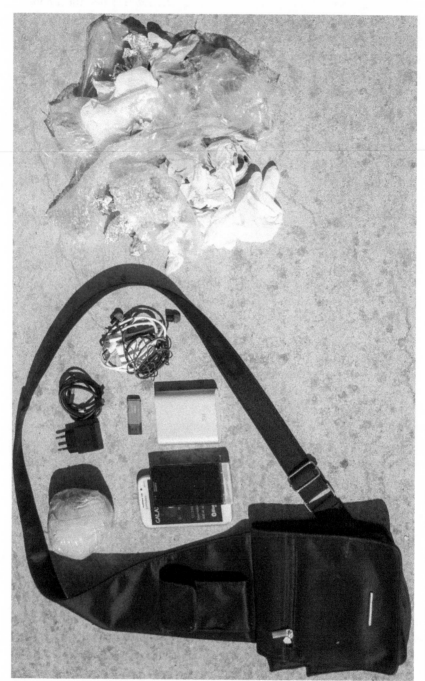

FIGURE 7.1. © Tyler Jump/International Rescue Committee

smartphones they carry. In the next section, I propose an alternative way of understanding refugees-smartphones relations and current conditions of precarity based on a new materialist framework. Within this framework, human suffering and vulnerability can be accounted for only when we take into consideration the discursive as well as the ontological relations between refugees and their environments. In this sense, we can understand the vitality of objects like smartphones within a more complex framing of humans and objects that do not simply support or mediate each other. Instead, they are co-constitutive of the precarious conditions that make up human life. Against the rhetoric of material assets, I suggest that we reassess the vital role of smartphones and redeploy human agency within complex relations that are representational and material at once (cf. Barad).

PRECARIOUS TECHNO-HUMAN ASSEMBLAGES

The division between body and tool has led to the questioning of precarity (as seen in the critics' comments on smartphone usage) or to revisions of the definition of precarity (as seen in the defenders' comments on the refugees' phone usage as a way of coping with uncertainty). However, framing the debate around bodies and tools with different symbolic capital represents a misreading, or an incomplete reading at best, of the refugee experience. To understand the fuller role of smartphones under current global conditions, we need to consider the relationship between humans and nonhuman things from a different perspective that recognizes how both are engaged with one another. This debate is not about refugees *with* smartphones, but about the choreography between migrant bodies and the things they carry. My proposition is that migrants with smartphones act together. Smartphones are neither tools that enact the will of the human body nor vehicles of human action. Instead, smartphones are co-constitutive of human life as much as the human bodies are. Together, they merge with other objects, practices, and entities to form techno-human assemblages that make human life matter. A failure to see these deep connections is what leads to the systemic and differential attribution of value to all human lives.

Iqbal is a teenager from Afghanistan who brought with him "1 pair of pants, 1 shirt, 1 pair of shoes and 1 pair of socks; shampoo and hair gel, toothbrush and toothpaste, face whitening cream; comb, nail clipper; bandages; 100 U.S. Dollars; 130 Turkish liras; smartphone and back up cell phone; SIM cards for Afghanistan, Iran and Turkey" (International Rescue Committee, "What's in My Bag?"). A pharmacist from Syria brought fewer objects with him:

"money (wrapped to protect it from water), old phone (wet and unusable) and new smart phone; phone chargers and headphones (plus extra battery charger); 16GB flash drive (containing family photos)" (International Rescue Committee, "What's in My Bag"). These are two survival kits among the many photographed by the IRC from the people who arrived on the shores of the Greek Island of Lesbos. With very little room on insecure boats and dinghies, migrants had to make tough decisions about the most important items that they could carry along on their journeys. While each survival kit varied from one individual to another, the IRC notes in its report that, almost without exception, the survival kits consistently contained a smartphone, a spare cell phone, or a charger that people were very keen on using immediately after they touched the ground. Yet, these objects *matter* neither as markers of privilege nor as indicators of well-being, but as vital objects during experiences of profound disturbances.

While viewers may look at the photographs of the survival kits to understand the difficult choices refugees make when they leave their homelands, these images, in fact, offer a glimpse into the vital assemblages of objects and bodies involved in dangerous transit experiences. Jane Bennett's new materialist framework helps us understand the ways in which we can look at the survival kits beyond a rhetoric of material assets to gain a more complex understanding of their vital role:

> An actant never really acts alone. Its efficacy or agency always depends on the collaboration, cooperation, or interactive interference of many bodies and forces. A lot happens to the concept of agency once nonhuman things are figured less as social constructions and more as actors, and once humans themselves are assessed not as autonomous but as vital materialities. (Bennett 21)

In other words, the migrant journey implicates the convergence of multiple agencies, both human and nonhuman. The human body is a "vital materiality" alongside the vital materialities of other "nonhuman things." The attention to matter does not focus on determinate objects, but on the relations between all co-constitutive elements that make up an interdependent web of shifting relations among human bodies, environmental elements, and infrastructural points. Bennett calls these interacting configurations "assemblages," and she notes that agency within these assemblages is ever-changing and emergent. In other words, "no one really knows what human agency is, or what humans are doing when they are said to perform as agents"; as there is always more to human agency than humans alone (Bennett 34). In this sense, it is hard to say who's driving the boats to the shore: the smartphone, the smuggler, the refugees, the waters, the GPS signals? According to Bennett's new materialist framework, all these vital forces engage and move things and bodies together.

Within material assemblages, Bennett recognizes the vitality of nonhuman things, yet not in the sense of crucial importance (as seen in the rhetoric of material assets). From a new materialist perspective, vitality is "the capacity of things—edibles, commodities, storms, metals—not only to impede or block the will and designs of humans but also to act as quasi agents or forces with trajectories, propensities, or tendencies of their own" (viii). To say that smartphones are vital objects in the migrants' journey means to acknowledge their force to affect the movement of human bodies. Moreover, this affectability is not the result of an instrumental function of one object that directly impacts human action. If the human body is matter, then the smartphone's vital materiality "runs alongside and inside humans" (Bennett viii), and alongside and inside other things as well.

The photographs of the survival kits capture some of these vital materialities. A comb and a smartphone, for instance, are not two isolated objects with different functionalities; their presence in the same survival kit tells a more complex story about what it means to move through precarious conditions. They encapsulate the kinds of agencies that are at play as refugees struggle to maintain their relations with familiar assemblages. Boats bring to the European shores movable fragments of people's previous life before the beginning of their journey, such as the pictures of family members on their phones. At the same time, these objects immediately form connections with new environments: phones with personal histories become constitutive elements of an uncertain life in new environments that involve other objects such as tents, clothes, food items, registration documents, and so on.

In light of Bennett's framework of vitality, to understand the more fundamental nature of "extreme precarity," we need to review the definition of precarity itself. As Jasbir Puar remarks, precarity "is not an identity, but rather a relation that is constantly shifting" (169). To take this claim further, precarity is embedded in a web of links with other people, things, and infrastructural entities that determine who is in danger and who is at bay, who is vulnerable or not. This is why questions such as "Where am I? Do you have Wi-Fi?" are so important. Upon arrival, Syrian migrants are trying to relocate themselves by understanding the new parameters of their being and by holding onto objects that *matter* for their existence. The interplay between the surviving body and its new environment demonstrates the process of a realignment of agencies and relations among people and things: refugees "are constantly worried about staying connected, finding access to wifi and phone charging,

and most of all about staying safe both online and offline" (Gillespie et al. 5). The struggle to break through conditions of vulnerability is reflected in the struggle to link up to new assemblages of things and people that keep the refugees within safe socio-material networks. The relations of connectivity and shared agency between the migrants and their new environments testify to the interdependent nature of human agency and the power of things to co-construct life (cf. Barnett and Boyle 7).

If Jane Bennett's notion of vitality helps us understand the nature of refugees' relations with other "things" in terms of co-constitutive assemblages, Karen Barad's concept of "intra-action" allows us to see why representations in the media distort refugees' precarious conditions and misdirect readers by fixating their attention on isolated objects (i.e., smartphones, in this case). According to Barad, "'intra-action' *signifies the mutual constitution of entangled agencies*" (33). Barad goes further than Bennett to problematize the boundaries of objects, arguing that "'things' do not have determinate boundaries, properties or meanings apart from their mutual intra-actions" (147). Such an example of indefinite boundaries can be found in the chilling testimony of a Syrian migrant: "'Three Iraqis wouldn't come. They said 'we can't swim.' One of those who stayed used Viber to phone his Dada from the boat. He said 'Hello Father, the boat is sinking so I will die.' It was his last message" (Reidy). A simple reading of this testimony would place the agency of the final message in the voice of the caller who used the smartphone as a way of reaching out to his father. But, who actually sent the message: the human body, the smartphone, Viber, the aerial infrastructures? In line with Barad's framework, it is the intra-action of all these and even more elements (boat, waters, the other people around the caller, etc.) that create a techno-human assemblage whose entangled agencies produced the final call.

If we are to revise the relations between human bodies and objects, we need to try to capture the intra-active relations between different entities instead of cause-and-effect relations. In an analysis of refugees' connectivity problems in the Za'atari camp, Schmitt et al. reveal the many forces at play behind the use of smartphones. Inside the community, the authors found significant access divides that depended on coverage gaps, restricted signals, fluctuating and unequal data speeds, the type of data carrier, and individuals' location in the camp. While Schmitt et al. are not directly interested in the ontological dimensions of the refugees' networks, the authors' attention to material and infrastructural elements uncovers physical entanglements and shifting relations among and within "social and technical systems" (2). The assemblages that make mobile connections possible within the camp entail the activation and cooperation of multiple entities within which the refugees play only a modest role. This is not to say that human agency is no longer important or effectual; to the contrary, "human beings are still relevant here; however, they are no longer singularly spotlighted" (Barnett and Boyle 6).

In a world of entanglements, Barad adds, "there is a vitality in the liveness of intra-activity, not in the sense of a new form of vitalism, but rather in terms of a new sense of aliveness" (177). Barad's notion of vitality is synonymous with the idea of aliveness—that is, meeting the world in its ever-changing rearrangements and reconfigurations. Along these lines, smartphones cease to be objects with identifiable properties and functionalities and become continuously entangled in new webs of relations depending on other intra-acting entities. In more concrete terms, smartphones cannot be separate tools in action without the agencies of phone connections, wires, Wi-Fi signaling, and software.

More importantly, smartphones continue to be reconfigured as they are engaged in new contexts. The testimony of another migrant reveals the techno-human assemblages of which the smartphone and the human body are but two entities: "I thought if I die on this boat, at least I will die with the photos of my family near me" (International Rescue Committee, "What's in My Bag"). What is the phone if not a hard-to-define materiality: a repository of memories, an object for living and dying with, a link to a past world, an extension of the human body, an ordinary device? The difficulty we have in fully answering this question is a good indicator that we take *matter* seriously. In fact, we don't even need to answer the question as we may end up searching for the proper functions of the phone. In Barad's terms, this means closing down other possibilities for understanding the full range of techno-human entanglements within which migrants are involved.

Because connecting to the world happens through relations rather than definite objects alone, precarity emerges from failed or failing assemblages inscribed in sociopolitical hierarchies of power. Not one, but a multitude of relations bring human bodies into fragile systems that are at the same time material (e.g., broken phones due to exposure to seawater), social (e.g., the complex monitoring registration systems), infrastructural (e.g., all the elements that make phone and Internet connections possible), technological (e.g., chargers and charging stations are equally important to the functioning of a smartphone), and political (e.g., the debate on the value of smartphones presented earlier in this chapter). Judith Butler makes a clear distinction between precariousness and precarity. While precariousness is the ontological condition of vulnerability shared by all human bodies, precarity refers to a complex system of sociopolitical circumstances that position the body "in terms of its supporting [and fragile] networks of relations" (Butler, "Bodily"

103). To put it differently, precarity emerges with constraining and oftentimes imposed relations onto one's body and the objects and their structures of support. Extreme precarity entails the systematic misalignment, ruptures, breakages, and dysfunctionalities of material entities to the point where "co-being and co-responsibilities" (cf. Barnett and Boyle 7) between humans and nonhumans are no longer possible. Therefore, precarious living, as often formulated in the public discourse, is the result of simplified and limited relations between discrete human bodies and objects with clearly defined properties that obscure or downplay more complex relations.

Refiguring precarity in the context of techno-human assemblages requires one further clarification: how do different technological structures and devices fit within a new materialist framework? I use the term "techno-human assemblages" not to single out the special role of technologies (both digital and nondigital), but as a way to describe the co-constitutive technological and human agencies. In the context of the Syrian refugee crisis, instead of reifying technologies into useful or problematic devices, we need to consider how techno-human assemblages reveal the entangled relations between technologies and human agencies with(in) social systems. From this perspective, smartphones become ordinary objects that will not help us understand refugees' precarious conditions unless we become more attuned to a wider range of practices (material, social, political) and complex relations from within the technologies engaged in the struggle for living.[5]

SEEING BEYOND IMAGES OF SMARTPHONES

As I have discussed in the first part of this chapter, many readers of social and news media come to learn about the refugee experience through articles, posts, and viral images. Distant from the points of arrival, readers encounter texts and photographs, tweets, and Facebook messages before they encounter the migrants themselves. Between the reader and the reality on the ground lie stories that capture only a part of the things lived, viral photographs from journalists or nongovernmental organizations, and the interpretations made possible by the readers' own frameworks of understanding. All these artifacts are "entities" in themselves in the techno-human assemblage of relations that entangle "us" (the readers) and "them" (the refugees). If public accounts and messages perpetuate conditions of precarity, is it possible to go beyond the limits of these representations? What kinds of artifacts, practices, and experiences would make us understand the complex nature of things that matter in experiences of forced displacement? In this section, I turn to photographs depicting refugees taking selfies, and I explore the possibility of breaking through public images in which we often get entangled.

Judith Butler explains that the process of precarity "acclimatizes populations over time to insecurity and helplessness" (Butler, *Notes* 15). Refugees' claims for humanitarian help are perceived as statements that make appeal to structures of *dependency*; that is, to survive, the refugees depend on the support that others can make available. At the same time, photographs published in the media that showed migrants taking selfies with their phones seemed to establish relations of *independence* from the viewers. This tense relationship between dependency and independence challenged the viewers' assumptions about refugees' vital needs. As shown in the first part of the article, many readers related to these images through the rhetoric of material assets; however, if we embrace a new materialist approach, we can situate these visual representations within larger assemblages that allow us to grasp the more complex web of relations between fragments of life.

Images of Syrians engaging with their phones were read as images of visual detachment from the viewers. At the end of their journey across the sea, the first thing the migrants did was to take a selfie to share with their relatives (Smith). The viewer is invited to look at these moments of celebration, but in doing so, the audience seems to act as an uninvited guest. There is no visual contact with the migrants because they are caught in the space between their bodies and the smartphones, leaving the viewer outside of the picture. With smiles on their faces, Syrians capture their moment of endurance in what seems to be a private encounter. The smartphones caught in photographs are always turned away from the audience, and the space they record does not include the frame of the viewer. The phone, in this case, acts as the screen that demarcates the migrants' world from the world of the viewer.

For those who critiqued the use of smartphones, the separation between the visual field defined by the phone and the field of the viewer became another proof that demonstrated Syrians' self-sufficiency. How can one make an urgency claim without looking at the viewer? How can these people need *us* when they do not engage with their audience? These relationships are crucial because they establish the grounds for political action. Photographs that demonstrate refugees' independent gaze become problematic for sustaining a discourse of political intervention grounded in claims of dependency and need. Taking a selfie is a political act of self-affirmation and self-representation, whereas taking on the refugee identity, as we have seen earlier in this chapter, is often viewed as a vulnerable position within the context of failed structures. According to feminist theorist Isabell Lorey, precarious living "denotes social positioning of insecurity and hierarchization, which accompanies processes of Othering" (qtd. in Puar 165). Precarity, in this sense, becomes the mechanism by which the refugee is expected to act as a dependable Other. Having a smartphone and taking a selfie, however, are social gestures that give the refugee the possibility to question the parameters of precarity and to express "individual autonomy and sovereignty" (Berlant 755). In other words, refugees with smartphones form one unit of human-thing relations represented as enacting autonomously, thus providing the proof of an enduring life.

Yet, these readings of the images are possible only within a narrow field of vision that focuses on predetermined relations between humans and things. The rhetoric of phones as tools provides a simple way for the readers to relate to (and in this case, to distance themselves from) the refugees' struggles. To move beyond these simple frames, we need to recognize the gap between representations and reality. In Barad's words, "images or representations are not snapshots or depictions of what awaits us but rather condensations or traces of multiple practices of engagement" (53). From a new materialist perspective, the images of selfies are but one set of objects or vital entities within a larger assemblage of images, texts, objects, practices, acts, and frames of reference that substantiate our relationships with the ontologies of refugees' lives.

So, is it possible to move beyond images of refugees taking selfies? My answer is yes, but only when we recognize that such practices caught on camera line up with many other practices, events, and circumstances that prevent vulnerable people from securing safe lives: sleeping in unsafe locations, losing family members on their journeys, having limited access to food and medication, and so on. The representations of these moments are equally critical and need to be brought in front of viewers' eyes to continually expand, challenge, and reframe public understandings of precarity. Only when we make visible the wider range of entities involved in experiences of human pain and survival will we be able to understand the struggle for life, the fragile nature of being, and the entangled relations between migrants and their environments. For this to happen, we need to ask not why refugees can afford smartphones, but for what purposes and through what means they use these devices. Under current conditions of unsettling global movements and digital connectivity, precarity settles within techno-human assemblages that perpetuate sociopolitical inequalities and mask the entanglements of being in an unsafe world.

UNSETTLING NEW GROUNDS: DIGITAL INEQUALITIES

In this chapter, I have used the debate over the vital role of smartphones as a way to better understand the notion of precarity within the context of the Syrian refugee crisis. While I have primarily focused on the phones for the purpose of the present analysis, the materialities that engage with the refugees' lives constitute an entire field of intra-active entities. From an ecological perspective (see Rickert 230), human action, or nonaction, can be accounted within systems of cooperating, or misoperating, material environments. When systems of relations begin to break apart, human life is no longer sustainable and extreme precarity emerges.

More importantly, precarity is not so much about the use or nonuse of technology alone. In fact, precarity does not go away when refugees use smartphones. The larger techno-human assemblages in which people try to find their way to safety show symptoms of other important failed relations that place refugees in vulnerable conditions and life-threatening circumstances. For this reason, to make visible current conditions of precarity, we need to examine techno-human assemblages, rather than remaining superficially focused on the symbolic relations between human agents and their devices (as seen in the rhetoric of material assets). In other words, once we recognize the material co-constitutive presence of digital technologies, what kind of new relations become possible? What can we find out about the refugees' experience if we move from looking at the phones from the outside to analyzing the practices and access points enabled from the inside of these technologies? What kind of mobilities are afforded by these material objects that position and (re)direct human movement in different configurations across the globe?

Access Now, for instance, is an advocacy group whose aim is to raise awareness about digital rights and to help "users at risk around the world." The group reaches out globally to influence policy makers and to advocate for "open and secure communications for all." This agenda recognizes digitality as part of the human condition, and at the same time, it tries to fight against the differential distribution of digital access as a human right. Smart gadgets are one among many other objects and forms of structural support that create the conditions for people to exert their rights to communicate with one another. Techfugees is another group of volunteers who work in the technology industry and try to create a global network of collaborators that bring in innovative ideas on how to "address the [refugee] crisis in ways where the technology world can bring its considerable firepower." These efforts reflect the realization among specialists that we do not have time to interrogate the presence of each digital technology or new device in the context of human crises. Instead, we should channel our efforts into engaging them to better the lives of so many people caught in insecure conditions.

Unfortunately, because smartphones are central to the migrants' way of connecting to the world, they have been co-opted into larger systems of human control. For example, operations of registration and humanitarian aid have become highly digitized processes. Precarity is locked in mobile phones, in the systems of surveillance that activate once migrants register into moni-toring systems. For instance, in Turkey, migrants need to go through a manda-tory process of SIM registration if they wish to gain access to hospital services, education, and other public services. According to Denis D. Aydin, mobile phone registration is automatically linked to one's passport and national ID, and this synchronicity of objects that enact one's identity threatens the pri-vacy and security of the refugees (Access Now). These systems are part of a new phenomenon, "digital humanitarianism," a form of intervention that seems to perpetuate rather than redeem the refugees from precarious living. Mark Duffield warns that new digital systems that aim to connect refugees with resources and new environments are, in fact, controlled remotely (5). Moreover, these systems lock the migrants into structures of dependence that perpetuate their dire circumstances: their location can be tracked, their finan-cial allowances are measured, and their identity can be compromised. Unfor-tunately, these techno-human assemblages do not raise many debates in the mainstream media, as the representations of these entangled relations are not as evocative as the accounts and photographs of stranded refugees and their survival kits (see Sontag 33).

Precarity seems to currently reside in the complex relationships between various forms of digital connectivity. The integrity of human life seems to build on techno-human processes and practices that open up new types of inequalities and insecurities: human control, individual surveillance, people monitoring, and so on. The potential of coming out of one's perilous condi-tions increasingly depends on what Gillespie et al. call "network capital"—"a stratified 'mobility regime' within which some individuals are rendered more mobile than others, and some individuals are completely immobilized" (10). The intricate configurations within techno-human assemblages constrain and create different degrees of dependability and vulnerability. In light of grow-ing anti-refugee sentiment and with the fear of uncertain global security, the challenge for rhetoricians and public activists is to confront such conditions of social instability, reveal the multiple relations of inequality, and recognize precarity in new material configurations.

CONCLUSION: HOW TO CARE FOR THINGS THAT MATTER

In *Frames of War*, Judith Butler claims that precarity has become one of the most enduring contemporary sociopolitical conditions that affects more and more groups of people across the globe. Precarity is a "politically induced con-dition in which certain populations suffer from failing social and economic networks of support and become differentially exposed to injury, violence, and death" (35). While many of us already know the violent effects of precarity on human lives, structural inequalities and precarious living persist against academic and public discourses that condemn them. In this chapter, I have proposed yet another argument on the nature of precarity, and I am aware that the ideas presented here may leave the reader with a lingering question: How should I now care for things that matter? If we are to take techno-human assemblages as our starting point rather than human bodies alone, how can we decide "When is life grievable?" (to echo Judith Butler's question).

These are important questions, and for the reader who wants to know what to do with a new materialist perspective, I find it imperative that I end my argument with a few practical suggestions on how we can change our ways of looking at *things* and valuing them differently. In fact, as Barad reminds us, we already have the ethical obligation to understand the world around us better simply by being a part of it, already entangled in relations of being with others (humans and nonhumans). In this sense, I propose here three concrete ways in which we can be part of a new materialist orientation toward the lives of others.

1. *Develop an attentiveness to things and an awareness of the symbolic boundaries of objects.* Jane Bennett states, "What is also needed is a cultivated, patient, sensory attentiveness to nonhuman forces operating outside and inside the human body" (xiv). This attentiveness requires that we retrain ourselves to see and continuously question where one object ends and where another begins, how objects intra-act, and how conditions of precarity emerge out of these always shifting and fragile relations. Clinging onto an object, a thing, or a phenomenon as proof of precarity is a dangerously reductive way of casting moral judgment and making decisions over others' fate. To measure precarity by the symbolic value of one thing means taking away even the right to call one's life precarious, and therefore worthy of human dignity and support.

2. *Change the lens of looking at the world.* I am not the first nor the last to present a critique against representationalism as a suitable epistemology.[6] A new materialist framework gives us a different way of knowing the world's vital forces, and it encourages curiosity for knowing more about the material configurations of human and nonhuman agencies. Seen through this lens, precarious conditions become more readily visible, and action can be deployed not just as one point of intervention, but also as a sustained plan of cooperative actions.[7]

3. *Look for assemblages rather than objects alone.* A life becomes grievable not when an individual has an object or not, but when being in the world becomes unbearable and almost impossible. When the material and discur-

sive assemblages systemically disconnect human bodies, objects, technologies, and (infra)structures, precarious living emerges out of these failed configurations. Precarity is about failed connective relations between humans and nonhumans. When such connective relations are controlled, monitored, or restricted, human life may no longer be a life worth living.

In line with Barad's cautionary remarks, the ethical guidelines offered above represent orientations and obligations rather than cause-and-effect actions. While the suggestions are definitely actionable, they do not overrely on human agency, nor do they come with the expectation of immediate measurable changes. In other words, caring for things that matter means working continuously on how we relate to techno-human assemblages. These relations become even more important when we are confronted with precarity, which is, as seen in this chapter, never the condition of the Other alone. We don't need to implicate ourselves, as we are already involved in this world through our being: "ethics is not a geometrical calculation; "others" are never very far from "us"; "they" and "we" are co-constituted and entangled" (Barad 179). What we need, though, is to recognize that precarity is not just an isolated state of being. Precarity lingers in all our evolving and shifting relations, and no measure of distance (epistemological, material, representational, etc.) can put a barrier strong enough to keep it at bay without more profound interventions into webs of fragile sociopolitical relations of power and inequality.

I have tried to enact these guidelines in my analysis of smartphones in the Syrian refugee crisis. I used this example as a case study to demonstrate the difficult work that still lies ahead of us. To see digital technologies (smartphones included) as part of structural inequalities or the fabric of precarious living requires that we revise our assemblages of objects, human bodies, and ethical values. Unfortunately, we may have already begun to learn these hard lessons in a painful way by watching and reading the last messages of Syrian civilians. What is the vital role of a smartphone for someone who writes to the world:

> the last massage. Thanks for everything. we shared many moments.
> The last tweets were from an emotiomal father. Farewell, #Aleppo
> Abdulkafi al-Hamdo (qtd. in Mackintosh)

NOTES

1. I use the term "refugees" and "migrants" to refer to people who crossed European borders as a result of displacement, war, violence, and terrorist threats in the context of the Syrian refugee crisis. Such terms have significant legal, political, and social dimensions (see Semmelroggen), which, due to length constraints, I cannot fully address in this chapter.

2. Not all refugees are in the possession of a smartphone at the point of arrival in Europe. Some may come with no mobile phones; others may carry basic devices with simple functionalities (i.e., the ability to make and receive calls or send and receive messages). However, in this chapter I analyze media representations that portray refugees using smartphones. While I do not have the space to fully problematize such generalizations here, these distinctions need to be further interrogated.

3. I use the term "matter" as both a verb and a noun to indicate the value of human life and its materiality at the same time.

4. Dykstra draws on Agamben's notion of "bare life," which is defined as human life sustained by meeting the basic necessities of the body (36).

5. For a similar argument, see Teston 266.

6. See Barad's extended argument against an overreliance on representationalism.

7. See, for instance, the work of Techfugees activists.

WORKS CITED

Abrougui, Afef, Dalia Othman, and Jillian C. York. "Digital Citizen: Special Edition on Refugees and Technology." Access Now. 2 Dec. 2015. <https://tinyurl.com/kyp2lll>. 1 Aug. 2016.

Access Now. "Migrants, Surveillance and Human Rights: How to Escape the Security Paradigm." *YouTube*. 1 April 2016. <https://tinyurl.com/lpxe7jp>. 1 Aug. 2016.

Agar, Jon. *Constant Touch: A Global History of the Mobile Phone*. Icon Books, 2003.

Azoulay, Ariella. *The Civil Contract of Photography*. Zone Books, 2008.

Barad, Karen. *Meeting the Universe Halfway: Quantum Physics and the Entanglement of Matter and Meaning*. Duke University Press, 2007.

Barnett, Scot, and Casey Boyle. "Rhetorical Ontology, or, How to Do Things with Things." *Rhetoric, Through Everyday Things*. University of Alabama Press, 2016. 1–14.

Bennett, Jane. *Vibrant Matter: A Political Ecology of Things*. Duke University Press, 2010.

Berlant, Lauren. "Slow Death (Sovereignty, Obesity, Lateral Agency)." *Critical Inquiry* 33.4 (2007): 754–80.

Butler, Judith. "Bodily Vulnerability, Coalitions, and Street Politics." *Critical Studies* 37 (2014): 99–119.

———. *Frames of War: When Is Life Grievable?* Verso, 2009.

———. *Notes Toward a Performative Theory of Assembly*. Harvard University Press, 2015.

———. *Precarious Life: The Powers of Mourning and Violence*. Verso, 2004.

Duffield, Mark. "The Resilience of the Ruins: Towards a Critique of Digital Humanitarianism." *Resilience: International Policies, Practices and Discourses* (2016): 1–19.

Dykstra, Tiffany. "Assemblages of Syrian Suffering: Rhetorical Formations of Refugees in Western Media." *Language, Discourse & Society* 4.1(7) (2016): 31–48.

Favell, Andy. "How Technology Is Helping Deliver Aid to Syrian Refugees in the Middle East." *ComputerWeekly.com*. October 2015. <https://tinyurl.com/obm2yyc>. 1 Aug. 2016.

Graham, Luke. "How Smartphones Are Helping Refugees in Europe." *CNBC*. 11 Sept. 2015. <https://tinyurl.com/mwohcme>. 1 Aug. 2016.

Gillespie, Marie, et al. "Mapping Refugee Media Journeys: Smartphones and Social Media Networks." The Open University. 13 May 2016. <https://tinyurl.com/mehnqub>. 2 Aug. 2016.

Harney, Nicholas. "Precarity, Affect and Problem Solving with Mobile Phones by Asylum Seekers, Refugees and Migrants in Naples, Italy." *Journal of Refugee Studies* 26.4 (2013): 541–57.

International Committee of the Red Cross. "Trace the Face: People Looking for Missing Migrants in Europe." 27 Aug. 2015. <https://tinyurl.com/kqsl3mn>. 1 Aug. 2016.

International Rescue Committee. "What Refugees Ask When They Arrive in Europe." *Medium.* 16 Oct. 2015. <https://tinyurl.com/meef79u>. 1 Aug. 2016.

———. "What's in My Bag? What Refugees Bring When They Run for Their Lives." *Medium.* 4 Sept. 2015. <https://tinyurl.com/kbz9sru>. 15 July 2016.

Lacohée, Hazel, Nina Wakeford, and Ian Pearson. "A Social History of the Mobile Telephone with a View of Its Future." *BT Technology Journal* 21.3 (2003): 203–11.

Mackintosh, Eliza. "Syrians Post 'Goodbye' Messages from Eastern Aleppo." *CNN.* 1 Dec. 2016. <https://tinyurl.com/mwvcgwu>. 2 Jan. 2017.

Marr, Bernard. "Big Data, Technology and the Middle East Refugee Crisis." *Forbes.* 15 Oct. 2015. <https://tinyurl.com/l8zqnrk>. 15 July 2016.

Mirowski, Philip. *Never Let a Serious Crisis Go to Waste: How Neoliberalism Survived the Financial Meltdown.* Verso, 2013.

O'Malley, James. "Surprised That Syrian Refugees Have Smartphones? Sorry to Break This to You, but You're an Idiot." *Independent.* 7 Sept. 2015. <https://tinyurl.com/pwgmmbh>. 15 July 2016.

Puar, Jasbir. "Precarity Talk: A Virtual Roundtable with Lauren Berlin, Judith Butler, Bojana Cvejic, Isabell Lorey, Jasbir Puar, and Ana Vujanovic." *TDR: The Drama Review* 56.4 (2012): 163–77.

Reidy, Eric. "'Hello Father, The Boat Is Sinking, So I Will Die.'" *Medium.* 14 Oct. 2015. <https://tinyurl.com/ogmm5hv>. 3 Aug. 2016.

Rickert, Thomas. "Afterword: A Crack in the Cosmic Egg, Tuning into Things." *Rhetoric, Through Everyday Things.* Ed. Scot Barnett and Casey Boyle. University of Alabama Press, 2016. 226–31.

Schmitt, Paul, Daniel Iland, Elizabeth Belding, Brian Tomaszewski, Ying Xu, and Carleen Maitland. "Community-Level Access Divides: A Refugee Camp Case Study." June 2016, <https://tinyurl.com/mnf6yvd>. 1 March 2017.

Semmelroggen, Jan. "Explainer: The Difference Between Asylum Seekers, Refugees and Economic Migrants." *The Conversation.* 4 Aug. 2015. <https://tinyurl.com/q757fxt>. 1 March 2017.

Smith, Jennifer. "Selfies on the Shore: Refugees in Lifejackets Celebrate on the Beach After Reaching Greek Island Where Thousands Are Waiting to Enter Europe." *MailOnline.* 6 Sept. 2015. <https://tinyurl.com/pda54qu>. 3 Aug. 2016.

Sontag, Susan. *Regarding the Pain of Others.* Picador, 2003.

Teston, Christa. "Rhetoric, Precarity, and Health Technologies." *Rhetoric Society Quarterly* 46.3 (2016): 251–68.

Von Habekuß, Fritz, and Stefan Schmitt. "Why Do You Need a Mobile Phone?" *Zeit Online.* 1 Oct. 2015. <https://tinyurl.com/pn7u488>. 1 Aug. 2016.

Wall, Melissa, Madeline Otis Campbell, and Dana Janbek. "Syrian Refugees and Information Precarity." *New Media & Society* (2015): 1–15.

Watkins, Jerry, Larissa Hjorth, and Ilpo Hoskinen. "Wising Up: Revising Mobile Media in an Age of Smartphones." *Journal of Media and Cultural Studies* 26.5 (2012): 665–68.

Williams, Audra. "Stop Shaming Syrian Refugees for Using Cellphones." *The Daily Dot.* 11 Sept. 2015. <https://tinyurl.com/jvkgurw>. 1 July 2016.

CHAPTER 8

The Non/Image of the Regime of Distortion

ADELA C. LICONA

IN HIS APRIL 2017 speech to U.S. Customs and Border Protection agents in Nogales, Arizona, U.S. Attorney General Jeff Sessions proclaimed a new "Trump era" to signal the U.S. Department of Justice (DOJ) crackdown on immigration. In his prepared remarks, he characterized migrants as depraved and violent and explicitly referenced "brutal machete attacks and beheadings" (Sessions).[1] Seven years earlier, then-governor of Arizona Jan Brewer made a related claim in a Fox News television interview with Greta Van Susteren, stating that Arizona simply could not "afford all this illegal immigration and everything that comes with it, everything from the crime and to the drugs and the kidnappings and the extortion and the beheadings" (*On the Record*). Brewer further falsely asserted that "Arizona's law enforcement agencies have found bodies in the desert either buried or just lying out there that have been beheaded" (*Sunday Square Off*). Shortly after Brewer's false claims, *Washington Post* journalist Dana Milbank wrote of the "tall tales emerging from Arizona" to highlight the unsubstantiated nature of Brewer's fabrications. Brewer's claims of im/migrant-as-beheader in the Arizona desert were proven to be altogether untrue.[2] Neither the border patrol, nor migrant-rights organizations, nor local law enforcement officials have ever been able to confirm that im/migrants crossing into the Arizona desert have beheaded anyone there. However, truth was never the point. These false claims functioned such that migrants crossing into Arizona through Mexico were seen and believed to be beheading people there. The productive force of this fiction cultivated fear that, in turn, produced what I term a non/image that circulated and was sustained through a neocolonizing social imaginary with material consequences for the (newly) vulnerable. The non/image is manufactured as an imagining, a conjuring, a fear. I invoke the forward slash (/) in the term non/image as a tool of both/and thinking. Non/image, written as such, includes both "non" and "image." It is a written term that refuses the idea that an image ever offers all there is to see.[3] It is a visual and affective rhetorical claim without (the need for) an actual referent that functions as a taken-for-granted given-to-be-seen and circulates as precarious rhetorics.[4] Such precarious rhetorics work as disciplining delimitations to, among other things, practices of looking that make im/migrants knowable and able to be seen as always only criminals and culprits and that secure violent conditions of their sustained vulnerability.[5]

Brewer's lies functioned through long-established and powerful rhetorical tropes, including im/migrant-as-criminal and desert borderlands-as-sites-of-territorial insecurity. They maintained associations of im/migrant with criminal and desert with terrorizing terrain while also sharpening the public focus from imag(in)ed im/migrant-as-*alien* to im/migrant-as-*illegal* and on to im/migrant-as-*beheading-terrorist* capable of (and culpable for) undermining national and state security especially in the borderlands. U.S. Attorney General Sessions' reproduction of and reliance on such tropes is evidence of the non/image's rhetorical force. Non/images need only be imagined to circulate as terrorizing images that are sustainable and substitutable in transnational contexts through what I term the "regime of distortion" (ROD).[6]

In a ROD, non/images are produced and also rhetorically productive.[7] Their distorting powers reveal a hegemonic project of state violence through enduring terrorist/terrorizing imaginaries with evacuative[8] implications. They function differentially to assign distinct de/valuations and vulnerabilities to particular human and nonhuman bodies (including bodies of land and bodies of knowledge). Brewer's false claim is an updated devaluation and distortion (related to but different from the long-standing trope of im/migrant-as-alien and im/migrant-as-illegal) that produces a terrorizing non/image of im/migrant-as-terrorist.[9] The given-to-be-seen is a conjured image, a non/image to be imagined, believed to be, and, therefore, seen, felt, and feared as always only a threat. The non/image circulates as an intelligible if fictive subject that is now apparently informing policy at the U.S. DOJ. When she finally did address her fictitious claim, Brewer stated that *if* she did say it, it was an error. She worked to explain her "error" as connected to her fear for "Arizona" and her expressed concern that the violence of Mexican drug cartels would spill over from Mexico into U.S. territory ("Jan Brewer"). Brewer's claim shifted the focus and substituted the conjured culprit from im/migrant-as-*beheading-terrorist* to an even more locally relevant spectacle of im/migrant-as-*invading-narco-trafficking-druglord*. In this instance, im/migrants were quickly given-to-be-seen as suspected members of Mexican drug cartels invading the United States. The rhetorical function of this particular transference was to reference the *possibility-cum-likelihood* of a territorial and terrorizing invasion into the United States and thereby to argue for the need for ever-greater border militarization, control, surveillance, and securitization. Through Brewer's rhetorical claim, value and vulnerability get redistributed, whiteness gets recentered as both corpus and territory, and a distinction is made between bodies that matter and those that don't.

In this chapter, I focus on the non/image of the fictive subject of the rhetorical claim made by Jan Brewer in 2010, and also briefly identify the fictive subjects of related passed and proposed legislation in Arizona at that same time, to illustrate how the ROD is both produced by and produces precarious rhetorics of notable flexibility.[10] The ROD is undergirded here by logics of seeing and believing that function as disciplining systems of perception.[11] Arizona's ROD emerged in what Mary Bloodsworth-Lugo and Carmen Lugo-Lugo refer to as "the 9/11 project," which implies the social reconfigurations that continue to occur under the auspices of a now deep-seated antiterrorist agenda and the "imperial era" and racialized nationalism it *renews*.[12] Brewer's claim and the legislative measures it engendered functioned so that im/migrants and, in time, any who *might* be seen as "reasonably suspicious," were given-to-be-seen as terrorists or not seen at all. In the ROD, practices of looking are constrained by the given-to-be-seen that is itself disciplined by specular logics predicated on false and limiting binaries.[13] These logics operate such that images and imaginings of people can be seen as *either* eligible for personhood and thereby worthy of social life *or* ineligible and so worthy of social death.[14] Human value, as Lisa Cacho argues, is "made legible in relation to the deviant, the non-American, the non-citizen, the nonnormative, the pathologized, and the recalcitrant—the legally repudiated 'others'" (18). Non/images in a ROD come into focus and gain currency through the social imaginary wherein non-normative others are ultimately seen as terrorizing and, therefore, always racialized subjects to be contained, deported, debilitated, or otherwise eliminated, which, in turn, sediments the urgent need for protection of particular and particularly valued populations in Arizona.

Non/images produced in Arizona's ROD have functioned to constitute powerful rhetorical arguments—visual arguments—for new regulatory techniques and biotechnologies of border control with transnational reach. As Wendy Hesford argues, specular logics often conspire with panoptic logics to

structure and delimit ways of looking and seeing (18). This specular disciplining functions to produce conceptual closures that are achieved through the
hardening of ideological support for the expansion of rights for some and the
curtailment of rights for others. To better understand how a non/image is re/
produced, I look to its rhetorical force and function—what it does, how it gets
distributed, and with what consequences—as key to the precarious rhetorics I
propose here. I end with a call for new practices of looking and seeing through
what I propose as wild refractions.[15] Such wild refractions constitute a queer
visuality that moves beyond the delimitations of a dichotomous optic and
refuses the structuring devaluations of the regime's given-to-be-seen. Such
refractions produce specular and sensate multiplicity and radical openness.[16]
They call viewers *to look, see, feel,* and *relate* differently, and to be moved *to
do* differently.[17]

THE NON/IMAGE AS VISUAL RHETORICAL ARGUMENT

Next, I consider how dominant discourses, especially at times of heightened
nationalism and as espoused by the talking heads and authorities of the state,
circulate co-constitutively with images to construct visual rhetorical arguments and how, together, they have come to have particular and consequential meaning. I am specifically interested in Brewer's reference to a fiction and
how that fiction, in and through the ROD, worked to constitute and conjure a
someone who didn't exist but could still be seen in the Arizona desert. To better understand how that fictive subject functioned as a non/image in the social
imaginary to become the unstated premise of the argument for increased border militarization and the expansion of border controls through stridently
restrictive legislation, I turn to visual rhetorical studies. In their edited collection *Defining Visual Rhetorics,* Charles A. Hill and Marguerite Helmers
explore the rhetorical function and force of visual images and their reliance
on strategies of identification to persuade. They begin from an understanding
that visual and verbal expressions work together to prompt a response from
an audience and then move to consider whether or not the visual itself can
constitute an argument. In his contribution to the Hill and Helmers collection,
J. Anthony Blair concludes that visuals can indeed make arguments. Specifically, Blair invokes Aristotle to consider how the art of rhetoric and argument
continues to be identified with Western conceptualizations of modes of persuasion, including demonstration. Demonstration's instrument, he reminds
readers, is the enthymeme: an argument in which an unstated premise or
taken-for-granted assumption can be and is left out. An enthymeme depends

on a particular kind of audience participation that effects its own persuasion as the audience actively or passively fills in the omitted premise according to prevailing norms and the affective intensities that produce and sustain them. In a ROD, the conditions for enthymematic argument are carefully cultivated. The unstated premise of the visual argument constructed through the non/image is a devaluing distortion secured through the active manufacturing of fears, insecurities, and suspicions.[18] Such distortions require a taken-for-grantedness of the given-to-be-seen. Within a ROD, the non/image functions as a potent visual argument. As in a regime of deportation, the fear manufactured in a regime of distortion is urgent to its productive and reductive force.[19]

In the ROD, both the im/migrant and the proper citizen are rendered vulnerable, but with very distinct valuations. In their vulnerability, proper citizens are marked as nationalist subjects who are deemed worthy and in need of protection, while im/migrants are marked as devalued necropolitical subjects unworthy of protection. Especially in times of heightened nationalism and nativism, non-normative Others are made to appear as threatening to the safety and well-being of normative citizen-subjects. The non/image of the im/migrant as beheading terrorist operates by sedimenting insecurity to secure the norms of neoliberal governmentality, including what Kim Rygeil refers to as the "biopolitics of citizenship," or those governing practices that establish the valuation of those seen and deemed worthy as responsible individuals (i.e., the good white citizen-subject) and the devaluation of those seen as worthy of detainment or deportation (i.e., the im/migrant-as-terrorist subject). Neoliberal governmentality depends on and reproduces individualization that, in turn, produces always racialized subjects to protect and those to be protected from. This differentiation is what Judith Butler is addressing when discussing the "geopolitical distribution of corporeal vulnerability," a radically inequitable distribution in the service of a sense of safety for some. It is what Yen Le Espiritu is referring to in her discussions of "differential inclusion" (47) and what Cacho is referring to when she considers how the "interconnected processes of valorization, devaluation, and revaluation (i.e., race, gender, sexuality, class, nation, legality, etc.) . . . work interdependently to reify value and relations of inequality as normative, natural, and obvious" (17). It is also akin to what Nicholas Mirzoeff refers to as the "necropolitical regime of separation" (495). In a ROD, the culprit produced as non/image argues for—is evidence of—the need for greater measures of securitization. The enthymeme or premise left out of this visual argument is that im/migrants are always and only terrorizing.

For the *On the Record* interview, Van Susteren and Brewer were broadcast live from southern Arizona with saguaro cacti, the Sonoran Desert's indicator species, as their dramatic backdrop. As a site of territorial dispute and conquest, the Arizona desert is tied to racialized anxieties that are inferred by the focused-upon isolated landscape in which these two women appear alone together. Brewer's interview setting, territory violently secured through conquest, implied the need for protections of U.S. citizenry, and specifically of white women threatened by the specter of a racialized im/migrant terrorist in the seeming-to-be increasingly dangerous Arizona desert and suddenly vulnerable U.S. territory. The tropes of im/migrant as criminal and of the Sonoran terrain as a site of territorial insecurity are tied to long-standing historical, colonial, racialized anxieties about human bodies and bodies of land and knowledge.[20] Here, again, is an unstated premise in the argument of the need for greater securitization of these contested spaces and histories of settler colonialism and for protection of the citizen-subject who rightfully belongs therein.[21] It is implied that these women, the proper citizen-subjects and legitimate reproducers of the nation and its values, and this land, the birthright of the proper and legitimate citizen-subject, need protection from the terrorizing im/migrants who must be deterred, detained, debilitated, deported, or otherwise made to encounter death-inducing conditions in terrain that is purposively cultivated as inhospitable and uninhabitable.

The TV interview included a compressed box zooming on and off the screen with B-roll footage of protestors, predominantly Latin@s, marching in the streets against anti-immigrant discourses and then-pending regressive legislation.[22] The juxtaposition of these images—two white women citizen-subjects, and a seemingly unruly mob of people of color—imag(in)ed a growing, disproportionate, and immanent racialized threat. Brewer's presence functions as a claim of rightful belonging for those rational individual citizen-subjects of the neoliberal state, and the footage of the protesters functions as evidence of the unbelonging of im/migrants as unruly mobs (incomprehensible in the neoliberal imaginary as individuals).[23] Such a scene reproduces the binary between civilization and chaos that undergirds settler colonial project(ion)s and generates what Frantz Fanon refers to as "aesthetic forms of respect for the status quo" (3). The status quo that becomes urgent to maintain disregards the fact that before the Treaty of Hidalgo, the earlier inhabitants of these terrains were indigenous peoples and Latin@s now broadly criminalized or otherwise erased.

As Susana Loza argues, the cultural production of the alien-Other reveals national anxieties about invasion and conquest (54). Tracing the production of non/images in Arizona's ROD illuminates their connection to settler colonialism.[24] Non/images circulate in this regime as extensions of colonial racial formations and fears that rely on colorized hierarchies to organize and divide life and death. The productions and assemblages of the non/image in the ROD are part of what Mirzoeff refers to as "a complex of visuality" that is itself implicated in the power geometries of the heteropatriarchical and settler colonial nation—always racialized, always sexed (476).[25] In this case, normative counterparts to these immigrant-subjects, those whom Brewer invokes and implies when she speaks on behalf of "Arizona," were simultaneously constructed in the social imaginary as the good citizen-subjects belonging in "Arizona" as good citizen-territory, both worthy and in need of state protection.[26]

Brewer's false claim functioned through the media to produce conditions for believing, seeing, and feeling.[27] As Sara Ahmed suggests, "the more signs circulate, the more affective they become" (45). In becoming more affective, their stickiness is revealed as related to resemblance—it sticks to any and all that resemble those monsters represented in and by the non/image.[28] Anti-immigrant sentiments that had been circulating in the state were sedimented in the rhetorical trope of im/migrant-as-beheading terrorist, which functioned to invoke distorted images and imaginings with staying power that could stick, but that could also be rather easily supplanted and, therefore, updated as needed. The non/image reveals itself, then, as a potent visual argument that can be made again and again.

PRODUCTIVE AND REDUCTIVE ASSEMBLAGES

The production of the non/image is secured and sustained within the ROD through fear implied and induced by authorized voices and visions as well as through legislative measures and media productions—all with conjuring powers. With each updated rhetorical trope, non/images were reassembled and reimagined and new terrorist-types requiring new measures and technologies of control. Such updated tropes introduce a constellation of newly distorted (and newly vulnerable) culprits to imagine, to believe in, to see, sense, feel, and fear.[29]

Distortions reached beyond subjects to space as well. The Arizona desert was and remains deadly terrain but *not* necessarily for the good citizen-subject of Brewer's expressed concern. Rather, through redistributed vulnerabilities, it is increasingly precarious for crossing migrants who through various borderlands policies were being, and continue to be, herded to and through the desert's most dangerous parts. According to Coalición de Derechos Humanos, a grassroots migrant rights organization, for the 2009–10 reporting period, the Pima County Medical Examiner's Office reported one of the highest numbers of migrant deaths resulting for those attempting to cross the desert's death corridor: 253.[30] Brewer's interview setting depicts a desert expanse of stark beauty; the focus is on a desert-scape as home territory rather than as death-inducing terrain for crossing im/migrants who routinely die in their efforts to cross. Such terrain is a place not experienced or seen by non-im/migrants and so is a "nowhere" in the dominant social imaginary. Here Butler's question comes to mind: "If someone is lost, and that person is not someone, then what and where is the loss?" (32). In a ROD, the loss of a "not someone" cannot be perceived and, because it occurs in a veritable nowhere, is not seen as a loss. The precarity at work here is such that an im/migrant subject can be seen as a circulating terrorist or won't be seen at all. It is cultivated fear and suspicion of the state-manufactured fiction and its non/image that serve to shift the focus away from the inhumane and increasingly precarious conditions of the Sonoran Desert for crossing migrants and from the reality of their deaths there.

As Cacho argues, media provides the tools that "enable us to see and simultaneously deny what we are seeing" (10). Through the distorting production of the non/image, Brewer affectively and effectively displaced the focus from im/migrants dying in the desert to those citizen subjects imagined as threatened by a fiction there. Those actively and actually made vulnerable in this desert terrain were imagined only and always as terrorists encroaching on space that was treated as threatened territory rightfully belonging to white U.S. citizen-subjects. Distortions were produced by and productive of generalized fear, which, as Butler notes, "works in tandem with the shoring-up of the sovereign state and the suspension of civil liberties" (39). Fear functioned through the ROD to produce powerful non/images circulating as arguments for curtailed human rights for those given-to-be-seen as terrorists and territorial invaders.

LEGISLATING DISTORTIONS

The circulation of the non/image served the emerging xenophobic climate and a regressive legislative agenda that counted on perpetually manufactured nativism as fear of non-normative Others of always only terrorizing and territorializing possibilities.[31] As Butler notes, it is at those times when the nation and its borders are recognized as more porous and permeable than what was previously imagined (something implied in Brewer's desert interview) that a radical desire for security—often accompanied by racial/ized hysteria—ensues (39). At such dispersals of fear, Butler argues, "everyone is free to imagine and identify the source of terror" (39).

The non/image circulated throughout the regressive legislative landscape of Arizona's Forty-Ninth Legislature. Conservative Arizona lawmakers made terrorists of im/migrants as well as any and all who could be imagined as "reasonably suspicious," including Latin@s, LGBTQ individuals, pregnant women of color, students of color, and teachers of color.[32] The disciplining and consequential effects in a ROD for anyone who is believed to be an im/migrant or otherwise seen as reasonably suspicious are central to Mirzoeff's discussion of the racialized divide that is instantiated any time a "citizen looks at a person suspected of being a migrant" (495).

SB 1070, Arizona's infamous anti-immigration law, introduced and stabilized the notion of the "reasonably suspicious" as common knowledge. Nonwhite bodies were broadly and increasingly feared and surveilled at this time, which occurred simultaneously with the legislated extension of the reach of police officers and everyday "citizens" as deputized immigration officials rendering the circulation of those able to be seen as "reasonably suspicious" even more vulnerable.[33] Before and especially since SB 1070, legislative proposals have produced a constellation of suspected terrorist types and tropes, from those given-to-be-seen as beheading-terrorists to mothers-of-color imagined as producers of babies-of-color as weapons (described in the "anchor baby" legislative proposal)[34]; to the intellectual imagined as a revolutionary racist invader (addressed in HB 2281, which banned Mexican-American studies); to the transgender person imagined as only and everywhere deviant (identified in SB 1045, the "bathroom bill"); and to those imagined as homosexual destroyers of family values (targeted by SB 1188, the "adoption preference bill"). Non/images were reassembled and recirculated as monstrous Others throughout and beyond the Forty-Ninth Legislature.

The social imaginary fuels and is fueled by such reassemblages, often manufactured from the remains of previously conjured monstrosities. The power of the non/image as precarious rhetoric is in its capacity to substitute one terrorizing type for another with redistributed vulnerabilities and differentiated valuations.[35] Cacho's concept of "transparent recognition" is at work in the transference of terrorizing traits across all the fictive productions that followed in the Arizona legislature (9). Non/images are reproduced through and as precarious rhetorics that, following Ahmed on affective economy, are effects of their own circulation. They stick in consequential ways to imagined and particular human and nonhuman bodies. In Arizona's ROD, the "reasonably suspicious" are imagined and seen as non-white, brown and black bodies, brown and black knowledges, queer, and all non-normative Others. The reasonably suspicious are racialized, pathologized, and criminalized to effectively divide the normative white citizen of belonging from the non-normative and unbelonging noncitizen of color.[36]

Through the ROD in Arizona, the alien morphed into a constellation of other legislated culprits that circulated as threatening and terrorizing non/images in the social imaginary. Brewer's assertion of im/migrants-as-beheading-terrorists and of headless bodies in the Arizona desert operated through the ROD to justify new practices of surveillance, biopolitics, and increased border militarization, to reassert the state's claim to land, to support an ethno-normative and singular vision of history, and to curtail the rights of any body or body of knowledge imagined and re/assembled as a terrorizing threat to the state. Brewer's claim was evidence of the argument she made for hyper-militarization and for an expanded role for the local police force to serve with at least partial authority of federal immigration officials. The legislative measures this inspired affectively and effectively moved the public to *productively* see conjured violences as real and as instigated by im/migrants who could only be reductively understood as *always already* and *always only* a threat to the safety and well-being of the rightful citizens of the state and its resources.

Then-governor Brewer, the legislature, and the media, together, populated the reservoir of social imaginaries with interchangeable non/images, thereby regulating what could appear and disappear, with repercussions for what could and should be seen, heard, felt, and even imagined. Importantly, those who could not or would not "see" the visual non/image of the im/migrant as always only terrorist became suspect themselves as not good citizens.[37] Images have long functioned as normative forces of racialized and spatialized "American nationalisms, cosmopolitanisms, and neoliberal global politics" (Hesford 3). The non/image that corresponded to Brewer's claim was produced to become instantly legible as a roaming terrorist in the social imaginary. Even if Brewer had wanted to debunk her deception, its fear-inflected circulation had already served a powerful rhetorical function.[38] The named citizenry of Arizona—those worthy of protection and social life—were being asked to see and to guard against unsubstantiated threats constructed as reasonable and as menacingly around every corner.[39] Seeing Others as suspicious appears in the ROD to be necessary ocular practices of the good citizen-subject lest they become reasonably suspicious themselves. The ROD functions, then, in and as the public sphere, which, as Butler notes, is "constituted in part by what can appear, and the regulation of the sphere of appearance is one way to establish what will count as reality, and what will not" (xx). Underpinning my ideas here regarding the non/image is a necessary reversal of the axiom from "seeing is believing" to "believing is seeing."[40] I work instead from an understanding that looking and seeing are always rhetorically mediated. The non/image was reassembled as the monstrous face of any brown or black, queer, student, teacher, im/migrant, trans*, non-normative Other so that the given-to-be-seen was a fiction in and of the desert rather than the reality of migrants dying there.

In carefully distinguishing transparent recognition from misrecognition, Cacho offers a helpful way to understand how people can come to be seen as "a fictional figure that people have made real and consequential," which can, in turn, provide justification for social abandonment and state-sanctioned violences (3). State action and intervention are seen as necessary and even benevolent curtailments in the face of terrorist and terrorizing subjects. In the context of a fear-inflected carceral state and a militarized border, this means always only seeing im/migrants as criminals and would-be terrorists. It also means *not seeing* the desert terrain as made increasingly perilous for im/migrants.

INTERSTITIAL REVISIONINGS AND REVERBERATIONS: CONSIDERING WILD REFRACTIONS AND RELATIONAL PROXIMITIES

My aim here has been to demonstrate the process and productive, even evacuative power of precarious rhetorics in the ROD and the specular logics that structure looking practices therein. It is there that the imagined non/image circulates as a given-to-be-seen and functions as an argument for the entrenchment of normative perceptions and perspectives as forces for new technologies of securitization and reinforced regulatory techniques.[41] As Hesford notes, "audiences draw on a host of historical associations, cultural narratives, structures of feeling and belief, and rhetorical expectations in their engagement with images as texts and their contexts" (57). I began with the always already monstrous, mythical, and fictional "(illegal) alien" as a criminalizing distortion that now insidiously extends to all non-normative bodies, their histories, their knowledges, and their spatialized contexts.[42] Assemblages of non/images shift in these affective and visual economies with implications for the promotion and production of life and "bare life." In focusing on the production of the non/image, I have worked to understand how a claim that could never be substantiated could function with such rhetorical force. Norms operate by producing not only ideals but also, importantly, "images of the less than human, in the guise of the human, to show how the less than human disguises itself, and threatens to deceive" (Butler 146). Here, then, is the rhetorical power of the non/image and its precarity: it can be made to be anything and anyone of un/belonging according to normative and nationalist revisions and neocolonizing imaginaries. As Butler also notes, "normative schemes work through providing no image, no name, no narrative, so that there never was a life" (146). And if there was a life, it gets erased, marginalized, or made terrorizing in and through the ROD. I have followed the production and even momentary stabilizations of such distortions and their newly imag(in)ed culprits in search of new practices of looking and seeing. Such practices must take into consideration the force and function of hegemonic viewpoints and normative perceptions as well as the oppositional specular logics of affirmation and denial upon which they are predicated.

I am moved to ask: What does it take to refuse the conceptual closure that precludes more than one way of looking and seeing and that enforces specular logics that are predicated on false and limiting binaries? What does it take to shift from the singular to the multiple? What if by looking at the particularized details of life, we simultaneously saw and felt the global forces of its production or prohibition? Practices of looking that allow the given-to-be-seen, in this case of the im/migrant, to be looked at beyond the either/or and, so, to be perceived and experienced as not only and not always pathological, criminal, or terrorizing. The insights of transnational, women of color, indigenous, and third-space feminism and the queer world-making possibilities they can inspire, particularly with regard to relational perceptions, relating across difference, and engagements with multiplicity, are vital to the search for new practices of looking, seeing, and sensing. I find it urgent in the expanding ROD and the rise in authoritarianism to answer Ruby Tapia's call to illuminate the (production of the) invisible pictures or non/images produced in dominance and to look at the multiple interstices or spaces between the production, circulation, and consumption of images and the normative practices of believing as seeing that produce them as reality.[43] To do so requires a recognition of the multiplicity of "material histories, social relations, and structural conditions" (Cacho 9) as well as of revisioning through refraction the relational interstices between assembled non/images, dominant discourses, norms, media productions, and social imaginaries. By refraction I mean to illuminate a kaleidoscopic multiplicity. The bent light of wild refractions creates conditions for dimensional illuminations and dispersals that depend upon radical openness and new ways of relating. Refractions can be relational modes of perceiving that, in complicating the hegemony of a singular ethno-normative historical record, serve to dislodge normative narratives and the hegemonic viewpoints they sediment to thereby effect new modes of relational perceptions and re-memberings.[44] A politics of wild refraction and relational proximity take place in the interstitial or third spaces between production, circulation, and consumption of non/images to call attention to that which has been made seemingly singular, naturally divided, and unrelated. Perhaps the task at hand is, as Butler proposes, "to establish modes of public seeing and hearing [and, I add, feeling] that might well respond to the cry of the [non]human within the sphere of appearance [where] the trace of the cry has become hyperbolically inflated to rationalize a gluttonous nationalism, or fully obliterated, where both alternatives turn out to be the same" (147). Experiences of seeing and practices of looking, then, must not and cannot be reductive, oppositional, or homogenizing acts, but rather, must be linked to a progressive visual politics that through a third-space borderlands framework rejects either/or ocular logics. To look and to see differently, and more, we must imagine, feel, and relate otherwise to one another, to histories and myths, to things, and to places. Key to these emergent conceptualizations is a deep engagement with other/Others' histories and with what Macarena Gómez-Barris refers to as "unbridled" life and forms of resisting and living otherwise, that can move us through contradictions and contestations to dislodge conceptual closures and become open to possibility (3). Through refraction and relational proximity, we can come to see and understand that our imag(in)ing of the Other must be decolonized. Perhaps Samera Esmeir's call to forge "concrete alliances with human beings [and, I add, nonhuman others] who await not our recognition but our participation in their struggles" might help us not only to affectively visualize but also to act on as of yet unimagined coalitional possibilities without a mandate for acquisition, extraction, or conquest (1545; see also Leanne Simpson). And maybe that is the urgency before us—to learn to live in relational proximity and to see through refraction multiplicities of bodies, bodies of land, and bodies of knowledge and not be terrorized by them.

Perhaps the distortion of the ROD itself is not the problem. Rather, it is its consequence of imposing and necessitating neat social orderings as deep divisions that create the conditions for distance from and opposition to Others. The shifts required of a cultivated and relational proximity[45] can produce their own distortions, and perhaps that is what is needed: more distortion, not less. To proximity and its distortions, I add refraction as it relates to what Gómez-Barris refers to as the "submerged" perspective, a distortion that can "differently perceive local terrains as sources of knowledge, vitality, and livability" (1). Such a perspective is a relational one that produces meaningful distortions through both relational proximity and refraction. Maybe new perceptions, touching proximities, and particularizations, never disarticulated from larger contexts and distances, can be accessed through refraction and relational proximity and their wild possibilities.[46]

To more fully consider the possibilities of wild refractions, I move from my previous work on notions of reverso[47] and the refracted gaze of multiplicity (as distinct from an inverted or oppositional gaze) through a politics of refusal[48] to a kind of counter-visuality[49] that rejects neocolonizing images and evacuating imaginaries that delimit what can be seen, known, and felt in a ROD. I want to consider a politics of looking, seeing, and sensing that, as Kaja Silverman argues, takes place at the threshold of the visible, and that Butler imagines as a practice of a sensate democracy. These are productive rather than reductive practices that treat the eye as an organ of touch to cultivate intimacies of awareness and feeling as well as moving possibilities and mobilizing potentials. Wild refractions and relational proximities, and the possibilities they imply, include the sensorial and the affective and call for particular attention to that which has been made seemingly inconsequential or otherwise erased. Such a politics of wild refraction is predicated on a relational rejection of a singular history and of the exceptional subject. It refuses the pull to create exceptional or even necessarily respectable subjects in order to avoid the good/bad dichotomy that is reinforced in a ROD. Perhaps wild refractions are related to the kind of intersectional and coalitional—interconnected—resistances, reverberations, and resonances re/emerging in this era of rising authoritarianism.[50] And perhaps, following Cacho, wild refractions and relational proximities can create the conditions for a kind of queer visuality that is related to a politics of deviance, and I add of decolonization, which is itself about criteria for acknowledging that which has been concealed and congealed in a ROD in order to recognize, reckon with, and see that which has been rendered invisible, alien, monstrous, or "dead-to-others" (166–68).[51] In her poem "Alien," Gloria Anzaldúa asks, "What if I loved the Alien, looked it in the face, said, 'Yes you are a part of me I cannot deny you, I cannot turn my back on you'" (33).[52] Yes, what if. . . ?

NOTES

The author thanks Eithne Luibhéid, Jamie A. Lee, Maritza Cárdenas, Karma Chávez, Ken McAllister, Ana Milena Ribero, Elizabeth Bentley, Anushka Miriam Swan Peres, Julie Swarstad Johnson, and her coeditors for their insights throughout this project.

1. Sessions's admonition with regard to the "Trump Era" was delivered in Arizona just one month after Trump's March 2017 "Executive Order Protecting the Nation from Foreign Terrorist Entry into the United States," which functioned to produce fear and suspicion of any persons entering the U.S. territory from countries framed as terrorist-sending. While he did not do so in his spoken remarks, Sessions's prepared remarks refer to the Arizona border as a "sliver of land" and to im/migrants as "filth." Such conceptualizations reinforce the tropes I have noted here. By referencing a "sliver of land," Session is feeding settler

state anxieties about ongoing territorial occupations; by referencing "filth," he is relying on another powerful rhetorical trope that pathologizes migrants as non-hygienic and as a public health menace. For a discussion of the related notions of virus and of the viral, see Coskan-Johnson in this collection.

2. While the media coverage of the total lack of veracity of Brewer's claim was not nearly as robust as the coverage of the claim itself, there were multiple media sources that reported on the fact of its untruth. See, for example, *Politico* (September 8, 2010; September 10, 2010); and *Washington Post* (July 11, 2010).

3. See Jafari Allen's explanation of the forward slash or "stroke" that can function to conjoin and to actively push terms apart toward "sharper focus."

4. For an extended treatment of the concept of the given-to-be-seen, see Silverman.

5. While "scapegoat" is a concept often used to describe how im/migrants are treated and seen in the public realm, I am persuaded by de Genova's use of "culprit." I think its relation to culpability through nativist rhetorics makes im/migrants appear culpable for conditions that can come to be seen as of their own making, thereby invisibilizing the macroeconomic and transnational forces that produce displacements and propel migrations.

6. I am indebted to the scholarship of Nicholas de Genova and collaborations with Marta M. Maldonado as these helped me to conceive of the ROD.

7. See W. J. T. Mitchell's discussion of the productive force of looking and of vision/visuality. He emphasizes the role of the image in constituting social reality and argues for understanding images as equal to language.

8. See Gómez-Barris.

9. The Alien and Sedition Acts were passed by the Federalist Congress of 1789, which produced the categories of "alien" and "alien enemy" and resulted in im/migrant deportations and obstacles to im/migrant voting. Interestingly, these laws also addressed those who sought to "procure any insurrection, riot, unlawful assembly." These acts were followed by the passage of Espionage and Sedition Acts, which, as Luibhéid notes, "gave government wide powers to crack down on . . . [those] considered 'undesirable' in some way" (14).

10. For other examples of regressive legislation proposed or passed by the Forty-Ninth Legislature, see also SB 1309 (required parental consent for students to participate in, among other things, sex education), and SB 1266 (which made youth sexting a class 2 misdemeanor punishable by up to four months in jail). For more thorough treatments of these legislative measures, see Brandzel; Licona and Soto; Luibhéid, Andrade, and Stevens; Chin; Russell.

11. For more on perception, see Sullivan's discussion of a "somatechnics of perception." She argues that "matter is inextricable from the I/eye that perceives it. In other words, perception makes 'matter' matter. It makes some-thing that is a no-thing become and as such it makes 'it' intelligible" (300).

12. While 9/11 is a marker of material significance, it is important not to isolate 9/11 as something new or altogether anomalous but rather to understand it as a moment of historic conjuncture and renewal. For more on the effects of post-9/11 policy on im/migrants, see de Genova.

13. For a discussion on specular logics, see Silverman.

14. See Cacho.

15. I refer to refraction as a consequence that is connected to the concept of reverso that I introduce in *Zines in Third Space: Radical Cooperation and Borderlands Rhetorics*. There I was working through ways of refusing the delimitations of binaries to better understand and engage multiplicity. I see now how my earlier idea of refraction is connected to looking and queer world-making practices.

16. For an excellent read on sensorial refusals, see Vargas.

17. I am inspired here by Avery Gordon's work on spectral hauntings and the idea that what has been "concealed is very much alive" (xvi). With the non/image, it is the diminishing reductions that have been concealed to produce a given-to-be-seen for the social imagi-

nary of a one-dimensional spectral figure that is worthy of slow and social death. Gordon argues that the hauntings of the concealed call us to action because "ultimately haunting is about how to transform a shadow of a life into an undiminished life whose shadows touch softly in the spirit of peaceful reconciliation" (208). In the ROD, this means a call to propose and develop new ways of looking and seeing that refuse the reductive distortions that produce and are produced by precarious rhetorics.

18. For an engagement through popular culture and video games of the dehumanizing effects of "the monstrous," see Kocurek.

19. For a further discussion of the consequences of fear, see de Genova.

20. See Saldaña-Portillo on the spatial productions of racial nationalism.

21. For an excellent discussion of spatialized concealments and racial-sexual differentiations made therein, see McKittrick.

22. My use of the "@" for "Latin@" follows those scholars and activists who use it to refuse the naturalized gendered dichotomy between masculinized and feminized terms, to acknowledge the role of language in maintaining such always-hierarchical dualisms, and to explicitly recognize gender fluidity.

23. See Ana Ribero on the possibilities in a politics of (non)belonging.

24. As Poole notes, monstrous Others in and of the United States are historic productions that have been present "from colonial times to the present" (4). These monsters, existing in and as non/images, reflect historic cultural anxieties as well as national obsessions and traumas.

25. On power geometries, see Massey.

26. For an illuminating discussion of the construction of "aggressive heterosexual patri[ots]," see Puar and Rai 117.

27. For a creative engagement with the consequences of failing to join in particular ways of seeing, see Cole.

28. For more on stickiness and feared bodies, see Puar.

29. For a discussion of "spectacle [as] capital accumulated to the point where it becomes image," see Debord 23.

30. Special thanks to Reyna Araibi, Kat Rodriguez, and Robin Reineke from the Colibrí Center for Human Rights for sharing the Pima County Medical Examiner's listing of border-crossing decedents whose remains have been recovered in the Arizona desert.

31. In the midst of Arizona's regressive legislative measure and in efforts to secure support for "anchor baby legislation," Arizona state legislator Russell Pearce introduced the related trope and non/image of the "illegal anchor baby" as homegrown-terrorist-in-the-making to shift from one non/image to another (in this case, the non/image is that of an illegal anchor baby, which does not and cannot exist) to sustain the fear of the Latina im/migrant in particular and to move state conversations to the questioning of jus solis. Such conversations were undertaken in the ROD, which served as the breeding ground for the notion of im/migrant-as-always-terrorist.

32. As Amy Brandzel points out, "all types of nonnormative experiences, identities, and bodies" are routinely scapegoated in defense of normative citizenship, which she notes is always exclusionary. She goes on to observe how the scope of such laws and legislative measures (as the ones I am addressing here) reveals the fear and threat felt by "proper" or "legitimate" citizen-subjects and the lengths to which they will thereby go to defend normative citizenship (2).

33. For more on the conflation of brown and black bodies with terrorists, see also Bloodsworth-Lugo and Lugo-Lugo.

34. For an elucidating discussion of this proposal, which conjured the image of baby-as-lethal-terrorist weapon, see Bloodsworth-Lugo and Lugo-Lugo.

35. For a provocative engagement with the idea of a "9/11 project" as a project that constructs im/migrants, and particularly Latina im/migrants, as threats to national security, see Bloodsworth-Lugo and Lugo-Lugo.

36. For a discussion of the "ascendancy of whiteness," see the introduction in Puar. For discussion of immigration control as key to the renegotiation of whiteness, see Luibhéid 6.

37. For an extended discussion on the ideological construction through which we see and know, see Mirzoeff's argument through which he underscores the people's consent to the status quo.

38. For more on the little difference such debunkings make, see Sturken and Cartwright.

39. For more on the context of growing fears wherein "individuals are asked to be on guard but not told what to be on guard against," see Butler 39.

40. For an article-length engagement with this reversal, see Morris.

41. As I finish this chapter, the false and fear-inflected rhetoric of Donald Trump has continued to re/produce terrorizing images of Muslims, Mexicans, transgender people, witch hunts, fake news, rigged elections, and more.

42. See news on Maricopa County Sheriff Joe Arpaio's disregard for judicial calls to stop his immigration enforcement patrols and to desist in racially profiling brown people, and on his failure to inform his officers about the judicial injunction.

43. Kaja Silverman's discussion of representational coordinates is helpful here as I believe the representational coordinates that produce the "given-to-be-seen" must necessarily be remixed in these wild refractions and queer ways of looking and seeing (221).

44. I am inspired by Silverman's suggestion that ways of looking informed through other people's memories can achieve the cessation of seeing an "alien other which must be colonized, exoticized, or phobically repelled" to achieve the thrilling prospect of another set of cultural possibilities. It requires, Silverman argues, a "cultural displacement, an estrangement from one's self, and from one's national coordinates" (192).

45. See Hayward on radical proximity.

46. My sense of wild here has been reignited by Jack Halberstam's discussion of queer wildness and its radical possibilities as conceptualized through an articulation of their own thinking with the works of José E. Muñoz and Tavia Nyong'o.

47. See Licona, *Zines in Third Space: Radical Cooperation and Borderlands Rhetorics*.

48. I have been inspired by Audra Simpson's work to think about the practice of a politics of refusal, which insists on multiple views from elsewhere/s.

49. See Mirzoeff.

50. On the reach and im/possibilities of the coalitional, see Chávez.

51. See Deborah Vargas on *lo sucio* as a Latino queer analytic.

52. For an extended engagement with Anzaldúa's *Light in the Dark / Luz en lo Oscuro* and with her relationship to the monstrous, see Bernadette Marie Calafell's *Monstrosity, Performance, and Race in Contemporary Culture*.

WORKS CITED

Agamben, Georgio. *Homo Sacer: Sovereign Power and Bare Life.* Stanford University Press, 1998.

Ahmed, Sara. *The Cultural Politics of Emotion.* Routledge, 2004.

Alien and Sedition Acts. The Avalon Project: Documents in Law, History and Diplomacy. <http://avalon.law.yale.edu/18th_century/alien.asp>.

Allen, Jafari S. "Black/Queer/Diaspora at the Current Conjuncture." *GLQ: A Journal of Lesbian and Gay Studies* 18.2–3 (2012): 211–48.

Anzaldúa, Gloria. *Light in the Dark / Luz en lo Oscuro: Rewriting Identity, Spirituality, Reality.* Ed. AnaLouise Keating. Duke University Press, 2016.

Blair, J. Anthony. "The Rhetoric of Visual Arguments." *Defining Visual Rhetorics*. Ed. Charles A. Hill and Marguerite Helmers. Lawrence Erlbaum, 2004. 41–61.

Bloodsworth-Lugo, Mary K., and Carmen R. Lugo-Lugo *Project(ing) 9/11: Productions of Race, Gender, and Citizenship in Recent Hollywood Films*. Rowan & Littlefield, 2014.

Brandzel, Amy L. *Against Citizenship: The Violence of the Normative*. University of Illinois Press, 2016.

Butler, Judith. *Precarious Life: The Powers of Mourning and Violence*. Verso, 2006.

Cacho, Lisa Marie. *Social Death: Racialized Rightlessness and the Criminalization of the Unprotected*. New York University Press, 2012.

Calafell, Bernadette Marie. *Monstrosity, Performance, and Race in Contemporary Culture*. Peter Lang, 2015.

Chávez, Karma. *Queer Migration Politics: Activist Rhetoric and Coalitional Possibilities*. University of Illinois Press, 2013.

Chin, Gabriel J. "SB 1070." Department of Mexican American & Raza Studies, University of Arizona, 2 Sept. 2010. Lecture.

Coalición de Derechos Humanos. <http://www.derechoshumanosaz.net/>.

Cole, Teju. "Fable." *The New Inquiry*. 1 Aug. 2016.

Colibrí Center for Human Rights. < http://www.colibricenter.org/>.

Debord, Guy. *The Society of the Spectacle*. Zone Books, 1995.

de Genova, Nicholas. "The Production of Culprits: From Deportability to Detainability in the Aftermath of 'Homeland Security.'" *Citizenship Studies* 11.5 (Nov. 2007): 421–48.

Esmeir, Samera. "On Making Dehumanization Possible." *PMLA* 121.5 (2006): 1544–52.

Espiritu, Yen Le. *Home Bound: Filipino American Lives Across Cultures, Communities, and Countries*. University of California Press, 2003.

Fanon, Frantz. *The Wretched of the Earth*. Trans. Richard Philcox. Grove Press, 2004.

Gómez-Barris, Macarena. *The Extractive Zone: Social Ecologies and Decolonial Perspectives*. Duke University Press, 2017.

Gordon, Avery F. *Ghostly Matters: Haunting and the Sociological Imagination*. University of Minnesota Press, 2008.

Halberstam, Jack. "Wildness, Loss, and Death." *Social Text* 32.4 (2014): 137–48.

Hayward, Eva. "Enfolded Vision: Refracting the Love Life of the Octopus." *Octopus: A Visual Studies Journal* 1 (2005): 29–44.

Hesford, Wendy S. *Spectacular Rhetorics: Human Rights Visions, Recognitions, Feminisms*. Duke University Press, 2011.

Hill, Charles A., and Marguerite H. Helmers. *Defining Visual Rhetorics*. Lawrence Erlbaum, 2004.

"Jan Brewer: I Made 'Error' in Beheadings Claim." *CBS News*. 3 Sept. 2010. <http://www.cbsnews.com/news/jan-brewer-i-made-error-in-beheadings-claim/>.

Kocurek, Carly A. "Who Hearkens to the Monster's Scream? Death, Violence, and the Veil of the Monstrous in Video Games." *Visual Studies* 30.1 (2015): 79–89.

Licona, Adela C. *Zines in Third Space: Radical Cooperation and Borderlands Rhetoric*. State University of New York Press, 2012.

Licona, Adela C., and Sandra K. Soto. "HB 2281: Key Points, Political Implication, and Local Mobilizations." *Encyclopedia of Latino/as in Politics, Social Movements, and Law*. Ed. Suzanne Oboler and Deena González. Vol. 2. Oxford University Press, 2016.

Loza, Susana. "Playing Alien in Post-Racial Times." *Monster Culture in the 21st Century*. Ed. Marina Levina and Diem My T. Bui. Bloomsbury, 2013. 53–72.

Luibhéid, Eithne. *Entry Denied: Controlling Sexuality at the Border*. University of Minnesota Press, 2002.

Luibhéid, Eithne, Rosi Andrade, and Sally Stevens. "Intimate Attachments and Migrant Deportability: Lessons from Undocumented Mothers Seeking Benefits for Citizen Children." *Ethnic and Racial Studies* 41.1 (2018): 17–35.

Marks, Laura U. *The Skin of the Film: Intercultural Cinema, Embodiment, and the Senses*. Duke University Press, 2000.

Massey, Doreen. "A Global Sense of Place." *Marxism Today* (1991): 24–29.

McKittrick, Katherine. *Demonic Grounds: Black Women and the Cartographies of Struggle*. University of Minnesota Press, 2006.

Milbank, Dana. "Headless Bodies and Other Immigration Tall Tales in Arizona." *The Washington Post*. 11 July 2010.

Mirzoeff, Nicholas. "The Right to Look." *Critical Inquiry* 37 (Spring 2011): 473–96.

Mitchell, W. J. T. *What Do Pictures Want?: The Lives and Loves of Images*. University of Chicago Press, 2005.

Morris, Errol. *Believing Is Seeing: Observations on the Mysteries of Photography*. Penguin, 2011.

On the Record with Greta Van Susteren. Fox News Channel. 16 June 2010. Television.

Poole, Scott W. *Monsters in America: Our Historical Obsession with the Hideous and Haunting*. Baylor University Press, 2011.

Puar, Jasbir. *Terrorist Assemblages: Homonationalism in Queer Times*. Duke University Press, 2007.

Puar, Jasbir K., and Amit S. Rai. "Monster, Terrorist, Fag: The War on Terrorism and the Production of Docile Patriots." *Social Text* 20.3 (2002): 117–48.

Ribero, Ana Milena. 2016. "Citizenship and Undocumented Youth: An Analysis of the Rhetorics of Migrant-Rights Activism in Neoliberal Contexts." PhD diss., University of Arizona.

Russell, Stephen T. "'Sexting' and SB 1266: Why the Law Matters for Families and Youth." *From Policy to Practice: Frances McClelland Institute for Children, Youth, and Families* 1 (2011): 1–4.

Rygeil, Kim. *Globalizing Citizenship*. UBC Press, 2011.

Saldaña-Portillo, María Josefina. *Indian Given: Racial Geographies across Mexico and the United States*. Latin America Otherwise: Languages, Empires, Nations. Duke University Press, 2016.

SB 1070, 49th Leg., 2nd Sess., Arizona Session Laws Ch. 113 as amended by HB 2162, 49th Leg., 2nd Sess., Arizona Session Laws Ch. 211. Section 1. Intent.

Sessions, Jeff. "Attorney General Jeff Sessions Delivers Remarks Announcing the Department of Justice's Renewed Commitment to Criminal Immigration Enforcement." Address to U.S. Customs and Border Protection agents, 11 April 2017, Nogales, Arizona.

Silverman, Kaja. *The Threshold of the Visible World*. Routledge, 1995.

Simpson, Audra. *Mohawk Interruptus: Political Life Across the Borders of Settler States*. Duke University Press, 2014.

Simpson, Leanne Betasamosake. "Land as Pedagogy: Nishnaabeg Intelligence and Rebellious Transformation." *Decolonization: Indigeneity, Education & Society* 3.3 (2014): 1–25.

Sturken, Marita, and Lisa Cartwright. *Practices of Looking: An Introduction to Visual Culture.* Oxford University Press, 2001.

Sullivan, Nikki. "The Somatechnics of Perception and the Matter of the Non/Human: A Critical Response to the New Materialism." *European Journal of Women's Studies* 19.3 (2012): 299–313.

Sunday Square Off. National Broadcasting Company. KPNX, Phoenix. 25 June 2010. Television.

Tapia, Ruby C. *American Pietas: Visions of Race, Death, and the Maternal.* University of Minnesota Press, 2011.

Vargas, Deborah R. "Ruminations on *Lo Sucio* as a Latino Queer Analytic." *American Quarterly* 66.3 (2014): 715–26.

PART III

RHETORICAL NAVIGATIONS

INSTITUTIONAL AND INFRASTRUCTURAL INSTABILITIES

CHAPTER 9

The Precarity of Disability/Studies in Academe

MARGARET PRICE

DISABILITY STUDIES (DS) is one of the most dynamic new fields in academe. It's also marked by paradoxes and inequities, to such a degree that Julie Avril Minich recently asked whether "the field's emergence as a major academic enterprise in the humanities is linked to the intensification of neoliberalism in higher education and health care." The rise of DS over the last thirty years has been accompanied by increasing gaps in power and access within the field— between scholars and activists; between White people and people of color; between those who receive university paychecks and those who rely on public benefits; and between those who are "functional" enough to hold jobs that include health insurance, and those who aren't.[1] The effects of these schisms are easily observable in the everyday spaces of DS. For example, at many DS-themed conferences, well-off professors lunch together in hotel restaurants while unfunded attendees, often living precariously on fixed incomes, eat non-perishable snacks out of their suitcases in the lobbies nearby. That unpleasant tableau is reenacted, in various forms, in all the realms of DS work—class-rooms, journals, university presses, public commons. I don't exempt myself from participation in these equity gaps. I'm a White disabled genderqueer, and at a conference I co-organized in 2013, an attendee stood up at the closing plenary and asked, "Why is it still so White?"

I refer to "disability/studies" in the title to signal that not only DS, but also disability itself, is marked by a complex kind of precarity in academe. The *field* of DS is doing quite well: universities are reporting new majors, minors, and graduate programs in DS; jobs calling for expertise in DS or crip theory are being announced; and special journal issues and conference themes abound. But disabled *people* in academic life seem to be struggling. Although statistics are hard to come by (especially for faculty), even partial or conservative estimates show that disabled faculty and staff are underemployed, while disabled students experience higher rates of attrition. Moreover, it increasingly seems that academic life itself is disabling: the U.K. *Guardian,* the *New York Times,* and a swath of academic studies record the increasing rates of mental health problems and other forms of debilitation on campuses (see Berg et al.; Clark et al.; Dolmage, *Academic*; Gill). Under neoliberal logic and governance, Berg et al. argue, "inequality becomes a *necessary* component of relationships between faculty members" (172, emphasis in original). In other words, some of the inhabitants of academe are built to break.[2]

Complicating the matter yet further, many forms of disablement are difficult to name, notice, or predict, and the people affected by those forms of disablement seem to be doing worst of all. One of the equity gaps in DS is between what I call "the accommodatable" and "the unaccommodatable." Accommodatable disabilities are noticeably present in university spaces, though embattled. But unaccommodatable disabilities—which could include chronic fatigue, chemical sensitivity, various cognitive impairments, or health disparities linked to environment, race, and class—inhabit a peculiar space, one that is usually not noticed. To be clear, I'm not saying that certain disabilities can be definitively labeled "unaccommodatable" for all situations and times; disability, as I explain in more detail below, is an emergent and situational phenomenon. Thus, these are not static examples that *always* illustrate unpredictability. For in fact, no disability is truly "predictable." For example, Dalia, a deaf and visually impaired faculty member, noted in an interview that she can't always predict whether or not it will be "a good lipreading day"— even though her disabilities might be assumed to be relatively consistent.[3] The point I'm making is that in the current academic system, some disabilities can be *made* to appear predictable enough to specify accommodation needs. Indeed, the structure and governance of academic "access" almost always mandates that sort of passing by requiring that accommodations be figured out and arranged ahead of time. Like Minich, I have an uneasy sense that DS perpetuates this inequity rather than alleviating it.

Through that perpetuation, disability studies has reached a point I call a "crisis of precarity." In this chapter, I explain why I think we are at this crisis point, and why I call it a crisis of precarity. I then turn to a series of interviews conducted with disabled faculty members. My analysis demonstrates how their stories of disablement illustrate DS's crisis of precarity, but also points the way toward a possible reshaping of DS and other academic disciplines aimed toward social justice. As I struggle to think about what "disability" means to me now—in this time of "slow death" and semi-bordered wars (Berlant; Erevelles; Puar, "Prognosis," "Coda"), in this time when Black people die sooner and experience much higher rates of disease and disability than White people (Williams; Pollock), in this time when working as a DS scholar confers "cultural capital," yet most disabled people live in poverty (Patsavas), and academic work seems to decapacitate us anyway—I find that I need a better way to be disabled, and a scholar/activist. I need a better way of doing what I want DS theory to do.

THE CRISIS OF PRECARITY IN DISABILITY STUDIES

Precarity involves not only the material conditions of vulnerability themselves (for instance, the presence of lead in a public water supply), but also two other key factors: first, infrastructures designed to *sustain* the vulnerability; and second, *obscurity* surrounding the constitutive conditions of vulnerability. To put it more simply, precarity occurs when certain inhabitants of a system are designed to be debilitated or broken (see Nakamura; Puar, "Coda" and "Prognosis"; Berlant), and when this debilitation remains obscure, that is, willfully hard to explain, and rhetorically not taken up. (On obscure disabilities, see Harnish; on rhetorical uptake, see Ratcliffe.[4]) Disability studies has long been familiar with the first factor, in which some inhabitants of a system are designed to be broken, but has not paid enough attention to the second, the problem of obscure, or unrecognized, disabilities.

By "recognition," I do not mean simply identifying something/someone by applying a label such as "blind"; as Wendy Hesford notes, that form of unrhetorical recognition tends to freeze subjects in falsely determinate positions and reifies binaries of self/other, inclusion/exclusion (41). Rather, I mean a rhetorically attuned form of recognition, one that recognizes the mobility of subjects, as well as the flow between persons, animals, objects, and environment (Hesford). Further, I argue that a strong focus on rights, which has characterized the U.S. (and some other) disability movements, tends to uphold the static binaries Hesford warns against, thus aggravating conditions of precarity for some disabled people. In the following section, I describe how those conditions of precarity play out within disability studies (and disability culture) along lines of predictability/unpredictability. First, however, I offer a brief history of rights-based work in disability activism and disability studies.

Disability studies in the United States[5] has interested itself strongly in the issues of accommodation and access. In doing so, it draws upon both the social-model disability movement in the United Kingdom, and the civil rights movement in the United States. Of the social-model movement, Tom Shakespeare notes that its emergence in the early 1970s was male-dominated, focused on the removal of physical barriers, and in general used as a "blunt instrument" (220) in drawing distinctions such as disability/impairment. The latter was understood, according to the early social model, to be a physical condition such as having paralyzed legs, whereas the former was understood to be the oppressions and limitations that arose from inaccessible environments and attitudes. This "blunt," sometimes simplistic, distinction has been critiqued by many scholars besides Shakespeare, including Eli Clare, Liz Crow, and Alison Kafer.

In the United States, the disability rights movement took up the social model and, while battling ableism and lack of access, often drew specific comparisons to the African American civil rights movement. This perspective emerged as the "minority model," which Harlan Hahn summarizes as the presumption that "disabled Americans are entitled to the same legal and constitutional protection as other disadvantaged groups" (35). When giving examples of those "other" groups, Hahn mentions African Americans, women, and Latinos.[6] Organizing across difference is a common strategy, and can be accomplished intersectionally, but the U.S. disability rights movement sometimes drew comparisons to other minority groups in reductive ways. Moreover, as Nirmala Erevelles points out, the early disability rights movement typically didn't consider people with "severe/cognitive disabilities," relying on liberal-humanist arguments that implied or stated that only those who met certain tests of humanness should have rights (151). As scholars in various disciplines have shown since then, the argument that people should "have" rights tends to reduce both the rights themselves, and the havers of them, into static entities—an approach that tends to shore up, rather than reduce, structural oppressions (see Hesford; Russell; Young and Quibell).

The discourse of individual rights fits neatly with discourses that flourish under neoliberalism: the classification of humans (and everything else) as economic actors or factors, the transformation of all energies into competitive moves aimed at in/equality, and emphasis on ideals of choice and autonomy (Brown). One effect of these moves is that the ability to be productive, in an economic sense, is considered a person's most important characteristic— indeed, is taken as evidence of whether one is a valuable person at all. The notion that severely disabled people are "better off dead" or "have no future" (Kafer) stems from this presumption that economic productiveness and value as a person are equivalent. The assumptions of neoliberalism are evident in academe, where, as Akemi Nishida explains, "hyper-productivity" is framed as normal, and "people's productivity is understood within the framework of individual capability, ability, and competency." If one's ability to hyper-produce within this framework falters, that is understood to be "an individual's responsibility to fix in private" (150).

Various commonplaces are used to encourage students, faculty, and in fact all inhabitants of university space to maintain their hyper-productivity, such as "resilience" (Aubrecht; Simard-Gagnon) and "wellness" (on wellness as a rhetorical trope, see Carey). The lean, mean, hyper-productive student or faculty member is, of course, also imagined as hyper-able. Disabled bodyminds in university space create a particular kind of dissonance, since these bodyminds are by definition not "fit" (on misfit, see Garland-Thompson). Hence, such bodyminds are rewritten as either able, or absent: sometimes through overcoming stories (see Kerschbaum et al.); sometimes through presumptions of fakery or malingering (see Brune and Wilson; Dolmage, *Disability Rhetoric*; Samuels, "My Body," *Fantasies*); sometimes by simply waiting for them to disappear through attrition, as a "population wearing out in the space of ordinariness" (Berlant 196).

Foregrounding the mechanisms of neoliberalism while thinking about inequity in DS reveals something rarely acknowledged: Accommodation in university space may actually shore up, rather than mitigate, the precarious position of disabled academics. In other words, accommodation itself may operate as a mechanism of inequity.

Both Melanie Yergeau et al. and Jay Dolmage (*Academic*) have argued persuasively that accommodation is tantamount to retrofitting. In other words, an accommodation is by definition a move put in place to address ("accommodate") some problem. Thus, it tends to operate in the neoliberal university more like an attempt at cure or eradication than like an attempt to actually include disability as part of university life (on inclusion, see also Ahmed; Titchkosky). *Access* is a broader, more diffuse concept than accommodation (Michalko), but "accommodation" and "access" tend to be conflated, especially when rights-based discourse is being used. In the next section I elaborate on this problem, and offer an alternative framework for understanding disability: *crip spacetime*.

THE UNACCOMMODATABLE

I'm not against either accommodation or access. I continue to appreciate and work toward both goals. Rather, I'm arguing that the way they are understood in specific times and places often leads to their being applied in limiting ways. Here's the rub: The imaginative logic of using accommodation as a means toward access relies on the assumption that disability is stable and knowable, not only in moments—for example, when confronting a step or a time limit or an uncaptioned video—but in *predictive* ways. Adaptation implies responding to an access need as it emerges; accommodation implies (and, in everyday academic life, almost always requires) the ability to say, "I can tell you what I'm going to need—in an hour, in a week, next semester."

Those of us who try to gain access in various environments, including higher education, have historically tended to trade upon whatever predictability we can muster—or masquerade. In other words, we have relied on a version of strategic essentialism (Spivak; Schmertz) in order to gain access, often working via the discourse of rights. Unfortunately, in doing so, we have enabled the creation of a dividing line between those whose disabilities are stable *enough*, predictable *enough*, to benefit from the protections of rights-based accommodation—and those whose are not.

Notably, the predictability-based model of access runs on linear time. I offer an alternative way of thinking about access: through a concept I call "crip spacetime." Crip spacetime turns its focus away from the human individual to focus on the spatial, the relational, the nonhuman animal or object, and the group. It is a concept drawn from material feminism, crip theory, and rhetorical ontology. It foregrounds questions such as these:

- Who can identify their own access needs in an understandable manner?
- Who can predict what sort of accommodation they'll need tomorrow, or next week?

And by implication, crip spacetime also demands that we ask: Who cannot?

Too often, those of us who practice DS, especially those of us who identify as scholar-activists, focus on moves like "get everyone in the room, ensure everyone has adequate means of communication"—and then forget that there is more to consider. Such moves are, of course, crucial. I will continue to fight for them, at my own university and at others. But I urge us to notice the ways that those moves, if thought of as endpoints, actually *increase* conditions of precarity within disability studies by encouraging a "rich get richer" dynamic. This is one of the inequities perpetuated within and through the discipline of DS: we tend to take "access" as an automatic good, define it narrowly within a particular neoliberal frame (see Berne), then enact it in ways that leave out and in fact erase many disabled people.[7]

To be clear, I am not arguing that we need *more* predictability in academic life in order to make it more accessible. Indeed, the effort to cram access into a metric of predictability is part of the problem I'm identifying. Rather, I am arguing that the spacetime of academe will always be unpredictable in the sense that it will always be "contested and contingent" (Maldonado and Licona 132) and constituted with the intra-activity of subject-objects (Barad; Kim). This is why it's crucial to take up a new way of thinking about how disability manifests through space and time. In the following section, I show how an understanding of crip spacetime helps expose the neoliberal logic that governs disability access in academe. The examples I offer are drawn from a survey/interview study of disabled faculty.

THE DISABLED FACULTY STUDY

I began researching disabled faculty in 2011 for several reasons. One was that, following the publication of *Mad at School,* I found myself receiving emails nearly every week from disabled faculty and graduate students who were having problems with "accommodations" that they could not figure out how to manage. Often, the writers had mental disabilities—since that was the topic of *Mad at School*—but at least as often, the writer addressed me because the accommodation they needed was difficult to discuss, or confusing in some way. Those situations required careful deliberation that took into account social, emotional, and spatial factors, as well as logical ones. For example, an employee with a professional services firm contacted me for help thinking through, and responding to, her workplace's attempt to offer accommodations.[8] Because of her impaired vision, she does not drive. Her job involves moving between work sites, so an alternate means of transportation was needed; her preference was to hire a car. However, her workplace proposed that instead, she could ride along with her manager (who did not always have the same schedule). In other words, not only would the employee have to engage in constant labor to ensure her transportation arrangements were in place, but she would also have to engage in a significant amount of social interaction in order to obtain her accommodation—interaction with her direct manager, no less. This example is one of literally thousands I know of that meet the letter of ADA law (pretty much) while ignoring socio-spatial issues of emotion, equity, and dignity.

Thus, I began the study of disabled faculty in 2011 because I realized much more needed to be explored. As time has gone on, I've realized that my findings call into question not only how academe operates but also what DS is and does. More and more, the battle for accommodation has become recognizable as one that's winnable only on narrowly defined terms. For example, one of the questions my coresearcher, Stephanie Kerschbaum, and I asked interviewees was: "If you could have any accommodation you wanted at work, what would it be?" It was striking to observe that some interviewees responded immediately and enthusiastically—suggesting objects, technologies, modified spaces—while others were at a loss even to imagine what accommodation might look like. This latter group were the interviewees who caused me to begin to think seriously about what Andrew Harnish calls "obscure" disabilities—those that can't be easily pinned to "needs" or "accommodations."

The Disabled Faculty Study was publicly launched in 2012 with an anonymous survey, coauthored with Mark Salzer, focusing on the experiences of mentally disabled faculty (Price et al.; Kerschbaum et al., "Accommodations"). The study's second phase, still ongoing, is a series of in-depth interviews with disabled faculty. We recruited faculty with a wide variety of self-identified disabilities, including blindness, deafness, mobility impairment, paralysis, mental illness, chronic pain, cognitive impairment, chronic illness, and others.[9] Our sampling method, "maximum variation" or "diversity" sampling, aimed at creating a group of interviewees who were as different from each other as possible. Thus, as our interviews progressed, we periodically reviewed the pool of volunteers and made specific efforts to ensure we included faculty inhabiting a wide range of positions in terms of gender, race, nationality, sexuality, class, age, rank, and type of institution, as well as type of disability. The key question for this sampling method is not "Who is typical or representative of a group?" but rather "Who is unimagined? What new questions might be asked through learning from the unimagined?"[10]

The following two subsections show how crip spacetime operates for disabled people in the academic workplace by highlighting two themes that were drawn from analysis of the data: *ambient uncertainty* and *the bodymind event*.

Ambient Uncertainty, or Not Knowing What You Don't Know

Ambient uncertainty is the sense of not knowing what's at stake when disclosing disability (or, more colloquially, "not knowing what you don't know").[11] Many of the faculty members we interviewed described the significant emotional labor required as they moved through situations in which disability and accommodation were almost never mentioned, except in a derogatory way (for example, other faculty complaining about "crazy" or "needy" students), and in which their own efforts to manage their disability identities were based upon laborious guesswork. Laurie, for example, who is a non-tenure-track faculty member teaching composition, mentioned a fear of not having her contract renewed if she were to ask for accommodations for her depression.[12] She didn't predict direct cause and effect, that is, "If I ask for accommodations, then I won't get renewed." Rather, she described an ambient sense of *potential* consequences. She stated,

> This is another issue about accommodations, you know, I am not tenured faculty or tenure-track faculty, and I don't know how comfortable I would be even in a fairly secure position that I'm in, disclosing and asking for accommodations, given the yearly contract issue.

Laurie explained that she is unlikely not to be renewed, since there is little competition for teachers of first-year comp at her school, "so that isn't stressful." And yet, "there's still this idea that maybe this is the thing that's gonna, you know, if I ask for accommodations." Note the omission in Laurie's sentence: "this is the thing that's gonna" is not followed by a verb clause such as "have a bad outcome"; rather, the clause that would have specified the consequence is left unspoken. Laurie picks up her sentence after "you know" as if the thought had been verbalized.

Many faculty reported a similar sense of vulnerability, and it was striking how often the faculty member's vulnerable feeling came from ambient cues rather than ones that could be pointed to directly. Another faculty member, Denise, who is blind, noted a feeling of being "at the mercy of other people" for all kinds of everyday needs—for instance, entering and leaving conversations.[13] This vulnerability is an important element of the way that disabled faculty members move through time and space at their jobs. Something as (seemingly) simple as a conversation at a faculty reception can become a strenuous test.

Thomas Rickert's theory of ambient rhetoric suggests that human agency does not direct situations. While human actions are an important part of the way that meaning takes shape in situations, "nonhuman entities and forces" are also important, and contribute to "the distribution of the materiality and energy that constitute the world" (221–22). In other words, agency is distributed, rather than manifesting only via human will. Thus, when Laurie or Denise describes an ambient sense of being vulnerable, that is not simply a feeling that may or may not be "true"; instead, the feeling itself is part of the reality and materiality of their situations. In crip spacetime, events unfold unpredictably, recursively, and in such a way that factors such as "just having a feeling about something" contribute to their outcomes. This is the spacetime that many of our faculty interviewees seem to operate in. However, when their experiences bump against normative assumptions about space and time (e.g., "Just tell us what you need!"), the clash of realities is painfully evident.

Some faculty interviewees chose not to disclose their disabilities at work, while others disclosed selectively, but then found that it was hard to track how that information might travel. For example, Nate, a White male tenured professor, expressed a sense of being the topic of clandestine conversations.[14] Nate had negotiated for enhanced mental health benefits when hired at his job, and some time later, found himself in a conversation with a colleague who wanted to ask questions about that process. As it turned out, the colleague had learned from another person in the department about Nate's accommodations—though Nate had never spoken to either of them on the subject. He stated, "That's what made me think that there is a kind of culture of wanting to suss out, maybe for good reason, but also just to know, to have people pinned down (rising inflection)." This culture can create for disabled faculty a sense of being perpetually investigated, and perpetually on the verge of being found out.

Many of the interviewees who described a similar sense of ambient unpredictability inhabited more marginal positions than Nate's. For example, Zoe, who was untenured at the time of the interview, noted her awareness of others' possible reading of her as "the stereotypical crazy Latina."[15] And Camille, also untenured, noted that because she sometimes isn't able to speak (due to cognitive impairment), this places her in a particularly disadvantageous position, since fluent language use is typically associated with fitness as a professor:[16]

> When you are a professor everything (Margaret: Yeah) depends on language so immediately people think you're crazy, it's a mental illness, or they made a mistake hiring you, and uh, how can you were articulated when you were uh giving your job talk and suddenly you can't release good English?

In this comment, Camille identifies two dimensions of precarity surrounding her periodic inability to speak. First, the fact that it involves loss of language is particularly difficult. As Joshua St. Pierre argues, dysfluency calls into question one's value as a person; that is, "the rational human materializes himself through the voice precariously" (333; see also Brueggemann on "the good man speaking well"). Any sort of dysfluency, whether it is impaired speech, not voicing aloud, speaking while working with interpreters, or "losing" speech intermittently, creates a precarious position for the non- or semi-speaker. The second dimension of precarity in the situation Camille describes is impermanence: her colleagues tend to assume that if a person speaks well at a particular moment in time, they should always be able to muster that same kind of speech at another time. There's a sense of "if you could be articulate and cognitively able an hour ago, why can't you do that now?"—with concomitant suspicion of those who appear to be "inconsistent." Colloquially, most academics understand that we all have "good days" and "bad days" for communication, but when that phenomenon is scaled up—for example, highly fluent language use is suddenly replaced by complete loss of speech or sense—the unpredictability involved is regarded as dysfunctional (and originating with the speaker) rather than routine (and originating with the conditions surrounding the speaker).

There is little understanding in mainstream academic life (and often, little understanding even within disability studies) of the intermittent, shape-shifting nature of many disabilities. As a result, Camille decided to pay for most of her own accommodations herself, rather than get into extensive conversations about why and when she needed them. (Although outside the scope of this chapter, it's worth noting that many interviewees mentioned the high level of surveillance attached to their disability accommodations.) That theme—"Use of personal resources to achieve accommodations"—appeared in many other faculty members' interviews as well.[17] Stacy Alaimo astutely notes that "the agency of the body demands an acceptance of unpredictability and not-quite-knowing" (250), and further notes that this unpredictability illustrates Barad's theory of material agency through intra-activity. However, building on Alaimo's insight, we should also acknowledge that the body's "demand" may not be honored, especially not in a governed space that urges all its inhabitants to be as "hyper-productive" (Nishida 150) as possible.

A Bodymind Event

The second theme I offer as an example of the precarity of crip spacetime is the bodymind event. Like ambient uncertainty, the concept of bodymind event was drawn from analysis of interviews. I define a bodymind event as a sudden, debilitating shift in one's mental/corporeal experience. Examples of such events might include a panic attack, being exposed to a toxic chemical or fragrance, abruptly realizing that an interpreter is not interpreting accurately, or hitting a bump with one's wheelchair and flipping over frontwards. Bodymind events are not located "in" bodyminds, but rather take place in crip spacetime; in other words, they are constituted through the particular conditions of space and time that contribute to the emergent meaning of a situation and what makes it disabling. In keeping with Rickert's theory of ambient rhetoric and Barad's of intra-activity, a bodymind event emerges through all the factors—human, nonhuman animal, object, space, and time—that compose a situation. Recognizing the importance of the bodymind event means being attuned to space as "a place of potential shock" (Maldonado and Licona 131).

Often, bodymind events involve loss of rhetoricity, that is, the ability to "make sense" to those around you and be received as a valid subject (see Lewiecki-Wilson; Prendergast; Price, *Mad*). Such was the case for Del, an autistic professor, who had "a complete sensory meltdown" when a fire alarm went off while she was teaching on the sixth floor of a building.[18] Ordinarily, Del is notified ahead of time for fire drills, because she knows the noise will trigger her. In this case, however, perhaps because it was an actual alarm and not a drill, no warning was given. I asked Del for more detail about what a meltdown is like, and Del responded, "It's physically dramatic. Like, I don't, I don't actually scream, but my body screams." She then went on to describe what happened as she and her students left the room:

> We had to use the stairs (Margaret: Mh-hm) and so you know how stairs are in a building which is mostly elevators. There's sort of an enclosed environment (Margaret: Yeah, yeah) um and concrete and stuff. And I, I don't really remember this but I heard from the students and also I could tell from my body afterwards from all the bruises, I was like pinballing down the stairs. (Margaret: Oh god! [laughing]) I was, I was (Margaret: Oh!) panicking so hard I was going down (Margaret: Oh!) like a pinball. . . . And so also I lost language.

Fortunately, in this instance Del was in a well-supported environment. Several of her students, one of whom has an autistic child, knew how to respond in this crisis. Thus, once the group got down the stairs, one student helped Del reach a place that was relatively protected from crowds and siren noises, while another student took charge of the class, ensuring they were safe and stayed together. When Del was able to speak again, she told them (with characteristic humor), "Okay, so you all aced the pop quiz on getting the melting-down autistic safely out of the building during a fire."

Although a meltdown is never a desirable event, Del's example is quite positive, as such events go. First, she had already identified to her students and colleagues as autistic, so the event did not serve as an instance of unwanted disclosure (which does often happen to disabled professors; see Vance). Second, she was among people who understood how to support her; that is, they and Del had the sort of nuanced and interactive relationship around access that Mia Mingus calls "access intimacy." Third, Del has a great deal of experience navigating professional situations in which her autism is a topic. This, along

with her sense of humor, enabled her to praise her students for their resource-
ful behavior during the shock of the fire alarm and Del's subsequent meltdown.

The bodymind event tends to break down the conventionally understood
boundary between "body" and "mind" (see Price, "Bodymind"). An example
of this characteristic comes from Iris, a professor at a large research university,
who described her experience of a brain injury as one of "disabling terror"
leading to a near-breakdown at work.[19] (She was untenured at the time this
story took place.) Although she had already disclosed and obtained accommodations for her "usual" disability, which involves mobility impairment and
pain, she later learned that she had a torn artery in her brain—an extremely
dangerous condition, which could have led to a sudden stroke or severe brain
damage. Iris described meeting with her chair and trying to explain the debilitating fear she was experiencing:

> My other stuff [with previous disabilities], you know, I was like, this is what's
> happening, and I was very professional. And this time I was very upset and
> I started crying, and that was really embarrassing? (rising inflection) Even
> though I know it happens (Margaret: Mh-hm) a lot for people in these situ-
> ations. And I felt like disclosing disability that I've been living with a long
> time [the mobility impairment and pain] . . . is very different from disclosing
> that I'm going through a scary medical crisis? (rising inflection)

In Iris's story, the debilitating "event" is a future event, existing largely in terms
of potential, but no less material for that (see Kafer). In present time, Iris said,
"I don't have symptoms from it. It's not physically debilitating me (Margaret:
It's scary, though), but it's terrifying." The labor associated with managing this
kind of disablement is, like the labor described in the previous section, largely
ambient and emotional.

It can be hard to get others to understand the materiality of this sort of
labor, and hence to consider it serious or real enough for accommodation.[20]
In the Disabled Faculty Study, a number of interviewees with multiple disabilities reported requesting accommodations on the basis of whichever of
their disabilities seemed most acceptable or understandable—discussing diabetes rather than bipolar disorder, for example, or explaining the needs surrounding a mobility impairment rather than those surrounding chronic pain
or addiction. (This strategy has been identified by Tara Wood as "selective
disclosure.") Indeed, Iris emphasized her awareness of her ability to appeal to
physical debilitation. She explained, "With every step of the way, I would say
the fact that I have a physical disability, a medically validated physical disability, has smoothed the way for me." Thus, although Iris spoke eloquently dur-

ing her interview about the ways that her brain injury was a *bodymind* event, not an event of the body *or* the mind, she was also candid about the fact that she often treated it as a physical event for the purposes of accommodation. In other words, she engaged in a version of disability "masquerade"—a concept from Tobin Siebers, which does not mean simple fakery, but rather *managing* one's disability disclosures (verbal, gestural, or otherwise) so that they accomplish what's needed in specific moments.

The appeal to physicality is no guarantee of accommodation, however. Nicola, whose chronic illness requires that her body not get overheated (lest she experience loss of motor control), once found herself teaching a class in a severely overheated room.

> It was like a two-hour class and I, I went in the room and I tried. I mean the room was like 90 degrees (Margaret: Oh god) and it was nobody's fault, it just, even the students were like, wow it's really hot in here. And within ten minutes I couldn't feel my hands, and I couldn't feel my feet, which for me is like a sign that things are going to go south really quick. . . . And I just like bolted out of the room and went to maintenance and was like please please help me. . . . I mean the guy could tell that basically I was just desperate.

In that case, the maintenance staff member turned on the air-conditioning in Nicola's classroom and she was able to resume teaching. However, as she pointed out during her interview, many of the accommodations she would like to request, including air-conditioning, are not often recognized or respected as needs; they are more likely to be framed as "preferences." The line between accommodations that are "needed" and those that are merely "desired" is often used against disabled people, and sometimes even used to pit disabled people against one another.

As I suggested near the beginning of this chapter, precarity can be understood (in part) as the structural sustainment of vulnerability in obscure conditions. Thinking about the precarity of disability in terms of crip spacetime helps de-obscure the experiences described by the faculty members in the Disabled Faculty Study. Crip spacetime forces us to confront the impossible-to-explain accommodation, or the access need that is considered "just a preference." It demands recognition of the intersectional identities of disabled people, including the ways that—for instance—those in less privileged positions of race, class, gender, and sexuality are more likely to be judged as angry, unreasonable, "crazy," faking, or disabled through their own fault. And it means that we must recognize the gaps in power/privilege that persist in DS as a discipline, as well as in academe more broadly—for example, between disabled people who (for whatever reason) can perform enough predictability to be "accommodatable," and those who can't.

CONCLUSION

My primary argument in this chapter is that if we understand that disabled people are often operating in crip spacetime, we will notice the central role predictability plays in efforts toward access in academe. And we will notice that it's a problem. Appealing to whatever form of predictability one can muster, or masquerade (Siebers), may allow a disabled person to achieve a greater degree of individual autonomy by enhancing their appeal to rights. However, such appeals have the simultaneous effect of further oppressing other disabled people—those who cannot offer such performances. Crip spacetime, as a framework that assumes events unfold through ambience and intra-activity, also assumes we are a part of a system of ethics that "emerge[s] from life as it is lived" (Rickert 223). That is, crip spacetime deals not only with space and time, but also with justice; the three are inextricable. Crip spacetime makes it obvious that we cannot rely on some individuals to articulate "needs" and others to bestow "accommodations" in order to achieve justice. Rather, we must find ways to move toward collective accountability.

What does collective accountability look like, and how might it actually work? Many reports from lived experience are available. One is Mia Mingus's story of attending the Allied Media Conference in Detroit with a group of twenty-two disabled people traveling together as a "pod." Mingus notes that the group's collectivity was grounded not in logistics but in feeling:

> [With collective access], when I say something is inaccessible, you don't just think "there's no ramp" or "there are no places to sit" or "there's no close, accessible, free parking." Instead, you *feel*. You feel the weight of what inaccessibility means to us. You understand inaccessibility to mean isolation, shame, exclusion, disappointment, loneliness, anger, privilege, sadness, loss of community and disconnection. ("Reflections")

Mingus's account foregrounds the sense of a collective ethics of access, demonstrating that that ethics is grounded in feeling; it also emphasizes that this work toward collective access is not always "successful" by conventional metrics, but works along a different scale, one that emphasizes solidarity: "If you can't go, then I don't want to go" (Mingus, "Wherever You Are").

Other examples of efforts toward collective access can be found in Hamraie ("Beyond"), on the website "Composing Access" (http://u.osu.edu/composingaccess), and in Nishida. And although we can identify common denominators in these examples, to some extent access must be rewritten with each new turn of crip spacetime. In my experience, if a group is *feeling* together the urgency of the need for shared access, that's when it tends to work better. No abundance of equipment, no carefully written policy, not even a big budget can replace that shared will, that shared sense of a need for justice. In her story about the "pod people" at the Allied Media Conference, Mingus emphasizes that their version of collective access grew in part from their shared sense of the "weight" of accessibility ("Reflections on an Opening"). If we recall that crip spacetime is a material and physical theory, as well as a discursive one, we will attend carefully to that weight, for it is the gravity that keeps us together.

NOTES

Thanks to those who have helped me slowly work out these ideas, especially the editors of this volume, Aimi Hamraie, Alison Kafer, and the reviewers.

1. These categories intersect significantly, of course. In pointing out the gaps between more- and less-enfranchised groups, my purpose is not to suggest that there are always distinct lines separating the groups. Rather, it's to point out the ways money and power tend to flow across populations and practices (toward some, away from others).

2. Precarity can be marked by this condition of *structurally governed vulnerability*. Precarity is recognizable not when some people *do* experience greater hazards, more acute health issues, and so on, but when infrastructures are *designed* (often subtly) to sustain conditions of unequal and unjust distribution. I am drawing this idea from Lisa Nakamura's concept of people and objects that are "designed to be broken." (See also Berlant; Puar, "Coda" and "Prognosis." See the next section for a longer discussion of what precarity entails.

3. This interview is part of the Disabled Faculty Study, described in more detail below. A few methodological notes: When conducting interviews, coresearcher Stephanie Kersch- baum and I adhered to an "accessible interdependent research paradigm" (Price, *Mad*). Accordingly, interviews took place in whichever medium participants identified as their preference, including face-to-face, videoconference, telephone (with captioning or sign interpretation), email, or instant message. Interviews took place in a mixture of oral, signed, and supported modes. We attended to the access needs of both interviewers as well as the interviewees. All interviewees are identified by pseudonyms, and in some cases, identifying details have been omitted. Quotes have been checked with the interviewee in question. The markup system for quotes involves relating interviewees' statements as they were spoken, signed, or typed, as accurately as possible (not omitting, for example, col- loquialisms such as "like"). When speech overlaps, the interviewer's words are shown in parentheses. Ellipses represent omitted words rather than pauses; pauses of two seconds or greater are marked with the notation "(pause)." Dalia's interview was conducted in sign, in person with Stephanie.

4. Although more work on precarity is urgently needed in disability studies, I am drawing on a long tradition of DS scholars whose work has contributed to theories of precarity without naming it as such. Such work includes Ellen Samuels's "My Body, My Closet" and *Fantasies of Identification,* and Tobin Siebers's *Disability Theory,* which serves as a foundational text for Harnish's theory of obscurity by pointing out that "the inability to disclose is, in fact, one of the constitutive markers of oppression" (97).

5. For the purpose of this chapter, I refer mostly to the U.S. educational system and U.S. legislation. Disability activism and disability studies have emerged along different lines in other countries, with varying degrees of emphasis on human rights (see Meekosha and Shuttleworth; Winter; Young and Quibell).

6. "Latinos" is Hahn's term.

7. Berne's article, which lays out a working draft for an approach to disability called Disability Justice, is written to apply to all disabled people. This article focuses mainly on disability within academe.

8. All anecdotes have been approved by their sources.

9. My use of these conventional, in some cases medicalized, labels is an example of "strategic essentialism," noted above (Spivak; Schmertz). When brevity and communication across diverse audiences are priorities, as they are here, I often use such labels, despite my scholarly and personal preference for more complex and nuanced ways of naming.

10. On "unimagined types," see Titchkosky.

11. The "ambient" concept in this theme, which draws upon the work of Thomas Rickert, is elaborated in my chapter "Un/Shared Space: The Dilemma of Inclusive Architecture."

12. In-person interview, conducted orally with Stephanie.

13. Telephone interview, conducted orally with Stephanie, working with captioning service (CapTel).

14. Videoconference, conducted orally with Stephanie.

15. Instant message (typed "chat"), conducted with Stephanie.

16. Videoconference, conducted orally with me.

17. The same theme, "using personal resources to achieve accommodation," was also evident in the findings from the survey of faculty with mental disabilities. This is worth noting, especially because a rhetoric of "faking" is often applied to disabled people who ask for accommodations. Rather than spending so much energy trying to figure out which students and faculty are "faking" disability, I suggest universities might turn their energies to asking why so many students and faculty pretend *not* to be disabled.

18. In-person interview, conducted orally with me.

19. In-person interview, conducted orally with me.

20. The labor surrounding disability often has a rehabilitative thrust. That is, the primary energy of this labor tends to be aimed at fixing, normalizing, and/or rescuing. See McRuer 121–22; Hamraie, *Building.* On the communicative labor carried out by disabled people, see Konrad.

WORKS CITED

Ahmed, Sara. *On Being Included: Racism and Diversity in Institutional Life.* Duke University Press, 2012.

Alaimo, Stacy. "Trans-corporeal Feminisms and the Ethical Space of Nature." *Material Feminisms.* Ed. Stacy Alaimo and Susan Hekman. Indiana University Press, 2008. 237–64.

Aubrecht, Katie. "The New Vocabulary of Resilience and the Governance of University Student Life." *Studies in Social Justice* 6.1 (2012): 67–83.

Barad, Karen. *Meeting the Universe Halfway: Quantum Physics and the Entanglement of Matter and Meaning.* Duke University Press, 2007.

Berg, Lawrence D., Edward H. Huijbens, and Henrik Gutzon Larsen. "Producing Anxiety in the Neoliberal University." *The Canadian Geographer* 60.2 (2016): 168–80.

Berlant, Lauren. *Cruel Optimism.* Duke University Press, 2011.

Berne, Patricia. "Disability Justice: A Working Draft." *Sins Invalid: An Unshamed Claim to Beauty in the Face of Invisibility.* 10 June 2015. <http://sinsinvalid.org/blog/disability-justice-a-working-draft-by-patty-berne>.

Brown, Wendy. *Undoing the Demos: Neoliberalism's Stealth Revolution.* MIT Press, 2015.

Brueggemann, Brenda Jo. *Lend Me Your Ear: Rhetorical Constructions of Deafness.* Gallaudet Press, 1999.

Brune, Jeffrey A., and Daniel J. Wilson. *Disability and Passing: Blurring the Lines of Identity.* Temple University Press, 2013.

Carey, Tamika. *Rhetorical Healing: The Reeducation of Contemporary Black Womanhood.* SUNY Press, 2016.

Clare, Eli. *Exile and Pride: Disability, Queerness, and Liberation.* South End, 1999.

Clark, Marlea, Wayne Lewchuk, Alice de Wolff, and Andy King. "'This Just Isn't Sustainable': Precarious Employment, Stress, and Workers' Health." *International Journal of Law and Psychiatry* 56, 30.4–5 (2007): 311–26.

Crow, Liz. "Including All of Our Lives: Renewing the Social Model of Disability." *Encounters with Strangers: Feminism and Disability.* Ed. Jenny Morris. The Women's Press, 1996. 206–26.

Dolmage, Jay Timothy. *Disability Rhetoric.* Syracuse University Press, 2013.

———. *Academic Ableism: Disability and Higher Education.* University of Michigan Press, 2017.

Erevelles, Nirmala. *Disability and Difference in Global Contexts: Enabling a Transformative Body Politic.* Palgrave Macmillan, 2011.

Garland-Thomson, Rosemarie. "Misfits: A Feminist Materialist Disability Concept." *Hypatia* 26.3 (2011): 591–609.

Gill, Rosalind. "Breaking the Silence: The Hidden Injuries of Neo-Liberal Academia." *Secrecy and Silence in the Research Process: Feminist Reflections.* Ed. Róisín Flood and Rosalind Gill. Routledge, 2010. 228–44.

Hahn, Harlan. "Accommodations and the ADA: Unreasonable Bias or Biased Reasoning?" *Backlash Against the ADA: Reinterpreting Disability Rights.* Ed. Linda Hamilton Krieger. University of Michigan Press, 2003. 26–61.

Hamraie, Aimi. "Beyond Accommodation: Disability, Feminist Philosophy, and the Design of Everyday Academic Life." *PhiloSOPHIA* 6.2 (2016): 260–71.

———. *Building Access: Disability, Universal Design, and the Politics of Knowing-Making.* University of Minnesota Press, 2017.

Harnish, Andrew. "'A Part of Me Died Suddenly': 'Minimally Invasive' Surgery, Illegible Disability, and Technocultural Confusion." Disability, Arts and Health Conference. Nordic Network for Gender, Body, Health. Bergen, Norway. 2 Sept. 2016.

Hesford, Wendy. *Spectacular Rhetorics: Human Rights Visions, Recognitions, Feminisms.* Duke University Press, 2011.

Kafer, Alison. *Feminist, Queer, Crip.* Indiana University Press, 2013.

Kerschbaum, Stephanie L., Rosemarie Garland-Thomson, Sushil K. Oswal, Amy Vidali, Susan Ghiaciuc, Margaret Price, Jay Dolmage, Craig A. Meyer, Brenda Jo Brueggemann, and Ellen Samuels. "Faculty Members, Accommodation, and Access in Higher Education." *Profession.* 9 Dec. 2013. <https://profession.commons.mla.org/2013/12/09/faculty-members-accommodation-and-access-in-higher-education>.

Kerschbaum, Stephanie L., Amber M. O'Shea, Margaret Price, and Mark Salzer. "Accommodations and Disclosure for Faculty Members with Disability." *Negotiating Disability: Disclosure and Higher Education.* Ed. Stephanie L. Kerschbaum, Laura T. Eisenman, and James M. Jones. University of Michigan Press, 2017.

Kim, Eunjung. "Unbecoming Human: An Ethics of Objects." *GLQ* 21.2–3 (2015): 295–320.

Konrad, Annika. "Access as a Lens for Peer Tutoring." *Another Word.* 22 Feb. 2016. <http://writing.wisc.edu/blog/?p=6454>.

Lewiecki-Wilson, Cynthia. "Rethinking Rhetoric Through Mental Disabilities." *Rhetoric Review* 22.2 (2003): 156–67.

Maldonado, Marta Maria, and Adela C. Licona. "Re-thinking Integration as Reciprocal and Spatialized Process." *Journal of Latino/Latin American Studies* 2.4 (2007): 128–43.

McRuer, Robert. *Crip Theory: Cultural Signs of Queerness and Disability.* New York University Press, 2006.

Meekosha, Helen, and Russell Shuttleworth. "What's So 'Critical' About Critical Disability Studies?" *Australian Journal of Human Rights* 15.1 (2009): 47–75.

Michalko, Rod. *The Difference That Disability Makes.* Temple University Press, 2002.

Mingus, Mia. "Access Intimacy: The Missing Link." *Leaving Evidence.* 5 May 2011. <https://leavingevidence.wordpress.com/2011/05/05/access-intimacy-the-missing-link/>.

———. "Reflections on an Opening: Disability Justice and Creating Collective Access in Detroit." *Leaving Evidence.* 23 Aug. 2010. <https://leavingevidence.wordpress.com/2010/08/23/reflections-on-an-opening-disability-justice-and-creating-collective-access-in-detroit/>.

———. "Wherever You Are Is Where I Want to Be: Crip Solidarity." *Leaving Evidence.* 3 May 2010. <https://leavingevidence.wordpress.com/2010/05/03/where-ever-you-are-is-where-i-want-to-be-crip-solidarity/>.

Minich, Julie Avril. "Enabling Whom? Critical Disability Studies Now." *Lateral* 5.1 (2016). <http://csalateral.org/wp/issue/5-1/forum-alt-humanities-critical-disability-studies-now-minich/>.

Nakamura, Lisa. "Afterword: Racism, Sexism, and Gaming's Cruel Optimism." *Identity Matters: Race, Gender, and Sexuality in Video Game Studies.* Ed. Jennifer Malkowski and TreaAndrea M. Russworm. Indiana University Press, 2017. 245–50.

Nishida, Akemi. "Neoliberal Academia and a Critique from Disability Studies." *Occupying Disability: Critical Approaches to Community, Justice, and Decolonizing Disability.* Ed. Pamela Block, Devva Kasnitz, Akemi Nishida, and Nick Pollard. Springer, 2016. 145–57.

Patsavas, Alyson. "Disabilities Studies Gains Cultural Capital? And Now What?" *The Feminist Wire.* 22 Nov. 2013. <http://www.thefeministwire.com/2013/11/disabilities-studies-gains-cultural-capital-and-now-what/>.

Pollock, Anne. *Medicating Race: Heart Disease and Durable Preoccupations with Difference.* Duke University Press, 2012.

Prendergast, Catherine. "On the Rhetorics of Mental Disability." *Embodied Rhetorics: Disability in Language and Culture.* Ed. James Wilson and Cynthia Lewiecki-Wilson. Southern Illinois University Press, 2001. 45–60.

Price, Margaret. "The Bodymind Problem and the Possibilities of Pain." *Hypatia* 30.1 (2015): 268–84.

———. *Mad at School: Rhetorics of Mental Disability and Academic Life.* University of Michigan Press, 2011.

———. "Un/shared Space: The Dilemma of Inclusive Architecture." *Disability, Space, Architecture: A Reader.* Ed. Jos Boys. Routledge, 2017. 155–72.

Price, Margaret, Mark Salzer, Amber M. O'Shea, and Stephanie Kerschbaum. "Disclosure of Mental Disability by College and University Faculty: The Negotiation of Accommodations, Supports, and Barriers." *Disability Studies Quarterly* 37.2 (2017). <http://dsq-sds.org/article/view/5487/4653>.

Puar, Jasbir. "Coda: The Cost of Getting Better: Suicide, Sensation, Switchpoints." *GLQ* 18.1 (2012): 149–58.

———. "Prognosis Time: Towards a Geopolitics of Affect, Debility and Capacity." *Women and Performance: A Journal of Feminist Theory* 19.2 (2009): 161–72.

Ratcliffe, Krista. *Rhetorical Listening: Identification, Gender, Whiteness.* Southern Illinois University Press, 2005.

Rickert, Thomas. *Ambient Rhetoric: The Attunements of Rhetorical Being.* University of Pittsburgh Press, 2013.

Russell, Marta. "What Disability Civil Rights Cannot Do: Employment and Political Economy." *Disability & Society* 17.2 (2002): 117–35.

Samuels, Ellen. *Fantasies of Identification: Disability, Gender, Race.* New York University Press, 2014.

———. "My Body, My Closet: Invisible Disability and the Limits of Coming-out Discourse." *GLQ* 9.1 (2003): 233–55.

Schmertz, Johanna. "Constructing Essences: Ethos and the Postmodern Subject of Feminism." *Rhetoric Review* 18.1 (1999): 82–91.

Shakespeare, Tom. *Disability Rights and Wrongs.* Routledge, 2006.

Siebers, Tobin. *Disability Theory.* University of Michigan Press, 2008.

Simard-Gagnon, Laurence. "Everyone Is Fed, Bathed, Asleep, and I Have Made It Through Another Day: Problematizing Accommodation, Resilience, and Care in the Neoliberal Academy." *The Canadian Geographer* 60.2 (2016): 219–25.

Spivak, Gayatri Chakravorty. Interview with Sara Danius and Stefan Jonsson. *boundary 2* 20.2 (1993): 24–50.

St. Pierre, Joshua. "Cripping Communication: Speech, Disability, and Exclusion in Liberal Humanist and Posthumanist Discourse." *Communication Theory* 25.3 (2015): 330–48.

Titchkosky, Tanya. *The Question of Access: Disability, Space, Meaning.* University of Toronto Press, 2011.

Vance, Mary Lee, ed. *Disabled Faculty and Staff in a Disabling Society: Multiple Identities in Higher Education.* AHEAD, 2007.

Williams, Richard Allen, ed. *Eliminating Healthcare Disparities in America: Beyond the IOM Report.* Humana Press, 2007.

Winter, Jerry Allen. "The Development of the Disability Rights Movement as a Social Problem Solver." *Disability Studies Quarterly* 23.1 (2003). <http://dsq-sds.org/article/view/399/545>.

Wood, Tara. "Rhetorical Disclosures: The Stake of Disability Identity in Higher Education." *Negotiating Disability: Disclosure and Higher Education*. Ed. Stephanie L. Kershbaum, Laura T. Eisenman, and James M. Jones. Ann Arbor: University of Michigan Press, 2017. 75–92.

Yergeau, Melanie, Elizabeth Brewer, Stephanie Kerschbaum, Sushil Oswal, Margaret Price, Michael Salvo, Cynthia Selfe, and Franny Howes. "Multimodality in Motion: Disability and Kairotic Spaces." *Kairos: A Journal of Rhetoric, Technology and Pedagogy* 18.1 (2013). <http://kairos. technorhetoric.net/18.1/coverweb/yergeau-et-al/index.html>.

Young, Damon A., and Ruth Quibell. "Why Rights Are Never Enough: Rights, Intellectual Disability and Understanding." *Disability & Society* 15.5 (2000): 747–64.

CHAPTER 10

"Are You Black, Though?"

Black Autoethnography and Racing the Graduate Student/Instructor

LOUIS M. MARAJ

AS USUAL, as I ease into a fresh semester at the Midwestern State University (MwSU),[1] I can count the Black-identified students in my second-year writing class on one hand: two men, one woman. The Black woman, Shaina—vocal—speaks to her biraciality, to one of her parents' experiences as a Black Caribbean immigrant, and calls out White privilege when necessary. One of the men is the typical Black male student I encounter at Midwestern State: shy, withdrawn, but willing to speak sometimes, though not always in debates directly related to blackness. The other Black man, T, outspoken, consistently challenges me in overt, often excoriating, ways. For the first time, he puts my blackness as an instructor at a historically White institution routinely up for open debate.

Unlike most Black men I encounter in other White spaces here, T performs "stereotypical" blackness: through his clothing, speech, and in ways through his writing. I remember gold chains with large pendants and felt pride knowing that T could dress like this in a classroom here—my classroom. He drops "nigga" frequently, nonchalantly, throughout discussions from the jump. That he says it so liberally in front of all the White students in my class engenders a kind of selfish confidence for me.

The first time T asks, "Are you Black?" in some discussion of a Black authored-text, I'm shook. At the front of the classroom, I feel coerced into disclosing my identities. Having worked through a positioning activity during the first week of class, asking students to consider their intersectional identities, T and my own pedagogies compel me to respond. I want to empathize—though this response requires public disclosure. I explain my background: I identify as Black, though ethnically I am both Afro- and Indo-Trinidadian. He doesn't push further.

My aunt and twin cousins visit from Trinidad. I invite them to see me teach. My immediate family never see me in this role, don't know my academic life, and my aunt is a retired schoolteacher whom I look up to. They sit as I review paragraph structure. My histories crisscross my present, living, as though its own body, with its own voice, in the classroom space—with my "Yankee" accent and flailing gesticulation—finally revealing another Lou, not the quiet, introverted child they know, here in "the States" at a major university, teaching (mostly) White kids how to write. Their videos and pictures document my teaching for the first time, letting me see myself as an English instructor while a Black Caribbean im/migrant[2] working in a privileged role. I proudly introduce my students to my relatives at the beginning of class and listen eagerly to their reaction to my teaching.

"#schoolboyLou" shows up on the margins of student assignments throughout the semester. T develops this nickname for me, which appears on his and other students' handwritten work. I never directly ask. I infer that T is "signifyin" on the name of LA rapper ScHoolboy Q. Although it seems subversive, I feel honored that a Black male student thought it his business to give me a new name, a Black name. Because it riffs on the name of a rapper associated with "wokeness," I think honor into what seems like his identification of me via urban Black masculinity. But such identification arises in the classroom as interrogation again, where, in a White space, we engage in some kind of antagonistic, verbal throwdown for blackness.

During group project presentations, I sit at the back of the room. T's group is next, and as he shuffles to the front of the class, he turns and asks in the lag between projects: "Are you Black, though?"

I sigh exasperatedly, "Uh, *yea.*" But before I can even vocalize that, Shaina, seated in between us, responds immediately: something along the lines of "He *already* told you he was Black. Why do you keep asking?" T ignores her, again engages with me, as I continue what must be a critical, staring-at-the-sun look at him. T's next question has me even more shook: "So, like . . . if this was plantation days, would you be in the house while I was in the field?"

•

I begin this story to give an intimate sense of how my experience as a Black im/migrant able-bodied male graduate student/instructor frames my analysis of rhetorical ecologies of race at White institutions. My blackness, articulated by me, perceived and engaged in material-discursive precarious rhetorics with others, cannot be separated from these spaces and communities within which I operate. When I use the word "space," I speak to ecological and environmental conditions that surround, constitute, and embody social intra-action and interaction. Karen Barad conceptualizes spatial meanings as co-constituted by such "agential intra-actions" between spaces' components, a concept integrating Marxist, feminist, and antiracist approaches (815, 810–11). But although I look to these (re)new(ed) materialist interests in spatial constitution, I foreground a fundamentally materialist analysis of racialized precarity through Black feminist thinkers who prioritized relationality long before scholarship's recent "new materialist turn."

Audre Lorde explains, for example, how "the quality of light" (environs/matter) shapes our subjectivities (*Sister* 36), while Patricia Hill Collins highlights the importance of alternative forms of community, stressing relationality through "connections, caring, and personal accountability" (222) to confront interlocking systems of oppression. This intersectional relationality arguably speaks to new materialists' recognition that "phenomena are caught in a multitude of interlocking systems and forces" and attempts "to consider anew the location and nature of capacities for agency" (Coole and Frost 9) in investigations of matter.[3] However, I emphasize the racialized precarities of embodied Black agential rhetorics in a Black feminist tradition, since, as Lisa Marie Cacho stresses, "criminalized populations and the places where they live *form the foundation* of the U. S. legal system, imagined to be the reason why a punitive (in)justice system exists" (5).[4] Spotlighting my Black im/migrant experiences through Black feminist autoethnography reveals the insidious ways that racialized precarity operates in U.S. educational spaces vis-à-vis/within that long-standing "(in)justice system."

Focusing on "everyday, taken-for-granted knowledge" (Hill Collins 32), I pick up and extend Margaret Price's notion of "kairotic spaces"—"the less formal, often unnoticed, areas of academe where knowledge is produced and power is exchanged" (60)—to spaces not traditionally considered "academic."[5] The above narrative demonstrates not only my inability to separate my subjectivity from this project but also the inevitably of being read racially based on my spatiality and positions within the institution. My relationship with T deeply puzzled me for a while: How could I be #schoolboyLou while also some kind of Black poser? Some house slave (contingent English instructor) for the White massa (MwSU)? What roles do the writing classroom—and, by extension, "White" campus spaces—our material identities, and our stories unfolding within them play in theorizing difference in rhetoric and composition? And what histories within the fields do those roles speak with, push against, draw from, and add to?

In this chapter, I center my autoethnographic stories to theorize antiracist agency within rhetoric, composition, and literacy studies. Such a move counters Krista Ratcliffe's view of autoethnography as "valuable" but "admittedly limited in its perspective" and separate from "academic research" in disrupting White supremacy in our fields (37). Autoethnography as a principal methodological orientation—rather than a cursory or introductory one—holds greater possibilities for these disciplines, as scholars of color and particularly Black scholars in it have demonstrated, as I will argue. Forwarded through a Black feminist intersectional lens (Lorde, Hill Collins, hooks), this chapter presents my stories as a Black im/migrant male student/instructor while situating them in a reflexive charted history of Black storytelling traditions within rhetoric, composition, and literacy studies. I mobilize and push forward that history, charting it from June Jordan's "Nobody Mean More to Me Than You and the Future Life of Willie Jordan" (1985) to Carmen Kynard's "Teaching While Black" (2015).

Within that tradition, my analysis considers how my identities embody and perform difference (and consequently institutional "diversity") for/against U.S. historically White institutions. Through this approach, I fracture understandings of the Black graduate student/instructor's precarious position at the historically White university, wrestling with how my meaning-making produces/negotiates within such White, capitalist, nationalist, heteropatriarchal spaces. "Precarization means more than insecure jobs," as Isabell Lorey shows; "by way of insecurity and danger, it embraces the whole existence, the body, modes of subjectivation" (1). In embracing my racialized precarity, I explore how I am criminalized in spaces of potential social death, building on Cacho's stance that in so doing, "empowerment comes from deciding that the outcome of struggle doesn't matter as much as the decision to struggle" (32). I present experiences to exhibit how educational spaces entangle my identities in a kind of self-defeating bind, all while working to subvert that paradox by embodying resistance. Through that presentation, this study calls on our disciplines to pay more attention to blackness and Black masculinity and ways that we might theorize the latter non-monolithically, beyond a toxically straight/stereotypically queer binary. I follow Simone Drake in approaching Black masculinity studies through Black feminist frameworks, imagining possibilities for intersectionality, complexity, and accountability.[6] In effect, I meta-theatrically perform resistance to these binds to emphasize and build on the roles of Black storytelling (its languages and literacies) in our fields. Like Adam Banks's "digital griot," I hope to demonstrate "a synthesis of deep searching (crate-digging) knowledge of the traditions and cultures of [my] community and futuristic vision" (155), mixing, remixing, and mix-taping the outlined tradition of *griot-as-scholar.*

As Mary Louise Pratt states, autoethnographic texts intertwine "appropriation of idioms of the metropolis or the conqueror . . . with indigenous idioms to create self-representations intended to intervene in metropolitan modes of understanding. Autoethnographic works are often addressed to both metropolitan audiences and the speaker's own community. Their reception is thus highly indeterminate" (35). Despite that potentially precarious reception, both White scholars[7] and scholars of color within our fields have embraced, and in some ways appropriated, women of color (and Black) feminism's application of autoethnography[8]—theorized/practiced by Audre Lorde, Gloria Anzaldúa, bell hooks, and others—in critiquing identity in educational spaces. Those scholars of color include Richard Rodriquez (*Hunger of Memory,* 1984), Victor Villanueva (*Bootstraps,* 1993), and Morris Young (*Minor Re/visions,* 2004), among several others. But here, within that subsection, I particularly prioritize the tradition of Black academics (or Blacademics) whose work in rhetoric and composition take up autoethnography, like these scholars of color, as their central methodological framework to extend this tradition through my own stories.

I highlight this long-standing, though unrecognized, foundation utilized by Blacademics in our field through the griot-as-scholar figure. Such a move follows on Banks's call to "build theories, pedagogies, and practices of multimedia writing that honor *the traditions and thus the people* who are still too often not present in our classrooms, our faculties, and in our scholarship" (13–14).[9] Autoethnographic orientations align with Afrocentric methodology that starts "with self-knowledge" and is "conducted through an interaction between the examiner and the subject. Cultural and social immersion are imperative" (Mazama 399). Moreover, Carter Godwin Woodson describes the storyteller's importance to African/diasporic communities. They—often older women—tell stories to youth to maintain posterity of the tribe's traditions. These persons, venerated in the community, play crucial roles in social functions and through daily performance of stories (ix–x). Storytelling, thus linked with both educational and everyday communal being, holds particularly esteemed value in customary Black knowledge-making.[10] I interrogate the functions of reflective stories that position Black rhetoricians and me within the griot-as-scholar tradition[11] to advance this project's Black feminist analytic that "affirms, rearticulates, and provides a vehicle for expressing in public" an already extant consciousness (Hill Collins 32).

I think through racialization as relational because, as Alexander Weheliye explains via Black feminists Sylvia Wynter and Hortense Spillers, relationality "reveals the global and systemic dimensions of racialized, sexualized, and gendered subjugation, while not losing sight of the many ways political violence has given rise to ongoing practices of freedom within various traditions of the oppressed" (13). Pursuing that analytic, I consider the conditions of particular environments and how they engage with bodies (and vice versa) to produce/ negotiate identity and meaning with/in them. Each of those bodies has stories to tell, and this chapter spotlights mine in particular. And more than simply acknowledging my subjectivity as significant in ongoing analysis, such a move calls attention to the human—positioned variously in privileged/marginalized ways in relation to the institution—involved in academic labor. My stories, transactional, dialectical, ecological, make me human. Audre Lorde sums it up best when philosophizing on her teaching: "So more than technique, I consider as basic my total perception. The poet as teacher, human as poet, teacher as human. They all feel the same to me. A writer by definition is a teacher" ("Poet" 182). To interrogate that "perception" means to engage in a process of Black storytelling, of autoethnography.

"IF THIS WAS PLANTATION DAYS" (CONTINUED)

As I calmly articulate why we shouldn't frame ourselves in relation to slavery, T makes his way to the front of the class. I can't help but think about our bodies' positionings in the space—T's resistance arising as he takes the front and I sit in the back row he usually occupies. Where is the house in this classroom? Where is the field? And though I readily dismiss the planation metaphor—because I don't want T to perceive himself as White chattel or to think myself some White overseer's lackey, lingering aloof over T on massa's behalf—deep down it holds some truth. Both Black bodies exist in relation to White authority, bound in different ways by and up in oppressive matrixes of domination: our exaggerated truths. While "the politics of slavery, of racialized power relations were such that slaves were denied their right to gaze" (hooks, *Black* 115), T, here, usurps that denial by racializing me as dominant through the academy's mechanisms.

By our last class, I have grown quite attached to this group. Having had particularly difficult, lengthy, delicate, and complex discussions about blackness, resistance, and their relationships to whiteness/institutional power, one day—prompted by Shaina's emotional response to a video on the Ferguson Uprising—I tell my story of being a victim of police brutality in Texas. I'm so comfortable I want to give this class a takeaway: on that final day, we watch parts of a documentary on racism. The clips address the "n-word," as well as the question "Are all White people racist?" Following our viewing of the former, T asks, "Do *you* say 'nigga'?" And before I can resp—"Are you Black, though?"

At this juncture, I need to know why. What motivates the question? What preoccupies T throughout the semester, so much that it manifests openly through these interjections? "I am. Like I explained before. Why do you keep asking this question, though?"

"Is it the color of my skin?"

"Is it the way I dress, or the way I speak?"

"Or is it that I'm standing in front of this classroom? What is it?"

"Because you're standing in front of a classroom," T explains. My position as an instructor at a historically White institution means that my blackness is inauthentic, out of place, or at the very least questionable. But it's my Black masculinity. And my lack of urban Black male performatives. How could I be *a Black man* teaching this shit? That a Black male student would think that Black masculinity couldn't be found in, or performed by, an English instructor at MwSU somehow implies that I am, in some ways, a whitewashed, feminized version of blackness—and it's true. But from his choice of my Black body's spatial location as the root of his questioning, rather than biological markers, or my material/linguistic racial/gender performance, T identifies an impossibility in the efficacy of my antiracist, intersectional Black agency. For him, because of my place in surrounding whiteness, which my White field substantiates and contributes to (Kynard, "Teaching" 3), my centering of blackness in teaching needs to be conspicuously critiqued. It is suspect.

BETWEEN POETRY AND RHETORIC

> The difference between poetry and rhetoric
> is being ready to kill
> yourself
> instead of your children.
> —Audre Lorde, *The Black Unicorn*, "Power" 108

In contending with T over Black language and our roles within institutional spaces, interrogating my affective responses as a Black instructor in relation to him, and bringing autoethnographic reflexivity to materialist analysis through a Black feminist lens, my reading here follows on teacher/scholar/poet June Jordan's. Her 1985 essay, "Nobody Mean More to Me Than You and the Future Life of Willie Jordan," wrestles with her experience teaching Black English to a mostly Black class.[12] Jordan's pedagogical reflection takes a sharp affective turn when one of her students, Willie, loses his brother to a police shooting. Utilizing the highly politicized teaching/learning of Black vernacular, Jordan and her students grapple with responding in protest. The essay deploys storytelling as a means to center topical issues significant to Black life and learning. It demonstrates Black autoethnography's potentials to weave through "the eloquence, the sudden haltings of speech, the fierce struggle against tears, the furious throwaway, and useless explosions" (135). Though different from my encounters with T, Jordan's relationship with her student demonstrates how Black pedagogical stories might help us think through Black identity, language, and their institutionalization—a critical aim of this project.

Prompting his suspicion to its climactic head, T's doubt about my saying "nigga"—a term fraught with histories of racialized violence and Black reclamation—underscores language's roles in racializing, classing, and gendering subjects. My relationship with T seemingly hinged on our individual/mutual, material-discursive relationships with the word, here, within a historically White space. The use of Black English situates us in, and reminds us of, debates within rhetoric, composition, and literacy studies surrounding the publication of a landmark Black autoethnographic text—Keith Gilyard's *Voices of the Self* (1991). Engaged in tensions on Black students' relationships with Black and standard English, Gilyard narrates his negotiations with literacy from "birth" to the end of high school in every other chapter of his monograph, carefully studying his sociolinguistic development in scholarly conversations in intervening ones. He justifies his methods by explaining the validity of autobiographical artifacts and a transactional analytical framework (12). In such a model, actively propelled by my own stories, subjects like T and me "continually [negotiate] with an evolving environment" (Gilyard 13). Though Gilyard frames his orientation as autobiographic, the study's scholarly analysis of his schooling in conversation with major, concurrent intellectual discussions characterizes *Voices* as a full-scale autoethnographic investigation into those discourses. Gilyard's book and Jordan's essay exemplify "critical autoethnographies" that "foreground a writer's standpoint and makes this standpoint accessible, transparent, and vulnerable to judgment and evaluation" (Adams et al. 89).

The vulnerability in reflecting on my exchange with T allows materialist analysis of various "voices" I embody as an able-bodied Black im/migrant male student/instructor in educational contexts. In the narrative, these include my "voices of the self," my own accentuated identity as a foreigner employed in a non-native space—aurally identifiable through speech—as a race-radical Black instructor, as a contingent laborer for the White institution, and as a male, privileged in a middle-class space through instructional authority. I wrestle with a similar desire as Gilyard's to embody the "hip schoolboy" in T's nickname "#schoolboyLou"—a persona "impossible to achieve" (160). On the selfsame notion of "voice," Jacqueline Jones Royster's (1996) "When the First Voice You Hear Is Not Your Own" capitalizes on meta-level prospects for autoethnographic storytelling to investigate "voice" as a "manifestation of subjectivity" tied not only to the spoken/written but also "as a *thing* heard, perceived, and reconstructed" (30). Working in the very mode she sees belittled by the White academy ("stories"), Royster multidimensionally critiques how academic spaces misconstrue voice—specifically hers—cleverly pushing against that distortion to fund her thesis. Likewise, "If This Was Plantation Days" shows how the classroom space in an ecology at MwSU works with/against my voiced identities, racializing my body in transactional contexts with notions of dominance and subordination. Royster's article operates alongside bell hooks's contemporaneous *Teaching to Transgress* (1994), which, through storytelling, extends sometimes beyond narrated personal responses to teaching/learning situations to active, reciprocal encounters with scholarship, countering various "systems of dominion" (10). hooks's call for instructors to "practice being vulnerable in the classroom, being wholly present in mind, body, and spirit" (14) parallels Royster's emphasis on the varied, intersecting ways voice can be embodied for Black feminist griots-as-scholars. In utilizing multiple angles of Black storytelling, both thinkers press Black autoethnography forward, demonstrating how subjectivity might be complicated through layers of analysis to resist institutional oppression.

Like Vershawn Young, in his article "Your Average Nigga" (2004) and subsequent monograph by the same name (2007), I stereotyped T based on his clothes, demeanor, and language. And while my initial reaction to T was optimistic, as opposed to Young's reaction to his "ghetto" student Cam ("Your" 699), that impression does not make my profiling any less harmful. Having grown up in a neighborhood unlike Cam's or Young's—mind you, not a "ghetto" in local parlance but one boasting a "drug zone," "pipers," and my mother's routine question, "That is gunshot ah hearin'?"—my relationship with U.S. Black masculinity differs from Young's, Cam's, and T's. Deploying autoethnographic techniques, Young's article contends that proponents of code-switching essentialize race construction, resulting in damaging consequences, particularly for Black urban males. The monograph pushes his use of this methodological orientation to other spaces in his personal and professional life, performing a "merger of what's often considered academic (and white) with what's considered creative (and raced)" (Young, *Your* 8, 10). Such emphasis on performativity and spaces in which performativity occurs marks *Your Average Nigga* as an amalgamation of critical autoethnography and "narratives of space and place" (Adams et al. 86).

Growing up, my situation differed from Young's in that school and bookishness were not necessarily socialized as feminine.[13] In postcolonial Trinidad and Tobago, parents, teachers, and even culture beat learning into us as a clear alternative to drugs, poverty, and violence. I distinctly remember the calypsonian Gypsy's refrain, "Little Black boy, go to school and learn, little Black boy, show some concern, little Black boy, education is the key, to get you off the street and out poverty." But I was an inside child from quite young and, because of mixed heritage, did not identify with the song when it was popular. My relatives' presence in "If This Was Plantation Days" also seemed, to me, to legitimize my blackness, particularly my im/migrant blackness and authority in an antiracist classroom. They were other Black bodies attesting to my racial and ethnic "authenticity." However, in T's struggle with me over Black masculinity, my im/migrant blackness undermined my (U.S.) Black masculinity—and perhaps contributed to T's doubt about my use of "nigga." The junctions of precarious bodies in particular temporalities and spatialities in both Young's and my analyses illustrate the dynamic capabilities of autoethnography within the griot-as-scholar lineage.

Methodologically, Young positions his text with *Voices,* explaining it as a predecessor, though he attempts to merge seamlessly autobiography and criticism, as opposed to Gilyard's chapter separations (11). Young also explicitly draws from W. E. B. Du Bois's *The Souls of Black Folk,* calling it a model for blending genres. Notably, Du Bois recalls first coming to the question prompting his formative theory of double-consciousness, which haunts this very project—"How does it feel to be a problem?"—in a "wooden schoolhouse" (1–2). His socialization within an educational institution teaches him, through reflective/reflexive interrogation, how to embody, affectively and materially, his precarity. Although Young frames *Your Average Nigga* as autocritography,[14] it might usefully also be considered Black autoethnography, working from that latter through self-aware attunement to subjectivity, identity formation, and genre manipulation. Young's performativity, reflexivity/reflectivity, attentiveness to space, and use of poetry[15] reveal a conscious propulsion of autoethnography and how it could be fruitfully employed in studying Black intersectional identity.

Following on Young's conspicuous and meta-level use of storytelling as a means to analysis, Carmen Kynard's scholarship exhibits Black autoethnographic methodologies in its prioritization of personal narrative in reflexive relation to academic conversation. It embodies critical self-awareness of her positionality as a Black race-radical griot-as-scholar and how that awareness shapes and furthers research. Kynard's *Vernacular Insurrections* (2014) intertwines several vignettes with revisionist histories of composition studies in relation to the Black Freedom movement. Calling her work "Intellectual Autobiography" (1), Kynard also foregrounds her language usage (like Young), claiming a "cross amalgamation of many styles and registers" from "high academese" to "high urbanese" (13). My above story in two vignettes and the critical reflections in proceeding sections similarly slip in/out of academic, colloquial Black U.S. and Trini dialect. Kynard explains the self-involvement required in Black autoethnography when she pronounces, "you are always right there in the mix, no matter how much you have been written out, spanning much wider than the token representation you have been allowed" (12), harkening back to Royster, and validating my humanization of the Blacademic in rhetorical ecologies of race.

While *Vernacular Insurrections'* organization reminds us of Gilyard's *Voices* in separating chapters featuring personal stories from explicitly critical conversations, Kynard's shifting deployment of language to story her work operationalizes and forwards the all-encompassing autoethnographic analytic offered in Young's scholarship. In her (2015) article "Teaching While Black," Kynard remains "conscious" in using "stories to understand and present the lives and literacies of students of color where [her] own cultural role as a *black female storyteller* enacts its own critical inquiry" (4).[16] Kynard's scholarship not only blatantly brings the Black feminist griot-as-scholar role to conversation, but it also reflexively marshals the inherent political Black agency and traditions from which it comes as a declarative, salient mechanism for scholarly analysis. Employing that mechanism, I re/mix autoethnographic frameworks from an amalgam of predecessors, pushing onward from Young and Kynard. My stories thus stand on their own as criticism and entertain academic conversation, fluidly navigating dialects, and eventually leave with only the creative (yet analytical) text.

In further interrogating why my "standing in front of a classroom" at MwSU caused intra-racial tension, I offer more stories to uncover and contextualize how my precarity embodies and performs difference, or fails to do so, on U.S. college campuses. These stories, like "If This Was Plantation Days," ask: How might my histories, identities, and experiences cut across spaces and temporalities to live difference? My materialist, Black feminist analysis follows purposefully on Royster's claim that individual stories placed against each other construct credible evidence, a basis from which "transformation in theory and practice might rightfully begin" (30). Building from the outlined griot-as-scholar tradition, I present them "as a stance of bearing-witness as more than just one individual's observations, but an indication of the levels of systematic racism that we do not address" (Kynard, "Teaching" 4). In so doing, I critique the institutionalization of race-radical Black thinking and de/constructions of my precarious intersectional identities, continuing to pose Du Bois's question: "How does it feel to be a problem?" while seeking agency through that push.

EMBODYING DIFFERENCE

"To the bleeding white man who jumped me"

for seeming the Black kid who mugged him
—for Trayvon Martin

Tell me my headstone reads "warhorse," I'm worth
its very concrete, my body before
it's emptied in latenight rainshower's burst
better unnoticed, in water, in war.
Tell me you've already heard my namesong's
encore: it means nothing, just like any
other. My mother, just another—wrong
for raising a thug like me—like every
one, mourns my name gone. No armor, no gun,
no well-tailored suit, no master's degree,
no eloquent president, no nation
post-race, no, see, not even a hoodie
protects me from *sob* stories my skin tells
in deep night, my heart, its own, loud, Black knell.

I think about Trayvon Martin a lot—maybe too much. I think about what he means to whom and why. Perhaps it is because a child, because of his clothes, skin color, and environment—because of his racializing assemblage—represented to a man some deviant problem. Weheliye contends that "the idea

of racializing assemblages construes race not as a biological or cultural classification but as a set of sociopolitical processes that discipline humanity into
full humans, not-quite-humans, and nonhumans" (4). I have sought repeatedly, through poetry mostly, to mull Du Bois's thesis question in relation to
Martin. With Weheliye's conception, this translates to "How does it feel to
be not-quite-human or nonhuman?" With Cacho's social death, it becomes:
"How does it feel to be criminalized?" In this section, I ask myself all three in
probing racial difference within college campus environments. While react-
ing to the alleged "colorblindness" of U.S. society during Obama's presidency,
the above poem arises from two particular incidents in 2015 and 2011. Both
occurred in "off-campus" areas[17] in the Midwest and Texas, respectively, and
demonstrate how I embody and affect certain precarious identities in particular environments.

The man to whom I dedicate this poem jumped me while walking home
one night three summers ago. Through the poem, I follow Audre Lorde's call
to "claim anger and to hear in anger a certain claim" (Ahmed 171). Like the
Black feminist thinker, "my response to racism is anger. I have lived with that
anger, ignoring it, feeding it, learning to use it" (Lorde, *Sister* 127). I return
from a White male friend's home after playing video games. As I continue up
the street where I live, three Black youth run by me. They wear an assortment
of shorts, T-shirts, and sneakers. In a college town, such scenes are common-
place late Saturday night, with bars buzzing, alcoholic energy quickly peaking.
I distinctly know, from my own experiences, that responses "to Black males in
common spaces, in public spaces, [send] powerful messages to [them] about
how their presence is unwanted" (Brooms 100). I continue until I notice a
White woman lying on the opposite curb, clutching her foot. I cross the street,
wanting to be an ally, offering help. She groans. I prod, asking, "Are you okay?"
I understand why a White woman, injured, lying on a curb at midnight, wants
nothing to do with a Black man in a country where media often re/casts Black
men as dangerous threats specifically to White women (and their sexuality)
(James 28). Fortunately, another man—a White man—approaches and asks
similar questions. We begin to find out she twisted her ankle.

With my back to the street, I'm shoved forward. I spin to a bloodied,
skinny, short White man, who shouts, "Gimme my shit! You took my fucking
shit!" I calmly explain that I don't know what he's talking about, but furiously
he again pushes his stained hands, now, into my chest, still shouting about his
"shit." I am almost twice his size (not a big man, not a fighter, I don't want to
hurl able-bodied anger against a vulnerable, injured person). As he continues
to aggravate me, the White man who stopped to help explains to the aggressor
that I'm not who he wants; "I think they went that way." The vigilante stares at

me blankly, recognizing in those few seconds that he profiled, picked a fight with, and assaulted me, before crossing the street, screaming into oncoming Saturday-nighters, "They took my shit!"—his "they" still "categorically [criminalizing]" the Black men he encounters that night (Cacho 23). As Brent Staples explains, there's "no solace against the kind of alienation that comes from ever being the suspect, against being set apart" (565). I walk a couple blocks home, remove my sneakers, shorts, and T-shirt, now bloody.

Within the campus environment, such vigilante action might be expected with the prevalence of the MwSU Public Safety Department's alerts via text messages, emails, and its website. These "safety notices," often racialized, give vague descriptions of Black men suspected of violent crimes, contributing to a vigilante culture that perpetuates White supremacy. The spoken word piece in this chapter's final section contains excerpts from one such alert. These announcements represent mechanisms by which historically White institutions criminalize Black males, placing us "under increased surveillance and control by community policing tactics on and off campus," rendering us "'out of place' . . . 'fitting the description' of illegitimate members of the campus community" (Smith et al. 562). The historically White institution's policies, which reflect the systemically inbuilt ideologies of most U.S. institutions, prompt affective responses from both Black males (paranoia, alienation, anger) and other members of on-/off-campus college communities about them. As Derrick Brooms highlights, fear of Black males in college environments aligns with how they are historically scripted (100). This narrative illustrates how embodying such identities within these rhetorical/material ecologies means wrestling with affects produced by oppressive institutional forces, as well as through gender performance.

The following night, another eye-opening, isolating incident speaks directly to individual behaviors that oppressive institutional environments birth (and vice versa), which undoubtedly feed into personal prejudices, a "most insidious danger" (Brooms 100). I go to a bar with the same White colleague from the night before to recuperate from my previous experience. At 2 a.m., while he smokes and chats up a woman, a bottle breaks amidst a small crowd across the street near another bar's patio. I step away briefly to use the bathroom and return to him on the phone. "White, Black, or Hispanic?" the other end asks—I could hear. "Black," he says. "Why would you *call the cops?* Why would you say *they are Black?*" He looks at me as most White folk do when confronted with ghosts of slavery and Jim Crow. Within sixty seconds, cops roll up. From the other side of the street, flanked by the man responsible for their presence, I see a White officer yell at, grab, and frisk a Black man walking by the nearby CVS. I see myself there, walking by that CVS as I hop off the bus daily. I recognize the disconnect that academia doesn't want me to. These particular acts of *seeing*—in eye contact with this colleague, with the previous night's vigilante, in living the distance between one side of the street and another—alert me to Du Bois's "Veil" mentioned throughout *Souls*. They make visible the color line that institutional White supremacy and colorblind policies and ideology invite us to ignore. They reveal the shaping of racialized, gendered, nationalized, dis/abled notions of material identities inherent in U.S. institutions that play into the re/active performance of these identities.

I specifically choose off-campus interactions that push institutionalization up against identity to foreground how the Black graduate scholar engages with kairotic spaces not seen in classrooms, conference presentations, or professionalization workshops. As sociologists indicate, Black male students in "campus-academic," "campus-social," and "campus-public" spaces routinely face microaggressions causing "racial battle fatigue (e.g., frustration, shock, anger, disappointment, resentment, anxiety, helplessness, hopelessness, and fear)" (Smith et al. 551). But, as David R. Williams et al. illustrate, we also experience macrostressors or racial macroaggressions. These traumas elicit the above range of affective responses that pile together, fashioning precariously racialized identities.

Monkey on Down[18]

I'm a monkey to you: joke, juggler, clown,
three races as they walk into a bar.
"Has anyone told you that you look, sound,
like Barack Obama?" Yes. My ears are
large. My skin's brown. Yes. I articulate
the slight academic jargon you like.
D'you like me to dance, twerk, dougie my skit
on out your white community? My bright
gold teeth skinned, jeweled dental treasure chest?
We sit. The black asks *ayo what's goin' down?*
The brown thinks *how do I best word this mess,*
an always already terrorist? Found
gut warns *bite down tongue.* Anger's insistence
tastes good. Chew the cud of most resistance.

Imagine a physical classroom where, as a student, you never meet five of the six assessors of your writing. They will evaluate through an online mechanism to which you submit your work, only knowing you through electronic documents. They do not know your name, what you look or sound like, when they open submissions. Unlike a strictly online course, your material identities matter within the classroom space to your instructor, but play little role in how meanings you produce might be "valued" (through grading) by the neoliberal university. While a graduate student/instructor in Texas, I teach for this program that removes student identifiers from submitted assignments. When not teaching a syllabus, texts, assignments, and rubrics standardized across all sections of this first-year writing course, I "document instruct": I grade online from a pile of work, unmarked.[19] Identical guidelines and material across all course sections ensure that my lived identities as an instructor, like my students', matter minimally as a vehicle for the information I deliver. In this colorblind institutional backdrop, I fall victim to racial profiling and police brutality, demonstrating how I am both "misrecognized as someone who committed a crime" while also "criminalized" through my Black im/migrant identities in being "prevented from being law-abiding" (Cacho 4).

On the first day of spring break 2011, I return with two White coworkers from a music festival to my home at 9 p.m. Having left at 2 p.m., with my roommate (a White woman from Dallas) away, the porch lights remain off. I fumble my keys in the dark. I use my phone's backlight to identify the right one and get inside. Sitting in the living room, loudly watching television, a bang interrupts casual conversation.

(Pause.)

Another bang. "Police!"

We exchange frantic glances.

Another bang. "Open this door!"

My colleague Ben shouts, "No!"

I'm taken aback, but Ben knows they need a warrant for intrusion. I don't.

Another bang. "Open this fucking door right now!"

When Ben shouts, "No! What's the problem?!," the cop explains, "I will kick in this door if I have to!" Reece relents. He opens to a hand, shoved, that yanks him out beyond eye-shot. Ben, closest to the door, gets ripped out next. I walk to it, and, by the hand, am raffed,[20] cuffed, face-slammed onto the concrete porch.

They check IDs. "I live here!" The White male cop takes my passport out my back pocket. I cut my dreads when I went for my new visa photo. My regrown dreadlocks couch my face from the ground. The passport, I suppose, seems sketch. In the barrage of questions, Ben asks, "Why is there a dog here?" "To bite your ass!" the White woman cop snaps. Still cuffed, I am dragged by the male officer through my living room. He asks about my roommate. Her framed pictures stare, an indictment. This is a nice White lady's home. The cop shoves me through each room, asks to see my mine, surveys my papers and poems: "You go by 'Lou'?"

He takes me back to the porch, sets me back on my face and stomach. They chat.

I panic.

I don't understand what's happening. I rock back and forth, screaming, "Help!" "Please!" "Why?!" The cops panic. Ben asks, "Can we tell him to shut the fuck up?" "Yes." "Lou, shut the fuck up!"

Eventually, they uncuff Reece. He again explains that all we did was go to a concert and come home. I live there. We ask for their names. They say only, "Next time, open the door when we fucking say to!" I eat my porch. I am humiliated. No record exists of the near-half-hour incident. All they offer at the station is a mostly blank sheet indicating a call was made: Three men; One suspicious with a light, opening the door; My body, profiled suspect. The rationale given by the cop I complain to, later on the phone: I would want the law to treat an intruder the way I was treated. They need to be brutal because the situation demands it. I, myself, ask to be brutalized.

PERFORMING DIFFERENCE

In "asking" to be brutalized, I succumb to what Sara Ahmed calls "a life paradox: you have to become what you are judged as being" in representing difference (186). Like my clash with T over our material-discursive relationships with "nigga," embodying and performing racially precarious rhetorics (above, through dreadlocks, my im/migrant identity, etc.) means being rendered non-law-abiding and less-than-human. In this section, I continue exhibiting this bind, which does diversity work for educational institutions that sustains dominant whiteness (Ahmed 33)—work built into neoliberal U.S. socioeconomic infrastructures for the racially precarious. I break completely from formal critical conversation, concluding only with a spoken word dedication to T.

Such a conclusion aims to facilitate (autoethnographic) scholarship in rhetoric, composition, and literacy studies that encourages, as Audre Lorde consistently does, knowledge-producers to take into account how "even the form our creativity takes" operates within oppressive matrixes. We must welcome work "which requires the least physical labor, the least material" (Lorde, *Sister* 116). In continuing the griot-as-scholar methodology, this chapter opens up what counts as valid knowledge-creation, situated within the complex systematic positions that Black folk (people of color, and other marginalized identities) occupy. I call on autoethnographers and non-autoethnographers "to consider the accessibility of their texts . . . asking what value or benefit our work might have for our participants and readers, as well as ourselves" (Adams et al. 44).

This creatively critical inquiry into my own racialized precarity as an able-bodied Black im/migrant male graduate student/instructor adds to Carmen Kynard's demand via LaNita Jacobs-Huey. I mobilize what the latter "described as the natives *'gazing and talking back'* in ways that explicitly interrogate *the daily operation of white supremacy in our field and on our campuses* rather than more performances of psychologically-internalized black pain for the white gaze" (Kynard, "Teaching" 14).[21] This chapter enacts that clap back, building on a tradition of resistant storytelling struggling to liberate our work, language, and daily material realities.

Selfie as #schoolboyLou
　　—for T

What you think this houseslave life bout?

Is not no skinning, grinning, or sipping tea. We work that kitchen, waiting: me, Uncle Langston, and Miss Audre. What you think we for, T? I pay my dues: I wear this skin like the blues I sing, fill the white man's drink when low.

What you think you know? T, they comin for all ah we.

"Safety Awareness Message: We are sharing this news on behalf of the [City] Division of Police for a crime that occurred in the off-campus area"

See, one mid-morning, rainy, I walk to my office from the on-campus gym. Cross the street when I come up upon a guided tour. It's always tours. T, I watch from the other side. A white man leads white parents in North Face and New Balance. He got stories—rehearsed—his mom's concern for his "safety," she texts. At night, on campus, he assures his white parent, his audience, "I feel very safe." But to keep you and me in check, MwSU's Campus Alert is "an awesome feature that informs us on these issues." I think bout Trayvon Martin shot by a vigilante in the rain. I stop.

T, they won't stop comin for all ah we. House or field, ain't matter the work we do for free.

"Suspect #1 is described as a black male in his 20's standing 5'6" and weighing 135 pounds. He was wearing white t-shirt and blue jeans."

Nah, you wouldn't wear a white tee. All black, the usual.

"Suspect #2 is described as a black male in his 20's standing 6'1" and weighing 180 pounds. He was wearing a black t-shirt, black baseball cap and blue jeans."

Maybe? You
taller than me. But you got that black beanie. Does it matter, T? What we wear, where we sleep, nigga, what we tryna be?

Schoolboy, houseslave, I'm just tryna be, aight?
"He aight," T writes on an eval, for the massa to see.

NOTES

1. I replace names for confidentiality. MwSU is a large Midwestern historically White institution. I tell autoethnographic stories from memory, recreating speech, acknowledging that stories change through re/telling.
2. I use "im/migrant" to demonstrate the precarity of U.S. noncitizenship.
3. Coole and Frost contend that materialist frameworks overlap with new materialisms as both "understand materiality in a relational, emergent sense as contingent materialization" (29). Especially attentive to that congruency, Barad contributes to a "robust account of the materialization of all bodies—'human' and 'nonhuman'—and the material-discursive practices by which their differential constitutions are marked" (810).
4. Emphasis Cacho's.
5. Though institutions border spaces for commodification, I argue those spaces operate with/against such bordering. "Off-campus areas," even while signaling separation, are inculcated in an institution's ecological meanings, since they remain relationally, geographically, and linguistically tethered to them. My study aligns with feminist geographers' "notions of space as paradoxical, provisional, contradictory, fragmented" (Reynolds 20).
6. I acknowledge able-bodied, straight, cis-gender male privileges, hoping to dismantle a tradition of their misuse. In centering Black women's scholarship, I theorize Black masculinity to work against essentialization of difference. This essay furthers scholarship at the intersections of race and gender/sexuality studies in our fields, like Eric D. Pritchard's.
7. Such as Hesford in *Framing Identities* (1999) and Rose in *Lives on the Boundary* (1989).
8. I use "autoethnography" to refer to autobiographic stories contextualized within the theorization of culture (ethnography) for knowledge production/negotiation. Adams et al. mark autoethnography distinct from autobiography due to its academic audience (36–37).
9. Emphasis mine.
10. While traditional griots use oral performance, autoethnography's performativity/reciprocity allows readers spaces to relate and respond (Calafell 8), dis/identify, riff, and clap back,

offering deviations from traditional ideas. As Barbara Christian spotlights, "people of color have always theorized . . . in the stories we create . . . since dynamic rather than fixed ideas seem more to our liking" (52).

11. The U.S. tradition dates back to Black knowledge-making by former slaves through autobiographic writings and speeches.

12. This charted history is inherently reductive. I choose Black scholars who represent the analytic for which I argue and speak in some way to my project's politics, welcoming further engagement with this history.

13. See Greene and Swenson's chapter in this volume on the feminization of soft skills.

14. Black autoethnography shares similarities with Kimberly Benston's "black autocritography" (284). However, I contend the former centrally analyzes the materiality of peoples and cultures (as opposed to literature) and represents more than slippages.

15. Young's second chapter features his poem "shiny," interrelating analysis of it. I extend this aspect of Blacademic autoethnography, acknowledging Young—and Lorde—as griot-as-scholar ancestors.

16. Emphasis mine.

17. Both incidents occurred within a one-mile radius of each respective campus.

18. Originally published at poets.org.

19. Groups of about six classes make up a work group. Six instructors grade from their pile. A classroom instructor thus has under a 20 percent chance of grading his or her own students' work.

20. "Raff" in Trinidadian dialect means to pull an object away (usually from another person) violently.

21. Emphases in original.

WORKS CITED

Adams, Tony E., Stacy Holman Jones, and Carolyn Ellis. *Autoethnography: Understanding Qualitative Research.* Oxford University Press, 2015.

Ahmed, Sara. *On Being Included: Racism and Diversity in Institutional Life.* Duke University Press, 2012.

Banks, Adam J. *Digital Griots: African American Rhetoric in a Multimedia Age.* Southern Illinois University Press, 2010.

Barad, Karen. "Posthumanist Performativity: Toward an Understanding of How Matter Comes to Matter." *Signs: Journal of Women in Culture and Society* 28.3 (2003): 801–31.

Benston, Kimberly W. *Performing Blackness: Enactments of African-American Modernism.* Routledge, 2000.

Brooms, Derrick R. *Being Black, Being Male on Campus: Understanding and Confronting Black Male Collegiate Experiences.* State University of New York Press, 2017.

Cacho, Lisa Marie. *Social Death: Racialized Rightlessness and the Criminalization of the Unprotected.* New York University Press, 2012.

Calafell, Bernadette Marie. "(I)dentities: Considering Accountability, Reflexivity, and Intersectionality in the I and the We." *Liminalities: A Journal of Performance Studies* 9.2 (2013): 6–13.

Christian, Barbara. "The Race for Theory." *Cultural Critique* 6 (1987): 335–45.

Coole, Diana, and Samantha Frost. *New Materialisms: Ontology, Agency, and Politics.* Duke University Press, 2010.

Drake, Simone C. *When We Imagine Grace: Black Men and Subject Making.* University of Chicago Press, 2016.

Du Bois, W. E. B. *The Souls of Black Folk: Essays and Sketches.* A. C. McClurg, 1903.

Gilyard, Keith. *Voices of the Self: A Study of Language Competence.* Wayne State University Press, 1991.

Hesford, Wendy S. *Framing Identities: Autobiography and the Politics of Pedagogy.* University of Minnesota Press, 1999.

Hill Collins, Patricia. *Black Feminist Thought: Knowledge, Consciousness, and the Politics of Empowerment.* Routledge, 1990.

hooks, bell. *Black Looks: Race and Representation.* South End, 1992.

———. *Teaching to Transgress: Education as the Practice of Freedom.* Routledge, 1994.

Jacobs-Huey, LaNita. "The Natives are Gazing and Talking Back: Reviewing the Problematics of Positionality, Voice, and Accountability among 'Native' Anthropologists." *American Anthropologist* 104.3 (2002): 791–804.

James, Joy. *Resisting State Violence: Radicalism, Gender, and Race in U. S. Culture.* University of Minnesota Press, 1996.

Jordan, June. "Nobody Mean More to Me Than You and the Future Life of Willie Jordan." *On Call: Political Essays.* South End Press, 1985. 123–39.

Kynard, Carmen. "Teaching While Black: Witnessing Disciplinary Whiteness, Racial Violence, and Race-Management." *Literacy in Composition Studies* 3.1 (2015): 1–20.

———. *Vernacular Insurrections: Race, Black Protest, and the New Century in Composition-Literacies Studies.* State University of New York Press, 2013.

Lorde, Audre. *The Black Unicorn.* Norton, 1978.

———. "Poet as Teacher, Human as Poet, Teacher as Human." *I am Your Sister: Collected and Unpublished Writings of Audre Lorde.* Eds. Rudolph P. Byrd, Johnnetta Betsch Cole, and Beverly Guy-Sheftall. Oxford University Press, 2009. 182–83.

———. *Sister Outsider: Essays and Speeches.* Crossing Press, 1984.

Lorey, Isabell. *State of Insecurity: Government of the Precarious.* Verso, 2015.

Maraj, Louis. "Monkey on Down." *Poets.org.* Academy of American Poets. 1 Sept. 2016. <https://www.poets.org/academy-american-poets/ohio-state-university-poetry-prize-2016>. 10 July 2017.

Mazama, Ama. "The Afrocentric Paradigm: Contours and Definitions." *Journal of Black Studies* 31.4 (2001): 387–405.

Pratt, Mary Louise. "Arts of the Contact Zone." *Profession* (1991): 33–40.

Price, Margaret. *Mad at School: Rhetorics of Mental Disability and Academic Life.* University of Michigan Press, 2011.

Pritchard, Eric D. *Fashioning Lives: Black Queers and the Politics of Literacy.* Southern Illinois University Press, 2017.

Ratcliffe, Krista. *Rhetorical Listening: Identification, Gender, Whiteness.* Southern Illinois University Press, 2005.

Reynolds, Nedra. *Geographies of Writing: Inhabiting Places and Encountering Difference.* Southern Illinois University Press, 2007.

Rodriguez, Richard. *Hunger of Memory: The Education of Richard Rodriguez: An Autobiography.* Bantam Books, 1983.

Rose, Mike. *Lives on the Boundary: A Moving Account of the Struggles and Achievements of America's Educationally Unprepared.* Penguin, 1990.

Royster, Jacqueline J. "When the First Voice You Hear Is Not Your Own." *College Composition and Communication* 47.1 (1996): 29–40.

Smith, W. A., W. R. Allen, and L. L. Danley. "'Assume the Position . . . You Fit the Description': Psychosocial Experiences and Racial Battle Fatigue Among African American Male College Students." *American Behavioral Scientist* 51.4 (2007): 551–78.

Staples, Brent. "Black Men and Public Space (1986)" *Essays in Context.* Ed. Sandra F. Tropp and Ann Pierson-D'Angelo. Oxford University Press, 2001. 564–66.

Villanueva, Victor. *Bootstraps: From an American Academic of Color.* National Council of Teachers of English, 1993.

Weheliye, Alexander G. *Habeas Viscus: Racializing Assemblages, Biopolitics, and Black Feminist Theories of the Human.* Duke University Press, 2014.

Williams, D. R., H. W. Neighbors, and J. S. Jackson. "Racial/Ethnic Discrimination and Health: Findings from Community Studies." *American Journal of Public Health* 98.9 (2008): 29–37.

Woodson, Carter G. *African Myths: Together with Proverbs.* Associated Publishers, 1928.

Young, Morris. *Minor Re/visions: Asian American Literacy Narratives as a Rhetoric of Citizenship.* Southern Illinois University Press, 2004.

Young, Vershawn A. *Your Average Nigga: Performing Race, Literacy, and Masculinity.* Wayne State University Press, 2007.

———. "Your Average Nigga." *College Composition and Communication* 55.4 (2004): 693–715.

Precarious Cooperation

Soft Skills and the Governing of Labor Power

RONALD WALTER GREENE and KRISTIN SWENSON

WORKPLACE SKILLS are ways to express what the Marxist tradition describes as a relation between labor power and labor. Labor power is an abstraction that describes the capacity to produce, while labor describes particular ways or forms of working. Labor power describes a potential power, while labor describes its actualization. Economic insecurity is a norm inherent in capitalism, not its exception (Neilson and Rossiter). However, in the United States, the breakdown of the Keynesian-Fordist compromises in the 1970s inaugurated a "new insecurity" (Wallulis 161–72) expressed in "the struggle to preserve employability in the present without past guarantees of secure employment" (161). This new insecurity generated a conceptual interest in precarity as a way to think and organize in new ways to generate new models of care and interdependence (Puar 166). At the same time, as Jonna and Foster write, worker precariousness "has a long history in socialist thought, where it is associated from the start with the concept of the reserve army of labor" (22). The struggle for employability provides a point of departure for this chapter.

How might someone prepare themselves for employability? Increasingly, many assert the value of soft skills for enabling people to secure a first job or hold on to a job, or as a crucial element for job advancement (Kamin 8). This chapter presents a rhetorical history of soft skills to explore their relationship to questions of employment and employability. As such, soft skills participate in a precarious rhetoric. As a way to reference workplace skills, soft skills are conceptually "fuzzy" (Matteson, Anderson, and Boyden 71). However, whatever else soft skills might include, today quality and effective communication is consistently central to their scope and function. Our argument is that the rhetorical history of soft skills illuminates a location of governance in the interpersonal/interactional/intersectional field of human social relations. As such, different ways to register labor power (communicative, cognitive, affective, and aesthetic) become constituted as soft skills in order to align labor power with organizational (capitalist) success. Moreover, we will describe how this interactional field is a governing space in which the productive power of cooperation requires the cultivation of soft skills by supervisors and the supervised. As a precarious rhetoric, the need to learn how to activate this interactional space to generate cooperation locates soft skills as a mode of "governmental precarization" (Lorey 13). Lorey argues that to appreciate the governance of precarity "makes it possible to problematize the complex interactions between an instrument of governing and the conditions of economic exploitation and modes of subjection, in their ambivalence between subjugation and self-empowerment" (13). Capitalism functions, in part, by appropriating and exploiting social relations—including the hierarchization of raced, sexed, gendered, and abled bodies—for its benefit. Attention to soft skills as a governing problem reveals an intersectional history (Collins and Bilge) of economic inequality as different populations become entangled in precarious relationships of cooperation.

The call for the cultivation of soft skills takes place in a rather contradictory form: On the one hand, soft skills exist as a precarious rhetoric that individualizes skill sets within the needs of an organization. Conversely, as a bundle of communicative, cognitive, aesthetic, and affective dimensions of labor power, soft skills succeed only when they promote cooperation. In other words, soft skills work less through promoting insecurity and more through cooperation and common tasks, emphasizing the interdependence of working with others. Soft skills exist as modes of "communicative labor" that harness the agency of communicative practices, genres, techniques, and technologies for generating value (Carlone 161; Greene 189; Hardt and Negri 29; Reeves 154; Spinuzzi, *Network* 17; Swenson 86). This communicative and immaterial labor is akin to the knowledge work "that involves thinking about, analyzing, and communicating things rather than growing or manufacturing things" (Spinuzzi, *All Edge* 60). As a way to index "communicative labor," soft skills are not limited to knowledge work because they increasingly inform all labor sectors, including retail, customer service, and manufacturing, but they also point to how relations of production increasingly transform the means of production, especially at the level of the firm or organization. The ontological politics of soft skills concerns whether these tools of cooperation can escape their command and supervision by and for capital. Put differently, we will maintain a critical posture toward the precarious rhetoric of soft skills to better appreciate their ambivalent relationship to economic exploitation.

To appreciate the rhetorical history of soft skills, we will explore a set of "precarity patterns" (Teston) generated by their invention and circulation. As Teston explains, "as our analytic attention increasingly turns toward complicated intra-actions between people, environs, and things, precarity as an analytic helps identify systemic inequities hiding out in a host of material discursive forces" (266). The pattern we discover in our research is one in which the value of soft skills is transformed from a disposable workplace skill to a necessary workplace skill. The story we share here begins in the United States Army and reveals how soft skills transfer precarity from a specific kind of labor to the precariousness of cooperation. In this move, soft skills become less associated with low skill labor and more with the managerial labor associated with the need to command, supervise, and lead others. One lesson from this history is that cooperation understood as "living labor" (Read 61–102), labor that relies on humans and their relationships with one another, has the potential to go rogue and escape its command (Greene 203). Finally, we trace the civilian uptake of soft skills in the 1980s to reveal a different precarity pattern that posits soft skills as a necessary skill for employability, yet maintains its privileging of particular bodies over others. The precarious rhetoric of soft skills circulates as a governmental prophylactic to the new insecurity.

SOFT SKILLS AND TECHNICAL SKILLS: THE U.S. ARMY AND MODERN WEAPONS

The concept of soft skills likely first appeared in differentiating the skills associated with occupations in the U.S. Armed Forces. In his 1957 biennial report, U.S. Army Chief of Staff Maxwell D. Taylor laid out a description of a two-year reclassification and retraining program that would

> balance their skills more effectively with the needs of modern weaponry and organizations. [In 1955] the Army had an excess of 27,000 noncommissioned officers trained in the less difficult skills while critical shortages existed in combat skills requiring long periods of training. . . . Approximately 60 percent of the overbalance in 'soft skills' . . . has been eliminated, and the imbalance is expected to end by October 1957. (39)

The scare quotes around "soft skills" suggests that the phrase is still new and, perhaps, without widespread acceptance. Taylor is not specific as to the skills he associates with soft skills, but we can infer that they are positions that do not require extensive training, and the skills are contrasted with those necessary for "the needs of modern weaponry and organizations." Moreover, these technical skills provide the key attribute for leadership. In a previous section of the report, Taylor describes how the "Modern Army" requires increased technical training:

> The process of training a new Nike battalion provides an example of how modern-day training is planned and executed. Almost a year before the missiles are manned at the site, qualified soldiers arrive at the US Army Air Defense School . . . for a 42-week technical school course of instruction. (14)

Technical skills, in contrast to soft skills, are associated with the training necessary, for example, to operate a surface-to-air Nike-Ajax missile. Moreover, General Taylor notes how the U.S. Army had undertaken an effort to increase the quality of its personnel by increasing the mental standards for enlistment because those in the lowest quarter "cannot be assigned to the growing number of technical tasks and responsible jobs in a modern Army" (37). The "modern" army signified by its new electronic weapons (i.e., Nike missiles) called forth a differentiation in the kind of labor required to successfully carry out the army's mission.

New weapons were partly responsible for the invention of soft skills. Applied to modern soldierly capabilities, "soft" skills were judged less valuable and more expendable than technical skills. In testimony before Congress, General Donald Booth, the army's assistant chief of staff for personnel, made more explicit the cognitive context that defined soft-skill soldiers: "For mental group 4, . . . around 24 percent of our personnel, we have restricted re-enlistments of that group because we are already over people in soft skills and we are trying to build up a higher average of person in the hard skills and the scarce skills where we need their services" (235). Working with General Booth's contrastive logics, soft skills differ from hard in being less critical and less rare. "Mental groups" distributed all soldiers on a psychometric norm, and category 4 bundled those who scored within the tenth and thirtieth percentile on the Armed Forces Qualification Test in the lowest acceptable category, known as "mentally marginal" (1967, Group IV on the Armed Forces Qualification Test p. 2). As Booth indicates, category 4 personnel were better assigned to soft skills than technical skills. Moreover, there is evidence to believe these rather crude instruments for normalizing labor worked to the disadvantage of African Americans and other minority groups (Appy 22).

Within the same time period, the Defense Advisory Committee on Professional and Technical Compensation, chaired by Ralph J. Cordiner, the chairman of General Electric, delivered its two-volume report to the secretary of defense in May of 1957 (Defense Advisory Committee). In a congressional hearing, Ralph Cordiner argued that the technical composition of the U.S. Armed Forces would determine U.S. national survival:

> Is the United States going to be ready, in an age of supersonic airplanes, nuclear weapons and intercontinental missiles, to defend itself against sudden attack? Or will this country be defended by a force of inexperienced military personnel who do not know how to command and operate modern weapons?
>
> . . . The United States has no choice but to meet the challenge of Communist technology and expend billions in the development of these scientifically advanced weapons; otherwise, the free nations will lie helpless before overwhelming Communist power. (16)

The stakes were high. To avoid helplessness in the face of communism, the armed forces needed soldiers with the capacity to acquire technical skills to operate advanced technological weapons. In contrast, soldiers with soft skills were technologically inexperienced, and hence their superfluity constituted a threat to national survival. The nation is made vulnerable by communism—and also by "mentally marginal" soldiers with soft skills in a nuclear age.

Karen Barad's conceptualization of "agential intra-action" is useful here to understand the "*causal relationship between specific exclusionary practices embodied as specific material configurations of the world*" and "*specific material phenomena*" (814, emphasis original). The "intra-action" between modern weapons, military personnel, and the "communist threat" generated an "agential cut" among military personnel (Barad 815): "the agential cut enacts a local causal structure among components of a phenomenon in the marking of the 'measuring agencies' ('effect') by the 'measured object' ('cause')" (815). The military measured the mental capacities of personnel to match skill-set potential (technical or soft) with available jobs. But this agential cut, distinguishing soft skills from technical skills, did not happen in a laboratory environment, it occurred in a macroeconomic and national security environment.

As the Cordiner Report came out of the administrative shadows, the job categories associated with soft-skill jobs became more defined. The *Washington Post* reported in 1957 that the reenlistment rate "for such 'soft skills' as truck drivers and cooks was twice as high as that for technicians" ("Pentagon Plans" A5). In the popular press and in congressional hearings, truck drivers and cooks became the jobs most associated with soft skills. The Cordiner Report avoided the term "soft skills" and instead bundled this labor under "supporting services" (45). Appearing before the U.S. Senate, Ralph Cordiner provided more insight: "Among the so called supporting services—and here I am talking about the cooks and truck drivers and other skills that are for the most part acquired easily, quickly, and inexpensive—first time reenlistments are in line with desired rates and it is obvious that the present incentives in this area are adequate" (20). Soft skills as supporting skills are imagined as easily acquired. Cordiner identifies a second problem with the current compensation system. It provides low incentives for improvement: "The easy jobs, requiring skills that are easy to acquire, offer as much reward as the jobs that take months and years of training and hard work" (21). Jack Raymond reported that the retraining program initiated by the U.S. Army to move soldiers from soft to hard skills was an effort to correct an imbalance between "administrative and clerical personnel" and to promote the reenlistment of skilled "electronics men" (32).

At the moment the term "soft skills" appears, soft skills are associated with military personnel of lower cognitive ability, with manual or administrative jobs that exist to support more critical personnel. Soft-skills soldiers are also more disposable due to the short time frame required to acquire the skills. This binary between hard and soft skills conceptually appropriates a division of labor premised on gendered and raced bodies. Soft-skill positions, and the bodies that occupy them, are there to serve and support the bodies that occupy the more valued technical and hard-skill positions. Laboring bodies are distributed; soft-skill workers move, feed, and care for the bodies of the cognitively essential. Therefore, the precarity pattern made manifest in the origin story of soft skills generates a "hierarchization of being" (Lorey 12), privileging the bodies with technical skills over those with soft skills.

SOFT SKILLS AS SURPLUS POPULATION: PRECARIOUSNESS AND THE INDUSTRIAL RESERVE ARMY

The Cold War provided the U.S. military with a need to reset the capacities that spoke to the subjective qualities of its labor force. Though, in 1958, the labor power of the U.S. Armed Forces was served by conscription, over 75 percent of both conscripts and volunteers left the armed forces after their initial tour of duty (Defense Advisory Committee). Thus, the labor problem was measurable in the kind of soldiers who reenlisted. To encourage reenlistment for the preferred technical skills, Congress authorized the armed forces in 1958 to implement "proficiency pay" to reward functional competence. Although applicable to all occupational specialties, proficiency pay could be higher for those with more technical skills than those with softer skills even within the same rank (Comptroller General of the United States). During the legislative hearings on proficiency pay, Congress asked this question:

> Could the Department of Defense indicate what administrative measures have been taken to ease the critical skills problem, such as retraining those holding so called soft skills and accelerating the promotions for those holding the hard-core skills? (842)

The question is relevant because it marks Congress's adoption of the term "soft skills," and the state's role in the governmental precarization of labor power. The state's role in military expenditures becomes a pathway for the institutional embedding of the idea of soft skills and the laboring bodies in soft-skill positions as less necessary and less valuable—therefore, less worthy of a wage increase.

The recognition that the army of 1958 reduced its surplus of soft-skill personnel reveals the precarity of labor in a specific Marxist sense. Karl Marx understood precariousness of labor to be built into the general law of capitalist accumulation: "the higher the productivity of labor, the greater is the pressure of the workers on the means of employment, the more precarious therefore becomes the conditions for their existence, namely the sale of their own labor-power for the increase of alien wealth, or in other words the self-valorization of capital" (798). As the productivity of labor increases (its quality or surplus value), fewer laborers are needed, partly due to the addition of machines to increase relative surplus value.

The precariousness of labor is generated by the surplus population of the industrial reserve army. The reserve army is at the mercy of capital's valorization process. Marx's proposition that capital accumulation increases as the variable cost of labor means that the industrial reserve army is both a cause and an effect of capital's ability to generate wealth. What often generates this wealth is the relative surplus value caused by technological advances in modes of production, such that fewer workers produce greater value. Thus, precariousness is materially wired into laborers' bodily existence, as the industrial reserve army helps to discipline the wage contract by constricting the cost of socially necessary labor. This undervaluation of certain bodies, especially those bodies that serve, support, and care for bodies deemed valuable and necessary, mirrors the stratification of laboring bodies in the social sphere (796). Soft skills index the precariousness of labor at that moment the military changes the way its force balance is valued and begins to promote and retain technical skills over soft skills. In this transaction, soft skills, and the bodies articulated to them, are made vulnerable and disposable.

The appearance of soft skills in the U.S. Armed Forces speaks especially to the precarity of soft skills. First, identifying soft skills as supporting services functions to feminize and racialize manual labor, providing a rhetorical mechanism for the embodied labor of driving and cooking to be devalued. Second, the more that military labor is associated with soft skills, the more this particular laborer is encouraged to retrain as a precondition of reenlistment (i.e., employability). As the technological composition of labor drives the armed forces' retention policy, soft skills are on the wrong side of the agential cut—to be returned to the industrial reserve army. Furthermore, there is a macroeconomic context that reminds us of the relationship between the military after World War II and the Fordist Keynesian compromise. In the United States, after World War II, the state tended to pursue a macroeconomic policy of "Military Keynesianism—that is, the policy of using the defense budget as a countercyclical and economic growth device" (Griffin, Devine, and Wallace S116).

One way it did this was to increase its procurement of new electronic weaponry, inventing a defense industry and supporting its industrial concentration as an element of monopoly capitalism (Baran and Sweezy 1966). Due to the union density in the defense industries at the time, military Keynesianism tended to support the skill labor of organized labor over unorganized and unskilled labor. The geopolitical and macroeconomic context provides reason to believe the agential cut between soft skills and technical skills intensified economic insecurity through the governmental precarity of those more closely aligned with manual labor, often aligned with the U.S. Army's effort to enlist those of lower cognitive ability (measured by inherently biased psychometric tests).

COMMAND AND COOPERATION: ARMY LEADERSHIP AND SOFT SKILLS

The reversal in the value of soft skills also has a military history. Its revision in military thinking can be traced to a U.S. Continental Army Command (CONARC) training conference on soft skills in the early 1970s. Soft skills were still contrasted with hard skills, but the soft skills had much less to do with occupation types than with job functions and behavior objectives. CONARC described soft skills as "job related skills involving actions affecting primarily people and paper, e.g., inspecting troops, supervising office personnel, conducting studies, preparing maintenance reports, preparing efficiency reports, designing bridge structures" (Volume II 4–5). In the 1970s, the military began a revaluation of soft skills by aligning them with communicative genres we associate today with knowledge work (Spinuzzi *Network*). More specifically, soft skills were embedded within the communicative labor of "command, supervision, counseling, and leadership" (Volume II 4). As such, the value of soft skills would be redeemed when the interpersonal interaction between supervisors and supervised became a site for promoting cooperation.

For CONARC, soft skills are more associated with mental or cognitive labor. Job skills closely associated with machines may be considered hard skills, but not because of their cognitive complexity or training time. Instead, "we can be specific what the machine operator ought to do if we know the situations or environments in which he[1] works, the purposes of his work in these situations, and the theories of operations of the machines he uses" (Volume II 13). In contrast, a "supervisor, or a leader or a counselor . . . is a people operator. He directs the activities of people toward the accomplishment of specified purposes in specified situations" (Volume II 13). The difficulty of learning soft skills is that unlike training someone to operate a machine, "operating" on people is much less codified and much more sensitive to situational dynamics. Soft skills are skills of interaction that, like communication, require a form of practical reasoning cultivated by knowledge and experience, but without a guarantee of success because each situation is unique. For example, when discussing the job functions and tasks needed for an ordnance officer, William Davis notes:

> When we attempted to identify what an officer does when he supervises and manages, we found a high degree of variability from position to position and from task to task. . . . In general, our approach has been to accept initially a rather general task statement and then proceed to more detailed behaviors much the same as we do when *identifying skills and knowledges* for hard skill tasks. This suggests to us that in truly soft skill areas, maybe it is the *skills and knowledges* that become the real training requirements. (Volume II 37–38, emphasis in original)

Hence, soft skills come to be defined as a specific kind of knowledge, and this knowledge is considered harder to learn than the technical skills associated with a machine.

As soft skills are reimagined by the army, they became a site for intervention and training. Since soft skills are now closely related to the management of people, it is necessary "to determine the critical interpersonal behaviors required from the supervisor, from the other workers, and the worker himself, in order to optimize the worker's job performance" (Volume II 15). The association of soft skills with the need to command, supervise, manage, and lead isolates interpersonal interaction as a site of governance, a training site for producing a labor power necessary for achieving organizational goals. It also places the reinvention of soft skills within a rhetoric of management and human resources.

As soft skills are attached to supervision, the Army Infantry School notes that soft skill proficiency is likely to traverse the mental and manual distinction between planning and execution. For example, "Preparation of a Unit CBR [Chemical, Biological, Radiation] plan might need to be broken down into more specific subtask like select personnel for the monitoring team . . . [and] the standard may differ for the same tasks between the doer and supervisor" (Volume II 48). Supervisors are more associated with mental-labor soft skills—the who/what/when/where/how of the plan's production—while the doers are associated with its execution and thus must "Preserve your Ability to Perform your Job" (Volume II 49). The situational characteristic of the successful deployment of soft skills holds a clue as to how they bridge the divide between planning and execution: soft skills make possible the cooperation between leader and led necessary for the accomplishment of organizational goals.

To make a more direct comparison with the Cordiner Committee era, recall how the popular press seized on cooks and truck drivers as examples of soft-skill labor and closely associated these with low-skill labor based on the limited training time required for performing the task. In one of its few identifications of job types, the Cordiner Report includes policing alongside drivers and cooks (10). When we jump ahead to the CONARC training schools, the U.S. Army Military Police School does not consider policing a soft skill. Instead, soft skills are crucial to the leadership training of noncommissioned officers. For example, Captain David Gardner reports, "We had to work into these tasks a requirement to insure the student could communicate, use information, and know exactly how much authority he is carrying around with him. We're emphasizing leadership as a direct one-on-one situation in which an influence attempt is directed at another" (Volume V 12). Regarding police training, leadership consists of "technical expertise, communicative skills, and derivation and use of information" (Volume V 13). Soft skills provide a pathway to leadership through a micro-rhetorical (interactional) process of influencing another. As such, soft skills are increasingly associated with communication and inquiry skills (information gathering and use).

THE PRECARIOUSNESS OF COOPERATION: LIVING LABOR AND ITS FLIGHT FROM COMMAND

The time between the Cordiner Report and the CONARC training conference is a difference of about fifteen years. Soft skills are no longer imagined as easy-to-learn and easily replaceable skills. Less attached to the problem of a surplus population, soft skills are less indexical of the precarity of "low skill" labor. Soft skills, in the early 1970s, are less about the flow of the industrial reserve army set free to move in and out of the U.S. military and more about how to harness the productive power of cooperation. Soft skills are interaction skills that are more abstract (more immaterial) than the labor power associated with particular occupations (drivers, cooks, radar technicians). The general character of soft skills requires situational judgment to best activate cooperation across the division of labor, in this case leaders and led. Our argument is that the precarity pattern associated with soft skills changes as the need for soft skills among leaders indexes the precariousness of cooperation. The precarity of cooperation is made manifest by Vietnam-era soldiers resisting their own embodied precarity in combat.

Marx provides insight about cooperation as a particular form of productive power. Cooperation, he writes, describes how "numerous workers work together side by side in accordance with a plan, whether in the same process, or in different but connected processes" (443). Just as the industrial reserve army borrows its tropological form from military labor, Marx uses a military metaphor to describe the productive labor of cooperation:

> Just as the offensive power of a squadron of cavalry, or the defensive power of an infantry regiment, is essentially different from the sum of the offensive or defensive powers of the individual soldiers taken separately, so the sum total of the mechanical forces exerted by isolated workers differs from the social force that is developed when many hands cooperate . . . we have . . . by means of co-operation . . . the creation of a new productive power, which is intrinsically a collective one. (443)

In cooperation more can be done—that is, more value can be produced—but the value of cooperation requires, according to Marx, supervision. Once again

Marx draws near the relationship between military soft skills and the capitalist mode of production:

> [The capitalist] hands over the work of direct and constant supervision of the individual workers and group of workers to a special kind of wage laborer. An industrial army of workers under the command of a capitalist requires, like a real army, officers (managers) and NCOs (foreman, overseers), who command during the labor process in the name of capital. The work of supervision becomes their established and exclusive function. (450)

The military provides an institutional location for how soft skills become integral to generating the cooperation necessary to meet organizational goals.

The initial appearance of military soft skills rooted them closer to manual labor and the precariousness of the industrial reserve army, the new pattern of aligning soft skills with leadership and supervision aligns soft skills to the "professional managerial class" (Ehrenreich and Ehrenreich 11). The managerial class supervises the active industrial army. Yet, as a managerial discourse, soft skills are less about making one form of labor more precarious than another (soft versus technical), but rather, more pointedly, about the precariousness of cooperation. The appropriate use of soft skills unleashes cooperation as the social productive power of labor to cooperate within and across the division of labor. As interactional skills, they are embedded in the communicative labor of command, supervision, leadership, and counseling. For CONARC, soft skills are about the uncertainty of command to capture the productive power of cooperation—the sum that is greater than its parts. Perhaps no organization was in more need of cooperation than the U.S. Army in 1972—a conscripted wartime army pinned down and pulling out of a losing war in Southeast Asia.

The CONARC proceedings are discreet about the conference's wartime context, but there are clues when the proceedings discuss how to include enlisted personnel in the execution of a plan. Recall how the execution of a chemical-biological-radiation plan required rank-and-file soldiers to preserve their ability to perform the job. Job performance required soldiers to avoid negative behaviors: "don't steal, don't gamble, don't use drugs, don't go AWOL, or don't fight with your buddies" (Volume II-49). In 1972, another "thou shall not" might have included: "Don't frag your commanding officer!" Eugene Linden reported, "Fragging is a macabre ritual of Vietnam in which American enlisted men attempt to murder their superiors. . . . Fragging has ballooned into an intraArmy guerilla warfare" (12).

Fragging and the fragmentation hand grenade created an alternative precarity pattern. In this case, the precariousness of cooperation is expressed in a different intra-action of weapon and personnel, revealing less the vulnerability of the GI or Viet Cong and more the command structure of the U.S. Army. Fragging was one of many "withdrawal symptoms" of the U.S. GI in Vietnam. As early as 1969, soldiers had declared an end to their cooperation: "We have come together as GIs United Against the War in Vietnam in order to organize ourselves to defend our rights and help bring all the troops home from Vietnam now!" ("Statement of Aims"). In the army of 1972, cooperation could no longer be guaranteed but needed to be cultivated; it required a leader with soft skills to better influence those under command.

In roughly fifteen years, the value of soft skills had gone through a hierarchical reversal: from dispensable low-level job skills in support of other soldiers to indispensable interactional skills necessary to lead soldiers. The value of this managerial structure was registered in the cooperation necessary to meet the army's organizational goals. This hierarchical reversal emerged alongside the resistance of army labor to be led into war. A new precarity pattern expressed itself as soft skills registered the organizational need for cooperation. Moreover, the resistance of soldiers being led into war demonstrated the breakdown of the army command structure and an alternative bottom-up form of cooperation against the war. By shifting soft skills to interactional encounters between people, the subjective capacity of soft skills emerged as a necessity for bending the productive power of cooperation in the direction of organizational needs and aims. Soft skills are less about identifying disposable labor than they are about providing the "people skills" necessary for getting the most from each and every person. Yet, in a wartime context, such cooperation demanded certain bodies be put in harm's way so that the army might succeed. Thus, as frontline soldiers challenged the authority of command, cooperation became a site of class struggle. CONARC's desire to generate leaders as "people operators" championed communication as a way to turn a conflict into cooperation.

The resignification of soft skills as a kind of managerial labor for inducing cooperation provides insight into how the army tried to respond to an authority crisis. The contingency of cooperation is revealed by the revolt of the army GIs who came together and organized outside of their command structure. Thus, the interactional zone of governance associated with soft skills expresses how cooperation exists as "living labor"—a subjective capacity of labor power that potentially exceeds its command, supervision, leadership, and counseling. The disciplinary power of the military command structure and the capitalist mode of production exist to channel this cooperative power, but the potential of soldiers working among themselves, for themselves and others, against the army command structure, turns this cooperation into an exodus from the war machine. The army's revaluation of soft skills reveals a managerial concern within the interactional terrain between leader and led. The relationship between those who command and those who follow commands illuminates a communicative site of governance, which is necessary for cooperation. Importantly, this interactional terrain reveals a set of possible counter-conducts that stage an antagonism between the cooperative power of living labor and the capture of cooperative power by command. That is to say that when the GIs organize and cooperate with one another and against their commanding officer, their cooperative power exceeds that of their commanding officer. The revolt of the GIs is a reminder that the precariousness of labor exceeds its capture by the command of capitalist accumulation as the cooperative potential of living labor generates a precarity pattern that constitutes a political agency of self-organization and freedom.

SOFT SKILLS AND EMPLOYABILITY

Beginning in the late 1980s, a new precarity pattern in the rhetorical history of soft skills emerged as youth (un)employment was identified as a problem. The lack of soft skills was isolated as a reason for youth unemployment. Like in the CONARC report in the early 1970s, soft skills are associated with interpersonal space of cooperation with an emphasis on "personal and interpersonal skills" (Office of Disability Employment Policy 35), with the addition of an affective dimension (a "positive attitude") to work. One might appreciate this affective dimension as the cooperative atmosphere of employees to attune themselves to the demands of the job and the goals of the organization.

The need to promote a curriculum that emphasizes soft skills expresses how soft skills are deeply implicated in the production of labor power and as a form of governmental precarization. In the 1980s, soft skills appeared as part of a complete package of necessary skills for youth employability. In speaking of a youth training program, Della Hughes prioritizes the relationship between soft skills and basic skills: "The [basic] skills cannot be taught in isolation. They must be surrounded by what we have tended to call 'softer skills'—learning how to make decisions, learning how to solve problems. Both skills training and the supportive soft skills must be put together in a package" (137). Here we can recognize the return of inquiry skills ("make decisions," "solve problems") to the bundle of soft skills and note how those skills are individualized in youth as a portfolio of skills (basic, soft, technical) to improve employability. The acquisition of soft skills is becoming, by the 1980s, an index of a young person's job readiness and as a way to improve U.S. economic performance.

The problem of youth employability provides another opportunity to return to the intersectional history of labor power implicated in the history of soft skills. First, youth notes a demographic particularity (16–24) associated with job entry. Second, youth unemployment might signify more than age. For example, in October of 1987, the youth unemployment rate of African Americans between the age of sixteen and nineteen was over 30 percent (U.S. Bureau of Labor Statistics). Moreover, in a racial reversal from the 1950s, when the military identified African American men with soft skills, employers in the 1980s and 1990s began to report that they "rated Black men poorly in terms of such [soft] skills" (Moss and Tilly). Though Cecilia Conrad has found that such a negative assessment of the actual soft skills of African Americans is impressionistic and lacked credible assessment (106), to be young, black, and male in the 1980s and 1990s was increasingly associated with lacking soft skills. Attention to soft skills as a governing problem reveals an intersectional history of economic inequality as racialized and gendered (Collins and Bilge). The intersectional character of soft skills provides more evidence about the racial and gendered history of the division of labor.

Today, youth employment demands that managers "bridg[e] the millennial soft skills gap" (Tulgan 1). Tulgan maintains the interactional focus of soft skills and their differential relationship to technical skills: "soft skills encompass a wider range of nontechnical skills ranging from self-awareness to people skills, to problem solving to respect for authority, citizenship, service and teamwork" (1). Soft skills combine individual dispositions and cooperation to the needs of an organization. The individualization of soft skills generates a concern about the imprecise character of the term and the need to separate skills from personality and disposition. The more that soft skills are removed from skills that can be taught and nurtured in experiential settings, the more they can be used to demarcate people by generating a social prejudice that some are more able than others to learn soft skills and fall in line with organizational expectations. The question of soft skills as a precondition for employment has led to a steady body of research concerned with how the personalization of soft skills discriminates against African American workers or maintains essentialist assumptions about gender differences (e.g., that women are better communicators) in coding some interactive service and retail jobs as women's work (Bailly and Léné). The contextualization of soft skills as individual job skills necessary for certain kinds of work generates a new precarity for those workers considered to lack those skills, and also slots those with those skills into a gendered and racial division of labor.

The call to overcome the soft-skills gap is fundamentally about youth commitment to the corporate organization and the need for them to fall in line with its command structure. As one manager told Bruce Tulgan, "When I was young and inexperienced, I may have been naïve or immature, but I knew enough to wear a tie, make eye contact, say 'please' and 'thank you' and 'yes sir' and 'yes ma'am' and when to shut up and keep my head down and do the grunt work without having to be told over and over again" (1). The beleaguered patriarch speaks. The soft-skill crisis is a crisis about decorous ways of communicating, respecting authority, and working without constant supervision ("told over and over again"). As such, the soft-skills gap risks organizational success:

> When employees have significant gaps in their soft skills there are significant negative consequences. Potentially good hires are overlooked. Good hires go bad. Bad hires go worse. Misunderstandings abound. People get distracted. Productivity goes down. Mistakes are made. Customer service suffers. Workplace conflicts occur more frequently. Good people leave when they might have otherwise stayed longer. It robs so many young employees of greater success and causes so many managers so much aggravation and so many unnecessary costs. (Tulgan 2)

The soft-skills gap makes cooperation much harder and more precarious for everyone, even if the blame for gaps in soft skills is placed on the shoulders of employees more often than employers. Tulgan's pitch is less for managers to improve their soft skills than for managers and leaders to prioritize soft skills in their organizational vision so that they may hire folks attuned to the success of the organization. The education in soft skills to a vast consultancy market speaks to how the governmentalized zone of interaction is also commodified to support a $160-billion industry in training and development (Association for Talent Development).

While consultants turn their attention toward managers as their target audience for cultivating a soft-skills training program, the U.S. federal government has designed a curriculum to promote soft skills to increase youth employability (Office of Disability Employment Policy). The curriculum includes lessons on developing communication, enthusiasm and attitude, teamwork, networking, problem solving and critical thinking, and professionalism. These skills were chosen because surveyed business leaders expressed the importance of soft skills over technical skills for workplace productivity. The skills deemed most important by businesses when surveyed by the National Association of Colleges and Employers (NACE) in 2008 were "communication skills, work ethic, initiative, interpersonal skills, and teamwork" (qtd. in Office of Disability Employment Policy 7).

The Office of Disability Employment Policy's curriculum includes a series of activities that accompany each skill set, and each skill is justified through a statement or two in a sidebar when the skill is introduced. For example, "Communication skills are ranked FIRST among a job candidate's 'must have' skills and qualities" (17). Enthusiasm and attitude are justified because "having a positive attitude in the workplace can help with potential promotions. Employers promote employees who not only produce, but also motivate others in the work place" (35). Teamwork notes the importance of cooperation: "The ability to work as part of a team is one of the most important skills in today's job market. Employers are looking for workers who can contribute their own ideas, but also want people who can work with others to create and develop projects and plans" (56). In terms of networking, "When it comes to finding a job, you've got to network! According to Cornell University's Career Center, 80% of available jobs are not advertised. These jobs are often referred to as the 'hidden job market'" (77). Networking produces the need to communicate with others. For problem solving and critical thinking, "Employers say they need a workforce fully equipped with skills beyond the basics of reading, writing, and arithmetic to grow their business. These skills include critical thinking and problem solving" (98). And finally, regarding professionalism, "Employers want new workers to be responsible, ethical, and team oriented, and to possess strong communication, interpersonal, and problem-solving skills. Wrap these skills up all together and you've got professionalism" (114).

As far as the Office of Disability Employment is concerned, the learning of soft skills is useful to those beyond the primary population in their care, those with physical and developmental disabilities. Yet, the particularity of disability reverses the original precarity pattern that associated soft skills with populations that scored in the bottom of a cognitive test. Soft skills proliferate and call on everyone to learn them for different purposes. For youth, they are operationalized and governmentalized as predominantly interaction skills organized into different categories of immaterial labor: communicative (communication, teamwork, networking); cognitive (problem solving and critical thinking); affective (enthusiasm and attitude); and aesthetic (professionalism). The teaching of soft skills transforms them into technologies for improving the cooperative potential of labor power. As abstract labor, communicative, cognitive, affective, and aesthetic labor improves cooperation by aligning this labor with the needs of the organization, but these technologies are ambivalent. Their ambivalence is, from our perspective, generated by the antagonism between soft skills as living labor and their command and control for particular organizational goals. However, because soft skills orient the interactional terrain between and among humans, they can potentially resist their individualization because they require careful attention to other people. The condition for Judith Butler's precarious vulnerability and interdependence (218) against precarity requires the living labor of cooperation, a productive power necessary for organizing collective projects of care and alternative forms of collective life.

CONCLUSION

As this chapter has demonstrated, the rhetorical history of soft skills owes part of its origin story to the U.S. Army in the 1950s and its need to shift the technical composition of its labor toward the need to learn how to use modern weapons. As such, soft skills were defined as less valuable than technical skills, lacking cognitive complexity, more manual in character, and, consequently, in less need. The U.S. Armed Forces took the lead in resignifying the value of soft skills in the 1970s. By assigning them to the interactional space between leader and led, soft skills become associated with the precarity of cooperation. Yet, cooperation turns out to be open to the creative potential of living labor to exceed its command and control. In the 1980s, soft skills belonged to a new precarity pattern associated with youth unemployment. The lack of soft skills is identified with a failure of employment and a threat to U.S. economic competitiveness in the new global economy. Soft skills remain deeply interactional as their value becomes embedded within communicative, cognitive, affective, and aesthetic modes of labor. These immaterial forms of labor power, however, are made concrete in terms of a set of human interactions marked by difference (race, class, gender). As labor power, soft skills exist in the abstract, but when actualized into the relations of production, soft skills must become more concrete. On the one hand, soft skills become associated with a skill deficit that is assigned to particular populations across the division of labor (youth, black men, managers). On the other hand, soft skills become more tightly feminized in retail work and customer service (white women). This intersectional history provides evidence for the claim that the precarity pattern embedded in soft skills assigns soft skills to the struggle for employability and increasingly individualizes and personalizes soft skills in a way that promotes economic inequality due to stereotypes about those with or without

252 • CHAPTER 11, RONALD WALTER GREENE AND KRISTIN SWENSON

soft skills. However, as the withdrawal of U.S. soldiers from the Vietnam War demonstrates, cooperation remains an ambivalent site of governmental precarization because it can be withdrawn from its command and control and used in alternative ways to promote human interdependence and differing forms of governing oneself and others.

NOTE

1. These documents clearly refer to the male sex, which is why we do not include a "*sic*" within the quotations.

WORKS CITED

Appy, Christian, G. *Working-Class War: American Combat Soldiers & Vietnam.* University of North Carolina Press, 1993.

Association for Talent Development. "164.2 Billion Spent on Training and Development by US Companies." 12 Dec. 2013.

Bailly, Frank, and Alexandre Léné. "The Personification of the Service Labour Process and the Rise of Soft Skills: A French Case Study." *Employee Relations* 35.1 (2013): 79–97.

Barad, Karan. "Posthumanist Performativity: Toward an Understanding How Matter Comes to Matter." *Signs* 28.3 (2003): 801–31.

Baran, Paul, and Paul Sweezy. *Monopoly Capital.* Monthly Review, 1966.

Booth, Donald. United States Cong. House. Subcommittee of the Committee on Appropriations. *Hearing on the Department of the Army Appropriations for 1958.* 85th Congress, 1st sess. Washington, DC: GPO, 1957.

Butler, Judith. *Notes Toward a Performative Theory of Assembly.* Harvard University Press, 2015.

Carlone, David. "The Contradictions of Communicative Labor in Service Work." *Communication and Critical/Cultural Studies* 5.2 (2008): 158–79.

Carnevale, Anthony. United States Cong. Joint Economic Committee. Subcommittee on Education and Health Hearings. *Competitiveness and the Quality of the American Work Force.* 100th Cong, 1st Sess. Washington, DC: GPO, 1988 (Statement, 29 Oct. 1987).

Collins, Patricia Hill, and Sirma Bilge. *Intersectionality.* Polity Press, 2016.

Comptroller General of the United States. *Report to the Congress; Military Retention Incentives: Effectiveness and Administration.* Department of Defense. General Accounting Office, 1974.

Conrad, Cecilia A. "Do Black Workers Lack Soft Skills?" *Building Skills for Black Workers: Preparing for the Future Labor Market.* Ed. Cecilia A. Conrad. University Press of America, 2004. 105–25.

Cordiner, Ralph. United States Cong. Senate. *Military Pay: Hearing Before a Subcommittee of the Committee on Armed Services on S. 2014,* 85th Congress, 1st. sess., Part 1. Washington, DC: GPO, 1957 (Statement, 21 Aug. 1957).

Defense Advisory Committee on Professional and Technical Compensation. *A Modern Concept of Manpower Management and Compensation for Personnel of the Uniformed Services: A Report and Recommendation for the Secretary of Defense, Volume 1—Military Personnel* (Cordiner Report). GPO, May 1957.

Ehrenreich, Barbara, and John Ehrenreich. "The Professional-Managerial Class." *Radical America* 11.2 (1977): 7–32.

GIs United Against the War in Vietnam. *GIs United Against the War in Vietnam: Statement of Aims.* The Sixties Project. Vietnam Generation, Inc., and the Institute of Advanced Technology in the Humanities. <http://www2.iath.virginia.edu/sixties/HTML_docs/Resources/Primary/Manifestos/GIs_United_aims.html>.

Greene, Ronald. "Rhetoric and Capitalism: Rhetorical Agency as Communicative Labor." *Philosophy and Rhetoric* 37.3 (2004): 187–206.

Griffin, Larry J., Joel A Devine, and Michael Wallace. "Monopoly Capital, Organized Labor and Military Expenditures in the United States, 1949–1976." *American Journal of Sociology* 88 (suppl.) (1982): S113–53.

Hardt, Michael, and Antonio Negri. *War and Democracy in the Age of Empire.* Penguin Books, 2004.

Hughes, Della. United States Cong. House. Hearings of the Select Committee on Children, Youth and Families. *Changing Economics in the South: Preparing our Youth.* 100th Cong. 1st Sess. Washington, DC: GPO, 1988 (prepared statement, 24 April 1987).

Jonna, R. Jamil, and John Bellamy Foster. "Marx's Theory of Working Class Precariousness—And Its Relevance Today." *Alternate Routes: A Journal of Critical and Social Research* 27 (2016): 21–45.

Kamin, Maxine. *Soft Skills Revolution: A Guide for Connecting with Compassion for Trainers, Teams, and Leaders.* Wiley and Sons, 2013.

Linden, Eugene. "Fragging and Other Withdrawal Symptoms." *Saturday Review* (8 Jan. 1972): 12–17, 55.

Lorey, Isabella. *State of Insecurity: Government of the Precarious.* Trans. Aileen Derieg. Verso, 2015.

Marx, Karl. *Capital: A Critique of Political Economy.* Vol. 1. Trans. Ben Fowlkes. Vintage Books, 1977.

Matteson, Miriam L., Lorien Anderson, and Cynthia Boyden, "'Soft Skills': A Phrase in Search of Meaning." *portal: Libraries and the Academy* 16.1 (2016): 71–88.

Moss, Philip, and Chris Tilly. "'Soft Skills' and Race: An Investigation of Black Men's Employment Problems." *Work and Occupations* 23.3 (1996): 252–76.

Neilson, Brett, and Ned Rossiter. "Precarity as a Political Concept, or, Fordism as Exception." *Theory, Culture & Society* 25.7–8 (2008): 51–72.

Office of Disability Employment Policy (ODEP). *Mastering Soft Skills for Workplace Success: Skills to Pay the Bills.* <https://www.dol.gov/odep/topics/youth/softskills/>.

"Paying Military Skills." *The Washington Post.* 18 Feb. 1957: A12. Proquest.

"Pentagon Plans Full Overhaul of Pay System, Based on Skills." *The Washington Post.* 26 Jan. 1957: A5.

Puar, Jasbir. "Precarity Talk: A Virtual Roundtable with Lauren Berlant, Judith Butler, Bojana Cevjíc, Isabell Lorey, Jasbir Puar, and Ana Vujanović." *TDR: The Drama Review* 56.4 (2012): 163–77.

Raymond, Jack. "Services Expand Lure to a Career." *New York Times.* 4 Oct. 1959: 32.

Read, Jason. *Micropolitics of Capital: Marx and the Prehistory of the Present.* SUNY Press, 2003.

Reeves, Joshua. "Automatic for the People: The Automation of Communicative Labor." *Communication and Critical/Cultural Studies* 13.2 (2016): 150–65.

Robles, Marcel. "Executive Perceptions of the Top 10 Soft Skills Needed in Today's Workplace." *Business Communication Quarterly* 75.4 (2012): 453–65.

Scheuer, James. "Letter of Transmittal." *The Education Deficit*, a staff report summarizing the hearings on "Competitiveness and the Quality of the American Work Force." GPO, 1988.

Spinuzzi, Clay. *All Edge: Inside the New Workplace Networks.* University of Chicago Press, 2015.

———. *Network: Theorizing Knowledge Work in Telecommunications.* Cambridge University Press, 2008.

Swenson, Kristin. *Lifestyle Drugs and the Neoliberal Family.* Peter Lang, 2013.

Taylor, Maxwell D. "Biennial Report of The Chief of Staff, United States Army: 1 July 1955 to 30 June 1957." *Army Information Digest* 12.9 (September 1957): 1–64.

Teston, Christa. "Rhetoric, Precarity, and mHealth Technologies." *Rhetoric Society Quarterly* 26.2 (2016): 251–68.

Tulgan, Bruce. "Bridging the Millennial Soft Skills." *Government Executive* (6 Oct. 2015): 1–3.

United States Bureau of Labor Statistics. *Unemployment Rate: 16–19 Years, Black or African American.* Accessed from Federal Reserve Back of St Louis. 8 Aug. 2017.

United States Cong. Joint Economic Committee. Subcommittee on Education and Health. *The Education Deficit: A Staff Report summarizing the hearings on "Competitiveness and the Quality of the American Work Force."* Washington, DC: GPO, 1988.

United States Cong. Senate. Subcommittee on the Committee on Armed Services Hearings on S. 2014, S. 3081, and HR 11470: *Changing the Method of Computing Basic Pay for Members of the Uniformed Services, to Provide term retention contracts for Reserve Officers and Other Purposes.* 85th Cong, 1st and 2nd sess. Part 2. Washington, DC: GPO, 1958.

United States Continental Army Command (CONARC). Soft Skills Training Conference: Proceedings of a Conference held at U.S. Army School Fort Bliss, Texas, 12–13 Dec. 1972. Five volumes.

Wallulis, Jerald. *The New Insecurity: The End of the Standard Job and Family.* SUNY Press, 1997.

CHAPTER 12

Complicit Interfaces

BECCA TARSA and JAMES J. BROWN JR.

THE EARLY DAYS of networked environments provided hope that racist, sexist, misogynist, and homophobic violence might be lessened in places where offline identities could be uncoupled from online identities. However, it has become clear that the design of our digital spaces has not stemmed violence. It has, at least in some cases, made things worse. Safiya Umoja Noble argues that the analysis of this problem can benefit from a methodology she calls "Black feminist technology studies," an approach that assumes the Internet is "not just a site of communications affordance, nor is it made equally and equitably available to all people. On the contrary, it is implicated in a number of environmental and oppressive conditions for Black life" (Noble). Noble's focus on issues of how environments are designed and maintained is linked to her interest in moving away from narratives of individual empowerment and toward a rethinking of how labor and resources shape our digital relations. Noble points us toward a way of understanding technical infrastructures as a party to, rather than a background for, our digital interactions. It is an approach that insists that infrastructures are arguments, and it is one that allows us to address the cruel precarity of digital spaces that are becoming increasingly unsafe for many people.

While any number of social networking websites might be seen as fostering and enabling these increasingly unsafe conditions, the social networking micro-blogging site Twitter has been the focus of a great many complaints in this regard. This is likely because sites such as 4chan and Reddit have long had reputations for catering to certain audiences and conversations while Twitter is used by a broad range of communities to share information and organize. While many might argue that Twitter is significantly different from 4chan (a bulletin board site that has gained media attention for its links to the Anonymous hacking collective, child pornography arrests, celebrity photo leaks, and much more), Twitter has shown a willingness to look the other way as users submit countless reports of harassment. In August 2016, Internet entrepreneur Jason Calacanis wrote an open letter in the voice of Twitter's CEO Jack Dorsey. Calacanis was frustrated with Twitter's weak response to users who were being harassed and abused and, in particular, to the racist and misogynist messages sent to actor Leslie Jones. Frustrated that Twitter seemed incapable or unwilling to address this problem, Calacanis took on the voice of the Twitter CEO in order to offer a speculative redesign of the Twitter interface.

Calacanis's redesign involved allowing all accounts to attain a "verified" status, a feature that at this point was only available to high-profile accounts (politicians, celebrities, etc.). Verified accounts allow users to confirm that, for instance, a celebrity account is legitimate and not a parody account. Calacanis (speaking as Dorsey) recognized that anonymity is an important resource for many and that the verified accounts feature would not be forced upon all users: "We all know that some voices need to be heard without revealing their identity. From political dissidents to parody accounts, anonymity has a place on the service" (Calacanis). However, he added that anonymity would no longer be used as a weapon for harassment. The redesign proposed by Calacanis would make it so that tweets from unverified accounts would be invisible unless a user chose to see them. This meant that, for instance, content posted by an unverified account in order to harass Leslie Jones would be blurred out (and thus not visible) unless Jones chose to see the content (see Figure 12.1). Upon viewing that content, Jones could choose to block the account, follow the account, or "collapse" the message (the content would remain but would be invisible to Jones). In addition, users wishing to have Twitter function as it typically does would have this option as well.

Calacanis's fictional letter is interesting for a number of reasons. First, he is proposing an easily implementable and feasible solution. In fact, Calacanis argued that he wrote the letter because it was "kind of embarrassing that Twitter can't figure this out on their own" (Calacanis). Of course, it seems likely that Twitter was fully aware of this potential fix and was choosing not to implement it, though the reasons for this are up for debate. Some would argue that such a fix is not in their financial interests, making certain content more opaque and difficult to view. Others would raise the question of

FIGURE 12.1. Graphical representation of Jason Calacanis's speculative redesign of Twitter.

"free speech," even though such an argument is absurd on its face: Twitter is not a government entity. Still others might argue that Twitter's choice not to act stems from a general lack of concern for issues of harassment and abuse by Silicon Valley companies that are run, in large part, by white men. But while we are interested in the embarrassing simplicity of this fix, our primary interest in Calacanis's letter is that it represents a speculative redesign of Twitter aimed directly at stemming abuse and harassment. In this chapter, we argue that such redesigns (and even redesigns that are less focused on utility and usefulness) offer an important method not only for those aiming to address issues such as online harassment but also for the study of precarity in general.

While precarity has not been the explicit focus of digital rhetoric research to date, the field of digital rhetoric does in fact have theoretical resources that help us build this bridge. One of us has written about the ethical predicament of hospitality in networked life, a framework that is in line with the work on precarity by scholars such as Judith Butler and Isabell Lorey. In *Ethical Programs*, Brown argues that networked technologies offer a stark reminder of hospitality, of the arrival of others before any conscious choice: "Prior to any attempt to make sense of our guest, that guest has already arrived, forcing a relation whether or not we have requested it" (2). Brown argues that networked software continually engages the question of hospitality, and he offers the notion of "ethical programs" in order to theorize how "both the computational procedures of software (a computer program) and the procedures we develop in order to deal with ethical predicaments (a program of action)" (5). While this work never invokes precarity as such, it builds from the same theoretical lineage as Butler. Like Brown, Butler uses Emmanuel Levinas's notion of the "face of the Other" to understand relationality, and Butler extends this notion to a discussion of precarity: "To respond to the face, to understand its meaning, means to be awake to what is precarious in another life, or, rather, the precariousness of life itself" (Butler 134). The predicament of hospitality, one that is unavoidable in any walk of life and not just digital spaces, exposes the precarity of all life.

As Lorey has argued, such precarity is not even confined to human existence. For Lorey, precarity is "a condition inherent to both human and non-human being" and that is "always relational and therefore shared with other precarious lives" (Lorey and Butler 37). Brown's discussion of ethical programs as both human and computational is concerned with this same question—it addresses the ethical predicaments of contemporary life by way of relation rather than by way of individuals. For Lorey, precariousness is, in the words of software developers, a feature and not a bug:

Recognizing social relationality can only be the beginning of an entry into processes of becoming-common, involving discussions of possible common interests in the differentness of the precarious, in order to invent with others new forms of organizing and new orders that break with the existing forms of governing in a refusal of obedience. (Lorey and Butler 42–43)

In order to invent from within the unavoidable predicament of precariousness, scholars should recognize that precarity is always relational and never situated in a human subject. The key feature of precarity in digital spaces is the radical exposure to the arrival of others regardless of choice (a situation that is exposed but not created by digital networks), and this exposure is enabled by what we call "complicit interfaces," the computational infrastructures that unavoidably open us to precarity but that also might be redesigned to reconfigure our relations to one another and to the systems themselves.

The reinvention of digital spaces is best demonstrated by Fiona Barnett, Zach Blas, Micha Cárdenas, Jacob Gaboury, Jessica Marie Johnson, and Margaret Rhee's theorization of a queer operating system. In "QueerOS: A User's Manual," they describe a queer computer operating system. As part of that description, they describe their idea of a queer interface. They argue that the common impulse to push past the interface to find hidden operations is "antithetical to a QueerOS." They do not advocate for opening up the black box (examining code or hardware) but instead for an interface that "would be expansive, proliferating the relationality allowed for by the inter-face, its interactivity, its nature as that which is between or among, that which allows us to enter one another and be in-formed—that is, to be shaped from within" (Barnett et al.). This interface is not about assuming a clear boundary between user and system and thus examining the black box as a stable system but rather is focused on "taking self-modification as its ontological premise, such that interaction with an interface might transform both the user and the system." The potential danger in this relational view, one that does not focus on boundaries but rather insists upon constant renegotiation of those boundaries, is that the interface disappears. However, the task of a QueerOS would be to ensure that the "mediating skin of the interface disappears but is not naturalized." The argument here is not for an interface that disappears in order to make one more "productive" or that allows for smooth interactions. Instead, a queer interface obliterates the clear boundary between user and system, understands the user-interface relation as mutually transformative, and never allows any single set of functions to be naturalized.

Speculative redesigns of our digital environments draw attention to how design enables and constrains activity—it suggests that no set of functions or features is "natural" and that each engagement with an interface is a new human-technology assemblage. This is of particular interest to those trying to address the problem of online harassment. Women and people of color receive a disproportionate amount of abuse online. A recent Pew Research Center study found that 40 percent of Internet users have experienced some form of harassment and that women are more vulnerable to sexual harassment and stalking online (Duggan). That same study found that young women are particularly vulnerable to harassment and attacks: "young women are uniquely likely to experience stalking and sexual harassment, while also not escaping the high rates of other types of harassment common to young people in general" (Duggan). In a recent study of its comments, the *Guardian* found that "since around 2010 articles written by women consistently attracted a higher proportion of blocked comments than articles written by men" (Gardiner et al.). Further, the story of Leslie Jones is not unique. People of color are routinely attacked online. Legal analyst Imani Gandy describes her experiences with a particularly vicious attacker:

> For the past two years, I have been harassed by someone calling himself Ass-holster, an anonymous Twitter asshole who, on most days, creates up to ten different Twitter accounts just so he can hurl racist slurs at me: I'm a "nigger," I look "niggery," I haven't earned my "nigger card," I'm a "pseudonigger," "fucking niggster," or "scab nigger." (Gandy)

Like others, Gandy argues that Twitter has shown little interest in preventing this kind of behavior. She has reported abuse and followed all of Twitter's procedures, and yet nothing has changed. She and others are forced to ask: Why bother? It is clear that young people, women, people of color, trans people, and others who identify as LGBTQ are targets for abuse, a problem that taints rhetorical exchange in just about every digital space. Those studying this problem can and should study hateful, racist, sexist language, but this will only get us so far. Scholars will also need to understand how computational systems enable such behavior, and this is why we are interested in speculative redesigns of what we call complicit interfaces, the software that enables harassment online. In many cases, digital environments are built in ways that allow harassers a uniquely rich set of tools for making someone's life a living hell. Adrienne Massanari has made this argument convincingly with regard to Reddit, demonstrating how the platform's upvoting and aggregating functions actually enable what she calls "toxic technocultures." Like Twitter, Reddit has shown little interest in building robust tools for victims, but more than this,

[Reddit's] system valorizes individual contributions and suggests that the site is democratic in terms of what material becomes popular. At the same time, such a system implicitly incentivizes certain activities that might gain karma for the Redditor: for example, reposts of popular material across multiple subreddits. (Massanari 9)

The ease with which one can set up multiple accounts and spread information across conversations (known as "subreddits") creates a welcoming environment for those looking to silence others. These interface design concerns even extend to Reddit administrators, who are typically hesitant to silence users or remove content. Thus computational systems conspire with human users to create toxic environments.

But even though our project is a rhetorical one focused on precarity in hospitable, networked spaces, it is worth pausing here to discuss why we find use in the term "speculative design." James Auger argues that a number of different terms and practices intersect with speculative design, including critical design, discursive design, design probes, and design fictions, but he sees all of these practices as attempts to "remove the constraints from the commercial sector that define normative design processes; use models and prototypes at the heart of the enquiry; and use fiction to present alternative products, systems or worlds" (Auger 11). Auger is concerned with "managing" speculation, especially when it comes to audience expectations and interpretations. If it extends "too far into the future," the audience has difficulty relating, and Auger argues that a speculative project requires that the designer ensure there is a bridge "between the audience's perception of their world and the fictional element of the concept" (12). Such projects should provoke and provide uncanny experiences, but provocations can and should be "managed" to prevent negative responses (14–15). Even though it mirrors arguments in rhetorical theory regarding attempts to manage and move audiences, Auger's approach to speculative design is a conservative one. Still, even if he argues for managing and crafting objects and expectations, he also pushes designers to build bridges to audiences so that "perceptions can be stretched or manipulated in precise and informed ways" (32). Benjamin Bratton offers a very different vision for speculative design. Bratton and Auger would agree that speculative design's focus is not prediction but rather how "to search the space of actual possibility (even and especially beyond what any of us would conceive otherwise)" (Bratton). However, Bratton critiques speculative designs that are too anthropocentric and thus not addressed to broader concerns that exceed contemporary human experience:

It takes a special kind of anthropocentric naiveté to fully entertain the idea that making all design "human scale" would be a long-term solution to anything but the most pedestrian problems. The futures that are probably most worth designing are those that exceed human phenomenology's intuitive scales of anatomically-embedded spatial navigation and the temporalities of organism life span. It is important to mobilize SD [speculative design] on behalf of conditions that are not-yet-existing here and now, and for that we must further shed local social history's mooring privilege.

Bratton argues that speculative designs should be tested by two different criteria. Does the project force the audience to question whether it is real, and does it force the audience to ask whether it is "the best thing or worst [thing] in the world"? For Bratton, if the latter question is unanswerable, the project is likely worth pursuing. Our own speculations fit this mold. In many cases, we are proposing features almost no one would want, but we follow Bratton in arguing that this is precisely what makes these proposals worth pursuing.

While the problem of online harassment would appear to be, in Bratton's words, a human-scale problem, we would argue that online harassment is most definitely not a "pedestrian" problem and also that it involves a number of extra-human forces and technologies. But our turn to speculation is not only about addressing so-called digital problems. In fact, there is no longer a clear line between online/offline or real/virtual spaces. More than a method for addressing online harassment, speculation is a key methodological tool for any scholar of precarity. Environments and tools are designed, meaning they nudge us in certain directions. By speculating about how they might be reimagined, we can provoke new kinds of behaviors, relations, and interactions. How can speculative design be used to address precarity, digital or otherwise? If Lorey is right that precariousness is the unavoidable ground from which contemporary political action emerges, then speculation provides a framework for imagining new possibilities and relations. How might we redesign and reimagine all kinds of spaces in order to denaturalize and reinvent the embodied experiences of users? This is a concern that has long been the focus of queer and feminist theorists, and it reaches beyond the concerns of digital spaces.[1] At the end of this chapter, we turn to work of Micha Cárdenas, who has taken up this speculative approach in spaces that cross the line between digital and non-digital interactions. Such work demonstrates that speculation can be understood as a tool for a broad range of work in precarity studies. While our focus is on digital rhetoric, precarity, and online harassment, we hope to model an approach that shows how speculative design is an essential tool for all scholars of precarity.

ACTIONARY AND REACTIONARY DESIGN

Sarah Jeong sets up a useful dichotomy for thinking about and combating harassment in her book, *The Internet of Garbage*. Harassment, Jeong suggests, "exists on two spectrums at once—one that is defined by *behavior* and one that is defined by *content*." It's the former, she argues, that we should be paying most attention to when it comes to designing and implementing policies for understand and combating the problem. Thinking in terms of content is what has led to our fixation on harassment as an issue of free speech. When the words are the substance of the problem, it's easy to see the issue as one of civil liberty. However, if we turn our attention to behavior, the problem becomes both more visible and more clear-cut: "seeing behaviors on the same spectrum becomes illuminating not because it teaches us how to punish, but how to design environments to make targets feel safe" (Jeong). What Jeong refers to as abusive "behavior," rhetoricians might liken to abusive actions—rhetorical actions that abuse and harass. As we will argue, such actions are encouraged by certain software functions and can be discouraged by redesigns of digital spaces.

The reporting mechanisms used by many platforms (toward which Jeong is decidedly skeptical) reflect the "content" perspective of harassment. The content is addressed, but the actions and behavior that gave rise to that content continue relatively unaffected, and likely unabated. The structure of many digital platforms makes the consequences for reported or banned content relatively limited. For example, users who are reported and banned from Reddit or Twitter for harassment can make another account in seconds, without even the need for an email address; the interfaces' support for such disposable "sock puppet" accounts does very little to discourage harassing behavior, despite the presence of mechanics for dealing with harassing content. Instead of this focus on harassing content, Jeong calls for tools that are focused specifically on behavior. In the terms we are laying out in this chapter, Jeong's approach is more focused on the precarity of hospitable infrastructures than on abusive discourse. A content-based approach would involve the rhetorical analysis of abusive speech, which is of course still necessary. However, we argue that this approach must be paired with one that takes up computational systems and how they invite certain behaviors. As an example of this kind of tactic, Jeong proposes that users who submit a large number of posts in a short amount of time be prompted with a pop-up window asking if they are sure they want to submit their message (Jeong). As abusive posts tend to be fired off fast and furious, such a measure is designed to combat this symptom rather than merely cleaning up the content it leaves behind. Such measures have some proven track record of success. Riot Games instituted a "Restricted Chat Mode" for its popular game *League of Legends,* in which users can only send so many messages per game. This method was so successful in curbing harassing behavior some users in fact requested to be placed on it of their own accord; once their abusive behavior was pointed out to them, they were eager to make use of a tool for learning to police and improve their participation in the community (Gera). In light of this, our speculative designs privilege behavior over content. In other words, our imagined interface prioritizes reducing abusive behavior over removing or obscuring abusive content.

Our speculations are further guided by a second dichotomy, that of actionary versus reactionary design. Interfaces designed to resist harassment frequently begin by implementing features that shift power to the potential victims once harassing behavior is already present. In other words, they offer reactionary design features. Such features include anonymous posting and its variations (discussed in more depth below), reporting and flagging options, and user verification mechanisms. These features allow victims in precarious positions to turn a potential threat into a measure of power over their environment by virtue of their position; the more threats there are to report, the larger their potential control over the discourse. In an interface where those tools are functioning as intended, precarity and the perspective it provides into what is and is not abusive behavior becomes a source of power.

Reactionary design plays a powerful role, but in many cases, these features feel like empty gestures, since they are not supported with the thoughtful design necessary to truly make them tools of counter-harassment. Anonymous or near-anonymous posting, for example, can easily cut both ways, protecting harassers as readily as (if not more so than) victims. And as discussed above, reporting features are frequently limited to a superficial role, removing the content but doing little to address the underlying behavior. As a result, reactionary design needs to be complemented by actionary mechanics that target, complicate, or obstruct potentially abusive behavior. Our notion of actionary design comes from Collin Brooke's discussion of "actionary rhetorics" in *Lingua Fracta.* For Brooke, rhetoric's value for theorizing digital media is in its capacity to invent: "As actionary, a rhetoric of new media should prepare us for sorting through the strategies, practices, and tactics available to us and even for inventing new ones" (Brooke 22). Like Brooke, we see rhetoric as an inventive framework, one that can help us move beyond designs that only address harassment after the fact.

In imagining what such a blended platform might look like, one that addresses both abusive content and behavior with actionary and reactionary mechanics, it's useful to consider what attempts at this already exist. Perhaps the most relevant for our purposes was Imzy, a social media platform designed with many of these same objectives in mind. Unfortunately, Imzy shut down operations in summer 2017, but its approach to design and harassment still offers an important example of how one might approach digital design. Imzy was an interface designed from the ground up to combat harassment. Its founder and CEO, Dan McComas, started the social platform after leaving Reddit. As Massanari's study makes clear, Reddit's software enables and harbors some of the ugliest types of Internet harassment. McComas believes that "the best way to curb harassment is to build a diverse user base and community standards from the start" (Newitz). And the commitment to these goals was plainly reflected in both the structure and the content of the platform. Lena Dunham's Lenny Letter and Black Girl Talking, for example, are two organizations that partnered with Imzy to manage their communities. "People tend to bring in people like themselves. If we waited a few years to address this," McComas said in an interview with Ars Technica, "we would already have a cultural norm, and that's hard to change" (Newitz). This mission is visible in many aspects of the platform's design. The feature of Imzy's interface that received the most attention was also the one most directly linked to precarity: its built-in "tip" mechanic, allowing users to easily send money to another user who had posted something they think has value. Aside from the obvious profit potential for the organization itself, the tip feature offered a concrete tool for encouraging and rewarding strong community moderation—a recognition on Imzy's part of the labor precarity that defines contemporary working conditions, especially in digital and cultural production (dePeuter 419). As anyone who's spent time in digital community spaces knows, effective and active moderation is key to building and maintaining positive, inclusive discourse. This can be a hard job, and all too often a thankless one—something the Imzy team recognized (Newitz). Designing a flexible tip mechanic directly into the interface empowers communities to establish their own norms for recognizing contributions to both conversations and the community that hosts them. In offering its communities a tool for financial recognition of labor, Imzy's interface resisted the tendency to conceptualize the work of digital production as "free labor" (Terranova), instead drawing attention to the precarious position of both those who perform is and those who rely on it.

But Imzy's design mechanics for resisting harassment went much deeper than simply offering incentives for users to combat it themselves. Its other features dealt predominantly with two issues: community formation and anonymity controls. This first set of mechanics, those for building and accessing communities, were designed to be the foundation of the Imzy platform.

Features for the first were immediately visible on joining the site, where users were asked right away to select specific communities to join (based on a checklist of interests). Content within all communities could *only* be viewed by members. This is a direct contrast to the structure of Reddit, where neither viewing nor posting content to a subreddit requires a subscription, a system that, as McComas, Massanari, and others have pointed out, makes communities easy targets for organized harassment by outsiders. Reasoning that "the core, devoted members of a group are often not the ones who make a community toxic, but rather the passers-by who may stumble upon a new community and leave disparaging remarks," Imzy's creators designed this opt-in-only feature as a means to expand the former category while limiting or eliminating the latter (Isaac). Imzy's community structure was an example of the kind of thoughtful design that results from approaching harassment as behavior rather than content. By designing to encourage investment in communities and discourage voyeurs, Imzy fostered a userbase that by nature behaved in a manner less prone to create abusive content. Should that user mechanic fail, there were other features, both actionary and reactionary, in place to correct the situation before such content accumulated and communities were irreversibly disrupted or overrun.

One such powerful reactionary feature was Imzy's approach to anonymity, yet another feature imagined in direct opposition to its creators' former employer. On Reddit, creating new usernames is extremely simple—"throwaway" accounts, designed for single or very specific uses and then (typically) discarded, are not only common but expected, a standard feature of doing business there. While this has some potential benefits (for example, allowing users to discuss personal or potentially identifying issues without fear of them being linked to their real identity through other information in their posting history), it is also a powerful tool for abuse. A single user can create what appears to the victim to be an army of abusers; harassment is uncoupled from consequences even for a user's digital identity within the site; trolls have access to endless identities with which they can perpetrate harassment. Imzy's design recognized the value of offering users multiple identities while also pushing back against the potential for misuse. Users were able to choose to post under a different username within a community, but they could only use one identity in that community. Users could also choose to post anonymously *without* logging out of their account; they still received notifications about responses to anonymously posted content, and any follow-up comments they made were posted under the same random, anonymous name. These posts could not be publicly viewed by others in that user's profile. In other words, anonymity functioned only protectively. It could not (at least not easily) be used as a tool for endless harassment. Likewise, this reactionary feature could be flipped for actionary use if needed: should a user engage in abusive behavior in one community, they were not protected by anonymity, and they could be restricted or banned across the platform as a whole. The cost of abusive behavior was much higher for the user, since they lost their presence and usernames in other communities as well. Abusing one community while enjoying the benefits of membership in another was not tolerated on Imzy, either by its users or by its code.

Imzy offers a valuable example of the power of thoughtful design to combat harassment. McComas and his team set out to deliberately consider the issue in their code, and the results were both innovative and protective. The features the site used are not exceptionally complicated or counterintuitive. These features stemmed from speculation about how an interface might protect a platform and its users from the ground up. Building from Imzy's example, our own speculations take this notion further, focusing on questions of embodiment. We speculate about interfaces that see harassment as an embodied behavior and therefore detectable and preventable via actionary features. Such features both exploit the unavoidable, precarious hospitality of online spaces while also aiming to address those who experience a disproportionate amount of online abuse.

EMBODIMENT AND SPECULATIVE DESIGNS

Bodies have an ugly, all-too-central place in the landscape of digital harassment. Revenge porn is perhaps the ugliest manifestation of this, where intimate photos of the victim are publicly displayed along with personally identifying information. Less dramatic but no less damaging, body shaming (whether connected concretely to images of the victim's body or merely in abstract) is another characteristic tool in the arsenal of online harassment. Such harassment, in both forms, is painfully visible on social news sites featuring content related to body positivity and media portrayals of the female body. Refinery29 publishes a series called the "Anti-Diet" about the ongoing quest of creator Kelsey Miller toward body positivity and intuitive eating; comments on these posts are thick with examples of both explicit body harassment, aimed at Miller herself, and more abstract harassment of those who defend her or share their own stories. Whether she is revealed in a photograph or a story, any woman who reveals herself becomes a target for overt and aggressive shaming. Victims are seen as possessing a physical body in addition to a digital identity, but harassers are too often nameless, faceless, and disembodied. We propose designing interface mechanics that forcibly embody harassers in their own view—reminding these harassers, if only in a small way, that they too possess a body and all the physical/aesthetic complications that come with it. Like any user, the online abuser cannot escape the physical actions demanded by most computational interfaces: the fingers feel the keys, the eyes track characters on-screen, the ears hear the strokes and screen reader software, the voice activates text-to-speech software. Whether conscious or not, harassment comes with its own set of physical and environmental preferences/habits—which are by nature tied to the needs and pleasures of the body. Our speculative redesigns are therefore in large part focused on the body of the harasser, as well as the environment of the harasser. These speculations highlight the precarity of any body, harasser included.

The features we have in mind would primarily fall into the "actionary" category, since they would attempt to actively reshape behaviors rather than police acts of abuse after the fact. These features reorient digital precarity and the behaviors it enables, making abusers and harassers aware of their own embodied affectability in networked environments. Such offensive features would be designed to, upon detecting signs of harassing behavior, turn the mechanisms of such behavior back onto the harasser themselves. What kinds of behaviors might be linked to harassment? We are imagining systems that draw on a broad of range of data gathered about a user's environment (weather, location data, pictures hanging on their walls) as well as user activities (pace of keystroke, other sites they have visited while posting comments on social media, length of time active on the site). Consider that it is entirely possible to design a system that uses a computer's front-facing camera to identify images hanging on the wall behind a user, conducts facial recognition on those images, and identifies them as family members. Perhaps the same system links the following data points: it's snowing outside, the user's keystroke pace has quickened significantly while they post aggressive messages to a stranger. A pop-up message might appear: "We're wondering what your sister, [name here], is doing right now? Perhaps she needs help shoveling her driveway?" Creepy? Absolutely. But even though such features are inspired by dystopian television shows like *Black Mirror,* they signal the outer edges of what's possible when considering speculative redesigns. Recall Bratton's question: Is this the best idea ever or the worst idea ever? If upon considering these speculative features such a question gives us pause, we're on the right track.

Our focus on the physical dimensions of the abuser's behavior opens up a number of other possibilities when it comes to speculative redesigns of social media spaces. As we suggest above, a user who is typing fast and furiously, contacting a user with whom they do not have a strong connection (someone they are not "friends" with or who does not follow them back), and not receiving any replies is quite possibly engaging in harassing behavior. There is, of course, no guarantee of this, but the advantage of a speculative approach is that we can worry less about these "false positives" than we would if we were enacting an actual interface change. In this speculative design, the user would be told that their typing rate has climbed by a certain percentage and that they are frequently contacting someone they don't know, and that person isn't responding. The system might be designed to lock that person's account for five minutes, preventing any activity and encouraging a "cooling off" period. The advantage of computational environments (and it must be said that this can be a distinct *disadvantage* as well) is that they can enforce rules computationally—rather than a law written in language that bars someone from using a website (something like what the courts have done to prevent hackers from returning to their activities once convicted), a software system can lock a user out. That lockout is again focused on the body of the user. It is an attempt to physically bar them from the activity. Of course, any system can be hacked and any rule might be circumvented, but this should not prevent us from considering how systems might deal with and prevent such behaviors. The embodied activity is foregrounded here, linking an increase in typing speed and a one-sided communication with a stranger to the likelihood of harassment, and then attempting to physically remove the person from the situation for a period of time. Lockout mechanisms are a fairly common feature in interactive media spaces—for example, Twitter will reject tweets submitted too rapidly on each other's heels; our design builds on this already familiar tool by taking further advantage of the computational environment to tie it to the specific user's practices. Rather than a one-size-fits-all rejection speed, we imagine a mechanic that responds to a change in practices. By tying the lockout to the potential abuser's own embodied typing and posting practices, the mechanic becomes more difficult to circumvent and more pointedly precarious—users cannot easily gauge where or when their actions will trigger a lockout, turning back on them the uncertainty their potential victims feel about where or when they might be subjected to attack.

In keeping with our user-facing approach, behaviors tripping an "abuse" or "harassment" flag would display a pop-up message over the current page with a message drawing attention to the behavior in question: "We noticed you've been hammering the keyboard unusually hard—maybe it's time for a snack break?" "It's pretty late to be sending [username] so many messages. Why don't you sleep on this one?" In addition to a simple close button, the box would also feature buttons for any relevant opt-in anti-abuse functions. For example, a target flagged for rapid-fire posting would be offered a button to activate limited posting for one hour. Rooted in the physicality of the target's behavior, this feature links the physical action to digital agency, pushing users to reverse the flow of abusive behavior by taking digital action—opting in or toning down—in response to a physically grounded triggering event. It also has the further advantage of being easily scaled according to the needs and values/priorities of the platform. In a space with a particularly vulnerable user base, or one that is particularly precarious due to media attention or coordinated attacks, each subsequent flag could be set to trigger increasingly explicit warnings and intrusive consequences. A community whose discourse expectations revolve around its commitment to unfettered free speech could disable scaling, allowing them to encode both expression and respect into the structure of their space.

The embodied behaviors of abuse also provide an opportunity for offensive disruption mechanics. A user engaging in such behaviors might find that control of their device's camera momentarily passes to the site, whose software then takes a series of pictures. A simple script chooses from among them the clearest portrait and assigns that image to the user as a profile image. For the next twenty-four hours, this image is displayed prominently on all the user's posts as well as any other page where their user information appears (profile page, newsfeed, etc.)—invisible to other users but unavoidable for the harasser themselves. While there is some debate over whether and when the tactics of trolls should be taken up for good, we feel that such turnabout is neither productive nor fair play; such unconsented exposure of the body is a violation regardless of circumstances (Phillips). Our goal is not to expose the harasser publicly, but to emphasize for them that they, like their victims, inhabit a physical (and physically imperfect) body. In our design, these embodiments would be invisible to other users, but obtrusive to the harasser themselves.

Obtrusive visual mechanics could also simply make content more difficult to read, and thus more difficult to engage with through abusive behavior. If a user is flagged for abusive behavior that then continues after they've received a warning pop-up, the interface could then become progressively more difficult to read. While there are many possible mechanics through which this could happen—blurring, dramatically shrinking or enlarging text, and so on—we like the idea of an interface that superimposes "stickers" over various parts of the pageview, with another added every minute until the user signs off for a designated "cool-down" period. (These stickers could be images of anything—the site's logo, for example, or random enlarged emojis.) Effectively the result is the same as being briefly banned, as after a few minutes the site will become impossible to use until the cool-down period runs its course. The difference, however, is that this method places that choice, however hollow, in the hands of the user. The appearance of the stickers is a clear sign that their behavior is not in keeping with the values of the site; the choice to persist in that behavior until the site becomes unusable is their own. Committing to harassment, this mechanic reminds them, is a choice.

We can also assume some relatively straightforward parallels with any typing-based interactive activity. Consider the small bodily pleasures of a good Facebook debate or Twitter exchange: the ping of notifications, the rapid click-clack of the keys, the haptic response from tapping submit, the immediate gratification of continuous interaction. These tiny physical sensations, through endless repetition, become tiny exterior analogs for interior pleasures: I am popular; I am productive; I am making myself heard. Disrupting that stream of physical feedback thus lessens those mental pleasures. Abusive behavior thrives on speed—firing off message after message, jumping from thread to thread, or even just a cycle of copy-paste-submit. This kind of behavior doesn't require speedy thinking, just speedy fingers and a broadband connection— and those fast-paced repetitive motions are part of the pleasure. Designing an actionary mechanic that targets that pleasure is simple: delay the rate of input allowed, record only every other keystroke, or activate a script that deletes any words that exceed an average (or reduced) typing speed every thirty seconds. (Since these roadblocks all present similarly at first glance, this feature could be scaled up by implementing multiple types to be randomly assigned each time the feature is triggered.) The experience of typing within the site instantly becomes tedious rather than titillating, and rapid-fire posting virtually impossible.

We imagine all users being subject to these features when first joining an online community, exposing all members to these mechanics. After this introductory period, assuming the user has not harassed or abused others, users would only experience such features when tracked behaviors trigger them. The hope would be that all users would understand that these invasive, actionary features are there to prevent undesirable behavior and that the software is a reflection of the values of the community. Such intrusive security mechanisms would, we believe, have a profound impact on harassing behavior—not only reducing it, but potentially encouraging its perpetrators to consider that behavior from a different perspective, bringing them toward a place of empathy with their potential victims by embodying those victims as themselves. But this potential coming-together relies on fairly intense security measures, ones we realize may seem antithetical to the goals of precarity scholarship. In other words, such a design neatly straddles Bratton's determining question for productive speculative design—appearing from one side the best thing, and from another the worst.

SPECULATIVE DESIGN AND PRECARITY STUDIES

As Micha Cárdenas has argued, we have had a curious set of priorities when it comes to constructing safe digital environments: "Why do we have better software to share pictures of lunch than we do to keep each other safe?" ("From a Free Software Movement"). Cárdenas has issued a call to designers to acknowledge that "the Internet era has not brought more safety but less" and has further argued that we should shift from arguments about "free software" (which focus on intellectual property) to ones about "free safety." A free safety movement would include

> people who want to figure out how to make transformative justice happen in increasingly networked societies, a movement that will develop networks for safety that don't rely on the corporations and police that daily perpetuate violence on our communities, a movement of people who will agree to keep each other safe from unjust forms of violence. (Cárdenas, "From a Free Software Movement")

Cárdenas has carried out just this kind of work with a number of projects, including one called Autonets, which attempted to create "autonomous communication networks for trans of color safety that do not rely on prisons, police, or corporations, inspired by the prison abolitionist movement" (Cárdenas, "Trans of Color Poetics"). The project involved creating garments and developing a system of gestures that Cárdenas and collaborators used during a live, public performance. Participants blended into a crowd and then used garments and physical gestures to communicate. Cárdenas notes that the project had its limitations, since the electronic components were expensive and not necessarily reliable; however, the project stills served as a useful speculative attempt to build embodied responses to the precarity of trans people of color. The project constructed both new objects and new gestures, both of which opened up discussions about how to build safety nets for those who need them. It is this speculative approach that we argue for in this chapter, putting forth a series of speculative redesigns for social media environments that are focused on creating newly imagined spaces. Those reimagined spaces highlight the precarity of all interactions, digital or otherwise, and they are put forth as arguments for how we can and should reimagine the ethics of our digital infrastructures and interfaces. Beyond conducting the rhetorical analysis of online discourse, which is of course a worthwhile project, we believe digital rhetoricians will have to directly engage questions of design as they begin to tackle the problem of online harassment.

Speculative design offers one possible way forward for digital rhetoricians who want to tackle the problems faced by the most precarious inhabitants of digital spaces. Software environments shape our behaviors—they contribute to rhetorical action. But more than this, our software environments are arguments. They put forth ideas about how relations should or should not happen, and for this reason they are squarely within the realm of rhetoric. Those who are most at risk of online harassment are fully aware of this fact. They experience the arguments made by our software environments on a daily basis as they attempt to deal with regular abuse and harassment. The rhetorical problem of harassment is (at least) twofold: it involves abusive discourse and it involves the environments that allow for the unfettered flow of that abuse. Our focus in this chapter has been on the latter, on the complicit interfaces that provide an entire tool kit for abusers and harassers. But more than this, we hope that this chapter performs the kind of speculative method that addresses the question of precarity in any environment. Through speculation, the unavoidable predicament of precarity becomes visible in new ways. Many of the features we suggest would almost certainly not be accepted by users and might not even necessarily foster a successful and stable online discourse community—because they distribute the precariousness felt keenly by the minority at all times across the majority, increasing the instability of digital participation to a fever pitch. But these speculations are a response to the calls of Lorey to embrace precarity as a tool of resistance, and this makes speculation a portable framework for exposing both the advantages and costs of such an embrace across a range of contexts—not just digital ones.

Speculation is a method that allows rhetoricians interested in precarity one way of imagining alternate futures and alternate public spaces. How might we redesign our environments so that they recognize behaviors rather than just policing abuse after the fact? What actionary methods are available as we imagine ways to build worlds that are simultaneously more welcoming and protective of those who most need protection? In her essay "Feminist Killjoys (and Other Willful Subjects)," Sarah Ahmed suggests that a "queer phenomenology" would allow us to understand how environments are only designed for the survival of certain people. She suggests that estrangement from one's environment is a daily reality for many, and a queer phenomenology allows us to hover over such estrangement rather than dismissing it as an aberration: "Phenomenology helps us explore how the familiar is that which is not revealed. A queer phenomenology shows how the familiar is not revealed to those who can inhabit it" (Ahmed). Ahmed's feminist killjoy is "the one who gets in the way of other people's happiness"—she is the one who continually reminds us that the world is only built for the survival of some (Ahmed). Our speculations operate from within this framework, but they are not just about disrupting the everyday. They are not reactionary; they are actionary. They are, in Ahmed's terms, a "world-making project," one that attempts to imagine things otherwise.

NOTE

1. In 1977, Carl Boggs coined the term "prefigurative politics" to describe "the embodiment within the ongoing political practice of a movement, of those forms of social relations, decision-making, culture, and human experience that are the ultimate goal." Boggs's term was an attempt to describe how communities imagine and articulate end goals of a Marxist vision for government and society without falling prey to "bureaucratic domination" (99–100). This framework has also been taken up by feminist and queer theorists and practitioners as they attempt to imagine community formations amongst communities with diverse interests and identities (see Anahita; Eder, Staggenborg, and Sudderth). Our own work intersects with this work on prefigurative communities, though our focus on speculation is an attempt to think about both practical questions (which tend to be the focus of work on prefiguration) as well as the utopic, dystopic, and fictional worlds exposed by speculative interfaces.

WORKS CITED

Ahmed, Sara. "Feminist Killjoys (And Other Willful Subjects)." *Scholar & Feminist Online* 8.3 (2010): n. pag.

Anahita, Sine. "Nestled into Niches: Prefigurative Communities on Lesbian Land." *Journal of Homosexuality* 56.6 (2009): 719–37.

Auger, James. "Speculative Design: Crafting the Speculation." *Digital Creativity* 24.1 (2013): 11–35.

Barnett, Fiona, et al. "QueerOS: A User's Manual." *Debates in the Digital Humanities*. N. pag. Web. 5 Dec. 2016.

Boggs, Carl. "Marxism, Prefigurative Communism, and the Problem of Workers' Control." *Radical America* 11.6 (1977): 99–122.

Bratton, Benjamin. "On Speculative Design." *DIS Magazine*. N. pag., n.d. Web. 5 Dec. 2016.

Brooke, Collin Gifford. *Lingua Fracta: Toward a Rhetoric of New Media*. Hampton Press, 2009.

Brown, James J. Jr. *Ethical Programs: Hospitality and the Rhetorics of Software*. University of Michigan Press, 2015.

Butler, Judith. *Frames of War: When Is Life Grievable?* Repr. ed. Verso, 2016.

Calacanis, Jason. "Evolving Twitter: A Message from Our CEO." *Recode*. N. pag., 14 Aug. 2016. Web. 5 Dec. 2016.

Cárdenas, Micha. "From a Free Software Movement to a Free Safety Movement." N. pag., n.d. Web. 5 Dec. 2016.

———. "Trans of Color Poetics: Stitching Bodies, Concepts, and Algorithms." *S&F Online*. N. pag., n.d. Web. 5 Dec. 2016.

de Peuter, Greig. "Creative Economy and Labor Precarity: A Contested Convergence." *Journal of Communication Inquiry* 35.4 (2011): 417–25.

Duggan, Maeve. "Part 1: Experiencing Online Harassment." *Pew Research Center: Internet, Science & Tech*. N. pag., 22 Oct. 2014. Web. 5 Dec. 2016.

Eder, Donna, Suzanne Staggenborg, and Lori Sudderth. "The National Women's Music Festival: Collective Identity and Diversity in a Lesbian-Feminist Community." *Journal of Contemporary Ethnography* 23.4 (1995): 485–515.

Gandy, Imani. "#TwitterFail: Twitter's Refusal to Handle Online Stalkers, Abusers, and Haters." *Rewire*. N. pag., n.d. Web. 5 Dec. 2016.

Gardiner, Becky, et al. "The Dark Side of Guardian Comments." *The Guardian*. 12 Apr. 2016. Web. 28 Oct. 2016.

Gera, Emily. "Riot Games Will Reward League of Legends Players for Not Being Jerks." *Polygon*. N. pag., 6 Jan. 2015. Web. 5 Dec. 2016.

Isaac, Mike. "Imzy Is a Kinder, Gentler Reddit. If It Can Stay That Way." *New York Times*. 8 June 2016. Web. 5 Dec. 2016.

Jeong, Sarah. *The Internet of Garbage*. Forbes Media, 2015.

Lorey, Isabell, and Judith Butler. *State of Insecurity: Government of the Precarious*. Trans. Aileen Derieg. Repr. ed. Verso, 2015.

Massanari, Adrienne. "#Gamergate and The Fappening: How Reddit's Algorithm, Governance, and Culture Support Toxic Technocultures." *New Media & Society* 19.3 (2015): 329–46.

Newitz, Annalee. "Imzy Is a Community Where People Pay Each Other for Being Nice." *Ars Technica*. N. pag., 22 May 2016. Web. 5 Dec. 2016.

Noble, Safiya Umoja. "A Future for Intersectional Black Feminist Technology Studies." *S&F Online*. N. pag., n.d. Web. 5 Dec. 2016.

Phillips, Whitney. *This Is Why We Can't Have Nice Things: Mapping the Relationship Between Online Trolling and Mainstream Culture*. Repr. ed. The MIT Press, 2015.

Terranova, Tiziana. *Network Culture: Politics for the Information Age*. Pluto Press, 2004.

CHAPTER 13

Pathologizing Precarity

CHRISTA TESTON

IN HIS 2015 State of the Union Address, President Obama announced support for a new medical model that leverages "advances in genomics, emerging methods for managing and analyzing large data sets . . . and health information technology to accelerate biomedical discoveries" ("Fact Sheet"). Among other purported advances, the White House's precision medicine initiative promised both prognostic accuracy and profitability. In theory, precision medicine suggests that health and healing can be achieved by marshaling the predictive power of genetic information. In practice, precision medicine mobilizes genetic differences as warrants for claims about at-risk bodies.

No person's genetic legacy is impervious to lead-laced water, rising sea levels, or political instability, however. In tandem with differences in human DNA are sociocultural, political, and environmental effects that condition the "slow death" (Berlant; Puar) of some communities. Bodies, biologies, geographies, histories, environments, economies, and sociocultural effects intra-act (Barad) in often unpredictable and unintended ways, and in ways that both sustain and limit life. Left unaddressed in President Obama's speech, therefore, are answers to questions about how and for whom genetic evidences will prove "precise." In precision medicine's biomedical backstage,[1] the complexity of infrastructural intra-actions are evinced in ways that, while expedient and efficacious, may be both racialized and reductive.

Rhetoricians of health and medicine critique medical practice for how it reductively constructs bodies in ways that often serve certain sociopolitical ends. But what backstage, material-discursive labor makes such reductions possible? Given that over the next decade precision medicine will envelop evidence-based medicine as the primary method for making medical decisions, what are the unintended consequences of precision medicine's fetishization of genetic evidence? What falls out of focus in such a medical model? To answer these questions, I mobilize precarity as an analytic for examining the biomedicalization of bodies.

Conversations that confront the biomedicalization of bodies and human health in medical rhetoric, medical humanities, and technical communication do not always attend explicitly to "relations of violence and inequality" (Lorey 38). I hope this chapter serves to amend such neglect by demonstrating the value of precarity as an analytic construct. Mobilizing precarity as an analytic makes palpable "the 'real-world' impact of our field's interrogations of medicine, health and illness" (Atkinson et al. 78).

The precision medicine initiative relies on proprietary scientific methods for taming biological information—in particular, genetic differences—into that which resembles actionable evidence. In other words, how genetic differences are characterized as evidence in support of a particular decision about future action hinges on a host of black-boxed,[2] behind-the-scenes techniques and technologies. Genetic scientists stage intra-actions between bodies, biologies, and technologies that are intended to evince and quantify genetic differences. After genetic differences are rendered legible in and by the biomedical backstage, assertions are then made about the vulnerability of some human bodies. Such assertions about a patient's genetic vulnerability aren't just clinically meaningful. They also have strong biopowerful[3] effects. As a result, some bodies' precarious positionalities—that is, their emplacement within extra-genetic material-discursive structures—are pathologized. One might say, then, that genetically vulnerable bodies are not only held hostage by their own biology; they're also held accountable for their own death.

Theoretically, there isn't anything novel about arguing that genetic evidence is (and always has been) used to mark some bodies as inherently weak, vulnerable, or inferior (see Condit; Happe; J. Lynch). In practice, however, the biomedical community has doubled down on the use of genetic differences as evidence for treatment options. The detection of genetic differences is precision medicine's evidential gold standard. Given the biomedical community's ongoing commitment to genetic difference as evidential grounds for care, this chapter describes how the material, biomedical backstage contributes to racialized medical practice. Locating in their genetic code the failure of some bodies to thrive pathologizes precarity.

Pathologizing precarity has serious consequences for certain human communities, especially for those who are disproportionately affected by failing networks of social and economic support. The pathologizing of precarity is a racialized act that permits assumptions about, for example, Native American populations' genetic vulnerability to alcohol abuse or African American women's genetic vulnerability to the deadliest form of breast cancer (see also Holloway, *Private Bodies*). As Karla F. C. Holloway argues, "In medicine and society, the most critical health indicator seems to be our zip code" ("Their Bodies" 127). Ultimately, a medical model that praises the predictive power of genetic differences risks neglecting other actionable evidence (e.g., zip codes)—evidence of the material-discursive conditions and infrastructures that exploit some human bodies' vulnerabilities.

To make the case that the precision medicine movement pathologizes precarity, I first unearth the backstage, material-discursive mechanisms that fortify genetic evidence. In other words, I analyze the rhetorical methods with which genetic scientists manufacture genetic difference. In so doing, I demonstrate that the evidence upon which the practice of precision medicine is based is not all that precise. Despite the appearance of technoscientific nuance, the rhetorical moves used to transform genetic differences into actionable evidence require scientists to synonymize: single nucleotide polymorphisms (SNPs) with human bodies; population labels with geographic location; and ancestry with race, ethnicity, and identity. Precision medicine's fetishization of genetic differences divorces human bodies from extra-genetic forces that condition the "injury, violence, and death" (25) to which Butler argues some populations are differentially exposed.

I conclude by exploring what it might look like to resist pathologizing precarity. What might it look like, in other words, to reframe certain communities' embodied vulnerability in terms of what Katie Oliviero, drawing on Cherrie Moraga and Gloria Anzaldúa, calls "theories in the flesh and differential vulnerabilities" (6)? Such reframing forces us (patients, practitioners, and critics alike) to understand our responsibility to one another as radical attunement and response to the very infrastructural powers that render some bodies more or less vulnerable over time and in varying contexts. Resistance to pathologizing precarity is not only a critical rhetorical practice; it is also an ongoing posture of responsibility that hears or is hailed by differential distributions of embodied vulnerability.

Genetic data from Indigenous communities and communities of color are increasingly mobilized in ways that warrant arguments about their cause of death as connected to an inherited legacy of corporeal disadvantage. In other words, individual human bodies are blamed for their collective, slow death. By describing how genetic scientists rely on computational cuts, logical tautologies, and the synonymization of geographical spaces with human populations, this chapter unearths genetic science's precarious rhetorics. In so doing, I draw attention to the coexistence of health disparities alongside so-called technoscientific progress within the medical-pharmaceutical industrial complex (Illich).

GENETIC EVIDENCE'S BIOPOWER

In "The Emergence, Politics, and Marketplace of Native American DNA," Kim TallBear asks: "How did it come to be that Native American bodies are expected to serve as sources of biological raw materials extracted to produce knowledge that not only does not benefit them, but may actually harm them by challenging their sovereignty, historical narratives, and identities?" (21). In the following analyses, I explore TallBear's question by investigating the material-discursive actors that are often overlooked or regarded only as epiphenomenal to science-in-the-making. I should note from the outset that I do not intend to characterize as unscrupulous scientists' methods for manufacturing evidence in the genomic backstage. I do, however, see a need for constant critical attention to how "all technologies have . . . strong 'bio-power' effect[s]" that "affect bodies and immerse them in social relations of power, inclusion and exclusion" (Braidotti, "Feminist" 67). As Pender argues, "For all of its scientific and technological advances, biomedicine continues to be an exclusionary enterprise that too often prioritizes corporate interests, leaving the health care needs of many unmet" (339). Genetic science's biopower effects are perhaps best illustrated in TallBear's (*Native American DNA*) study of how DNA evidences are used to negate Indigenous populations' rights to land and sovereignty. Specifically, TallBear describes how DNA evidence has been used "to constitute history and identity in ways that risk indigenous land and governance rights" (203). TallBear's work presents a clear case of how genetic evidences are used to govern bodies in ways that empower state-sponsored institutions while disadvantaging members of local communities.

One of the reasons genetic evidences become suasive, biopowerful artifacts is because DNA is imbued with what Kramer calls "biological facticity" (99). In other words, genetic information is assumedly neutral, natural, and unaffected by "culture and discourse" (Happe 137). Genetic evidence is assumed to inhabit a kind of "'prediscursive' reality" (137). In turn, a body's biology becomes a "common sense marker of difference" (135). Genetic infor-mation's biological facticity has profound implications for the care of what the medical-pharmaceutical industrial complex regards as non-normative, or diseased, bodies. In divorcing a body's biological materials from the extra-biological conditions that bear up and make possible bodily being (Rickert), genetic evidence is used either to endorse racist ideologies or to support anti-racialist research agendas (see Reardon and TallBear).

To understand how bodies of color are deemed more or less vulnerable because of their biology—what Celeste Condit calls race-based biological infe-riority (385)—requires first that we acknowledge a human body as "a medium with specific properties that drive and shape discourse both in the moment and through time" (387). For Condit, bodies are "moved by . . . cultural and socio-political interests" (388). Ways in which bodies become mediums for race-based ideological arguments have consequences for contemporary care practices. Kelly Happe argues that when genetic scientists construct a "racialized other," they simultaneously constitute the "grounds by which consent to a racialized order (by the privileged) can be secured" (138). Racialized order by the privileged has helped to create what is now collectively referred to as health disparities.

Disparities among Black, Indigenous, and other human communities whose bodies are marked as "other" result in different medical treatments and disproportionately negative disease outcomes: "Differential treatment of those already presumed to be biologically and culturally discrete, and thus infe-rior, results in different disease outcomes" (Happe 147). Race-based presump-tions about human bodies—presumptions that I argue are staged through a series of material-discursive intra-actions in the biomedical backstage—helps to explain why a commonsense response to why more Black women than White women are dying from the most aggressive form of breast cancer is because of Black women's DNA (see Warner et al.). Jayna Brown argues in "Being Cellular: Race, the Inhuman, and the Plasticity of Life" that "ableism and racism are imbricated within scientific advances" (326) and "black, queer, and disabled people . . . are painfully aware of the way power is present in any attempt to represent material reality" (337). As precision medicine uses genetic differences to make claims about at-risk bodies, what values are built into its biomedical backstage? Asked another way: What material-discursive labor conditions corporeal futures under the guise of so-called precision? How does such labor make it possible to pathologize precarity and, in turn, mute the effects of differential "allocations of power, resources, and inequali-ties" (Oliviero 6)?

For the purposes of this project, I draw on Isabell Lorey's definition of precarity, which she describes as "a structural category of ordering segmented relations of violence and inequality" (38). Using precarity in this way draws analytic attention to the material-discursive conditions that structure health disparities. Under this definition, there is not, nor could there be, an antidote for precarity. According to Lorey, precarity is a social condition determined by relational differences produced through our interdependencies with others (Lorey, qtd. in Puar 172). The effects of precariousness, in other words, are felt unevenly among certain communities. While precarity is, as Butler describes, "a generalized condition," it is also "the condition of being conditioned" (23). One cannot ignore its uneven distribution. Depending on the degree to which precarious conditions are normalized by certain regimes of power (e.g., governments, economies, institutions), some persons' precariousness is made more or less visible, relevant, and insufferable. Said simply: At the same time that some communities are safeguarded from precariousness, others are abandoned to it.

Certain communities are abandoned to precariousness when the "privilege of protection is based on differential distribution of the precarity of all those who are perceived as other and considered less worthy of protection" (Lorey 22). Abandonment to precariousness first requires that a person be perceived and subsequently marked as different or Other. Once markers of difference are established and enacted, institutional actors—that is, the medical-pharmaceutical industrial complex—have grounds to distribute resources to those who fall within agreed upon boundaries of normality. Lorey refers to the process of precarization as "segmentation." What results from the segmentation of some lives from others is a pervasive anxiety—specifically, "an anxiety towards others who cause harm, who have to be preventively fended off, and not infrequently even destroyed, in order to protect those who are threatened" (21). Precarious rhetorics emerge from such anxieties. Such anxieties contribute to pathologizations of precarity.

To explore how abandonment to precarity manifests itself materially, consider the following: In 1991, Dr. Samuel Broder (the U.S. National Cancer Institute's then-director) declared poverty a carcinogen. More than a decade later, the Surveillance, Epidemiology, and End Results Program (which provides statistics about cancer diagnoses and deaths) continues to report that "49.5% of African Americans, 47.5% of American Indians/Alaskan Natives, and 40.7% of Hispanics/Latinos lived in census tracts with a poverty rate of over 20% compared with 7.0% of non-Hispanic Whites and 16.0% of Asian Americans/Pacific Islanders" (Ward 80). And today, a life expectancy gap of 15.4 years continues to exist between urban Black males and Asian males in the United States (Gehlert and Colditz 1810). A medical model that fetishizes individuals' genetic differences systematically neglects attention to the carcinogenic effects of poverty on particular communities. How, then, might the persistence of health disparities correlate with the very tactics deployed in the biomedical backstage? How are precision medicine's technoscientific segmentations then imbued with explanatory power?

To explore these questions, I trace how the process of precarization unfolds in genetic science's biomedical backstage. That is, I investigate how genetic scientists manufacture markers of difference that then warrant claims about some bodies' biological vulnerability. The stakes for such a project are high. Decisions about the distribution of material and human resources in health care and public policies are warranted by genetic evidence and concomitant claims about embodied vulnerability.

ANALYTIC RATIONALE

To trace how the process of precarization unfolds in the biomedical backstage, I examine precision medicine's primary evidential source: genetic tests. Genetic testing involves dominant discourses (Condit; Pender) and "mundane architectures and economies" (Lynch) that condition how biomedical practitioners identify, assess, and characterize human bodies. To understand how dominant discourses, mundane architectures, and economies condition claims about embodied vulnerability, I follow Michael Lynch's recommendation to conduct a rhetorical ontography—that is, an inventory of "the furniture of the world." Specifically, Lynch invites researchers to "mundanize epistemology, ontology, ethics and aesthetics" and trace their "historicized and situated" nature (2–3). In an effort to mundanize the ways in which genetic evidences are manufactured and used to make claims about bodies at risk, I borrow Thomas Rickert's rich rhetorical construct, ambient rhetoric.

Ambient Rhetorics

Ambient rhetorics are the "conditions that give rise to our ongoing perceptions and understandings of the world" (Rickert xiii). Accounting for ambient rhetorics requires that we attend to "nonhuman aspects of place," for they are "both more dynamic and more integrated into our practices than we have recognized them to be" (43). To illustrate the suasiveness of ambient rhetorics, Rickert describes the mutually beneficial relationship between a vineyard's soil and the growth of grapes for wine (ix–x). But more than a decade before Rickert's vineyard/soil illustration, Ladelle McWhorter asked us to consider the suasiveness of dirt. In particular, she argues that all living things come "from the activity of that undifferentiated, much maligned stuff we call dirt" (167). Drawing on both Rickert and McWhorter, I ask: What are the characteristics of the material-discursive soil from which genetic evidences hail? What material-discursive methods do genetic scientists employ when creating evidential order from complex embodied and sociocultural intra-actions? And how do such methods lend themselves to the pathologizing of precarity?

Accounting for how quotidian, ambient rhetorics (such as how genetic scientists negotiate changes in matter, movement, and time) have significant consequences for human bodies—what Stacy Alaimo refers to as "trans-corporeality" (238)—requires a nuanced analytic approach. This approach should enable critiques that document "the entangled territories of material and discursive, natural and cultural, biological and textual" (Alaimo 238). TallBear makes a convincing case that genes are often seen as "autonomous, objective things" (*Native American DNA* 70). Such an assumption ends up "obscuring and displacing the social relations between the humans and . . . nonhumans involved in the production of such objects" (70). By focusing on scientists' methods for attuning to genetic difference, I hope to resist such obfuscations.

Asking questions about the material-discursive soil from which genetic evidences hail is crucial—especially since rhetoricians of science and medicine have demonstrated the impossibility of isolating nature from other constitutive forces. The very concepts of "nature," "material," "genes," and "bodies" are shaped by "a historically and culturally specific set of concerns that have distilled themselves into particular lexicons of material-discursive facticity" (Willey 12). I argue that when genetic scientists attune to human bodies' differences, they rely on historically entrenched, value-laden, material-discursive methods for manufacturing scientific facts. Backstage biomedical methods discipline biological materials in a way that not only makes genetic evidence clinically meaningful but also renders at-risk bodies governable.

Rhetorical Attunement

Given the messy and complex ambient rhetorics that are always already present in even the most sterile laboratory, and remaining mindful that "the human is always intermeshed with the more-than-human world" (Alaimo 238), one methodological solution to the problem of studying genetic science's biomedical backstage is to deploy analyses that do not isolate an object of study, such as the gene, from its environment. Rather, I embrace a tactic that allows me to more holistically account for overlapping contributors to what the precision medicine movement calls genetic evidence; such contributors include bodies, biologies, geographies, and technologies.

To delve deeper into the material-discursive lineages from whence genetic evidence hails, I take as my object of study genetic scientists' methods of rhetorical attunement. Rhetorical attunement draws attention to the "ensemble of material elements bearing up, making possible, and continually incorporated in the conducting of human activity" (Rickert 93). Attuning is a way of listening, discerning, or noticing. While Latour and Woolgar argue that the very process of constructing scientific facts "*involves the use of certain devices whereby all traces of production are made extremely difficult to detect*" (176, italics in the original), by mobilizing Rickert's notion of attunement as a part of my analysis, I unearth such traces of production. To summarize: I endeavor to interrogate the promise of precision medicine through an analysis of the everyday, ambient contributors to genetic scientists' methods of rhetorical attunement.

RHETORICAL ATTUNEMENT IN THE BIOMEDICAL BACKSTAGE

The precision medicine movement posits that health, healing, and even cures for cancer can be located in human DNA. Interestingly, the German word on which the English words "heal," "cure," and "mend" are based—*heilen*—does not just mean healthy, whole, and uninjured. *Heilen* bears an additional connotation: to castrate, tame, make useable, or remove the wildness (see Lorey 57). While much of contemporary, allopathic medical practice involves locating and acting on deviations from an embodied norm or standard, such practices derive from backstage techniques that require biomedical scientists to tame, make useable, or reclaim the wild, broken body. Such activities afford the segmentation (Lorey 21) of some bodies from others. In this section, I unearth genetic scientists' methods for taming, making useable, or segmenting (for the purpose of policy making and decision making) human bodies based on genetic differences. I will show that methods for attuning to matter, movement, and time in the biomedical backstage have significant effects on how certain bodies are characterized as at-risk. As readers engage with forthcoming technical descriptions, pay close attention to the material-discursive methods that genetic scientists employ when attuning to difference. Genetic scientists' use of the single nucleotide polymorphism (or SNP), reference materials, algorithms or computational code, ancestry informative markers (or AIMs), populations, geographical location, and frequencies enable the process of segmentation in the biomedical backstage.[4]

SNPs and Reference Materials

To manage the sheer scope of the big data project that is genetic testing, scientists must splice DNA into fragments.[5] Most laboratories employ a version of next-generation sequencing that involves identifying SNPs (pronounced "snips") for the purpose of comparison. When compared with SNPs from a previously collected and analyzed database of genetic data, or reference materials, differences and similarities between the two are detected. After using algorithms to detect patterns of similarity or difference between a patient's SNPs and SNPs from reference materials, genetic scientists posit probabilities about an individual's genetic makeup and their risk for developing certain diseases.

Where, exactly, on a chromosome a genetic scientist directs their full attention—whether because of limitations in time, technology, cost, or some other reason—ultimately shapes resultant findings. Genetic evidences are, as Sheila Jasanoff describes, "co-produced" in the biomedical backstage. When Jasanoff and others in science and technology studies characterize scientific labor as co-production or co-constitution, they are drawing our attention to the ways in which science and technology are "interwoven with issues of meaning, values, and power" (29). To understand genetic materials, human actors must partner with them in ways that are enmeshed in a host of otherwise black-boxed assumptions. Allowing for some things to fall out of view is necessitated by scientists' desire to make manageable and thereby narrow the scope of their analytic gaze. We see this with the very practical decision to employ SNPs as analytically meaningful objects of study. Every act of revealing for the sake of seeing genetic difference also involves an act of concealing. Such material-discursive acts of revealing/concealing in the biomedical backstage yields the pathologizing of precarity.

Reference materials are powerful actors in the production of genetic evidence. It might help to think of them as a genetic scientist's methodological plumb line or evidential heuristic. As a genetic scientist's methodological plumb line, reference materials help to stabilize (for now) how differences are detected, thereby shaping claims that can be made about whose bodies are more or less genetically vulnerable. Once SNPs from reference materials are collected and compared, scientists identify genetic markers that, based on comparisons to other genetic materials, appear to be correlated with a wide range of diseases—such as certain kinds of cancers, type 2 diabetes, and alcoholism. Findings from genetic tests hinge on the richness of a laboratory's reference material database. Notably, not every genetic testing laboratory uses the same database of reference materials. Aware of the as of yet unstandardized nature of reference materials, and acknowledging that "the regulation of DNA tests . . . is complicated and in flux," the National Institute of Standards and Technology recently developed reference materials "that could be used by laboratories to determine whether their machines and software were properly analyzing a person's genetic blueprint, or genome" (Pear). These standardized reference materials cost $450 a vial and include 10 micrograms of DNA from a woman of European ancestry who lives (or at one point lived) in Utah.

Unearthing both the emergence of the SNP as an evidentially revealing object of study and scientists' reliance on reference materials provides a glimpse into two "practices of knowing" (Meißner) employed by genetic scientists. In both practices, the work of manufacturing genetic evidence in the biomedical backstage requires scientists to attune to some phenomena while censoring others. For both Barad and Meißner, the act of attuning to some phenomena while censoring others performs an agential cut. Importantly, the human actor is not the center of agential cutting. In fact, recognizing one's place within the human and extra-human performance of an agential cut requires accountability and responsibility—"not because we do the choosing . . . but because we are an agential part of the material becoming of the universe" (Barad 178). In other words, genetic materials are not mere material marionettes enlivened by human actors' scientific strings (Teston, *Bodies*). Rather, the laboratory, through a host of ambient, agentic contributors, stages an intra-action (Barad) between matter, movement, and time that is evidentially suasive. Such material-discursive enactments imbue genetic evidence with explanatory power.

Algorithms and Ancestry Informative Markers

Seeing differences between SNPs under investigation and SNPs within a laboratory's reference material database is quite challenging, not only since all humans possess the same genes but also because the sequence of human bodies' genes is 99.5 percent alike. To see distinctions between individual patients' genetic materials, scientists look for unique genetic expressions, or what they call "ancestry informative markers" (AIMs). Ancestry informative markers may be mere patterns, or they might involve, for example, the mutation or deletion of genetic material.

Just as SNPs and reference material are co-produced in the biomedical backstage, so, too, are AIMs. That is, AIMs are both manufactured and detected using algorithms that are written to identify similarities and differences between the reference materials and the DNA sample under study. Computational algorithms, or what James J. Brown might call "difference machines," are composed in such a way that genetic scientists both detect and produce patterns of similarity and difference. In other words, the coding languages that make difference detection possible are not merely a way of rendering a priori differences visible. Rather, computational code helps to perform or enact genetic variation. Algorithms transform otherwise benign biological materials into evidentially suasive actors. They help realize "certain possibilities . . . over others" (Brock 5). Nelson and Robinson summarize it in this way:

> Algorithms and computational mathematics are used to analyze the samples and infer the individual's admixture[6] of three or four statistically constituted categories—sub-Saharan African, Native American, East Asian, and European—according to the presence and frequency of specific genetic markers said to be predominate [*sic*] among, but importantly, not distinctive of, each of the original populations. (113)

Here, Nelson and Robinson indicate that algorithms and computational mathematics are crucial to manufacturing AIMs in the biomedical backstage. Computational cuts configure "the conditions of possibility" (Meißner). But such computational cuts are neither fixed nor finite. The practice of computational cutting in the biomedical backstage plays a crucial role in pathologizing precarity. In particular, the practice of performing a computational cut hinges on a host of value-laden assumptions about definitions for and boundaries of both population and place. I explore these assumptions in the next section.

Population and Place

To meaningfully mobilize reference materials for the purpose of constructing algorithms capable of comparing genetic materials, scientists first analyze and map materials onto geographical regions that correlate to a particular population label. Such an act may seem a straightforward process of characterizing, labeling, and enacting criteria for quantifying difference and similarity. However, this process is complicated by several factors. To begin with, note Nelson and Robinson's final assertion above: AIMs are *predominate* [*sic*] *among* but *not distinctive of* original populations. So, when genetic scientists rely on the correlation between AIMs and population labels to make decisions about computational cut-making criteria, they collapse quantity with type. Markers of genetic difference are predicated on discursive synonymizations of persons and place, or population and geography. Such synonymizations are the material-discursive conditions that structure precarious pathologies.

Synonymizing geographical spaces with particular populations, and then drawing inferences about common characteristics—or AIMs—is the quintessential example of evidential co-production in the biomedical backstage. When scientists attune to differences in this way, they can then make claims about the genetic association between a specific population and life-threatening health conditions, such as the link between Caucasians of European descent and a genetic vulnerability to neuroblastomas (Diskin et al.). Correlating genetic differences with place-based population labels is argumentatively problematic, however: "the use of SNPs for group identification is founded upon allelic variations already selected to show group identification" (Montoya 58). As many critics have pointed out, such a move or agential cut hinges on logical tautology. To illustrate the circular reasoning inherent in the use of place-based population labels that aid genetic scientists in attuning to genetic difference, consider the following examples.

Logical Tautology A. "SNPs A, B, and C are (found in) X group. SNPs A, B, and C are found in person Y. Therefore, person Y is of X group" (Montoya 58).

This same brand of circular logic allows scientists to make the following argumentative associations.

Logical Tautology B. "Most of the time, group X's members share SNPs A-C, and group Y's members share SNPs B-D. Therefore, group X is genetically different from group Y" (Montoya 58).

Such tautological reasoning collapses the complexity of intra-actions between bodies, environments, economics, politics, time, place, subject, object, content, and category.

Using population-based categories to attune to genetic differences in the biomedical backstage also assumes that premodern humans' geographical locations and group memberships remained stable over time. Because populations' geographical locations, cultural traditions, and ways of living were (and are) in constant flux, Dennis O'Rourke, a former president of the American Association of Physical Anthropology, warns against relying on such a method for attuning to genetic difference. For example, differences between populations regarding certain cultural traditions, such as burial practices, affect the availability and subsequent representativeness of certain populations' genetic materials. O'Rourke even goes so far as to describe premodern human populations as "ephemeral." These complexities and ephemeralities are left unaccounted for in the biomedical backstage. Using premodern populations (whose emplacement, positionality, and community memberships were in constant flux) as evidence of ancestry and then mobilizing that evidence to segment some bodies from others is, in O'Rourke's words, "arbitrary." Of the struggle associated with trying to identify biological difference from ancestral data, O'Rourke says, "This difficulty stems from the fluidity of individual and group identities in time and space. Individuals may change ethnic identities, and hence group membership will complicate assumptions of demographic continuity over time" (104). Given the instability if not inaccuracy of the ancestral data that scientists use in the biomedical backstage, one might ask how anything about a medical model based on genetic data could ever be characterized as "precise."[7] Human communities' constant geographic and definitional flux simply cannot be captured, quantified, and standardized in the biomedical backstage. Attempts to do so pathologize precarity.

The inaccuracy of claims to precision isn't the only thing with which advocates of precision medicine must contend. They must also address the ethical responsibilities associated with attuning to genetic differences in the ways I describe above. Methods for attuning to genetic difference I've described thus far link ancestry with place and population. As a result, geography, ethnicity, ancestry, and even race are often (although not always) collapsed in the biomedical backstage (for more on this phenomenon, see Ali-Khan et al.). Collapsing geographical location, or place, with ethnicity, ancestry, and race has profound effects on how contemporary human communities are characterized (and, ultimately—pathologized).

Consider TallBear's research wherein the collapsing of tribe and race resulted in disastrous effects for Indigenous populations. "An Anishinaabee with too many non-Anishinaabee ancestors won't count as part of an Anishinaabee 'population,' thus bringing a tribal/First Nation category of belonging into conflict with a geneticist's category" (TallBear, "Emergence" 24). Tension between categories erected in the biomedical backstage and narratives of belonging among actual human communities reinforces the precarization of human bodies—especially when scientific categories are framed as "precise" and community narratives are (dis)regarded as mere story. What results is not only the erasure of Indigenous communities' own methods for negotiating embodied similarities and differences, but also serious consequences for how and where certain communities may materially dwell and secure conditions required for living.

Frequencies

Thus far, I've described how genetic scientists use population and place when characterizing and correlating differences between and among the SNPs under study and the genetic information embodied by a laboratory's chosen reference material. In this section, I describe how discursive markers such as "mutation" and "variation" are assigned and thereby structurally condition the pathologizing of precarity for certain communities.

What is considered a potentially life-threatening genetic mutation versus a mere genetic difference is a function of frequency. That is, once SNPs have been compared and associated with a particular population, and after AIMs have been detected and characterized, genetic scientists calculate how common a DNA sample is among the population to which it has been assigned. Essentially, scientists ask: How frequently does a genetic difference occur within and outside of the population from which this genetic sample hails? If the difference occurs in greater than 1 percent of the population, then that difference may be characterized as relatively benign, or in technical terms, a mere polymorphism. If, however, the frequency of that difference occurs in less than 1 percent of the population to which the genetic sample under study is associated, genetic scientists are inclined to categorize such a difference as a mutation. Depending on the frequency of a genetic difference, inferences are made about a patient's embodied vulnerability to certain conditions.

Using frequency as the method by which the category of mutation is assigned points to the co-constructed nature of the discursive marker, "genetic mutation." That is, there is nothing inherently or biologically deviant about differences in a particular DNA sequence. How differences are characterized as "deviant," thereby placing a body at risk, is a matter of how often that difference appears in a particular population. While reliance on statistical frequency sounds like the most objective and scientifically sound method for leveraging serious claims about genetic differences, such a tactic black-boxes the complex intra-actions that had to occur in the biomedical backstage to make such frequencies possible. To open the black box that is a claim about genetic mutation based on statistical frequency, recall the methods that create the conditions for seeing difference and pathologizing precarity in the first place. Specifically, recall the following:

- SNPs embody only a small fraction of an individual patient's actual genetic makeup.
- Reference materials embody only a small fraction of whole populations' actual genetic characteristics.
- Algorithms are co-constructed difference machines that rely on population labels in order to perform computational cuts.
- Population labels are assigned by synonymizing ancestral data with geographical location.
- But geographical location, time, and group membership are never static.

The statistically calculated frequencies upon which claims about genetic difference and embodied vulnerability are made are, at best, tenuous. And yet, this method of attuning to genetic difference facilitates the segmentation of some bodies from others.

Scientific realities are enacted in the genomic backstage through a host of value-laden attunements to matter, movement, and time. Methods used to materialize genetic evidence do not simply transport scientific knowledge and experience; they *transform* such knowledge and experiences (Berg and Mol 244; see also Teston, *Bodies*). In other words, more than tools, translation, or transport of a priori genetic differences, precision medicine's evidences hail from attunements to matter, movement, and time that have strong biopower effects on both individual human bodies and whole communities—effects that condition claims about a body's risk of disease. TallBear makes the case that "genetics discourse can be used to 'other,' that is to represent some living human beings as not normative, as the sources of the raw materials of science, as the ancient, remote, less evolved, less enlightened ancestors of more modern living people" (*Native American DNA* 202). Indeed, genetics discourse can be used to Other. But the biomedical act of Othering, itself, is conditioned by a host of material-discursive assumptions, categories, and agential cuts.

CONSTRUCTING CONDITIONS FOR CARE

The analyses above indicate that genetic evidence's suasive power relies on reductive material-discursive premises. These are precarious rhetorics. So much falls out of focus within a medical model that reduces the complexities of human life and change over time to algorithms and other forms of syllogistic reasoning. Such reductions pathologize precarity. In his book, *Making the Mexican Diabetic: Race, Science, and the Genetics of Inequality*, Michael Montoya argues that when medicine emphasizes risk factors based on genetic evidence, practitioners erase "the socioeconomic, historical, and political contexts of populations affected by disease" (87). Subsequently, policies are made about how and for whom care is provided.

Precision medicine seeks out reasons for disease in human bodies' genetic codes. But as many feminist scholars argue, "in order to 'be,'" bodies "must rely on what is outside" (Butler 33). Reliance on what is outside—the condition of being conditioned—makes some bodies more or less vulnerable. It makes sense to ask, therefore: What ambient rhetorics (e.g., economies, histories, politics) act on and co-produce human bodies in such a way that whole communities are deemed "disposable others" (Braidotti, *Transpositions*; Teston, "Rhetoric, Precarity")?

Nadine Ehlers argues that within the "medico-discursive model of health," human bodies' vulnerability to disease is often understood as "a shortcoming—one that discursively positions the subject as weak or unfortunate—and as that which marks the subject as potentially beyond the normative standards of being" (119). And yet, precision medicine seeks to find genetic links, and in turn, obfuscate attention to ambient or extra-genetic contributors to human health. This is evidenced by the search for genetic links between alcoholism and some Indigenous communities, type II diabetes and some Mexican communities, and stage IV breast cancer and some African American women. Building on Montoya and Ehlers, I argue that the genomic backstage seeks answers to embodied vulnerability in vulnerable subjects themselves, rather than in the external, extra-genetic conditions that bear up and make possible conditions required for securing life.

Precision medicine, through its reliance on certain methods for attuning to difference in the biomedical backstage, will continue to fortify material-discursive conditions by which some bodies are characterized as weak or unfortunate, and therefore non-normative. What might it look like, then, to practice care in a way that resists pathologizing precarity? What might it look like to practice care in a way that is attuned to "segmented relations of violence and inequality" (Lorey 28), our connection to the environment and to one another, and extra-genetic toxicities that condition life and death? How might contemporary care practices acknowledge "the differential distribution of symbolic and material insecurities" (Lorey 21) that are left unaccounted for in precision medicine's biomedical backstage?

From epigenetics to environmental effects on human health, we know that the human genome is neither fixed nor finite. Genetic materials are malleable actors affected by ambient matter(s), movement, and time. Once we bear witness to ambient rhetorics' suasiveness—or, in this case, genetic materials' malleability and manipulability—it requires "deeper transformations in our lived relations to the world in ways that in turn attune us differently to world" (Rickert 239). Given how important matter, movement, and time are for genetic scientists in the biomedical backstage, we must attune differently to extra-genetic contributors to human health and well-being. One way to accomplish this is, as material feminists argue, to enact a "form of accountability, based on a strong sense of collectivity and relationality, which results in a renewed claim to community and belonging" (Braidotti, *The Posthuman* 191). Under a rubric of relationality, precision is a fiction.

Pathologizing precarity involves the biomedical search for correlations between genetic materials and certain human communities' embodied vulnerability to disease. But what happens when such searches are unsuccessful? More often than not, the biomedical backstage fails in its attempts to manufacture correlative links between allelic variations and a particular disease. For example, in this chapter I have referenced narratives in both the popular press and public discourse that suggest a genetic link between alcoholism and Indigenous communities. Geneticists have failed to find such a link. Enacting a material feminist form of accountability requires we ask, therefore: What claims do genetic tests' *null results* have on us?

Maia Szalavitz reminds us that the "firewater" myth has its origin in the "racist ideology that fueled colonialism," as evidenced by a letter written by Thomas Jefferson to a chief in which Jefferson argued: "Spirituous liquors are not in themselves bad. . . . But as you find that your people cannot refrain from an ill use of them, I greatly applaud your resolution not to use them at all" (qtd. in Szalavitz). The firewater myth points to how powerful state-sponsored actors intra-act with biologies, histories, environments, and other ambient contributors in ways that exploit human vulnerabilities. A medical model that neither permits the exploitation of human vulnerabilities nor abandons communities to precariousness accounts for the ways that "environmentalism, human health, and social justice cannot be severed" (Alaimo 262). Such a medical model responds to communities' slow death—even when hypotheses about correlations between individual members' genetic differences and disease fail.

As epideictic rhetorics about the promise of precision medicine endure, researchers, critics, and medical practitioners must remain attuned to how arguments warranted by genetic evidences about at-risk bodies pathologize precarity. Pathologizing precarity is the biomedical equivalent to victim blaming. A medical model that does not pathologize precarity includes as a part of its pedagogy, training, and practice an awareness of ambient contributors to care that exist both beyond the laboratory and within and beyond human bodies. A medical model that does not pathologize precarity finds itself hailed by extra-human contributors that condition the "slow death" of certain populations (Puar 169). It makes do with and acts on the evidences it has on hand—for example, relationships between zip codes and long-term exposure to lead in water, and proximity to nuclear power plants and firearms.

Finally, claims about at-risk bodies based on genetic evidence reify narratives of "neoliberal humanist notion[s] of the individual body-subject" (Atkinson et al. 77). Because human bodies are "porous and not discretely bounded"

(Jayna Brown 326), the hope for precision in medical practice is simply untenable. A medical model that does not pathologize precarity recognizes that "human corporeality, and materiality itself," is "something that always bears the trace of history, social position, region, and the uneven distribution of risk" (Alaimo 261). Such a model does not seek to frame infrastructural injustices as individual suffering (Fassin; see also Athey, Ferebee, and Hesford). Care for human communities requires ongoing negotiations with constantly changing biologies, histories, environments, politics, and economies. The flux and flow of such constantly changing infrastructures both bear witness to and condition corporeal futures.

NOTES

1. My use of "backstage" in this chapter points to Erving Goffman's investigation into differences between communication in the frontstage versus communication in the backstage. The latter is reserved for insiders. For Ellen Barton, backstages in medical contexts are limited to those who "co-construct" medical discourse and decisions (71).
2. I'm drawing on Bruno Latour's construct, "black box," which is a term "used by cyberneticians whenever a piece of machinery or a set of commands is too complex" (2–3). Black boxes collapse complexity into mere input and output. They coalesce disorder into something that "resembles an organised whole" (Latour 131).
3. According to Foucault, bodies are ways of controlling individuals and populations. Using medical knowledge, those in positions of power aim to produce citizens that are economically productive. To do this, medical knowledge harvested from bodies becomes grounds upon which claims of normality and abnormality may be made. Foucault's notion of biopower is a way of regulating and fitting individual bodies into norms that are warranted by statistical analyses.
4. I focus on these seven material-discursive contributors to the manufacturing of genetic evidence in the biomedical backstage not to elide the "larger operations of power" (Willey 13) in which genetic science takes place, but rather to manage the analytic scope of this chapter. If readers are interested in reading more about the broader contexts of institutional power in which genetic science is located, see chapter 5 in Teston (*Bodies*).
5. As Lori Andrews and Dorothy Nelkin argue: "Such language reflects a set of cultural assumptions about the body: that it can be understood in terms of its units, and that these units can be pulled from their context, isolated, and abstracted from real people who live in a particular time, at an actual location, in a given society" (qtd. in Montoya 155).
6. As TallBear ("Emergence") notes, the very notion of an "admixture" implies that there was or could be a genetically "pure" population. Population purity or genetic originality is, as TallBear argues, "at odds with the doctrine of evolution, of change over time, of becoming" (23). Attuning to differences in the biomedical backstage appears to require, therefore, the suspension of contingency, emergence, and change.
7. Fatimah Jackson says it best: "How will inaccurate and inadequate genetic-ancestry information be reconciled with the promise of personalized, precision medicine when the latter depends on accurate and comprehensive genetic ancestry data?" (280).

WORKS CITED

Alaimo, Stacy. "Trans-corporeal Feminisms and the Ethical Space of Nature." *Material Feminisms.* Ed. S. Alaimo and S. Hekman. Indiana University Press, 2008. 237–64.

Ali-Khan, Sarah E., Tomasz Krakowski, Rabia Tahir, and Abdallah S. Daar. "The Use of Race, Ethnicity and Ancestry in Human Genetic Research." *HUGO Journal* 5 (2011): 47–63.

Athey, Stephanie, K. M. Ferebee, and Wendy S. Hesford. "Introduction: The Poisoning of Flint and the Moral Economy of Human Rights." *Prose Studies* 38.1 (2016): 1–11.

Atkinson, Sarah, et al. "'The Medical' and 'Health' in a Critical Medical Humanities." *Journal of Medical Humanities* 36.1 (2015): 71–81.

Barad, Karen. *Meeting the Universe Halfway: Quantum Physics and the Entanglement of Matter and Meaning.* Duke University Press, 2007.

Barton, Ellen. "Discourse Methods and Critical Practice in Professional Communication: The Front-Stage and Back-Stage Discourse of Prognosis in Medicine." *Journal of Business and Technical Communication* 18.1 (2004): 67–111.

Berg, Marc, and Annemarie Mol. *Differences in Medicine: Unraveling Practices, Techniques, and Bodies.* Duke University Press, 1998.

Berlant, Lauren. "Slow Death (Sovereignty, Obesity, Lateral Agency)." *Critical Inquiry* 33.4 (2007): 754–80.

Braidotti, Rosi. *Transpositions: On Nomadic Ethics.* Polity, 2006.

———. "Feminist Epistemology After Postmodernism: Critiquing Science, Technology and Globalisation." *Interdisciplinary Science Reviews* 32.1 (2007): 65–74.

———. *The Posthuman.* Polity Press, 2013.

Brock, Kevin. "Enthymeme as Rhetorical Algorithm." *Present Tense* 4.1 (2014): 1–7.

Brown, James J. "The Machine That Therefore I Am." *Philosophy and Rhetoric* 47.4 (2014): 494–514.

Brown, Jayna. "Being Cellular Race, the Inhuman, and the Plasticity of Life." *GLQ: A Journal of Lesbian and Gay Studies* 21.2–3 (2015): 321–41.

Butler, Judith. *Frames of War: When Is Life Grievable?* Verso Press, 2009.

Condit, Celeste. "Race and Genetics from a Modal Materialist Perspective." *Quarterly Journal of Speech* 94.4 (2008): 383–406.

Diskin, Sharon J., et al. "Copy Number Variation at 1q21. 1 Associated with Neuroblastoma." *Nature* 459.7249 (2009): 987–91.

Ehlers, Nadine. "The Dialectics of Vulnerability: Breast Cancer and the Body in Prognosis." *Configurations* 22.1 (2014): 113–35.

"Fact Sheet: President Obama's Precision Medicine Initiative." Press release, Office of the Press Secretary, The White House. 30 Jan. 2015. <https://www.whitehouse.gov/the-press-office/2015/01/30/fact-sheet-president-obama-s-precision-medicine-initiative>.

Fassin, Didier. *Humanitarian Reason: A Moral History of the Present.* University of California Press, 2012.

Gahlert, Sarah, and Colditz, Graham A. "Cancer Disparities: Unmet Challenges in the Elimination of Disparities." *Cancer Epidemiology, Biomarkers & Prevention* 20 (2011): 1809–14.

Goffman, Erving. *The Presentation of Self in Everyday Life*. Harmondsworth, 1978.

Happe, Kelly. *The Material Gene: Gender, Race, and Heredity after the Human Genome Project*. New York University Press, 2013.

Holloway, Karla F. C. *Private Bodies, Public Texts: Race, Gender, and a Cultural Bioethics*. Duke University Press, 2011.

———. "Their Bodies, Our Conduct: How Society and Medicine Produce Persons Standing in Need of End-of-Life Care." *Journal of Palliative Medicine* 19.2 (2016): 127–28.

Illich, Ivan. *Limits to Medicine. Medical Nemesis: The Expropriation of Health*. Marion Boyers, 2002.

Jackson, Fatimah LC. "Genomics: DNA and Diasporas." *Nature* 529.7586 (2016): 279–80.

Jasanoff, Sheila. *States of Knowledge: The Co-Production of Science and the Social Order*. Routledge, 2004.

Kramer, Anne-Marie. "The Genomic Imaginary: Genealogical Heritage and the Shaping of Bio-convergent Identities." *MediaTropes* 5.1 (2015): 80–104.

Latour, Bruno. *Science in Action: How to Follow Scientists and Engineers Through Society*. Harvard University Press, 1987.

Latour, Bruno, and Steve Woolgar. *Laboratory Life: The Construction of Scientific Facts*. Princeton University Press, 1986.

Lorey, Isabell. *State of Insecurity: Government of the Precarious*. Verso Press, 2015.

Lynch, John. "Articulating Scientific Practice: Understanding Dean Hamer's 'Gay Gene' Study as Overlapping Material, Social and Rhetorical Registers." *Quarterly Journal of Speech*, 95.4 (2009). 435–56.

Lynch, Michael. "Ontography: Investigating the Production of Things, Deflating Ontology." Paper prepared for *Oxford Ontologies Workshop, Said Business School*, Oxford University, 25 June 2008. 1–12.

McWhorter, Ladelle. *Bodies and Pleasures: Foucault and the Politics of Sexual Normalization*. Indiana University Press, 1999.

Meißner, Hanna. "Conversing with the Unexpected: Towards a Feminist Ethics of Knowing." *Rhizomes* 30 (2016).

Montoya, Michael. *Making the Mexican Diabetic: Race, Science, and the Genetics of Inequality*. University of California Press, 2011.

Nelson, Alondra, and Joan H. Robinson. "The Social Life of DTC Genetics: The Case of 23andMe." *Routledge Handbook of Science, Technology and Science*. Ed. D. L. Kleinman and K. Moore. Routledge, 2014. 108–23.

Oliviero, Katie. "Vulnerability's Ambivalent Political Life: Trayvon Martin and the Racialized and Gendered Politics of Protection." *Feminist Formations* 28.1 (2016): 1–32.

O'Rourke, Dennis. "Anthropological Genetics in the Genomic Era: A Look Back and Ahead." *American Anthropologist* 105.1 (2003): 101–9.

Pear, Robert. "U.S. Introduces New DNA Standard for Ensuring Accuracy of Genetic Tests." *New York Times*, 14 May 2015.

Pender, Kelly. "Genetic Subjectivity In Situ: A Rhetorical Reading of Genetic Determinism and Genetic Opportunity in the Biosocial Community of FORCE." *Rhetoric and Public Affairs* 15.2 (2012): 319–49.

Puar, Jasbir. "Precarity Talk: A Virtual Roundtable with Lauren Berlant, Judith Butler, Bojana Cvejic, Isabell Lorey, Jasbir Puar, and Ana Vujanovic." *TDR: The Drama Review* 56.4 (2012): 163–77.

Reardon, Jenny, and Kim TallBear. "'Your DNA Is *Our* History': Genomics, Anthropology, and the Construction of Whiteness as Property." *Current Anthropology* 53.S5 (2012): S233–S245.

Rickert, Thomas. *Ambient Rhetoric: The Attunements of Rhetorical Being.* University of Pittsburgh Press, 2013.

Szalavitz, Maia. "No, Native Americans Aren't Genetically More Susceptible to Alcoholism: Time to Retire the 'Firewater' Fairytale." *The Verge.* 2 Oct. 2015.

TallBear, Kim. "The Emergence, Politics and Marketplace of Native American DNA." *Routledge Handbook of Science, Technology, and Society.* Ed. D. L. Kleinman and K. Moore, 2014. 21–37.

———. *Native American DNA: Tribal Belonging and the False Promise of Genetic Science.* University of Minnesota Press, 2013.

Teston, Christa. *Bodies in Flux: Scientific Methods for Negotiating Medical Uncertainty.* University of Chicago Press, 2017.

———. "Rhetoric, Precarity, and mHealth Technologies." *Rhetoric Society Quarterly* 46.3 (2016): 251–68.

Ward, Elizabeth, et al. "Cancer Disparities by Race/Ethnicity and Socioeconomic Status." *CA: A Cancer Journal for Clinicians* 54 (2004): 78–93.

Warner, Erica T., et al. "Racial and Ethnic Differences in Breast Cancer Survival: Mediating Effect of Tumor Characteristics and Sociodemographic and Treatment Factors." *Journal of Clinical Oncology* 33.20 (2015): 2254–61.

Willey, Angela. "A World of Materialisms: Postcolonial Feminist Science Studies and the New Natural." *Science, Technology, & Human Values* 41.6 (2016): 1–24.

CONTRIBUTORS

EDITORS

WENDY S. HESFORD is a professor of rhetoric at The Ohio State University, with affiliate appointments in comparative studies and women's, gender, and sexuality studies. She is the author of *Framing Identities: Autobiography and the Politics of Pedagogy* (University of Minnesota Press, 1999), for which she received the W. R. Winterowd book award, and *Spectacular Rhetorics: Human Rights Visions, Recognitions, Feminisms* (Duke University Press, 2011), for which she received the RSA book award, and is currently completing her third monograph, *Violent Exceptions: Children's Human Rights and Humanitarian Rhetoric*, forthcoming from The Ohio State University Press. Hesford has coedited two book collections with Wendy Kozol, *Haunting Violations: Feminist Criticism and the Crisis of the "Real"* (University of Illinois Press, 2001) and *Just Advocacy: Women's Human Rights, Transnational Feminisms, and the Politics of Representation* and coauthored a textbook, *Rhetorical Visions*, with Brenda J. Brueggemann (Prentice Hall 2007). Hesford has published in a range of journals, including *Biography, College English, Feminist Formations, Humanity, PMLA,* and *Signs,* among others.

ADELA C. LICONA is associate professor of English and interim director of the Institute for LGBT Studies. She is affiliated faculty in gender and women's studies, Institute of the Environment, and Mexican American studies. She is coeditor of *Feminist Pedagogy: Looking Back to Move Forward* (Johns Hopkins University Press, 2009), author of *Zines in Third Space: Radical Cooperation and Borderlands Rhetoric* (SUNY Press, 2012), and has published in such journals as *Antipode, Transformations, Journal of Latino-Latin American Studies, Annals of the Asso-*

ciation of *American Geographers and Sexuality Research and Social Policy,* and in *Critical Studies in Media Communication.* Adela was the 2015–16 cochair of the National Women's Studies Association Conference, is editor emeritus of *Feminist Formations,* and serves on the board for *Feminist Formations, QED: A Journal of GLBTQ Worldmaking, Spoken Futures/The Tucson Youth Poetry Slam,* and the *Primavera Foundation.* In 2010, she was awarded a Ford Foundation grant to fund the Crossroads Collaborative, a think-and-act research, teaching, writing, and outreach collaborative dedicated to advancing research, graduate training, public conversation, and ultimately social change in the areas of youth, sexuality, health, rights, and justice, which she codesigned and codirected.

CHRISTA TESTON is associate professor of English and director of Business and Technical Writing at The Ohio State University. Teston is author of *Bodies in Flux: Scientific Methods for Negotiating Medical Uncertainty* (University of Chicago Press, 2017). In 2015, she coedited (with Brian McNely and Clay Spinuzzi) a special issue of *Technical Communication Quarterly* focused on contemporary research methodologies in technical communication. In 2010, her article "A Grounded Investigation of Genred Guidelines in Cancer Care Deliberations" won the National Council of Teachers of English award for best article reporting qualitative or quantitative research in technical communication. Teston has published articles on medical rhetoric and deliberative decision making in the *Journal of Medical Humanities, Technical Communication Quarterly, Written Communication, Present Tense: A Journal of Rhetoric and Society,* and *Rhetoric Society Quarterly.* Teston serves on editorial boards for *Written Communication* and *Rhetoric of Health and Medicine.*

CONTRIBUTORS

JAMES J. BROWN JR. is associate professor of English and director of the Rutgers-Camden Digital Studies Center. His research and teaching focus on digital rhetoric, new media studies, and electronic literature. His book, *Ethical Programs: Hospitality and the Rhetorics of Software* (University of Michigan Press, 2015), examines the ethical and rhetorical underpinnings of software platforms such as Twitter and MediaWiki, and he has also published essays on computation, rhetoric, and writing in journals such as *Philosophy and Rhetoric* and *Computers and Composition.*

GALE COSKAN-JOHNSON is associate professor of Writing and Rhetoric in the Department of English Language and Literature at Brock University in Ontario. She is affiliated faculty of the Social Justice and Equity Studies (SJES) MA Program and the PhD in Interdisciplinary Humanities. She teaches classes in rhetorical theory, histories of rhetoric, theories of social justice, public address, and transnational mobility. Her current research examines tensions that emerge in national and international discourses of sovereignty and transnational migration. Her work can be found in the collections, *Discursive Framings of Human Rights: Negotiating Agency and Victimhood,* edited by Jonas Ross Kjærgård and Karen-Margrethe Simonson and *Serendipity in Rhetoric: Writing, and Literacy Research,* edited by Peter Goggin and Maureen Daly Goggin and to be released in April of 2018. She has published scholarly articles in *Amerikastudien / American Studies, Encultura-tion: A Journal of Rhetoric, Writing, and Culture, Cultural Studies ↔ Critical Meth-odologies, Present Tense: A Journal of Rhetoric and Society*, and *Studies in American Indian Literature*. She has an article forthcoming in *JAC: A Journal of Rhetoric, Culture, and Politics*.

RONALD GREENE is professor and chair in the Department of Communication Studies at University of Minnesota. Over the last twenty years, he has pursued a research project on the different material modalities of rhetoric. He is the author of Mal-thusian Worlds: US Leadership and the Governing of the Population Crisis (West-view, 1999) and over fifty book chapters and articles in such journals as Cultural Studies, Communication and Critical/Cultural Studies, Critical Studies in Media Communication, Philosophy and Rhetoric, Argumentation and Advocacy, Quar-terly Journal of Speech, and Rhetoric Society Quarterly. His 1998 essay, "Another Materialist Rhetoric" won the Charles H. Woolbert Research Award for distin-guished scholarship "that has stood the test of time and has become a stimulus for new conceptualizations of communication phenomenon."

LAVINIA HIRSU is lecturer in the School of Education at the University of Glasgow. With a background in rhetoric and composition, Hirsu is currently developing interdisciplinary research that draws upon literacy studies and digital literacies, theories of cultural diversity and social justice, and applied linguistics, with a particular interest in translanguaging and translingualism. She has completed an evaluation for the Sharing Lives, Sharing Languages project developed and imple-mented by the Scottish Refugee Council and is part of two international networks that work toward social integration and resilience in contexts of migration, dis-placement, and environmental crises. Her research has appeared in *Computers and Composition, Peitho*, and *JAEPL*.

ARABELLA LYON is professor of English at the University at Buffalo. Lyon has an impressive list of awards and publications. In 2014, her book *Deliberative Acts: Democracy, Rhetoric, and Rights* (Penn State University Press, 2013) was awarded the "Rhetoric Society of America Book Award." Lyon also coedited (with Lester C. Olson) *Human Rights Rhetoric: Traditions of Testifying and Witnessing* (Rout-ledge, 2012) and authored *Intentions: Negotiated, Contested, and Ignored* (Penn State University Press, 1998). Lyon's work has also appeared in *Rhetoric Review, JAC: A Journal of Rhetoric, Culture, and Politics, Rhetoric Society Quarterly, College English, College Composition and Communication*, and *Philosophy and Rhetoric*.

LOUIS M. MARAJ is assistant professor of rhetoric and composition in the Department of English at the University of Pittsburgh. His scholarship lies at the intersections of rhetorical theory and history, critical race theory, digital media studies, and critical pedagogies. Specifically, his work focuses on notions of blackness in aca-demic spaces and centers blackness in frameworks for antiracist agency. He is an award-winning poet and cofounder of Digital Black Lit (Literacies/Literatures) and Composition.

SARA MCKINNON is associate professor of rhetoric, politics, and culture in the Department of Communication Arts at the University of Wisconsin–Madison. McKinnon's research and teaching is in the areas of intercultural rhetoric, globalization/transnational studies, legal rhetoric, and transnational feminist theory, with expertise in critical rhetorical and qualitative methods. Her book, *Gendered Asylum: Race and Violence in US Law and Politics* (University of Illinois Press, 2016), charts the emergence of gender as a political category in U.S. asylum law within the context of broader national and global politics. Her essays have appeared in *Women's Studies in Communication, Text and Performance Quarterly,* and the *Quarterly Journal of Speech.*

ALEXANDRA SCHULTHEIS MOORE is professor of English and codirector of the Human Rights Institute at Binghamton University (State University of New York). Moore is the author two monographs, *Vulnerability and Security in Human Rights Literature and Visual Culture* (2015) and *Regenerative Fictions: Postcolonialism, Psychoanalysis, and the Nation as Family* (2004), as well as five coedited collections: the *Routledge Companion to Literature and Human Rights* (with Sophia McClennen, 2015); *Teaching Human Rights in Literary and Cultural Studies* (with Elizabeth Swanson Goldberg, 2015); *Globally Networked Teaching in the Humanities* (with Sunka Simon, 2015); *Theoretical Perspectives on Human Rights and Literature* (with Elizabeth Swanson Goldberg, 2012); and *Witnessing Torture: Perspectives of Torture Survivors and Human Rights Workers* (with Elizabeth Swanson Goldberg, 2018). Her essays have appeared in numerous edited collections as well as journals that include *ARIEL: A Review of International English Literature, College Literature, Feminist Formations, Genders, Humanity, International Journal for Human Rights, Journal of Human Rights, Radical Teacher, South Asian Review,* and *Tijdschrift/Frame.*

KIMBERLEE PÉREZ is assistant professor of performance studies in the Department of Communication at the University of Massachusetts Amherst. Her interests include the politics of belonging and coalition, intimacy, personal narrative, and solo performance. She is coauthor of *Answer the Call: Virtual Migration in Indian Call Centers* and is currently working on a book titled *Queer Intimacies: On the Politics of Belonging in Performance.* Her research has been published in *Text and Performance Quarterly, QED: A Journal of Queer Worldmaking, Liminalities, Performance Research, Journal of International and Intercultural Communication,* and other journal and book collections.

MARGARET PRICE is associate professor of English and director of Disability Studies at The Ohio State University. She is the author of *Mad at School: Rhetorics of Mental Disability and Academic Life* (University of Michigan Press, 2011), which was awarded the Outstanding Book Award from the Conference on College Composition and Communication (2013). Price's coauthored work, "Multimodality in Motion: Disability and Kairotic Spaces," published in *Kairos,* was awarded the 2014 Accessibility and Digital Composition award from the Computers & Composition Digital Press. Recently, Price has published in *Enculturation, Disability Studies Quarterly, Composition Studies,* and *Hypatia: A Journal of Feminist Philosophy,* as well as the collection *Disability Space Architecture: A Reader* (Routledge, 2017). Price is currently at work on a monograph titled *Crip Spacetime*.

AMY SHUMAN is professor of English at The Ohio State University. She is the author of four books: *Storytelling Rights: The Uses of Oral and Written Communication Among Urban Adolescents* (Cambridge University Press, 1986); *Other People's Stories: Entitlement Claims and the Critique of Empathy* (University of Illinois Press, 2010); and (with Carol Bohmer) *Rejecting Refugees: Political Asylum in the 21st Century* (Routledge, 2007) and *Political Asylum Deceptions: The Culture of Suspicion* (Palgrave Macmillan, 2018). She is a Guggenheim Fellow and the recipient of Ohio State University's Distinguished Scholar, Distinguished Teaching, and Distinguished Service Awards. Her research focuses on narrative, political asylum, artisan pedagogies, and disability.

KRISTIN SWENSON is associate professor and chair in the Department of Critical Communication and Media Studies, Butler University; affiliated faculty member in the Gender, Women, and Sexuality Studies Department. Swenson's work examines subjectivity, affect, agency, and gender in contemporary forms of labor. In her book, *Lifestyle Drugs and the Neoliberal Family* (Peter Lang Press, 2013), she contends that direct-to-consumer advertisement of pharmaceuticals function to align our affect with contemporary demands of work in neoliberal capitalism. Her work has appeared in a variety of journals, including *Communication, Culture and Critique,* and *Baltic Journal of Law and Politics.*

BECCA TARSA is an assistant teaching professor in the Writing Program at Georgetown University. She teaches courses on digital writing and visual rhetoric. Her research focuses on extracurricular student writing, digital literacy and rhetoric, multimodal composition, and the teaching of writing. Her research on digital interfaces and literacy activity can be seen in *College English.*

BELINDA WALZER is assistant professor of Rhetoric and Composition at Appalachian State University. Walzer teaches courses on community writing and social justice rhetorics. Her research focuses on rhetorics of resistance, temporality, and human rights. Her scholarship can be found in the *Routledge Companion to Literature and Human Rights* (2015), *Teaching Human Rights in Literary and Cultural Studies* (MLA, 2015), and a special issue of *College Literature* focused on Human Rights and Cultural Forms. She has also published in *Rendezvous Journal of Arts and Letters* and *Philosophy & Rhetoric.*

INDEX

abuse, 26, 258, 270; alcohol, 278; human rights, 22, 111; online, 267, 268, 269

access, 14, 162, 194, 195, 205, 206; intimacy, 202; predictability-based model of, 196, 197

accommodation, 192, 194, 195, 199, 200, 203, 205; affordable, 148; battle for, 198; disability, 201; physicality and, 204; rights-based, 196

Ackerman, Spencer: reporting by, 36, 37

actionary, 268; design, 263–67

Adelman, Robert M., 128

African Americans: breast cancer and, 278, 280, 292; discrimination vs., 248; poverty and, 281

Agamben, Giorgio, 24, 166n4

agency, 44, 154–55, 158, 159, 164, 238; Black, 222; digital, 270; entangled, 157; independent nature of, 157; physical, 270; political, 126; shared, 141; unwilled, 112; victimization and, 3

Ahmed, Sara, 174, 176, 195, 228, 273–74

akairos, 6, 7, 24, 25; as ambient invention, 28–30; kairos and, 29–30; textual strategies of, 30–38

Alaimo, Stacy, 201, 283

al-Assad, Bashar, 1, 2

Aldebs, Alhadi, 149

al-Hamdo, Abdulkafi, 165

al-Sisi, Abdel Fattal, 2

Althusser, Louis, 45

Alyokhina, Masha, 93, 94, 95, 96

ambient rhetoric, 282, 283, 291, 292; theory of, 199–200, 201

ancestry informative markers (AIMs), 284, 286–87, 288, 290

Anzaldúa, Gloria, 129, 142n7, 181, 216, 278

appropriation, 45, 82–83, 84, 88, 90, 95, 97, 216; coalition and, 9, 83, 85, 92; cultural, 13

Arendt, Hannah, 130, 135, 136, 142n7

assemblages, 178; productive/reductive, 174–75; racializing, 224; techno-human, 11, 153–55, 157–59, 162, 163, 164–65, 260

asylum seekers, 2, 9, 10, 108, 116, 118; attacks on, 105, 106, 107, 117

Athey, Stephanie: torture narrative and, 35

Auger, James, 261

autoethnography, 13, 15, 215, 216, 230n1; Black, 21, 214, 219, 220, 221, 222, 229, 230n8

CPSIA information can be obtained
at www.ICGtesting.com
Printed in the USA
LVHW04s1029250818
587942LV00003B/3/P